Progress in
Applied Social Psychology

Volume 1

Progress in
Applied Social Psychology

Volume 1

Edited by
G. M. Stephenson
University of Kent at Canterbury
and
J. H. Davis
*University of Illinois
at Urbana-Champaign*

SCHOOL OF
CALIFORNIA
PROFESSIONAL
PSYCHOLOGY
LOS ANGELES

JOHN WILEY & SONS
Chichester · New York · Brisbane · Toronto

British Library Cataloguing in Publication Data:
Progress in applied social psychology.—(Wiley
   series on progress in applied social psychology)
   Vol.1
   1. Social psychology
   I. Stephenson, Geoffrey Michael
   II. Davis, James Henry
   301.1   HM251   80-41694

   ISBN 0 471 27954 4

Phototypeset by Dobbie Typesetting Service, Plymouth
and printed in the United States of America

List of Contributors

ICEK AJZEN   *University of Massachusetts at Amherst, USA*

THOMAS D. COOK   *Department of Psychology, Northwestern University, USA*

ARTHUR J. CROPLEY   *University of Hamburg, Federal Republic of Germany*

ROBYN M. DAWES   *Psychology Department, University of Oregon, USA*

SHARI SEIDMAN DIAMOND   *Department of Psychology, University of Illinois at Chicago Circle, USA*

WILLEM DOISE   *FPSE, University of Geneva, Switzerland*

MARTIN FISHBEIN   *Department of Psychology, University of Illinois at Urbana Champaign*

JAMES FREMMING   *Department of Psyhology, Northwestern University, USA*

CAROLE J. HERHOLD   *Department of Psychology, University of Illinois at Chicago Circle, USA*

DIAN-MARIE HOSKING   *Management Centre, The University of Aston, England*

JOHN M. INNES   *Department of Psychology, University of Adelaide, Australia*

CHRISTOPHER K. KNAPPER   *University of Waterloo, Canada*

GABRIEL MUGNY   *FPSE, University of Geneva, Switzerland*

JOHN ORBELL   *Political Science Department, University of Oregon, USA*

ANNE-NELLY PERRET-CLERMONT   *FPSE, University of Geneva, Switzerland*

BERNADETTE ROBINSON   *Faculty of Educational Studies, The Open University, England*

DEREK R. RUTTER   *Social Psychology Research Unit, University of Kent at Canterbury, England*

JOHN C. TURNER   *Department of Psychology, University of Bristol, England*

TOM R. TYLER   *Department of Psychology, Northwestern University, USA*

Contents

SECTION C — RESEARCH REPORT

Preface

This *Series* stems from the conviction that good theories may be improved by application, and that the development of an applied social psychology can and will be important to strong theory and research in the general area of social psychology. Such a view is perhaps more fashionable than it used to be, but the failure of social psychologists to come to grips with social issues and social problems has from time to time been discouraging. For example, industrial relations has emerged as a vigorous discipline in Great Britain and in the United States, especially the former. In Great Britain the focus has been on ideology, history of trade unions, and the economics of wage bargaining, the major aim being to elucidate the structure of the formal relationship between the principal antagonists. The relationship of this structure to the lives of the individuals who comprise the system — i.e. the social psychological dimension — has been almost entirely neglected. As a consequence, the academic pursuit of industrial relations has largely failed to be of practical assistance in the formulation and implementation of policy.

It is not surprising that young social psychologists have not been recruited to the field of industrial relations, given the extensive neglect of the real world by research in theoretical areas most directly relevant to the discipline—social exchange, bargaining, intergroup relations, power and influence. It is a melancholy but short-lived experience for social psychologists to read through the relevant literature in the hope of discovering examples of theoretical studies—of bargaining, risky shift, or minority influence to name three currently popular topics—based on, or even discussed in relation to, particular organizational contexts. The same tale can surely be told in respect to other applied disciplines—medicine, law, education, administration, to name but a few.

It is not our intention that this *Series* should argue against either theory in social psychology or the importance of laboratory work. On the contrary, we believe that good applied social psychology will stimulate theoretical discussion and advance, and that laboratory experiment has an irreplaceable role, as John Turner persuasively argues in the opening chapter of this Volume. Perhaps we could do no better than to quote Kurt Lewin who addressed some fundamental problems of research in social psychology which revolved around the very issues we are discussing here concerning theoretical and applied social psychology. The last line of that quotation has become very famous indeed, but one could argue that the preceding text speaks as succinctly to the issues.

> It would be most unfortunate if the trend toward theoretical psychology were weakened by the necessity of dealing with natural groups when studying certain problems of social psychology. One should not be blind, however, to the fact that this development offers great opportunities as well as threats to theoretical psychology. The greatest handicap of applied psychology has been the fact that, without proper theoretical help, it had to follow the costly, inefficient, and limited method of trial and error. Many psychologists working today in an applied field are keenly aware of the need for close cooperation between theoretical and applied psychology. This can be accomplished in psychology, as it has been accomplished in physics, if the theorist does not look toward applied problems with highbrow aversion or with a fear of social problems, and if the applied psychologist realizes that there is nothing so practical as a good theory. (Lewin, 1951, p.169.)

The contents of Volume 1 broadly reflect the kind of studies and contributions we hope the *Series* will attract — general theoretical and methodological discussions, substantial research reports, and theoretical discussions of empirical areas, both well defined and exploratory. Although we shall be soliciting manuscripts directly, we would like this *Series* to be responsive, and to reflect current perceptions of priorities generally. Hence, we invite submissions and suggestions, and in both we welcome controversy.

Finally, we would stress the *international* bias of the *Series*. European social psychologists have in the past twenty years or so felt the need for an independent conceptual and empirical effort, feeling that the concentration of resources and personnel in North America might lead dangerously to intellectual domination of the field. Their concern stems from the perception that social psychology does not always flourish independently of its social context, and that to be effectively applied it must engage prevailing concerns in its cultural milieu. It is the belief of many European social psychologists that their work conveys a 'social dimension' which is lacking in North American social psychology, and that this has deep historical roots. The development of different cultural traditions in social research does not, however, diminish interdependence, nor eliminate common concerns. Rather, this realization of multiple cultural interdependencies emphasizes the need for comparative effort and often for collaborative work. For these reasons we intend to emphasize international representativeness as the *Series* progresses.

December, 1980   Geoffrey Stephenson
                                                                                  James Davis

REFERENCE

Lewin, K. *Field Theory in Social Science* (Ed. D. Cartwright), Harper and Brothers, New York, 1951.

SECTION A

Theoretical and Methodological

Progress in Applied Social Psychology, Volume 1
Edited by G. M. Stephenson and J M. Davis
© 1981 John Wiley & Sons, Ltd.

1

Some Considerations in Generalizing Experimental Social Psychology

JOHN C. TURNER

Department of Psychology, University of Bristol, England

INTRODUCTION

At the same time in 1957 that Campbell introduced the concept of external validity, he noted in a relatively matter-of-fact fashion the conflict between laboratory control and the representativeness of experimental data. A few years later Campbell and Stanley (1966) drew attention to the doubts 'frequently expressed' about the applicability of the results of highly artificial experiments. In a few more years again, experimental social psychologists were having to defend their work explicitly against the interrelated charges of artificiality and irrelevance (e.g. Mills, 1969). In the latter years of social psychology's well-advertised 'crisis' (Elms, 1975), critics have found headier issues to discuss, but, nevertheless, a central and remaining source of disquiet has been the extent to which experimental social psychology can provide a deep, challenging or powerful analysis of social behaviour in its social context (e.g. Argyris, 1975; Gadlin and Ingle, 1975; Gergen, 1973, 1978a, 1978b; Israel and Tajfel, 1972). Even as the crisis ebbs, there is little abatement in the doubts expressed about the role of artificial laboratory experiments.

This chapter will attempt to answer at least some of these doubts by discussing in some depth the generalization of social psychology from the laboratory to the real world. Where possible, the theme will be related to problems in applying experimental social psychology.

Initially we shall suggest that laboratory artificiality is the most important source of current disquiet. The several forms of both laboratory artificiality and research generalizability will be elucidated. We shall then discuss, respectively, whether laboratory control, 'ecological validity' and 'mundane realism' are useful or not for generalization from experimental to real-life contexts. Our conclusion will be that experimental social psychology does generalize to the real world, but primarily on a theoretical rather than empirical basis, and that laboratory artificiality promotes theoretical progress. Finally, some general implications for applying social psychology will be considered.

Methodological imperialism needs to be disclaimed at the outset. There is no suggestion that any single research method should predominate in social psychology. This is a pseudo-issue, since every method has its value for certan purposes. Social psychological research is conducted on a broad front and hence, quite properly, is multi-methodological. Our focus on the laboratory experiment is explicitly from this perspective.

It is worth noting immediately that although there has been much argument that the laboratory experiment is an inadequate or inappropriate research method for social psychology, the evidence advanced for this claim has tended to be indirect. A research method is judged primarily by its results and so cannot properly be rejected without a direct assessment of the theories and data which it has produced. Yet, thus far, the findings of experimental social psychology still stand undemolished. Indeed, no *systematic* theoretical and empirical survey of the field seems ever to have been attempted. The critics have been preoccupied with meta-theoretical and ideological issues (e.g. Argyris, 1975; Gadlin and Ingle, 1975; Gergen, 1973; Israel and Tajfel, 1972; Sampson, 1978) and specifically methodological matters (e.g. Miller, 1972; Rosenthal and Rosnow, 1969). However useful these discussions may be, they are not persuasive, with a few exceptions, as an assessment of the extent to which laboratory experimentation into social behaviour actually works. Moreover, experimental researchers themselves, who presumably should know, still in the main display few doubts on this score. The laboratory experiment retains its dominance in theoretical research (Gergen, 1978b), which research continues to thrive, and has shown itself able to assimilate innovative theory generated by analysis of social psychology's ideological themes (e.g. Moscovici, 1976, *vis-à-vis* Moscovici, 1972, or Tajfel, 1978, *vis-à-vis* Tajfel, 1972 and 1976).

Furthermore, despite the popularity of the contention, no empirical evidence has been forthcoming to support the hypothesis that a laboratory science can produce theoretical truths which do not extend to real life. Social psychological processes in the laboratory do not appear to be separated from those in the field by a Chinese Wall. Innumerable studies have shown beyond all reasonable doubt that laboratory-based theories can have predictive validity in the field (e.g. in 1978, Baron and Ransberger; Baum *et al.*; Grush *et al.*; Isen *et al.*; Kandel; Mann *et al.*; McCauley and Stitt; McGuire *et al.*; etc.). And, of course, we take it for granted that the journey can be made successfully in the opposite direction. Numerous experimental hypotheses have rested on the assumption, subsequently confirmed, that real world phenomena can be effectively reproduced in the laboratory. Cialdini *et al.* (1978), for example, make this the basis of an explicitly 'ecologically derived' research strategy for social experimentation.

On the other hand, there appear not to be any instances of sound laboratory theories being rejected, because, on being correctly applied in the field, they were discovered to be spurious. Any theory may be elaborated or disconfirmed by new information at any time, since scientific truth is never more than approximately valid. Moreover, it is especially likely that field research will contribute to revising laboratory theories because real-world settings are nearly always more complex than experimental ones. This is one positive way in which field research complements experimental work. However, results are not necessarily spurious or artifactual because later research may amend the conclusions drawn from them. Thus far, experimental theories have not been discovered to be misleading fantasies inspired by trivial responses found solely in the laboratory. They do not tend to be falsified in the real-world *merely* because they were developed in the laboratory. It seems reasonable to suppose, therefore, on empirical as well as philosophical grounds, that laboratory and field are parts of the same real world and that social psychological phenomena in both places follow the same natural laws.

It seems, in fact, that the doubts about the social relevance of experimental social psychology spring from more intangible considerations than the scientific validity of its ideas. Two arguments in particular stand out for their currency.

The first is that social psychology has failed to live up to (somebody's) expectations as an applied science. It tends often to be assumed that the subject has had a disproportionately small impact on society and that this results from an excessive preoccupation with basic research. This hypothesis is then elevated to the status of self-evident proof that experimental social psychology does not generalize to real social conditions or that, if it does, it is too trivial to matter. There are at least three clear weaknesses in this position.

Firstly the actual extent of applied social psychology and the rate at which it is expanding tend to be ignored or underestimated. Applied social psychology is very much alive (e.g. Argyle, 1980; Deutsch and Hornstein, 1975; the present volume; or simply peruse copies of *American Psychologist*, *Contemporary Psychology*, or the *Journal of Applied Social Psychology*). In Britain, for example, a recent survey of social psychological research (Compendium of British Research in Social Psychology, B.P.S. Social Psychology Section *Newsletter*, nos. 1 and 2, 1978) demonstrates that easily less than half seems to be motivated primarily by theoretical as opposed to practical considerations. This distinction in terms of subjective purpose is crude (there is no implication that theoretical research is impractical or that applied research is atheoretical), but it serves to make the point. Furthermore, this is by no means a new state of affairs. According to one distinguished social psychologist: 'the most important single influence on the development of [American] social psychology up to the present came from outside the system itself . . . [from] the Second World War and the political upheaval in Europe which preceded it' (Cartwright, 1979, p.84). He argues that social psychology became established as a legitimate field worthy of public support through its contribution to 'the solution of problems faced by a nation at war'. Amongst many such problems, Cartwright enumerates: 'Building civilian morale and combatting demoralization; domestic attitudes, needs and information; enemy morale and psychological warfare; military administration; international relations; and psychological problems of a wartime economy' (p.84). He goes on to say that this applied work provided concrete examples of the practical usefulness of social psychology and a mass of new information, 'but I must add, not much in the way of theory' (p.84). Thus, it seems that a major impetus to the development of social psychology has been its efficacy as an applied science. If there are problems in applying social psychology, it seems as implausible now as it ever was that they result from too much pure research.

Cartwright's survey of the war-time experience in the U.S.A. provides evidence that social psychology can have an important influence on society where there are sufficient incentives and resources for its message to be heard. There is similar evidence for experimental research. To mention merely three instances: there is the role of research into intergroup relations on American desegregation policies (Jones, 1972; Stephan, 1978), into persuasion and attitude change on advertising and propaganda techniques (Argyle, 1980; Argyris, 1975), and into leadership and group dynamics on the whole art of social management (Argyle, 1980). In psychology at large, the same point is made even more dramatically by the societal impact of Behaviour Modification, which Krasner (1979) for one is tempted to describe as revolutionary (cf. Kazdin, 1978), the applied product of laboratory research into learning processes.

Secondly, it is usually forgotten that there is neither a scientific nor an ideological consensus about what constitutes a social problem and even less about what social or applied problems are, in principle, social psychological as opposed to political, economic or moral for example. Therefore, there are as yet no common criteria for measuring the success or failure of applied social psychology. The development of specifically scientific and technological standards for assessing the effectiveness of social psychological applications is a difficult but important task. Too often experimental social psychology is condemned by critics because it has not provided political solutions to what are essentially political problems. At the very least it needs to be clear that the discipline may not be making the contribution to social life which is scientifically feasible because, for ideological reasons, some people may not wish it to, whereas others may be zealously applying it to the wrong areas.

Thirdly, there is the simple point, related to the above, that the approximate validity of a social psychological theory is a necessary but not sufficient condition for its successful application. Sound application also depends upon expertise in applying pure theory to concrete settings and generating its specific technological implications (Varela, 1971), and on society's willingness to encourage and implement the mooted social changes. It is naive to believe that these conditions are always met. Indeed, it is not implausible to suppose that experimental social psychology's contemporary social role has much more to do with society than with its technological potential. The concept that society waits with bated breath to apply every new social psychological finding holds true only in certain restricted areas. The general point is that what has not been applied is not necessarily inapplicable. There are many obstacles to applying the results of pure research which have nothing to do with their scientific importance or potential social relevance.

The second argument, mentioned at the outset, is at first sight more compelling, because it is based on two correct premises. It declares that the laboratory experiment is an inherently artificial setting and hence that it cannot but produce artificial behaviour. From this it is wrongly concluded that experimental social psychology can neither be generalized to nor applied in the spontaneously complex conditions of social reality. If correct, this argument would make laboratory experimentation an intellectually futile activity and excuse any reluctance to learn how its results might be applied. Therefore, this chapter will attempt to rebut it.

FORMS OF LABORATORY ARTIFICIALITY
IN SOCIAL PSYCHOLOGY

What are the precise forms taken by laboratory artificiality? Classical experimental design is characterized by the manipulation of one or more variables under conditions where all others are controlled (eliminated or held constant) in order that the effect of the manipulated variable can be observed independently of confounding influences (cf. Boring, 1969; Gillis and Schneider, 1966). In this way, any observed effect can be assumed to have been caused by the manipulated factor. A laboratory experiment is simply one in which the investigator has created the exact conditions he or she wants to have in order to realize a particular expression of this ideal state of affairs (Festinger, 1953, p.137).

There is no doubt, therefore, that laboratory experiments attempt deliberately to manipulate and interfere with the normal workings of nature. In fact, there are at least five distinct senses in which they can be artificial and which have been considered important.

1. Laboratory experiments are *man-made, contrived situations* rather than settings which occur spontaneously in nature. An important specific sense in which this is true is that the variation in the independent variable usually

indicates an active *manipulation* of nature in order to produce some cause-and-effect relationship.

2. They represent a *controlled simplification* of the conditions under which some empirical phenomenon would normally or naturally occur. Variables which interact with the independent variable are prevented from operating in order that its pure or isolated effect may be observed.

3. To a lesser or greater degree they lack *mundane realism*, a term coined by Aronson and Carlsmith (1968) to refer to the empirical similarity between events and conditions in the laboratory and those likely to occur in the real world.

4. Their subjects, situations, and findings are usually *ecologically invalid* or *unrepresentative* in that they are not randomly sampled from some wider universe of subjects and settings in which the effect of interest is thought to occur.

Brunswik (1955) introduced the concept of ecological validity to describe the degree to which one ecological variable correlated with, was representative of, or functioned as a cue to some other ecological variable. Ecology was the 'natural-cultural habitat of an individual or group' (p.198). The methodological meaning of ecological validity intended here approximates that original sense: it indicates the degree to which some experimental effect or other aspect of the experimental setting can be considered as an 'ecological instance' randomly sampled from and hence empirically representative of some given natural universe. Ecological validity or empirical representativeness will be used solely in this precise sense hereafter.

5. Laboratory experiments are potentially *reactive*. They are capable of changing some phenomenon merely through the process of investigating it.

Reactivity will be defined as the degree to which some methodological characteristic intended as a passive record of behaviour acts as a stimulus to behavioural change (Campbell and Stanley, 1966, p.9).

This problem can be illustrated by Schrauger and Schoeneman's discussion of studies investigating the effects of feedback from other people on the self-concept (Schrauger and Schoeneman, 1979, p.564). The basic finding is that subjects change their self-evaluations to bring them more into line with the opinions expressed by others. However, these changes tend to be measured in the presence of the experimenters. Thus, subjects may change their measured self-descriptions, not because their private self-concepts have been altered, but because they do not want to disagree publicly with the opinions of the evaluators. The results may not be due to manipulated feedback *per se* but to the presence of the experimenter, something which was intended to be a 'passive record'.

Probably the most dangerous source of reactivity in social psychology experiments is the fact that they constitute a special class of social situations with their own institutionalized form and social psychological dynamics

(Miller, 1972). For example, the participants may enact subject and experimenter roles or experience motives, beliefs, and attitudes uniquely aroused by the experimental setting. Reactivity will be used here in this specific sense to describe problems of 'evaluation apprehension' (Rosenberg, 1969), 'demand characteristics' (Orne, 1962), 'experimenter effects' (Rosenthal, 1966), or other contaminating subject orientations which may arise because experiments may be subjectively strange, unusual, or odd.

In general, laboratory experiments strive for and are defined by controlled manipulation and simplification, incur mundane irrealism and ecological invalidity incidentally, and actively combat reactivity. To assess the impact of these properties we need to examine what is meant by the generalizability of experimental results. Probably the most influential single answer has been provided by Campbell's (1957) concept of external validity.

THE BASES OF EXTERNAL VALIDITY

Campbell (1957) distinguishes between the internal and external validity of experimental designs. Internal validity asks: 'did in fact the experimental stimulus make some significant difference in the specific instance?' (p.297). It indicates the degree to which the study approximates the ideal conditions of classical experimental design in allowing the unequivocal causal attribution of the observed effect to the experimental treatment rather than some extraneous variable confounded with it. External validity asks: 'to what populations, settings and variables can this effect be generalized?' (p.297). Campbell states that it refers to the generalizability, representativeness, and even the applicability of the experimental effect with respect to other settings.

The criterial question above seems to define external validity as *direct generalizability*, i.e. the degree to which experimental data (results, findings, or effects in an empirical sense) can be extended directly to other social settings. This appears to be the main meaning which Campbell attributes to the concept. This is illustrated by his well-known and much-endorsed argument that 'internal and external validity are to some extent incompatible, in that the controls required for internal validity often tend to jeopardize representativeness' (Campbell, 1957, p.297) and that external validity is improved by 'that maximum similarity of experiments to the conditions of application which is compatible with internal validity' (Campbell and Stanley, 1966, p.18). His position, therefore, is that laboratory artificiality threatens external validity by making experimental settings unlike real-world conditions.

Now it is certainly true that internal validity requires an experiment to be unlike real life. The intention is to show the empirically isolated effect of some stimulus by simplifying the conditions under which it normally occurs. Thus, it follows immediately that the more successfully is this intention realized, and so relevant conditions simplified, the fewer the normal, real world settings to which any observed effect can be directly extrapolated. Therefore, if this is what Campbell means, then external validity is clearly intended to indicate direct generalizability. It seems to equate with the immediate empirical generality or representativeness of some experimental effect with respect to real-world settings.

This is an unsatisfactory definition — which has caused a certain amount of confusion — for both specific and general reasons. The laboratory experiment's special role is to demonstrate isolated causal connections between a few variables at a time. Such effects are by their nature singular, infrequent, and unusual events. If this were not so, if they were common, spontaneous occurrences, a special research method would not be necessary to observe them. Properly speaking, therefore, internal validity does not threaten their empirical generality but simply describes the necessary pre-conditions for their detection, which are that a few variables be manipulated where all others are held constant. In other words, the purpose of laboratory experimentation precludes findings with much inductive generality. This being the case, it is unsatisfactory to employ this criterion for the method when the latter's primary objective must frustrate it. (Not surprisingly, experimenters themselves have paid little attention to direct generalizability in practice. They have not, for example, tended to seek as much mundane realism as possible in their studies, as Campbell advises. Indeed, some researchers have explicitly rejected both mundane realism and direct generalizability as desirable objectives for experimentation, e.g. Aronson and Carlsmith, 1968; Carlsmith *et al.*, 1976; Festinger, 1953; Kruglanski, 1975; Mills, 1969.)

The general objections to equating external validity with empirical generality run as follows. The practical purpose of striving for externally valid research is to be able to predict, on the basis of the results, what is likely to happen in some real-life setting. We want to know what will happen before it happens — for example, we need to know the likely consequences of some social policy before and not after we implement it. Moreover, we do not care in the least if what we predict does not correspond empirically to our observed experimental effects. All that matters is that the experimental results provide information which improves our real-world diagnosis. We wish for generalizable rather than merely general results in the twofold sense that they are anticipatory of future events and predictive of more than their own empirical repetition. External validity in this sense asks the question: which property of experimental data provides the basis for predictive generalizations to as yet unobserved as well as observed populations, settings, and variables?

Thus, external validity is not the same as empirical generality because the latter is always, strictly speaking, a statement about the past. An empirically general finding is one that has already been observed on a number of occasions or in several places in a similar form. We have to check out our facts *before* we can describe an effect in this way and our description summarizes those facts or past observations. External validity, however, has to do primarily with as yet unknown facts. Neither can empirical generality provide a direct basis for external validity: some effect is not more likely to be observed in the future to the degree that it has been observed in the past. This is the logical fallacy of induction. It is not true that the more populations, settings, and variables in which an experimental effect has been found, the more to which it can be extrapolated. The fallacy can be demonstrated by rephrasing the statement as, for example: all the swans that I have ever seen are white and therefore all the swans that I will ever see or that exist are white.

Campbell and Stanley themselves (1966, p.17; Campbell, 1969) point out that the problem with an inductive basis for generalization is that generalization always involves extrapolating into a realm that is not represented in one's original sample. We observe some effect under given conditions and assume that it will be reproduced under similar circumstances. Unfortunately, new or as yet unobserved situations always differ in several ways from previously sampled settings. It is always possible that some novel characteristic will prove causally relevant to the determination of the effect and so inhibit or modify it. Since generalization is directed exactly at new and *ipso facto* different settings, it is logically never fully justifiable.

The scientific solution to this state of affairs is to theorize—to attempt to discover the laws which govern some phenomenon. These laws indicate which conditions are theoretically relevant to the determination of an effect and so which similarities and differences between settings are causally important and which can be disregarded as trivial. We generalize an effect from one setting to another by assuming that they are identical in theoretically important ways and that our theory is correct. Any specific generalization may prove wrong either because our theory is disconfirmed by some novel observation or because our factual analysis of the conditions obtaining in the setting to which it is desired to generalize is inaccurate. The important point is that generalization is never a purely inductive exercise but always rests implicitly or explicitly upon some theoretical analysis.

It is nevertheless the case that, for certain purposes, a direct empirical basis for generalization can be approximated through representative sampling. A sample becomes representative to the degree that it contains all the important features of the universe to which it is desired to generalize. This minimizes the extent to which extrapolation goes beyond the original sample. By the same token, it tends to transform generalization from a predictive into a descriptive exercise.

The problem is that the larger the empirical differences between some sample and its intended universe, the more that representative generalization becomes predictive and so needs to be based on theory to be accurate. Some empirical differences are almost impossible to avoid. Time is one important example. Political opinion polls, for instance, will often survey voting intentions week by week or even day by day up to the date of some election because, however representative, a sample on day 1 cannot predict with confidence opinions on day 2. As we know from experience, there is a big difference between an accurate description of voting intentions at the exact time a poll was conducted and actual voting behaviour at an election. Sound predictive generalization in this instance awaits the necessary theoretical advances.

Thus, the search for a purely inductive form of external validity, for empirical results which generalize directly to a large number of real world conditions, leads inevitably to the transformation of the concept into something like Brunswik's (1955) ecological validity. Campbell undoubtedly sees the empirical representativeness of a result as an aspect of its external validity. However, his views are antithetical to Brunswik's in some important respects and, as we have seen, Campbell and Stanley are well aware that generalizability needs a theoretical basis. Thus, their ostensible definition of external validity is to some extent at odds with their substantive arguments. The definition to be adopted here will be in line with the latter.

Two particular meanings will be distinguished which derive from Campbell and Stanley's explication of the specific factors which threaten the generalizability of experimental data. Firstly, there are factors which are methodological threats, i.e. extraneous variables in the experimental setting which are likely to interact with the independent variable and so produce effects restricted to the experimental situation with which they are uniquely associated. Thus, *external methodological validity* can be defined as the extent to which an experimental effect can be generalized, under theoretically appropriate conditions, to non-experimental settings. Secondly, there are theoretical threats, i.e. the dangers of incorrectly interpreting the conceptual and theoretical meaning of an experimental effect. As described above, the appropriate generalization of an effect depends upon its theoretical significance being known. Even the simplest finding cannot be generalized directly to nominally identical variables unless it has been 'conceptually purified' (Campbell, 1957, pp.309–10; Campbell and Stanley, 1966, pp.32–34; Carlsmith *et al.*, 1976, pp.61–81). Therefore, *external conceptual validity* can be defined (inclusively of its methodological counterpart) as the extent to which the conceptual and theoretical meaning of an experimental effect is known so that it can be generalized systematically to theoretically identified conditions. Such generalization may be indirect as well as direct in that a theoretically identical effect may be predicted to take different empirical forms under systematically different real-world settings.

External validity will be used in the above senses in the rest of this paper and distinguished sharply from direct generalizability or ecological validity. External conceptual validity is considered to be the fundamental form of generalizability of an experimental effect. We shall now examine more precisely whether internal and external validity are incompatible.

DOES INTERNAL VALIDITY THREATEN EXTERNAL VALIDITY?

Methodological Issues

Methodological threats to external validity are trivial, extraneous variables, specific to the experimental setting, which are likely to interact with the independent variable and so influence its effect. Such an effect does not generalize beyond the experimental setting to real-world situations because these trivial variables are not present in the latter to interact with the stimulus which was the independent variable. Four examples of such threats are noted by Campbell and Stanley (1966, pp.5–6):

(1) the reactive effect of testing in which pre-testing subjects might increase or decrease their sensitivity to the experimental stimulus (this threat seems now less plausible, cf. Campbell, 1969; Lana, 1969);

(2) the interactive effects of subject selection biases and the experimental variable;

(3) the reactive effects of experimental arrangements which make subjects aware that they are participating in an experiment; and

(4) multiple treatment interference in which the effects of different treatments applied to the same subjects are likely to interact.

Pre-testing and multiple treatment effects are relatively easy to eliminate or measure in the laboratory experiment. Representative subject samples, on the other hand, are usually thought neither necessary nor desirable (see the later section on ecological validity). Selection biases which are potentially interactive in theoretically interesting ways are discovered and explored through the systematic sampling of distinct subject groups, whereas those of no interest are avoided in the same way.

Therefore, the only plausible methodological route by which internal validity might tend to threat external validity is through reactivity. Specific reactive effects are always possible in social experimentation, and competent researchers seek to eliminate them in the same way that they seek to eliminate any other plausible, alternative explanations of their data. How this is accomplished will depend upon the particular theoretical and empirical circumstances which make a specific reactive process plausible in a given instance. Reactivity becomes especially dangerous only if we suppose that it is sufficiently pervasive as to be impossible to eliminate as an alternative explanation of any given experimental data. It might be, for example, that subjects' mere awareness of being experimental subjects always caused them to respond differently to the independent variable than they would have without such an awareness. The situation has, indeed, sometimes been pictured as if the laboratory unleashed mysterious, indefinable processes of social influence so that the subjects were always able and motivated to divine and confirm the experimenter's hypothesis independently of its validity.

Recent evidence makes this hypothesis of pervasive reactivity in laboratory experimentation much less plausible than it once seemed (e.g. Barber, 1976; Barber and Silver, 1968a, 1968b; Crano and Brewer, 1973, pp.67–89; Kruglanski, 1975; Milgram, 1972). It has not been established, for example, that experimenters can confirm hypotheses unintentionally through some intangible process of communicating expectations to subjects. Crano and Brewer (1973, p.84) suggest that most experimenter expectancy effects can probably be explained by systematic errors in observing, recording, or analysing data or by the provision of cues to subjects as to the correct response through some form of verbal or non-verbal reinforcement. Kruglanski (1975) concludes from his empirical review of reactive dangers such as 'evaluation apprehension' and 'demand characteristics' that subject artifacts have not been adequately demonstrated. He finds that there do not appear to be pervasive sources of subject artifacts associated with psychology experiments and that only two specific sources produce pervasive effects, which do not necessarily tend towards confirming the hypothesis. The latter sources are providing the subjects with a hypothesis and/or cues to the socially desirable or typical response.

It would seem, then, that the only reactive effects which are likely to be pervasive are rendered implausible by standard experimental procedures, for it is normal practice to attempt to minimize data errors, disguise hypotheses, and eliminate clues to the socially desirable, expected or typical response. In fact, experimental social psychology has developed a battery of weapons for coping with reactivity. There are three main approaches.

1. General styles and strategies of experimentation such as the 'deception study' to conceal the theoretical hypothesis and even the fact of experimentation, 'experimental realism' to encourage spontaneity and decrease self-consciousness (Carlsmith et al., 1976, p.81), complex or non-obvious hypotheses, post-test only research designs, unobtrusive field studies and cumulative, multiple experimentation across laboratories.

2. The procedures of systematic replication and extension of an experimental effect which define normal theoretical research. These procedures and the related practice of 'multi-operationalism' purify the conceptual meaning of an effect by eliminating plausible, alternative conceptualizations such as reactive effects (Campbell and Stanley, 1966, pp.32–34; Carlsmith et al., 1976, pp.61–81; Kruglanski, 1975).

3. Methodological procedures and techniques such as keeping experimenter and subjects blind to the hypothesis and experimental condition, separating the dependent measure from the experimental setting, running conditions simultaneously in one session, reproducing instructions to subjects mechanically, etc.

Thus, social psychologists have developed sophisticated defences against reactivity. This is not to say that an experiment need employ all the above defences to be sound. On the contrary, it is only necessary and desirable that it be proof against plausible as opposed to possible dangers. Possible dangers, like other possible alternative explanations, are logically infinite in number. It would paralyse scientific research to worry about what is merely possible. The more rewarding and scientifically difficult task is to distinguish between plausible and implausible processes in the light of available evidence. What constitutes a sound study from this perspective is decided much more by social psychological theory and common sense than methodological ritual. Finally, it needs to be stressed that some hypothetical reactive process must be attributed definite and falsifiable empirical features before it can be considered plausible.

Reactive processes are an important topic of research in themselves and have, in fact, been studied experimentally. The main methodological point, however, is that although reactivity is a problem which cannot be dismissed, it does not represent a pervasive, unitary process and so can be coped with. In the self-concept studies mentioned earlier, for example, the reactive artifact is easily tested by separating the dependent measures from the overt experimental context or even by varying the presence of the experimenter. The cumulative information gained from coping with reactivity provides both new methodological standards for experimentation and a better understanding of reactive processes in their own right.

In conclusion, it is well within the normal competence of experimental social psychologists to produce effects with external methodological validity. Laboratory artificiality does not appear to generate reactive effects which intrinsically vitiate the experimental method as applied to human subjects, whereas pre-testing, selection bias, and multiple treatment interference are less problematic for laboratory experimental than other forms of social research. Even particular reactive effects can be combated through conceptual purification and other measures which depend upon controlled manipulation and simplification. The controls necessary for internal validity may tend to facilitate external methodological validity.

Theoretical Issues

Experimental effects generalize directly to real-world conditions which approximate experimental settings in theoretically relevant ways. Since such settings are designed to embody theoretically simpler conditions than those which obtain in most natural instances, it follows that experimental effects can rarely be extended directly to real-world situations. (Where this is possible, the researcher should ask him- or herself why the experiment was conducted.) This is the specific reason why the external validity of experimental designs cannot be reduced to the empirical or direct generalizability of their results. Laboratory experiments are constructed to generate singular, artificial events which neither duplicate nor are representative of real-world happenings. Their empirical findings are artificial in at least two specific ways: they tend to be unnaturally isolated or pure and innovative or novel. Effects with these properties are sought because they are extremely valuable for theoretical research.

This can be illustrated by considering very crudely and schematically how an experimenter develops a theory about some complex, real-world phenomenon. The research can be described in terms of three interrelated stages: simple causal analysis, conceptual purification, and theoretical synthesis. The description is idealized since we are concerned with the logic of the research process, not its much more untidy and capricious reality. Similarly, developments are depicted as if they took place in isolation from other kinds of research and the values, intuitions, and naive observations of the experimenter. This, too, is a necessary licence.

The first stage is to disentangle causal from spurious relationships between empirical events by manipulating potential causes in isolation from factors which normally co-vary with them. The experimenter breaks down the complex, empirical phenomenon into separate causal components. This does not imply that natural events are merely the sum of isolated causal components. Causal analysis is not intended to simulate reality but to discover the theoretical significance of important variables as a first step towards predicting natural events.

The second stage is the conceptual analysis or purification of isolated causal components. Any empirical variable is always a complex package of correlated variation on multiple dimensions. It is impossible, therefore, to create an experimental variable which does not have multiple empirical attributes and hence potentially multiple conceptual meanings (Campbell and Stanley, 1966, pp.32–34; Carlsmith et al., 1976, p.61). To find the conceptual meaning of some experimental effect, the researcher must discover which aspects of the independent and dependent variables are responsible for their causal connection. In particular, the researcher must determine whether the effect is produced by the theoretically important attributes which he or she intended to manipulate in the experimental variables or by the theoretically irrelevant attributes confounded with them.

This is achieved through cumulative, systematic experimentation to replicate and extend some result. The basic procedures are:

(1) to hold constant the theoretically relevant aspects of an experimental variable and vary systematically the theoretically irrelevant aspects — it being predicted that the same effect will be observed; and

(2) to vary systematically the theoretically relevant and hold constant the theoretically irrelevant aspects — it being predicted that systematically different but theoretically expected effects will be observed.

These procedures are employed on independent and dependent variables, within and between experiments, and separately or simultaneously — the systematic replication of variables is also often known as 'multi-operationism'

(Crano and Brewer, 1973, p.6). Experimentation continues until all but one of the conceptualizations of the effect have been rendered implausible. If the predictions are disconfirmed, then the effect is appropriately reconceptualized.

Conceptual analysis proceeds through the systematic exploration of the limits of some effect across a range of empirical conditions. The result's conceptual meaning is thus the succinct, theoretically represented summary of the accumulated facts about the extent to which it does and does not generalize to specific populations, settings, and operationalizations. The transformation of simple causal components into conceptually pure effects facilitates the elaboration and testing of theoretical syntheses.

Theoretical synthesis is directed at abstracting general laws from the conceptual meanings of the observed effects. The researcher seeks the principle or process by which the experimental effects operate. To do this, he or she must combine or integrate several different findings into one natural invariance functioning under systematically different conditions. As abstract theoretical propositions, laws go beyond the empirical generalities observed in nature and summarize the conditions theoretically relevant to their operation. They postulate how as yet unobserved as well as observed effects are invariant with respect to some theoretically identified but not necessarily actual range of settings.

To test such a law, the experimenter constructs laboratory conditions which model what is theoretically possible in social reality rather than simply record what everybody knows already to be there. Settings are designed which are at the extremes of theoretically relevant dimensions in order to produce theoretically expected but empirically novel effects. Such effects may be non-obvious because they have never before been clearly observed in nature; they are persuasive support for a theory since they demonstrate that it is explanatorily heuristic and powerful in practice.

They are also a direct stimulus for the discovery and elaboration of new laws. The researcher can design experimental settings which push theoretical knowledge to its very limits by modelling the enigmas which exist at the frontiers of understanding. The result may be theoretically as well as empirically novel effects which the researcher must now seek to assimilate.

Thus, artificially isolated and novel effects define each important stage of theoretical experimental research. Their isolation takes the forms of simple causality, conceptual purity, and theoretical extremity, and they become more novel correspondingly. At no stage does the experimenter attempt to duplicate the real-world effects of variables. This, paradoxically, is why he or she can advance relatively rapidly to a theoretical understanding of the processes implicated in their operation. The experimental social psychologist generalizes from data to the real world indirectly on the basis of that theory. The complex natural phenomenon is predicted as the outcome of relevant laws operating under the specific circumstances that obtain in the natural setting, including the particular values of the observed causal factors. Just as the research has not been constrained by the need to simulate reality, so neither are predictions limited to results observed in the laboratory. Indeed, the ultimate goal is the development of powerful theories which transcend the available empirical reality and so allow its purposeful reconstruction. The retreat into the laboratory is a purely tactical one designed to equip the researcher with new, critical weapons with which to confront everyday reality.

This can be illustrated by considering some research on intergroup behaviour. Common sense (and theory) suggest that an important factor in intergroup conflict is conflicting group interests for scarce, objective resources. However, one variable always confounded with intergroup relations in real life is social categorization *per se*, i.e. the mere awareness of ingroup-outgroup membership. Tajfel *et al.* (1971) isolated this variable experimentally and to their surprise discovered that it alone was sufficient to cause gratuitous intergroup discrimination in which the ingroup was favoured over the outgroup.

Systematic replications included demonstrating that the effect was not due to interpersonal similarities and differences between ingroup and outgroup members. It was found even when subjects were divided into completely 'minimal' groups on an explicitly random basis (Billig and Tajfel, 1973). Systematic extensions included showing that the intergroup discrimination decreased when subjects were able to respond to others as 'individuated' persons rather than solely as group members (Wilder, 1978). Research in different methodological paradigms also reinforced the conclusion that the intergroup categorization was the effective conceptual variable.

The effect can be explained as a compound product of a cognitive process whereby subjects attribute characteristics to themselves and others on the basis of their category or group memberships and a motivational process whereby they seek intergroup differences which favour the ingroup to increase their self-esteem (Turner, 1978). These processes imply the law that group members tend to accentuate similarities within groups and differences between groups on any stimulus dimension which they perceive to correlate with ingroup-outgroup membership. This allows the derivation of a non-obvious principle about intergroup conflict. Assuming that people tend to perceive their needs and goals as correlated with ingroup membership, then *social categorization per se should cause people directly to perceive their objective interests as similar and cooperative within groups and different and competitive between groups.* Common sense, in other words, may only be half right: intergroup conflict may be reciprocally determined by objective group interests and the mere fact of an ingroup-outgroup division.

The theoretical hypothesis explains why conflicting interests and different group memberships tend to be confounded in real life. To test the hypothesis, therefore, requires an unnatural situation in which people's actual cooperative or competitive interdependence is varied independently of their ingroup–outgroup membership. We can imagine some experiment with four conditions in which, to maximize their economic self-interest, subjects should either (1) cooperate with ingroup and compete with outgroup members; (2) compete with ingroup and cooperate with outgroup members; (3) cooperate with both ingroup and outgroup members; or (4) compete with ingroup and outgroup members. The study is hypothetical, but we can speculate on the basis of some evidence that the result might well indicate that subjects tend to cooperate with ingroup and compete with outgroup members relatively independently of objective reward structures.

Such a result would have important theoretical and applied implications, not because it would generalize directly to many real settings — there are many complicating factors which make this problematic — but because of the theoretical principle it would illuminate. For this reason these implications extend beyond the observed findings.

For example, suppose that some large organization is afflicted by inter-departmental rivalry which reduces efficiency. One sensible policy would be to invent new and stress old cooperative interdependencies (superordinate goals) between the departments and encourage as much cooperative interaction as possible. If our theoretical principle is correct, this might only work in the short term, if at all, for two groups can easily cooperate whilst still retaining their separate identities. What would matter would be whether the policy contributed to the fusion of the departments into one psychological group or reinforced the salience of ingroup–outgroup membership. If the latter, then there would remain a pervasive tendency for the departments to perceive their interests and even reinterpret cooperative ones as competitive. A better policy might be to work directly at the level of psychological group membership and adopt measures to create a superordinate group identification. These would evidently depend on the particular situation, but could include inventing some common group label, providing it with high everyday visibility (badges, uniforms) and ensuring that members experienced common fate, shared threat and so on as well as cooperative interaction. This new policy follows from the working hypothesis that the merging of subgroups into one superordinate group should cause people to perceive competitive subgroup interests as intragroup, cooperative interests. If the basic principle described above is valid, then so should be this hypothesis, even though it has not itself been demonstrated experimentally. Similarly, it is worth noting that a theoretical explanation of laboratory intergroup discrimination can be used to promote an exactly opposite state of affairs in the real world.

The research above began with a non-obvious finding. This is typical in that theoretical synthesis continually feeds back into causal analysis. It is a fundamental strength of experimentation that it can probe everyday reality to make it appear strange, abnormal, and unfamiliar, for there are few better ways of gaining insight into ordinary processes than by pushing them to produce extraordinary results. Social change, after all, requires that the *status quo* be seen as contingent and hence modifiable. Thus, artificial effects play a positive, creative role in disconfirming received wisdom and stimulating new ways of thinking.

Laboratory artificiality, therefore, as embodied in the controlled manipulation and simplification of some causal effect and measured by the concept of internal validity, contributes to the theoretical analysis of experimental data often to the same degree that it threatens their empirical generality or representativeness. Artificial effects are deliberately sought for their clear theoretical meaning and it is the theoretical meaning of a result which defines the settings, populations, and variables to which it can and cannot be generalized. Thus, internal validity actively promotes external validity at the same time that it sacrifices ecological validity and mundane realism. In the next two sections we shall consider whether ecological validity and mundane realism improve the generalizability and applicability of experimental results.

REPRESENTATIVE DESIGN AND ECOLOGICAL VALIDITY

Brunswik (1955) has argued that systematic or experimental design should be replaced by 'representative design'. The latter is characterized by the observation of empirical relationships as they occur spontaneously in nature through the random sampling of real-world settings. The results describe empirical relationships exactly as they are found in the context of their naturally occurring concomitant variation, i.e. they are confounded or unconfounded as the case may be. The purpose of this procedure is to generate ecologically valid data, i.e. findings which are empirically representative of what obtains in some natural–cultural environment or ecological universe.

It must be stressed that neither representative sampling nor correlational research techniques are necessarily indicative of representative as opposed to systematic design. The main difference is that representative design observes the relations between factors as they are varied or not by an ecology, whereas systematic design is directed at making causal inferences by observing the effects of varying factors on the basis of the researcher's theory. The latter is often accomplished by correlational methods and the representative sampling of theoretically identified variables. Brunswik's arguments for representative design are complex and need not concern us. His position is important because it takes the search for direct generalizability to a logical extreme. Our *sole* concern in this section is to assess whether empirical representativeness provides a solid basis for the predictive generalization of some finding. It is not the intention to denigrate representative design, or descriptive, correlational surveys in general, as a useful research method, nor to suggest that correlational methods cannot be employed for systematic causal analysis.

There seem to be at least four fundamental limitations upon ecological validity as a form of generalizability (Hilgard, 1955; Mills, 1969, pp.426-27; Postman, 1955; Selltiz *et al.*, 1959, pp.125-27).

1. Representative design passively records naturally confounded relationships between variables. It provides descriptive, correlational data. Correlation does not necessarily indicate causality and so ecologically valid relationships may nevertheless be causally spurious.

2. Ecological validity is not a strategic alternative to external validity, but depends upon systematic causal theory to be any more than a statistical concept. Any interesting ecology contains a potentially infinite number of instances which it is impossible to sample representatively. The researcher must restrict the ecological universe to some finite class of settings. Inevitably and consciously or unconsciously, the researcher will define the universe in terms of his or her current theory: he or she will select ecological instances to represent variation along the situational dimensions which are considered causally relevant to the events being studied. The sample represents the universe which represents the theory. If the theory is incorrect, the universe will tend to include causally irrelevant and exclude causally relevant settings and so bias the result. Yet, since the result pretends to reflect nature, it will often seem to confirm the researcher's original theory. The researcher may attempt to be atheoretical by selecting ecological settings simply because they contain some specific natural variables, but this merely recreates the same problem at second remove: the results will still tend to redescribe the implicit, theoretical presuppositions inherent in the definition of those natural variables.

3. Ecologies are not usually causally homogeneous: they tend to contain multiple causal variables which often interact to produce some natural correlation. Thus, the ecologically valid correlation may disguise the actual relationship between two variables in different specific locations in the ecology. A result may be true for the ecology as a whole and yet theoretically incorrect and inapplicable in practice in any particular ecological instance.

4. Fully representative design is impossible and difficult even to approximate. The researcher must always settle for less than an investigation of some natural phenomenon under all relevant conditions. Ecologically valid data tend to be expensive in time, money, and effort even where the so-called ecology has already become so restricted as to question whether the concept is applicable.

To illustrate the third point, let us hypothesize an ecological universe in which cohesiveness interacts with group norms to influence the productivity of industrial work-groups. Cohesiveness increases productivity where group norms favour high performance at work, but decreases productivity where group norms favour low performance. We can suppose, too, that some investigator employs representative design to discover the natural correlation between cohesiveness and productivity but, unfortunately, is unaware of the role of group norms. It is obvious, firstly, that since the ecology must be restricted to, for example, the work-groups in one town, industry, or large factory, a biased result may be obtained. It may be found, for instance, that cohesiveness, is positively correlated with productivity. Yet, should the researcher attempt to apply this finding and recommend to management that group cohesiveness be increased, the actual consequence could be a decrease in productivity. What matters is the specific groups to which the policy is applied, not the effect of cohesiveness on the empirically representative group.

It is obvious, secondly, that even if the researcher accidentally samples the theoretically appropriate ecology, the unbiased result may be yet more misleading. The investigator may now discover, quite correctly, that there is a zero correlation between cohesiveness and productivity. This average correlation disguises the fact that there is a positive relationship between cohesiveness and productivity in half the ecology and a negative relationship in the other half. The researcher may assume, in consequence, that cohesiveness has no causal influence on productivity and draw incorrect theoretical and applied conclusions.

This example also makes it clear that, to make some progress, the investigator has to abandon the search for representative truths and subject his data to systematic, theoretical analysis. This task is facilitated by data which have been sampled systematically on explicit theoretical grounds in the first place. Systematic design, or some approximation to it, would have fared much better in this field context.

For example, it would have taken just one sound experiment on one homogeneous, unrepresentative sample of subjects to have discovered that cohesiveness was capable of a causal effect on productivity. Further research could have attempted to falsify this result as rapidly and efficiently as possible by replicating it upon new subject groups within the ecology which were as different as possible both from each other and the original sample. In consequence, contradictory findings could have soon emerged. Despite a popular misconception, inconsistent results are extremely valuable and exciting in theoretical research, for they indicate the hidden influence of some, as yet unidentified, theoretically important condition. The researcher finds that condition by comparing and contrasting the studies which produce the different results. Eventually the importance of group norms would have been noticed and this factor would have provided the clue to the integrative, conceptually general law that cohesiveness increases adherence to group norms. This law, in turn, would have permitted relatively sophisticated applied recommendations directed at selective changes in both group cohesiveness and social norms. Research can always go wrong, of course, whatever the design, but the important point is that the utilization of small, homogeneous subject samples, deliberately chosen to represent systematically the possible variations within some population, is a sound and cost-effective strategy for generating theoretical progress and social applications. What matters is not that each sample represents the whole, but that, as a whole, the several samples represent variation along the important dimensions which define the ecology.

Ecological validity, therefore, is a secondary or subordinate form of generalizability which cannot replace but presupposes external validity to be useful. It is worthwhile for accurate factual description of natural correlations in some whole setting, but does not necessarily convey much predictive understanding of the real world. Systematic or experimental design, on the other hand, is not concerned to describe nature in its spontaneously occurring, empirically chaotic form. It analyses the conceptually pure regularities which lie below the surface confusion. Thus, experimental effects become representative in their conceptual and theoretical content rather than empirical form. They become more representative of and applicable in the real world in so far as they embody some more abstract and general law.

From this point of view it is crucial to distinguish between ecological validity in Brunswik's sense and the *ecological importance* of some social psychological law. Ecological importance can be defined as the degree to which some social psychological law is sufficiently general for some practical purpose in a specific ecological setting. For example, the law that cohesiveness increases conformity to group norms is more important in the above ecology than the law that cohesiveness increases productivity. The latter law is valid but it is a lower order, restricted law which applies only in some parts of the relevant applied context; other, same level laws apply in other parts. This ensures that the antecedent conditions postulated by this law tend to interact with background features of the ecology to produce effects unpredicted by the law and which frustrate planned social applications. For example, management may provide work-groups with an extended lunch-break, assuming that this will increase cohesiveness and so productivity. The policy may work in small factories but not large ones, because these locations facilitate the development of different group norms. To management, working solely with a valid but ecologically unimportant law, the result will be demoralizing confusion. On the other hand, the law that cohesiveness increases conformity to group norms is sufficiently general that it happily predicts all the observed effects of this policy. It directs attention to all the ecological factors which must be manipulated or measured to ensure that some applied policy has predictable and desirable consequences. Management only need this single law for their practical purpose in this ecology because it demonstrates that what appeared previously to be complex interactions between variables are in fact a simple invariance operating under systematically different and theoretically identifiable conditions.

The concept of ecological importance is fully compatible with the theoretical purpose of social psychological experimentation and yet stimulates a constructive relationship between theoretical and applied research. It has three distinctive advantages over the concept of ecological validity as a way of describing the ecological usefulness of experimental effects and laws. Firstly, it does not create misconceptions that the generalizability of experimental data is a matter of their empirical representativeness. Secondly, it does not lead to the unwarranted denigration of experimental laws by implying that they are invalid merely because they may be as yet too restricted to be useful in practice. Thirdly, the discovery that some law is ecologically unimportant can provide a direct stimulus to theoretical research to develop higher order theories more in tune with applied needs.

Gergen (1978b) argues that experimental effects are swamped in the real world because natural events are multiply determined; he, therefore, advocates research methods which can detect higher order interactions between many variables. Although, as we have agreed, this premise is correct with respect to effects understood purely as specific empirical relationships, it is nevertheless one-sided in ignoring their theoretical content. Theories transform complex interactions into main effects by conceptualizing them more simply at a higher level of abstraction. Thus, whether some real event is more or less multiply determined depends upon the power of the explanatory laws available and experimental effects hold in the real world in so far as they are conceptualized appropriately to embody some ecologically important law. There is no special merit in merely detecting highest order, real-world interactions (for which common sense observation often suffices), since they can be factually specific, theoretically confusing, and impractical to work with. Causal and conceptual analysis, by whatever method, is necessary to develop laws precisely as heuristic devices for avoiding the measurement and prediction of natural events as complex interactions.

Laboratory and field research are complementary and both necessary in this work. For example, the ecological importance of some sound laboratory law could be determined by the systematic sampling of its effects in specific real-world instances through either experimental or correlational methods. Such instances could be selected to represent ecological dimensions which seem important on theoretical, intuitive, and applied grounds. The law's predicted outcomes could then be mapped against observed effects to discover the settings within which it held. The purpose would not be to invalidate the law but to discover the background conditions with which its antecedent conditions interacted. Such interactions would be demonstrable proof that some novel theoretical synthesis was required which would transform them into the simple effects of some higher order law. At this point, research could well return to the laboratory to solve a problem which although purely theoretical would nevertheless be responsive to applied needs. Thus, in line with the concept of external conceptual validity we can advocate the notion of ecological importance as determined by the systematic sampling of field settings.

MUNDANE REALISM, EXTERNAL VALIDITY,
AND THE APPLICABILITY OF EXPERIMENTAL RESULTS

Does mundane realism improve external validity? Should the laboratory experiment be an empirical analogue or simulation of some real-world setting? However much a laboratory experiment has been made to resemble a real-world setting, it is evident that they are nevertheless two different settings in which therefore different results may obtain. What actually matters for similar effects to occur is that the experimental and real setting are theoretical rather than empirical analogues of each other. Yet, it is obvious that if a researcher has a sufficiently adequate theory that he can be sure that he has constructed a theoretical analogue of real-world events in the laboratory, then it is pointless to do so. The thing to do in this instance would be to use the theory directly to predict real-world events.

Assuming, therefore, that the researcher begins with an uncertain theoretical understanding, does mundane realism contribute to the external validity of some experimental effect? There is not, in fact, any general answer. It depends upon the particular experimental instance and the specific real setting that is being simulated. Methodologically speaking, mundane realism may decrease reactivity by making subjects more relaxed and less suspicious; on the other hand, it may increase it by making the theoretical hypothesis obvious. Similarly, it may or may not increase 'experimental realism'—the degree to which experimental settings are involving and impactful (Aronson and Carlsmith, 1968)—since some real settings have to be taken seriously whereas others can be very boring. Experimental realism is more important than mundane realism just as are the other characteristics of experiments already discussed with respect to eliminating reactivity. Mundane realism becomes useful for external methodological validity in so far as it contributes to these other characteristics.

Conceptually speaking, too, mundane realism is neither necessary nor sufficient for external validity. Experimental manipulations with mundane realism tend to be gross, empirically complex stimuli. Thus, they may sometimes help to purify an effect conceptually by demonstrating it over a large amount of theoretically irrelevant variation. On the other hand, complex, realistic stimuli are often associated with multiple conceptual meanings which can confound the theoretical interpretation of their effects. The fundamental point is that the basic means whereby experimentation elucidates the theoretical meaning of empirical relationships is to manipulate and isolate them under conditions theoretically dissimilar to natural settings. The apparent, empirical similarity between experimental and real situations is essentially irrelevant from this perspective; it matters only in so far as it contributes to or hinders attainment of this objective.

It is nevertheless true that, all things being equal, an experiment which attempts to simulate a real setting empirically is more likely to be its theoretical analogue. Thus, mundane realism does make it more likely that an experimental effect will generalize directly to the simulated, real situation. Such a result may extend to the specific, simulated setting, but no other; it may therefore be an applicable but not necessarily empirically general or generalizable result. Should experiments be designed to achieve specific applicability in this sense?

Let us hypothesize an applied field setting in which an investigator wishes to implement some social change or policy, X, in order to achieve a state of affairs, Y. A laboratory experiment is carried out to see whether the theory that X causes Y is plausible. The experiment is made an empirical analogue of the field situation in the hope that whatever happens in the laboratory will also be found in real life. Unfortunately, although this strategy might work, the investigator will not know whether it has or not until the social change is implemented; only then can it be determined whether the experiment was a theoretical as well as empirical analogue. In this case the experiment was, of course, pointless since X was as much a shot in the dark after as before it.

Let us suppose that X produces Y in both laboratory and field. This argues but does not make it certain that laboratory and field are theoretical analogues of each other. Unfortunately, they may still not be analogues of the researcher's theory. It may be that Y was caused by some extraneous, but not unimportant, variable confounded with X in both the experiment and reality. Precisely because the experiment has been designed to duplicate reality exactly, it will tend to reproduce the variables naturally confounded with X or Y. Thus, although the experiment looked successful, it did not actually contribute any additional information to that obtained by implementing the social change. The researcher's theory is no more and no less plausible than it would have been without the experiment; what was learned is exactly repeated in the laboratory; what was unclear in the field remains confused in the experiment.

This becomes more obvious if X does not produce Y in either laboratory or field. The researcher's social policy has proved a failure; he or she has lost a theory and is probably no wiser than before as to why it was inadequate and with what to replace it. The researcher has the useless consolation that the experiment probably did duplicate the applied context in some important by unknown theoretical respect. This factor cannot be identified because experiment and field resemble each other in too many ways. Of course, the researcher may not implement X in the field if it does not produce Y in the laboratory. This would be sensible caution. Unfortunately, the investigator still does not know whether the theory is wrong in reality or whether the experiment failed to be a theoretical analogue. He or she knew that the theory might be wrong at the outset and the experimental effect has simply confirmed but not resolved this doubt. As for the latter query, there is little choice but to implement the real X to find out.

The experiment will in fact only provide materially useful information that throws light on the investigator's theory if it produces different results from those which obtain in reality. The researcher now knows that experiment and field differ from each other in some hitherto unknown but important theoretical respect which he or she needs to identify. The discovery of this factor will probably have implications for theoretical expectations about whether X will cause Y in reality. Thus, there was only a point in doing the experiment if, accidentally, it failed to be a theoretical analogue of the field. The limitations of this trial-and-error strategy for applicable results are evident: the research which is supposed to justify the social policy cannot be interpreted until the policy has been implemented; whether or not the policy succeeds, the research may not improve our theoretical understanding of why; and, finally, since the research succeeds in being informative, at best accidentally, it may well provide trivial theoretical insights.

The alternative is to employ the experiment for its proper purpose of testing theoretical hypotheses. The researcher should identify the real-world conditions relevant to the effect of X on Y in the light of current social psychological knowledge. He or she should attempt to predict the effect of X under those and other intuitively relevant conditions by considering in particular how the antecedent conditions of laboratory-based laws might tend to interact with each other in the field and with other salient variables hitherto neglected in theoretical research. The search for intuitively plausible, confusing interactions between real-world factors is directed at identifying where theoretical analysis and synthesis are most necessary in the double sense that undoubted theoretical ignorance is likely to sabotage social application. The experimental hypothesis would be addressed to closing what the researcher has determined to be the most important theoretical gap in social psychology relevant to the particular applied problem. Whatever the outcome, the researcher would have contributed to theoretical understanding and also improved the chances of correctly predicting the real-world effects of X. The important point, again, is not simply that pure research can remain primarily theoretical and yet be responsive to applied needs, but also that applied problems have a role to play in stimulating higher order theorizing as a counterweight to the fragmentation which tends to occur in the laboratory.

CONCLUSION

The conclusion is that the laboratory experiment is primarily a technique for theoretical research and that experimental social psychology generalizes to the real world through extending its theories—not its empirical data—to new social contexts. Festinger (1953) made these points some years ago, but recently they seem to have been often forgotten.

This is evident in two recent critiques of experimental social psychology

(Gergen, 1973; Argyris, 1975). Gergen argues that general laws are not possible because historical change such as the development of public awareness about social psychological predictions invalidates the underlying theories by changing social behaviour. Schlenker (1974) refutes this position by pointing out that empirical generalizations (which may be historically specific) should not be confused with abstract, universal propositions (basic laws or processes). The latter do not include historically specific facts in their formulations and have a conditional 'if–then' form: if certain antecedent conditions are realized, then particular consequences follow, but different, equally lawful, consequences follow from other relevant antecedents. Thus, general laws, far from being incompatible with historical change, must predict changes in social behaviour under systematically different, historical conditions. The reactive effects of public predictions are not a special case. If some law predicts A from B, but some unforeseen event such as public awareness of that prediction (C) produces D instead of A, the law is not invalidated since B and BC constitute different antecedent conditions. Reactivity would only be problematic if it were unlawful so that neither the original nor any other theory could predict D from BC—which is both implausible and inconsistent with existing theories of reactive processes such as, for example, 'evaluation apprehension'. Laws are thus historical in the specific sense that their effects obtain only when necessary antecedent conditions are historically present, but transhistorical in that effects vary with systematic changes in relevant conditions (which may be correlated with time) but not with time *per se*. To argue that psychological or other processes vary with time *per se* is to postulate nature as arbitrary rather than lawful. This denies *a priori* the possibility of a psychological science—which would seem like shutting the stable door after the horse has bolted.

Argyris has the opposite worry that public awareness of experimental social psychology will tend to validate it by perpetuating historically specific forms of social behaviour. He argues that its theories are imbued with the currently dominant value system or 'model' for action because, firstly, they describe social reality uncritically (we have discussed extensively why this is not the case) and, secondly, laboratory experimentation requires social practices congruent with the model. The latter point is, to say the least, contentious, since, for example, methodological control is confused with an ideologically motivated power relationship between experimenter and subjects. However, even ignoring these premises, his conclusion that social applications of experimental results must tend to recreate the social conditions under which they were obtained is fallacious. Again, this confuses empirical generalizations with abstract, theoretical propositions. The generalization of theories is not restricted to the empirical effects upon which they were based: their applied value is that they make new social realities possible by specifying the necessary alternative conditions for novel empirical relationships. Furthermore, since theories prescribe what is possible and not simply what is, the applied policies derived from them reflect the social objectives, moral values, and ethical choice of the researcher and his or her client. No theory dictates or excuses the politics of derived applications—this is guilt by association and lets the applied researcher off the ethical hook.

The real obstacles to generalizing to applied contexts are relatively straightforward. They are limitations in basic theory, factual ignorance of the exact conditions which obtain in complex, real situations including our lack of suitable measurement techniques, and lack of practical control over relevant conditions. At present, theory is fragmented and molecular: there are innumerable lower and middle order laws but few general theories which are also non-vacuous. This state of affairs partly explains why real situations look complicated and difficult to measure. Powerful, ecologically important theories reveal the lawfulness in events that otherwise would appear chaotic and so simplify the task of particularistic analysis by directing attention towards the variables that actually matter. Whether social psychology can create powerful, heuristic laws is an empirical question to be resolved through research rather than *a priori* argument. Thus far, however, a psychological science of human social behaviour has proved not only possible but also in some respects surprisingly successful; so there is reason for optimism.

It would surely be foolish to reject the laboratory experiment at the very moment that the development of social psychology has made theoretical research perhaps more necessary than before. Ecologically important laws will not appear simply because research takes place in field settings for applied purposes. Such laws have to be produced as much as discovered and are more likely to be relatively abstract, theoretical propositions, invisible to the naked eye, than concrete and particularistic, descriptive generalizations.

On the other hand, as stressed at the outset, laboratory experimentation must be seen in a multi-methodological context where its role is complemented by the strengths of other methods, and vice versa. The laboratory itself is empty and, ultimately, research is always ecologically derived. The real world provides the raw material of facts, problems, and theoretical insights. Field research and naturalistic or naive observations generate the issues for experimentation and test and amend its theoretical conclusions, whereas laboratory research provides direction in field work and refines the interpretation of its results. Furthermore, laboratory and field are undoubtedly complementary in the development of theory. The conceptual analysis of experimental effects dictates multi-methodologism as surely as multi-operationism: powerful variables require the analytic precision of the laboratory and the ecological robustness of the field. Perhaps more importantly, field and applied research are necessary to combat theoretical fragmentation: to identify the ecological boundaries of laboratory laws, stimulate theoretical syntheses, and provide direction to theoretical progress by drawing attention to the gaps in systematic knowledge which really matter. None of this implies that, to be responsive to applied needs, experimental social psychology need or should lose its character as basic research. On the contrary, the diminution of pure research, whether in laboratory or field, would harm applied as much as theoretical objectives (cf. Schlenker, 1974). The more powerful the laws produced by pure research, the more fundamental their possible social applications. To restrict the search for basic theory is, at the same time, to limit social change to relative inertia and reduce practical usefulness to the circumscribed and partisan needs conventionally accepted by some at a specific historical moment.

Perhaps the most important source of pessimism over the prospects for applying social psychology seems to derive from a misconception about its role. It is sometimes considered to equate with curing society's ills. Some class of social events is defined by somebody as a 'social problem' and social psychology is then expected to be able to ameliorate the situation. The assumption seems to be that if social psychology works, it ought to be able to solve all of society's problems. Unfortunately, social problems are rarely defined on the basis of social psychological criteria; more usually, they are selected by means of political and ideological value judgements. This means not only that the patients frequently dispute that they are ill, but also that the disease, such as it is, is often more clearly political, economic, or cultural than social psychological. It seems implausible that social psychology should be able to make more than a minor contribution to solving the problems of other social sciences and somewhat unfair to expect otherwise. It is also, of course, politically naive of social psychologists to suppose, as they sometimes seem to, that racial prejudice or class conflict, for example, can be eliminated by purely psychological means.

This does not mean that social psychology cannot solve important problems nor that it should not be ambitious in its subject matter. Some humility and open-mindedness is needed, however, to ascertain scientifically and empirically the boundaries of social psychological phenomena and their level of operation in relation to other social sciences. The discipline's potential as an applied science can only be realized if some thought is given to the kind of contribution to social change which it can actually make. It should be recognized, therefore, once and for all, that it is neither the only nor the primary social science. Indeed, in some respects, it is the most 'natural' of the 'social' sciences. It is not especially an ideological discipline in the sense that it is not suited to setting the goals for human society as do politics, history, or philosophy. Neither would it seem especially suited to playing an ameliorative role as if it were a form of 'social medicine' which could cure political ills. (Nevertheless, social psychologists should certainly study all relevant settings and make what contribution they can.) Applied social psychology might be better fitted to being something like a science of social engineering.

It would not usurp politics in this role but would inevitably be subordinated to it in terms of feasible objectives — which in turn would demand that political and social goals be explicit and acceptable. Its function would be to optimize social institutions and practices by employing specifically social psychological theory to analyse and reconstruct social arrangements to ensure the better achievement of their goals. Social psychology has large resources in this respect which seem as yet little developed. Whether or not this analysis is correct, the real point is, as above, that social psychology's applied potential cannot be properly tapped if it is used in ways for which it is not suited and not used in ways for which it is suited. Inappropriate aspirations for applied social psychology will lead to demoralization, whereas objectives in harmony with the nature of the discipline may well lead to greater success than is presently anticipated.

ACKNOWLEDGEMENTS

The author wishes to thank Rupert Brown and Don Taylor for their useful comments on an earlier draft of this article.

REFERENCES

Argyle, M. (1980) 'The development of applied social psychology', in *The Development of Social Psychology* (Eds. R. Gilmour and S. W. Duck), Academic Press, London.

Argyris, C. (1975) 'Dangers in applying results from experimental social psychology', *American Psychologist*, **30**, 469-85.

Aronson, E. and Carlsmith, J. M. (1968) 'Experimentation in social psychology', in *The Handbook of Social Psychology* (Eds. G. Lindzey and E. Aronson), 2nd edn, Vol.2, Addison-Wesley, Reading, Mass., 1-79.

Barber, T. X. (1976) *Pitfalls in Human Research: Ten Pivotal Points*, Pergamon Press, New York.

Barber, T. X. and Silver, M. J. (1968a) 'Fact, fiction and the experimenter bias effect', *Psychological Bulletin Monographs*, **70**(2), 1-29.

Barber, T. X. and Silver, M. J. (1968b) 'Pitfalls in data analysis and interpretation: A reply to Rosenthal', *Psychological Bulletin Monographs*, **70** (2) 48-62.

Baron, R. A. and Ransberger, V. M. (1978) 'Ambient temperature and the occurrence of collective violence: The "Long Hot Summer" revisited', *Journal of Personality and Social Psychology*, **36**, 351-60.

Baum, A., Aiello, J. R., and Calesnick, L. E. (1978) 'Crowding and personal control: Social density and the development of learned helplessness', *Journal of Personality and Social Psychology*, **36**, 1000-11.

Billig, M. and Tajfel, H. (1973) 'Social categorization and similarity in intergroup behaviour', *European Journal of Social Psychology*, **3**, 27-52.

Boring, E. G. (1969) 'Perspective: Artifact and control', in *Artifact in Behavioural Research* (Eds. R. Rosenthal and R. L. Rosnow), Academic Press, London, 1-11.

Brunswik, E. (1955) 'Representative design and probabilistic theory in a functional psychology', *Psychological Review*, **62**, 193-217.

Campbell, D. T. (1957) 'Factors relevant to the validity of experiments in social settings', *Psychological Bulletin*, **54**, 297–312.

Campbell, D. T. (1969) 'Perspective: Artifact and control', in *Artifact in Behavioural Research* (Eds. R. Rosenthal and R. L. Rosnow), Academic Press, London, 351–82.

Campbell, D. T. and Stanley, J. C. (1966) *Experimental and Quasi-Experimental Designs for Research*, Rand MacNally and Co., Chicago.

Carlsmith, J. M., Ellsworth, P. C., and Aronson, E. (1976) *Methods of Research in Social Psychology*, Addison-Wesley, London.

Cartwright, D. P. (1979) 'Contemporary social psychology in historical perspective', *Social Psychology*, **42**, 82–93.

Cialdini, R. B., Cacioppo, J. T., Bassett, R., and Miller, J. A. (1978) 'Low-Ball procedure for producing compliance: Commitment then cost', *Journal of Personality and Social Psychology*, **36**, 463–76.

Compendium of British Research in Social Psychology, B.P.S., 1978, Social Psychology Section *Newsletter*, nos. 1 & 2.

Crano, W. D. and Brewer, M. B. (1973) *Principles of Research in Social Psychology*, McGraw-Hill, London.

Deutsch, M. and Hornstein, H. A. (1975) *Applying Social Psychology*, Laurence Erlbaum Associates, Hillsdale, N.J.

Elms, A. C. (1975) 'The crisis of confidence in social psychology', *American Psychologist*, **30**, 967–76.

Festinger, L. (1953) 'Laboratory experiments', in *Research Methods in the Behavioural Sciences* (Eds. L. Festinger and D. Katz), Holt, Rinehart and Winston, New York, 136–72.

Gadlin, H. and Ingle, G. (1975) 'Through the one-way mirror: The limits of experimental self-reflection', *American Psychologist*, **30**, 1003–10.

Gergen, K. J. (1973) 'Social psychology as history', *Journal of Personality and Social Psychology*, **26**, 309–20.

Gergen, K. J. (1978a) 'Toward generative theory', *Journal of Personality and Social Psychology*, **36**, 1344–60.

Gergen, K. J. (1978b) 'Experimentation in social psychology: A reappraisal', *European Journal of Social Psychology*, **8**, 507–27.

Gillis, J. and Schneider, C. (1966) 'The historical preconditions of representative design', in *The Psychology of Egon Brunswik* (Ed. K. R. Hammond), Holt, Rinehart and Winston, New York, 204–36.

Grush, J. E., McKeough, K. L., and Ahlering, R. F. (1978) 'Extrapolating laboratory exposure research to actual political elections', *Journal of Personality and Social Psychology*, **36**, 257–70.

Hilgard, E. R. (1955) 'Discussion of probabilistic functionalism', *Psychological Review*, **62**, 226–28.

Isen, A. M., Schalker, T. E., Clark, M., and Karp, L. (1978) 'Affect, accessibility of material in memory, and behaviour: A cognitive loop?', *Journal of Personality and Social Psychology*, **36**, 1–12.

Israel, J. and Tajfel, H. (1972) *The Context of Social Psychology: A Critical Assessment*. Academic Press, London.

Jones, J. M. (1972) *Prejudice and Racism*. Addison-Wesley, Reading, Mass.

Kandel, D. B. (1978) 'Similarity in real-life adolescent friendship pairs', *Journal of Personality and Social Psychology*, **36**, 306–12.

Kazdin, A. E. (1978) *History of Behaviour Modification: Experimental Foundations of Contemporary Research*, University Park Press, Baltimore, Md.

Krasner, L. (1979) 'History of a revolutionary paradigm?', *Contemporary Psychology*, **24**, 1–2.

Kruglanski, A. (1975) 'The human subject in the psychology experiment: Fact and artifact', in *Advances in Experimental Social Psychology* (Ed. L. Berkowitz), vol.8, Academic Press, New York, 101–47.

Lana, R. E. (1969) 'Pretest sensitization', in *Artifact in Behavioural Research* (Eds. R. Rosenthal and R. L. Rosnow), Academic Press, London, 121–46.

Mann, L., Paleg, K., and Hawkins, R. (1978) 'Effectiveness of staged disputes in influencing bystander crowds', *Journal of Personality and Social Psychology*, **36**, 725–32.

McCauley, C. and Stitt, C. L. (1978) 'An individual and quantitative measure of stereotypes', *Journal of Personality and Social Psychology*, **36**, 929–40.

McGuire, W. J., McGuire, C. V., Child, P., and Fujioka, T. (1978) 'Salience of ethnicity in the spontaneous self-concept as a function of the ethnic distinctiveness in the social environment', *Journal of Personality and Social Psychology*, **36**, 511–20.

Milgram, S. (1972) 'Interpreting obedience: Error and evidence (A reply to Orne and Holland), in *The Social Psychology of Psychological Research* (Ed. A. G. Miller), Free Press, London, 138–54.

Miller, A. G. (1972) *The Social Psychology of Psychological Research*, Free Press, London.

Mills, J. (1969) 'The experimental method', in *Experimental Social Psychology* (Ed. J. Mills), Macmillan, London, 407–48.

Moscovici, S. (1972) 'Society and theory in social psychology', in *The Context of Social Psychology* (Eds. J. Israel and H. Tajfel), Academic Press, London.

Moscovici, S. (1976) *Social Influence and Social Change*, Academic Press, London.

Orne, M. T. (1962) 'On the social psychology of the psychological experiment with particular reference to the demand characteristics and their implications', *American Psychologist*, **17**, 776–83.

Postman, L. (1955) 'The probability approach and nomothetic theory', *Psychological Review*, **62**, 218–25.

Rosenberg, M. J. (1969) 'The conditions and consequences of evaluation apprehension', in *Artifact in Behavioural Research* (Eds. R. Rosenthal and R. L. Rosnow), Academic Press, London, 280–250.

Rosenthal, R. (1966) *Experimenter Effects in Behavioural Research*, Appleton, New York.

Rosenthal, R. and Rosnow, R. L. (1969) *Artifact in Behavioural Research*, Academic Press, London.

Sampson, E. E. (1978) 'Scientific paradigms and social values: Wanted — a scientific revolution', *Journal of Personality and Social Psychology*, **36**, 1332–43.

Schlenker, B. R. (1974) 'Social psychology and science', *Journal of Personality and Social Psychology*, **29**, 1–15.

Schrauger, J. S. and Schoeneman, T. J. (1979) 'Symbolic interactionist view of self-concept: Through the looking glass darkly', *Psychological Bulletin*, **86**, 549–73.

Selltiz, C., Jahoda, M., Deutsch, M., and Cook, S. W. (1959) *Research Methods in Social Relations*, Revised edn., Holt-Dryden, New York.

Stephan, W. G. (1978) 'School desegration: An evaluation of predictions made in Brown v. Board of Education', *Psychological Bulletin*, **85**, 217–38.

Tajfel, H. (1972) 'Experiments in a vacuum', in *The Context of Social Psychology* (Eds. J. Israel and H. Tajfel), Academic Press, London.

Tajfel, H. (1976) 'Exit, voice and intergroup relations', in *Social Psychology in Transition* (Eds. L. Strickland, F. Abound, and K. Gergen), Plenum Press, New York.

Tajfel, H. (1978) *Differentiation Between Social Groups: Studies in the Social Psychology of Intergroup Relations*, Academic Press, London.

Tajfel, H., Flament, C., Billig, M., and Bundy, R. (1971) 'Social categorization and intergroup behaviour', *European Journal of Social Psychology*, **1**, 149–75.

Turner, J. C. (1978) 'The experimental social psychology of intergroup behaviour: A theoretical review', Paper presented to B.P.S. Social Psychology Section conference on the Social Psychology of Intergroup Behaviour, 18 November, University of Bristol. To appear in J. C. Turner and H. Giles (Eds.), *Intergroup Behaviour*, Basil Blackwell, Oxford, in press.

Varela, J. A. (1971) *Psychological Solutions to Social Problems* Academic Press, New York and London.

Wilder, D. A. (1978) 'The reduction of intergroup discrimination through individuation of the outgroup', *Journal of Personality and Social Psychology*, **36**, 1361–74.

SECTION B

Theoretical Review

Progress in Applied Social Psychology, Volume 1
Edited by G. M. Stephenson and J. M. Davis
© 1981 John Wiley & Sons, Ltd.

2

Social Dilemmas

JOHN ORBELL

Political Science Department, University of Oregon, Eugene, Oregon

ROBYN DAWES

Psychology Department, University of Oregon, Eugene, Oregon

INTRODUCTION

In the *Wealth of Nations* (1776), Adam Smith set out how the self-interested pursuit of gain by individuals can work to the advantage of the whole. In two of the best known quotes:

> It is not from the benevolence of the butcher, the brewer, or the baker, that we expect our dinner, but from their regard to their own interest. We address ourselves, not to their humanity but to their self-love, and never talk to them of our own necessities but of their advantages (Book 1, p.18).

> As every individual, therefore, endeavours as much as he can both to employ his capital in the support of domestic industry, and so to direct that industry that its produce may be of the greatest value; every individual necessarily labours to render the annual revenue of the society as great as he can . . . . By preferring the support of domestic to that of foreign industry, he intends his own security; and by directing that industry in such a manner as its produce may be of the greatest value, he intends only his own gain, and he is in this, as in many other cases, led by an invisible hand to promote an end which was no part of his intention (Book 4, p.477).

Individuals might be selfish and self-seeking, but that is not a problem for the society in which they live. On the contrary, the steadfast pursuit of individual gain is the best assurance of gain for the whole. In Smith's world there is a happy harmony between individual and society.

More than one hundred years previous to Smith's great work, Thomas Hobbes enunciated a very different logic. In *Leviathan* (1651) Hobbes worked out an inquiry into the origin of and justification for government that was based on what he thought society would be like in the *absence* of government — his 'state of nature'. Like Smith's, his world is peopled by selfish, self-seeking individuals, but the consequences of their selfishness are very different. Each person can pursue the goals that all desire (wealth, power, and glory) by production, but each can also pursue them by predation on others in the society. Since there is nothing to prevent predation, all individuals must adopt a defensive stance toward their fellows, if not one that is openly predatory itself. Any individuals who do not, who act in a peaceable manner, who turn the other cheek, will rapidly find that they are incurring unacceptable costs; at best they will have turned down the gains they could make through their own predation, but at worst they will lose their own possessions and perhaps even their own lives. The problem is that mutual predation produces a social disaster:

> There is no place for Industry; because the fruit thereof is uncertain; and consequently no culture of the Earth; no navigation, nor use of the commodities that may be imported by Sea; no commodious Building; no Instruments of moving, and removing such things as require much force; no Knowledge of the face of the Earth; no account of time; no Arts; no Letters; no Society; and which is worst of all, continuall feare, and danger of violent death; And the life of man, solitary, poore, nasty, brutish, and short (*Leviathan*, pp. 64–65).

In the terminology of contemporary game theory, predation or a war-like stance toward one's neighbours is the *dominant* strategy for all but is associated with a *suboptimal* social equilibrium. Nobody wants the 'war of every man against every man' but the logic of everyone's situation produces behaviour that, in the aggregate, makes that war inevitable.

The Hobbesian logic has attracted considerable attention in recent years, finding its clearest statement in various models of ecological disaster and in the economic theory of collective goods. In the former category, Garrett Hardin's classic 'Tragedy of the commons' (1968) is perhaps best known. In his unhappy model, individual farmers have access to grazing ground that is held in common by all. Each can make a personal profit by adding successive cattle to the commons and each continues to do so. The choice 'add another animal' does involve costs in terms of pasture consumed and damage done to the commons, but those costs are absorbed by the collectivity, not the individual. This ability of individuals to ignore some of the costs their action generates means that they will be more likely to indulge in that action and, since the opportunities are the same for all, that is what all will do. But as a result, in aggregate, far greater costs are likely to be generated than individually absorbed benefits and, eventually, the commons will be destroyed.

Once again, the social equilibrium is (decidedly) suboptimal. Once again nobody in the society wanted that outcome. But once again selfish individuals are led inexorably to behaviours that produce that outcome by consideration of their individual incentives.

Similar logic is contained in the modern theory of collective goods that has developed largely since the work of Samuelson (1954, 1955). A 'collective good' is a product that, once produced, is available for consumption by all; exclusion from the benefits of consumption is impossible. The problem with such goods is that, if production is left to the uncoordinated efforts of individuals, they will often be produced in quantities less than the demand that does exist in the community, and in extreme cases they will not be produced at all.

Individuals can be counted on to reveal their demand for 'private goods' (goods for which exclusion *is* possible) by their price bids and, as a result, the total purchased is likely to match total demand. But before they make similar bids in the case of collective goods, they will consider two possibilities. First, they will consider the possibility of being a 'free rider' on the productive efforts of others—since exclusion is impossible, they might not have to pay the costs of production in order to enjoy the benefits of the good in question. Secondly, they will consider the possibility of being a 'sucker' who makes a contribution to the cost of a collective good when nobody else does, perhaps ending up carrying the whole cost. If they pay attention to either concern, they will end up making 'price bids' substantially less than their true evaluation of the collection good in question, perhaps no contribution at all. Paradoxically, therefore, even though a demand exists in a community for a particular public or collective good, the members of that community might not take the necessary action in order to produce it (Olson, 1965).

Notice that Hardin's commons case can be interpreted in these terms. A viable commons is a collective good from the benefits of which individual farmers cannot be excluded. But the price of maintaining that collective good (which everyone wants maintained) is individual restraint—and if one individual pays that price others may not (making him a 'sucker') or, alternatively, if other individuals do pay the price, a given individual can enjoy the commons without paying himself (making him a 'free rider'). Conversely, of course, the logic of collective 'bads' works the same way. If a collective 'bad' is a generally *un*desired product that, once produced, can be consumed by all, and if *refraining* from its production involves a cost to the individuals, we can expect individuals to *over*produce. Why should I exercise restraint when others might not? And if others do exercise restraint, I can enjoy the fruits of their restraint (the absence of the 'bad') without having to contribute to its cost. Obviously, pollution of the commons is a collective bad in this sense, and the Hardin case can be understood in such terms, as well.

What is the critical difference between the happy model of relationships between individual and society that is found in Smith's work and the far more unhappy models of the Hobbesian state of nature, the commons, and collective good production?

It does not lie in assumptions about human selfishness but in the 'third party effects' or 'externalities'. For Smith, when two individuals engage in an exchange, all costs and benefits are 'internalized' by the respective parties — that is to say, parties to the exchange must consider all the costs and benefits the exchange involves. It is thus a reasonable prediction (if the individuals are rational and concerned with the efficiency of their actions) that they will only engage in those exchanges or productive decisions that involve a net increase in wealth for themselves *and therefore that involve a net increase in the social product*. Negative effects (costs) are borne by individuals alone, not by the society.

Alternatively, in the other models that have been sketched, the individuals are able to impose some of the costs generated by their action on others in the society and, freed from at least some cost constraints, will make decisions that are privately beneficial (rational) but may be publicly or socially harmful. Thus, in the Hobbesian state of nature individuals will find predation to be rational behaviour precisely because the costs of their own action (a contribution to the war of every man against every man) can be largely avoided by themselves. Similarly, individuals will find adding further animals to the commons to be rational for themselves because they can avoid most of the costs of that decision (a contribution to the decline of the collective resource). In the collective goods–collective bads case, individuals will find that not contributing to the production of the collective good is rational for themselves, because the cost of providing the good can be passed on to others.

Notice importantly that it is not the simple presence of external costs that is at issue. If external costs are slight, the behaviour generating them might still be socially efficient as well as privately efficient. Only if total cost (external and internal) exceeds total benefit (internal) will the society be headed toward eventual disaster. In summary, when negative externalities are not present to this degree, individually rational behaviour is also likely to be socially rational. When they are present, individually rational behaviour is likely to be socially irrational.

It is customary, at least among economists, to view such situations as cases of 'market failure' since it is no longer possible to rely — as market models do — on the free and untrammelled choices of individuals to produce optimal behaviour. But, as Schmid (1978, p.47) has pointed out, they might just as well be regarded as cases of 'collective failure' since they describe situations in which groups or collectivities are unable to reach their collective goals. Of perhaps more importance is the empirical issue: What is the incidence and impact of 'market success' and 'collective failure' for a given society? If 'market success' is usual, then problems of collective organization will not be particularly pressing. But if 'collective failure' is usual, then the organization of a society for joint or collective action will be of critical importance.

For it is *organizational* problems that are raised by these models. Hobbes, for example, is raising the question: How might a society of self-interested individuals be organized so that they can coexist together in mutually profitable ways? And Hardin is raising the question: How might a society of self-interested individuals be organized so that ecological disaster can be avoided? And the models of collective goods and collective bads, perhaps the most general of all, are raising the general question: If exclusion from the benefits or costs of goods is not possible, how might a society be organized to ensure that goods it generally wants are provided and that goods it generally does not want are not provided?

In this chapter we will not fight the terminological issue—although our bias is that the 'collective failure' perspective is most appropriate. Nor will we argue the empirical issue about the incidence of 'market success' and 'collective failure' although it seems to us that, increasingly, modern society is having to face the latter kind of problem. Rather, we will discuss the variety of ways in which 'collective failure' might be avoided in general. Models such as those discussed above are, of course, descriptions of hypothetical worlds that might exist; they are statements of potential if a whole set of limiting conditions are met. But in real-world situations, while that potential is undoubtedly sometimes realized, that is not always the case and societies learn (more accurately, the individuals who comprise societies learn) to change the situation in critical ways so that the potential is *not* realized. We will first identify changes that will be sufficient to produce different—and happier—predictions from the various models of social dilemmas and discuss how these changes are realized in real-world situations. We will then present a formal statement of social dilemma logic and review some of the findings from experimental social psychology with a bearing on the 'avoidance' problem.

ALTRUISM

If we are interested in modifying our models so that they give more satisfactory predictions to social outcomes, there are two broad things we can do: we can modify the assumptions about human motivation on which they are built or, keeping those assumptions intact, we can modify the structure of incentives to which individuals respond. In real-world situations that contain social dilemma potential, what mechanisms might produce such changes in motivation or incentive?

Altruism is clearly a possibility, but we must be careful what we mean by that. If we mean 'behaviour that benefits someone else or the group as a whole' we must recognize that such behaviour can happen for good selfish reasons. Adam Smith's entrepreneur, for example, benefits others when he engages in an exchange (others would not freely close the deal if that were not the case). But if we mean the motivation to benefit others we are not talking about behaviour itself; it would be meaningful, for example, to talk about a 'misguided altruist' who is motivated to benefit others, but fails in behavioural terms.

Since the assumed selfishness of players in the various social dilemma games is an assumption about motivation and not about actual behaviour, we will use the term *altruism* to describe a motivation, not a behaviour. Will altruism be sufficient to eliminate the potential of social dilemma situations? Clearly, that depends on the dilemma in question and on the degree of altruism that characterizes our players. If the members of a family are altruistic with respect to other family members they will not impose external costs on each other and, therefore, social dilemmas in the family will be avoided. But such 'family altruism' will not eliminate social dilemmas in general, since the family as an actor in the wider society might well be prepared to impose the most grievous costs on other families or the society as a whole.

There is also the question of the altruist's motivation to benefit himself relative to his motivation to benefit others (whatever the particular set of others involved). A 'pure' altruist, of course, will be motivated to benefit others no matter what the cost to himself. Clearly, this is the motivational goal that many religious systems have for their members (Campbell, 1975). But what trade-off can be expected between benefit to others and cost to self? How much personal cost will individuals absorb in order to improve the situation of others? Presumably, there are degrees of altruism with individuals at one extreme being willing to absorb large personal costs to produce trivial benefits for others, and individuals at the other extreme being unwilling to absorb any but the most trivial costs for even the most substantial benefits returned to others.

Some minimum of communication among members of a group will often be necessary if altruism is to help resolve social dilemma situations. Even the most dedicated altruist must have some information about what it is that others value before he or she sets out to act in their benefit, and that will not always be available; the Biblical command to do unto others 'as you would have done unto yourself' offers a rule of thumb but not an infallible one since others will not *necessarily* like what I like. In a similar vein, altruists (even the most dedicated ones) will often find it useful, perhaps critical, to know how much cost they must each absorb if the group goals are to be reached. Given goals are likely to require only some contribution from individual group members, and without information about the appropriate size of their contributions, members might over-contribute. Or, perhaps more likely, they might wrongly anticipate that more is required than they are willing to contribute, and not contribute when more accurate information about cost would have a happier result. Accurate communication about the altruistic motivations of others in the group might also alleviate fears held by altruists themselves about the social futility of whatever costs they might be willing to bear. In general, if altruistic motivations do exist, particular organizational conditions (perhaps effective leadership) seem likely to facilitate their being expressed in terms of behaviour.

The empirical question (*Are* humans motivated to improve the payoffs of others?) has received considerable theoretical attention in recent years from the new discipline of sociobiology, where it has aroused considerable controversy. Some sociobiologists, Campbell (1975) for example, believe that biological evolution has led to fundamentally selfish human beings since altruism would be systematically selected against in a Darwinian world. They do not deny the existence of *behaviour* that benefits others (people adopt children, help each other out of ditches, give money to charity, sacrifice themselves in war, and so on) but argue that such behaviour is the product of 'social evolution' that has produced normative and religious sanctions in its support; for Campbell, there is a conflict between biological evolution that has produced selfish motivations and social evolution that has operated (perhaps more accurately, is capable of operation) in support of cooperative or helping behaviour. Trivers (1971) has proposed that a socially imposed norm of reciprocal altruism will in fact make the altruistic act have more survival value than appears from its typology. And Blaney (1976) has noted that whatever shapes a society's beliefs (the selfish interests of those in charge?) women in all societies prefer men who are altruistic and brave to those that are self-centred and cowardly. At least to this extent, social evolution would result in a selection of altruistic traits, traits that might not fare well in a 'warre of all against all'.

In contrast, other sociobiologists hypothesize mechanisms by which altruism in and of itself may result in genetic propagation, even if not through direct reproduction. Those proposing that such survival works through 'group selection' ultimately benefiting the individual currently (in 1980) have few adherents, but many others (e.g. Alexander, 1980) have proposed 'kin altruism' as a plausible genetic link to all altruism. People share genes with their close relatives and to the degree to which they—even in the celibate roles of priest or maiden aunt—help relatives survive, they enhance the probability of their own genes propagating. Hence, to the degree that such altruistic concern is genetic and limited to close kin (nepotistic), it would be expected to *increase* through genetic selection and, therefore, would be a surviving human trait.

Obviously, human nature is describable in terms of some mix of altruism and selfish motivation, and just as obviously, evolution and genetic selection have much to say about what we should expect. In the absence of consensus among evolutionary theorists, however, it is sufficient to point out that *some* significant motivation to benefit others, even at cost to oneself, would lead us to expect less willingness to impose external costs on others and greater ability of groups to reach their common goals than is predicted under the starkly selfish motivations characteristically assumed in models of social dilemmas.

SUPPLEMENTARY PAYOFFS: BRIBES, THREATS, AND OTHER ALTERNATIONS OF THE PAYOFF MATRIX

If we grant that real-world players *are* motivated in the selfish manner assumed by models of social dilemmas, and if so-motivated players *are* confronted with the structure of costs and benefits described in the various social dilemma games, then the social disasters those models predict are quite inevitable—the war'of every man against every man will prevail, the commons will be destroyed, and collective goods in general will not be provided. Unless we abandon the rules of logic (or unless there is some logical flaw in the various models), real-world processes will work in the same way as their model analogues. It follows, therefore, that real-world societies populated by individuals who are not altruists in the sense just discussed must find some way of modifying the cost–benefit payoff schedules confronting their members if they are to avoid social dilemma situations and the outcomes they produce. Individual incentives must be changed so that the game is not a social dilemma game. There are several possible sources of such additional rewards and punishments.

Legal Systems—The State

Thomas Hobbes used the analysis of the state of nature that was sketched earlier as the basis of a justifying theory of the state that is still fundamental in Western political theory. He assumes that people will value social peace above everything else; in his terminology, it is a 'first and fundamental law of nature' that people will 'seek peace and follow it' (Hobbes, p.140). What will purposive goal-oriented (or, in the modern term, 'rational') people do when they recognize the 'solitary, poore, nasty, brutish and short' condition that the logic of the state of nature has brought them to?

Hobbes argues that people in the state of nature will recognize that there is no way out of their situation short of *Leviathan*, a government with sufficient power to force people into peaceable ways. In this recognition, they will agree (Hobbes's 'social contract') to the establishment of such a government—an empirical prediction, but more importantly a normative argument since it provides a justification for strong government that is based on the consent of the governed. People will all *prefer* such an all-powerful government because social peace, something they all desire, is only possible if all people are coerced to behave peaceably.

The important point in the present context is that, under Hobbes's *Leviathan*, individuals (now they are 'citizens') are no longer confronted with the social dilemma logic that confronted them in the state of nature. If they choose against predation and in favour of peaceable ways they will be better off *as individuals* than if they were to do otherwise because they avoid jail or worse. That is to say, if *Leviathan*'s punishments and rewards are sure, an individual contemplating predation will have to add punishment and reward to his or her anticipated costs and benefits and, being no less rational than before, he or she will now opt against predation. People are not suddenly converted into altruists by *Leviathan*; they are just obliged to deal, as selfish maximizers, with a different situation, one that leads them to socially desirable behaviour rather than socially undesirable behaviour. Society has solved its most fundamental problem by organizational change, not by changing the individuals that comprise it.

Government is certainly *one* source of rewards and punishments sufficient to bring an individual's payoff schedule into harmony with the achievement of collective goals. Hardin's solution to the tragedy of the commons is 'mutual coercion mutually agreed upon' and that could certainly involve government; in fact, many commentators have drawn the implication from Hardin's prescription (and its obvious parallels to the Hobbesian logic) that government is the only solution to the tragedy of the commons (in particular, Ophuls, 1973, 1977; Heilbroner, 1974). In the more general case of collective goods—social peace in the Hobbesian analysis can be regarded as a collective good (Orbell and Rutherford, 1974)—government is often proposed as the means to ensure their provision, and arguments for and against an expanded role for the state are based on the perceived incidence of collective good–bad problems and the inability of societies to deal with them efficiently by market mechanisms (see, for example, Taylor, 1976; Buchanan, 1968, 1971, 1975; Frohlich *et al.*, 1971; Olson, 1965). People seldom contribute taxes to government voluntarily, and coercion is necessary if the collective good for which taxes pay are to be provided at all. Similarly, people will continue producing such collective bads as pollution unless they are forced to stop—either by direct prohibition and the associated punishments, or by taxation imposed on the behaviour in question—and government can mobilize sufficient force to obtain the desired behaviour.

From one perspective, social dilemma problems exist when public and private modes of property ownership exist side by side in a society, when an individual can make a *private* profit from exploiting a *public* resource. It follows that they can be avoided by either making all things owned in common (in which case the individual benefits not all from exploitation) or by making all things owned in private (in which case there is no public resource to exploit). By the latter logic, for example, if all the land in Hardin's commons were privately owned by individual farmers who had the right to reap all profits from their particular parcel—and who had the obligation to suffer all the costs associated with use as well—individuals would have a clear incentive to make decisions that were publicly as well as privately efficient. By imposing more costs than they reaped benefits, the farmers *themselves* would suffer; they would be absorbing all the costs of their decisions, not passing them on to the wider community. Under such circumstances, Adam Smith's unseen hand would guide individual decisions into harmony with collective wealth. Arguments for this kind of solution to 'commons problems' have been made for the national forests and a range of other situations in which property rights to particular pieces of what was previously a commons could be specified, but it is important to remember that such a solution is limited by the nature of the resource in question. Under present technological capacity it is not possible, for example, to 'privatize' the air we breathe.

An important literature dealing with the origin, character, and impact of various patterns of property rights has developed in recent years, and the role of the state in the creation and specification of property rights has been a central issue. Without reviewing this large and rapidly growing body of work (see, importantly, Schmid, 1978; North and Thomas, 1973; Demsetz, 1966, 1967; Coase, 1960), we can notice that any specification of property rights requires coercion from some quarter if it is to operate to guide individual choices into socially productive avenues. In Hobbes's state of nature, it would not fundamentally change things if all property were simply allocated to particular individuals; without enforcement of those property rights, predation would still be the dominant strategy for individuals, and the war of every man against every man would continue unabated.

Coercion from some source is clearly a necessary condition if a fully specified set of property rights is to have its desired consequences, and the Hobbesian 'problem of order' must be solved before Smith's untrammelled exchange between profit-seeking individuals can have the effects Smith predicted—as, indeed, Smith himself recognized. The question is: If the state is a sufficient condition for such coercion, is it a necessary one?

Normative Systems

Hobbes's answer was unequivocally *yes*—the state is a necessary condition for the avoidance of the social dilemma logic inherent in the state of nature. But Hardin's more cautious prescription of 'mutual coercion, mutually agreed upon' is more satisfactory. Coercion sufficient to resolve most social dilemmas is available from other sources than the state, most obviously from normative systems.

Like the legal systems of the state (and like 'conscience' — to be discussed below), normative systems involve rules specifying what behaviours are correct and what are incorrect; both the state's legal systems and normative systems would specify, for example, 'exercise moderation' or perhaps 'graze only X cattle on the commons' as rules governing the behaviour of individuals in a commons situation. And, like the state's legal systems, normative systems back up those rules with rewards and punishments hopefully sufficient to persuade rational (and selfish) individuals into the paths of righteousness. Are the years in prison, fines, medals, and executions that the state can offer of more or less potency to persuade individuals in those directions than the black looks, personal rejections, praise, and trips 'to Coventry' that normative systems can offer? It is impossible to give a definitive answer, but there is no doubt that rewards and punishments mobilizable by normative systems can be formidable; Shils and Janowitz (1953) long ago showed, for example, that the pressures of acceptance and rejection by one's own comrades were sufficient to persuade soldiers in the German army to continue fighting even in the face of likely death. And there are, of course, endless studies of small group dynamics that reinforce the same point.

The difference is rather in the mechanics by which coercion is mobilized in the two cases. In the legal systems associated with the state, rewards and punishments are administered in a centralized manner with specialists, normally paid by the collectivity, being responsible for that administration. Although citizens (supposedly) can make citizens' arrests, the job is usually left to policemen; in fact, citizens' arrests happen very rarely. Most countries have laws explicitly prohibiting amateurs (vigilantes) from making judgements about the violation of laws and certainly from passing out rewards and punishments — such things are the express province of the state's representatives. The logic by which collectivities allocate resources to pay such specialists has been spelled out by Frohlich *et al.* (1971); briefly, such specialists can be the means by which a generally desired collective good is actually realized, but in order to ensure that they do what is expected of them, it is necessary to pay them a sufficient amount to make it worth their while (unless they are altruists, and experience suggests that they rarely are).

Alternatively, normative systems are characterized by the *decentralized* administration of whatever rewards and punishments are involved. While specialists carry the costs of administering the laws of the state, all members of the collectivity are potentially involved with the administration of the rewards and punishments required under normative systems. Thus, for example, some universities allocate the task of handing out anti-cheating sanctions (widespread cheating being regarded as a collective bad) to specialists — the faculty — while others leave it to decentralized administration by the students themselves. Similarly, while quasi-legal systems concerned with professional ethics do exist, much enforcement of sanctions against unprofessional behaviour is left in a decentralized manner to the members of the professional population in question.

Clearly, there are problems with normative systems. While, as we have suggested, the sanctions themselves might be formidable—quite sufficient to induce the desired behaviour if imposed—imposition itself will often be uncertain and erratic. The logic of failure is, once again, social dilemma logic. While all members of some society might recognize the desirability of inducing a particular kind of behaviour, and while they all might accept the necessity of given rewards and punishments being mobilized to that end, if there are any substantial costs associated with actual enforcement they will have an incentive not to carry those costs themselves; they will prefer that others in the population do so (they will try to be 'free riders') or they will fear doing so when nobody else does (they will fear being 'suckers'). The problem will be apparent to anyone who has observed academic departments organizing their graduate programs. Faculty (usually) all recognize the desirability of graduate students having a demanding experience in graduate school, and will avow their support for the general principle in appropriate public meetings. But when it comes to the necessity of their individually carrying the costs involved in producing such a programme (rejection by students, empty seminars and the like) they will often back down—with the result that the programme is *not* demanding. Only if the rewards from enforcement (the esteem of one's colleagues and the Dean, for example) are sufficiently great will the desired behaviour be generally forthcoming.

But there are serious problems with the centralized enforcement of the state, too. Policemen, judges, politicians, bureaucrats, and prison wardens all cost money and it is quite possible that such costs will be greater than the benefit they provide in terms of collective goods produced (social dilemmas avoided). For example (Goodman, 1972), the state of New York recently spent $750,000 more than the estimated loss from forgery for a mandatory system of photo ID cards for welfare recipients. Similarly, for them to do their job at all they must be accorded a measure of coercive capacity, and there is always the possibility of their using such power to the collective *disadvantage* as well as the collective *advantage* (Tullock, 1974). Niskanen (1971) and others have developed a theory of bureaucracy based on the assumption that bureaucrats maximize, not the welfare of the society, but their own welfare and that of their bureau. Presumably, well-designed constitutions can minimize such dangers, but there are problems with even the best designed constitutions. If government is weakened (by a system of checks and balances, for example) out of fear of what it might do to harm the collectivity, there is always the possibility that it will not have the capacity to do the things the people want it to do. As L. J. Sharpe (1973) has emphasized, 'functional effectiveness'—the capacity to act—is an important and often valuale attribute of governments. Majority rule is often taken as an appropriate device for deciding what a collectivity should do, but as Orbell and Wilson (1978a, 1978b) have shown, majority rule is likely to produce anything, from the very best in terms of the social product to the very worst, for the range of social dilemmas in which the incentive to engage in socially damaging behaviour is more than 50 percent of the social damage that is done by that behaviour. For social dilemmas in which the 'undesirable incentive' is short of this, majority rule can be expected to work better, but it will normally be difficult to predict in advance of 'constitutional choice' the kinds of social dilemmas with which a society will be faced.

As players who know themselves to be in social dilemma situations come to experience the failures of formal legal systems and the state, they can be expected to feel the hostility and disillusionment that political scientists term 'political alienation'. And as they come to experience the failures of normative systems, they can be expected to feel the uncertainty and disorientation that sociologists call 'anomie'.

In general, while the decentralized enforcement characteristic of normative systems makes such systems an uncertain tool for the satisfactory resolution of social dilemmas, the centralized enforcement characteristic of the state and formal legal systems makes that alternative of uncertain value, too. What can be said for conscience?

Conscience

The rewards and punishments necessary to bring the behaviour of selfish and rational individuals in social dilemma situations into conformity with social goals *can* be mobilized by the behaving individuals themselves. Rather than by paid specialists as with the state, or by one's fellow citizens as with normative systems, individuals can bring rewards and punishments to bear on their own cost–benefit calculations, thereby influencing the directions of their own behaviour. This is what we will call 'conscience'. Notice, importantly, the difference between the manner in which altruism works and the manner in which conscience works. The altruist says, in effect: "I am acting in conformity with social goals because I am interested in the welfare of others." But the person driven by conscience says, in effect: "I am acting in conformity with social goals because, in net, I feel like a better person for doing so." In the final analysis, therefore, the conscience-driven person is acting as a rational and selfish miximizer — a behavioural model no different from that assumed previously. He or she is simply responding to 'internalized' rewards and punishments. H. L. Mencken is reported to have said that "conscience is the inner voice that warns us that someone may be looking." (Alistair Cooke, 1955, p.231). Perhaps. But it is also capable of punishing us for socially irresponsible behaviour and rewarding us for socially responsible behaviour when we know quite well that nobody is looking.

There are, of course, problems with conscience, too. To resolve social dilemmas in ways consistent with social goals, conscience must wield internalized rewards and punishments often of substantial magnitude. When the cost of being a sucker is a high probability of death (as perhaps in the Hobbesian state of nature, or more realistically for soldiers in battle), or when the incentives to free ride are very large (as once again for a soldier in battle), conscience might be a thin reed for a society to lean on. And conscience is not cost-free; manifestly, societies spend large sums of money in efforts to instil 'right' values into their young—and sometimes their not-so-young.

But conscience does have a great advantage over the state and centralized legal systems in that it avoids many administrative costs, and over normative systems in that it avoids the free-rider problems associated with decentralized enforcement. No doubt, the most satisfactory situation for a society is to have legal systems, normative systems, and conscience all working in the same direction and reinforcing each other's directives. Certainly a society in which these three mechanisms are at odds with each other can expect trouble.

A Caveat

We have been discussing how rewards and punishments wielded by the state, normative systems, and conscience can be sufficient to bring the behaviour of selfish and rational individuals into conformity with social goals. Those rewards and punishments are, of course, also capable of bringing behaviour into conformity with different goals—those of an elite subset in the society, for example. Our concern is simply with the resolution of social dilemmas and, by definition, a social dilemma involves a goal that all members of the community can subscribe to equally. Social peace in the Hobbesian state of nature, preservation of the commons, and the provision of collective goods are all specified in the models outlined above as truly *social* goods. But, as the Marxists remind us, government and normative systems (religion) can be used to the selfish advantage of the few and it is also clear that the few can be quite capable of manipulating the rewards and punishments of conscience to that end, as well.[1] The analysis above says nothing about the possibilities for selfish and rational individuals to exploit their fellows through control over the machinery of government, normative systems, and conscience. They are patently considerable.

A FORMAL STATEMENT OF SOCIAL DILEMMA LOGIC

Most experimental investigations of behaviour in social dilemmas have concentrated on subjects' responses in iterated two-person prisoners' dilemmas. The formal logic of this well-known game locates it in the same family as the social dilemmas discussed above. As originally formulated by Luce and Raiffa (1957), it involves two prisoners charged with committing the same crime. They are locked in different cells unable to communicate with each other. Each is told that his punishment depends on his decision to confess or deny the joint execution of the crime, but that the severity of the punishment depends on the simultaneous decision of the other. Punishments are structured (by a devious prosecutor) so that the best outcome for a given prisoner is to confess when the other does not (the state's evidence tactic); the second best outcome is to deny when the other denies as well (coordinated outcome); the third best outcome is to confess when the other does also; and the worst outcome is to deny when the other confesses. The problem—and the dilemma for each prisoner—lies in the conflict between what is optimal behaviour for himself and what is optimal for the two-person 'society'. By looking after his own interests, a prisoner is led to confess, and has the chance of being a winner if the other denies. But if each follows this strategy, each will end up in the second-to-worst situation. And between them they will serve more years in prison than they would given any other outcome.

In our view, however, the iterated two-person prisoners' dilemma has three characteristics that make it unique and not representative of the social problems we wish to explore here.

1. In the two-person prisoners' dilemma (iterated or not) all harm for defection is visited completely on the other player; harm is focused rather than spread out. In Hardin's commons and other games like it, gain for defecting behaviour (individually rational but socially suboptimal) accrues directly to the self while harm is diffused over a considerable number of players.

2. In Hardin's commons defecting behaviour may be anonymous; it is not necessarily so, but the possibility is there. In the two-person game, in contrast, each player knows with certainty how the other has behaved. This necessary knowledge is unique to the two-person situation.

3. Each player has total reinforcement control over the other in the iterated two-person dilemma. That is to say, each player can 'punish' the other for defection or cooperation (behaviour that is socially optimal if individually suboptimal) by choosing defection on the subsequent choice, and can 'reward' the previous choice of the other by choosing cooperation. Thus, each player can attempt to shape the other's behaviour by choice of defection and cooperation, while partially determining his or her own outcome by that same choice. The situation is very complicated. In fact, Amnon Rapoport (1967) has shown that if subjects really can influence each other's subsequent choices, then the iterated prisoners' dilemma is not a dilemma at all! So if subjects believe that they have such influence, it is not a dilemma to them. This degree of 'influence potential' is unique to the two-person iterated dilemma.

When the number of people involved approaches two (three or four), there might be some potential for shaping others' behaviour, but the potential effectiveness of doing so is clearly diluted. Notice that this inability of a single player to shape the behaviour of others in the game is analogous to the inability of any single producer–entrepreneur to define prices in a perfect market (Buchanan, 1965). In a market involving any considerable number of producers, all producers (but not consumers) have an interest in collusion to keep prices up or quality down, but it is difficult for any one player to bring successful pressure on others to that end. Collusion in markets involves social dilemma logic and, as is well recognized, collusions are more and more difficult to sustain as numbers increase.

Owing to the specificity of harm, the lack of possible anonymity, and the potential use of one's own behaviour to shape the other's behaviour, two-person iterated prisoners' dilemmas cannot be considered representative of the general category of social dilemmas. In what follows we will limit our concern to investigation of dilemmas involving three or more people.

Let $D(m)$ be the payoff to the defectors in an N-person game where m players cooperate, and let $C(m)$ be the payoff to the cooperators when m players (including themselves) cooperate. A social dilemma game is characterized by two simple inequalities.

1. $D(m) > C(m + 1)$.

That is, the payoff when m other people cooperate is always higher for an individual who remains a defector than for one who becomes the m plus first cooperator (m goes from 0 to $N - 1$).

2. $D(0) < C(N)$.

That is, universal cooperation among the N players leads to a greater payoff than does universal defection.

The statement of condition no. 1 in game theory language is that defection *is a dominating strategy*. But if everyone chooses that dominating strategy, the outcome that results is one that is less preferred by all players to at least one other (e.g. that resulting from universal cooperation). Since according to game theory all players should choose a dominating strategy, the result is termed an *equilibrium*. (No player would want to switch his or her choice.) Because the outcome dictated by the dominating strategy is less preferred by all players to the outcome of unanimous cooperation, this outcome is termed *deficient*. Hence, *a dilemma game is one in which all players have dominating strategies that result in a deficient equilibrium*. Two games developed for experimental research illustrate this point.

The 'Take Some' Game

Each of three players simultaneously holds up a red or blue poker chip. Each player who holds up a red chip receives $3.00 in payoff, but each of the three players *including that player* is fined $1.00 for that choice. This is the negative externality. Each player who holds up a blue chip receives $1.00 with no resultant fine. Three blue chips being held up provides a $1.00 payoff to all players (and a social product of $3.00) while three red chips being held up provides a zero payoff for all (and a zero social product). At the same time, however, each player reasons that he or she is best off holding up a red chip, because that increases the fines he or she must pay by only $1.00 while increasing the immediate amount received by $2.00 ($3.00 - $1.00). In this game, one 'takes some' from others as a consequence of choice analogous to the choice involved in the decision to pollute (Dawes *et al.*, 1974).[2]

The 'Give Some' Game

Each of five players may keep $8.00 from the experimenter for himself or herself or give $3.00 from the experimenter to each of the other players. Again it is a dilemma because if all *give*, all get $12.00 (4 × $3.00) while if all *keep*, all get $8.00; yet it is clearly in each player's individual interest to keep. In fact, each player is getting $8.00; yet it is clearly in each player's individual interest to keep. In fact, each player is getting $8.00 more by keeping than by giving. This game is based on the research of Bonacich (1972). Notice that the 'give some' game is analogous to the game of collective goods provision mentioned earlier, and that the 'take some' game is analogous to Hardin's commons (or the logic of collective *bads*).

The 'take some' and 'give some' games can be presented in matrix form displaying the payoffs to defectors and cooperators as a function of the number of cooperators (Table 1).

Table 1

The 'take some' game			The 'give some' game		
Number of cooperators	Payoffs to defectors ($)	Payoffs to cooperators ($)	Number of cooperators	Payoffs to defectors ($)	Payoffs to cooperators ($)
3	—	1.00	5	—	12.00
2	2.00	0	4	20.00	9.00
1	1.00	-1.00	3	17.00	6.00
0	0	—	2	14.00	3.00
			1	11.00	0
			0	8.00	—

In addition to properties 1 and 2 (above), the 'take some' and the 'give some' games have three further properties:

A. $D(m + 1) - D(m) = c_1 > 0$.

B. $C(m + 1) - C(m) = c_2 > 0$.

C. $D(m) - C(m + 1) = c_3 > 0$.

In the 'take some' game, $c_1 = \$1.00$, $c_2 = \$1.00$, and $c_3 = \$1.00$. In the 'give some' game, $c_1 = \$3.00$, $c_2 = \$3.00$, and $c_3 = \$8.00$.

If we were to plot the payoffs for defection and cooperation as a function of the number of cooperators, properties A and B state that both functions are straight lines with positive slopes (see Schelling, 1973; Hamburger, 1973). Property C states that these slopes are equal. Condition no.1 (that an additional cooperator makes less than had he or she remained a defector) follows directly from property C, and condition no.2 states that the right-hand extreme of the cooperating function is above the left-hand extreme of the defecting function.[3] Graphically, a social dilemma exists when the D payoff function is above the C function for its entire length and the right extremity of the C function is higher than the left extremity of the D function. It is apparent that a very wide range of configurations meet this specification. Schelling (1973) has discussed many such configurations and given a host of imaginative examples.

Hamburger (1973) has shown that dilemma games having properties A–C are equivalent to games in which each participant simultaneously plays identical two-peraon prisoners' dilemma games having property C (termed 'separable' in the literature) against each of the remaining $N-1$ participants. Dawes (1975) has shown that they are also equivalent to the algebraic expression of the 'commons dilemma' described by Hardin (1968). In Figures 1 and 2 we plot the payoffs for our version of the 'take some' game and the 'give some' game, respectively.

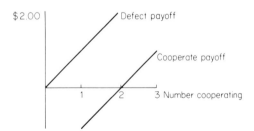

Figure 1

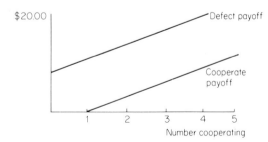

Figure 2

It is apparent that individuals *can* be better off under defect than under 'all cooperate'. In our three-person 'take some' game, the lone defector makes more than all the 'all cooperate' payoff, and in our five-person 'give some' game defectors make more than the 'all cooperate' payoff when there are as many as three of them.

But it is also apparent that not all individuals can do this at the same time. Should they all try, all will make the 'all defect' payoff, which is inferior to the 'all cooperate' one. A given individual will rank outcomes thus: one (me) defect is most desirable; 'all cooperate' (me included) is next most desirable; 'all defect' (me included) is third; and one (me) cooperate is worst. We can predict, therefore, that selfish maximizing individuals will try and devise ways of ending up as the sole defector (or one of a privileged few) and that strategic interaction, bluffing, manoeuvring and all kinds of deceit will characterize human behaviour in these situations. *But we can also predict that the same selfish maximizing individuals will try to find ways by which their societies can end up at the 'all cooperate' outcome—or at least N - 1 (namely me) cooperate.*

FINDINGS

Involvement

While any correlation between the 'ecological validity' of an experiment and the degree of subject involvement is far from perfect, the assessment of such involvement is certainly an important factor in evaluating a domain of studies. When social dilemma games are played for substantial amounts of money, subjects are *extremely* involved. In 1972, Bonacich ran two conditions of five-person 'give some' games; in both conditions $c_1 = c_2 = \$0.25$; in a 'low temptation' condition c_3 ranged from \$0.01 to \$0.20 across five trials, while in a 'high temptation' condition it ran from \$0.01 to \$0.75, with a special trial at the end where subjects could win up to \$16.00 by betraying their groups. In both conditions, communication was allowed, and the subjects made ample use of evaluative terms ('cheat', 'screw', 'greed', and 'fink' being the four most common). In a later study (1976) Bonacich used larger amounts of money, which resulted in even more striking involvement. All subjects, in five-person groups, played two games; in the first $c_1 = c_2 = c_3 = \$0.30$, while in the second, which was not a uniform game, any defection resulted in no payoff to cooperators and a payoff as high as \$9.00 to a single defector.

Bonacich writes (1976, p.207):

> During the coding of the tapes we noticed occasional joking threats about what the group would do to a noncooperator; he would not leave the place alive, they would push him down the stairs as he left,

they would beat him up, they would write a letter to the student newspaper exposing his perfidy, or they would take him to small claims court. These threats could be intimidating and could suggest how angry the group would be toward the noncooperator.

Dawes *et al.* (1977) conducted an experiment involving even larger amounts of money; subjects played just once. Total cooperation resulted in $2.50 for each of their eight-person groups, total defection resulted in no payment to anyone; $c_1 = c_2 = \$1.50$, and $c_3 = \$8.00$, a substantial monetary incentive to defect. Some groups could communicate while others could not. Dawes *et al.* (1977, p.7) write:

> One of the most significant aspects of this study, however, did not show up in the data analysis. It is the extreme seriousness with which the subjects take the problems. Comments such as, 'If you defect on the rest of us, you're going to have to live with it the rest of your life,' were not at all uncommon. Nor was it unusual for people to wish to leave by the back door, to claim that they did not wish to see the 'sons of bitches' who double-crossed them, to become extremely angry at other subjects, or to become tearful . . . .

> The affect level was so high that we are unwilling to run intact groups, because of the effect the game might have on the members' feelings about each other. The affect level also mitigates against examining choice visibility (NB in experiments involving high stakes). In pretesting we did run one group in which choices were made public. The three defectors were the target of a great deal of hostility ('You have no idea how much you alienate me!,' one cooperator shouted before storming out of the room); they remained after the experiment until all the cooperators were presumably long gone.

Experimenters whose payoffs consist of points to be converted to trivial amounts of cash or course credits do not report the affect level of their subjects. It may also be high, but we suspect that if it were it would be mentioned.

Whether or not high stakes and affect are necessary to reach valid conclusions about behaviour in social dilemmas is a question that cannot be answered *a priori*, but depends in part upon a general finding of congruent or disparate results across high involvement and low involvement studies. As yet, there are not enough investigations in the field to know.

Certainly most of the situations in which we are interested involve high affect — e.g. that experienced by one of us (RMD) during the 1974 gasoline crisis as friend and neighbour after friend and neighbour became a 'regular customer' of some service station that closed its tanks to the general public once enough such customers were obtained.

Most social dilemmas we face are involving. While it is not clear that the experiments using minimal payoffs yield results different from those using more substantial payoffs, we see no reason for researchers with access to money to continue using mills or hypothetical dollars as payoffs. It makes no sense to spend large amounts of money for summer salaries, secretaries, computer terminals, and research assistants, and then motivate the subjects with microscopic amounts of money or course credits, when it *could* make a difference. (Subjects motivated primarily by boredom may give systematic data, but not those relevant to the hypotheses of the experimenter.) Moreover, using substantial amounts of money as payoffs obviates the ethical problem of giving course credits — more credits for more points (more defection?).

Communication

The salutary effects of communication on cooperation are ubiquitous. In the first experiment by Bonacich reported above, communication was allowed in all groups, and 93 percent of the choices were cooperative. In the second experiment, there was a 94 percent cooperation rate. Bonacich did not run a no-communication control group (because he was not studying the effects of communication *per se*), but Dawes *et al.* (1977) did. They found 72 percent cooperation in their communicating groups (which consisted of two different types to be described shortly) as opposed to 31 percent in their no-communication groups (which also consisted of two types).

Using points as payoffs, Rapoport *et al.* (1962), and Bixentine *et al.* (1966) found that communicating groups cooperated more.[4] Brechner (1977), Edney and Harper (1978, in press), and Harper (1977) studied behaviour in variable games in which players took or refrained from taking points from a common pool that could replenish itself in proportion to the number of points remaining. They found that groups able to communicate cooperated more, with the result that more points were 'harvested' from the pool.

Using a hypothetical uniform business game (in which manufacturers could cooperate against consumers), Jerdee and Rosen (1974) found that communication enhanced cooperation, but in a uniform game in which subjects 'should act as if each point were worth $1', Caldwell (1976) did not. Caldwell did find, however, that a communication condition in which subjects could sanction defectors did result in greater cooperation. But his findings about communication *per se* were in the right direction — although not significant — and, as he wrote, 'Perhaps with real money subjects would be less inclined to treat the experiment as a competitive game' (p.279).

What is it about communication that leads to more cooperation? While most of the studies mentioned above simply pitted communication against no communication, Dawes *et al.* (1977) attempted to study the effects of various aspects of communication. They argued that there is a hierarchy of at least three aspects involved in any face-to-face communication about dilemma problems. First, subjects get to know each other as human beings (humanization); secondly, they get to discuss the dilemma with which they are faced (discussion); and thirdly, they have the opportunity to make commitments about their own behaviour and to attempt to elicit such commitments from others (commitment). Commitment entails discussion, and discussion in turn entails humanization.

Dawes *et al.* (1977) ran four types of groups: those that could not communicate at all, those that communicated for ten minutes about an irrelevant topic (they were asked to estimate the proportion of people at various income levels in Eugene, Oregon), those that could discuss the problem but could not ask for public commitments, and those that were required to 'go around the table' and make public commitments after discussion. The first two types yielded cooperation rates of 30 and 32 percent, respectively, while the last two had rates of 72 and 71 percent. Thus, humanization made no difference — at least not personal acquaintance based on a ten-minute discussion (the average amount of time that the discussion and commitment groups spent on the problem). Surprisingly, commitment made no difference, but it must be remembered that this commitment was one forced by the experimenters rather than one arising spontaneously from the group process. (Moreover, *every* subject promised to cooperate, which is the only reasonable statement to make no matter what one's intentions.)

Group Size

All experimenters who have made either explicit or implicit comparisons of dilemma games with varying numbers of players have concluded that subjects cooperate less in larger groups than in smaller ones. Rapoport *et al.* (1962) and Bixentine *et al.* (1966) simply noted the low degree of cooperation in their three- and six-person games and stated that it is less than in comparable two-person prisoners' dilemmas. But they had no strict criterion of comparability. Marwell and Schmidt (1972) studied two- and three-person uniform games with c_3 equal in each and found less cooperation in the three-person game. Unfortunately, c_1 and c_2 were not equated, being twice as large in the two-person as in the three-person game (which resulted in the 'expected values' of cooperation and defection being identical if the other players were to respond in a fifty-fifty random manner). Harper *et al.* (unpublished manuscript) compared one-, three-, and six-person groups in the variable dilemma involving pool replacement. They found that cooperation decreased with group size, but it is not clear what the results for a 'one-person group' test — other than the intellectual ability of a single individual to solve the replenishment problem in an optimal manner given the experimenter's replacement rule.[5]

The problem is, of course, how to 'equate' N- and N'-person games varying 'only' group size. Games may be described by a variety of parameters. (In fact, different investigators have investigated the effects of differently defined parameters in the two-person iterated prisoners' dilemma game *ad nauseam*.) Which parameters should, then, be held constant when comparing N- and N'-person games? A natural candidate in uniform games is c_3, but even that as a constant can be disputed on the grounds that with harm spread out over more people in larger games the monetary motive to defect should increase. There is no mathematical or structural solution to the equating problem, just solutions that are reasonable from the point of view of ecological validity.

Anonymity Versus Public Disclosure of Choice

Three studies have compared private with public choice (Bixentine *et al.*, 1966; Jerdee and Rosen, 1974; Fox and Guyer, 1978); all found higher rates of cooperation when choice was public. While the difference between anonymity and public disclosure in these studies is not striking, they used minimal payoffs — and given the involvement obtained with significant amounts of money, we suspect that the difference would be much greater were the payoffs more significant.

Expectations About Others' Behaviour

We have been able to find only two studies that collected subjects' expectations about whether others playing the game would cooperate or defect (Tyszka and Grezlak, 1976; Dawes *et al.*, 1977). There are two possible predictions. To the degree to which a subject believes others *will not* defect, he or she may feel it is possible to obtain a big payoff without hurting others too much. This desire to be a 'free rider' (or 'greed' as Coombs, 1973, terms it) could result in a negative correlation between the propensity to cooperate and beliefs that others will. To the degree to which a subject believes that others *will* defect, he or she may feel that it is necessary to avoid a big loss by defecting himself or herself. The desire to 'avoid being a sucker' (or 'fear' as Coombs, 1973, terms it) could result in a positive correlation between the propensity to cooperate and beliefs that others will. In fact, both studies report a positive correlation.

There is one other interesting finding in both. Defectors are more accurate at predicting cooperation rates than are cooperators. But Dawes *et al.* (1977) found that they were *not* more accurate at predicting specifically who would cooperate and who would not. This apparent discrepancy between base rate accuracy and specific accuracy can be best understood by considering the predictions of the outcome of coin tosses. A person who predicts heads 50 percent of the time will be correct only 50 percent of the time despite a perfect base rate accuracy; a person who predicts heads 100 percent of the time will also be correct 50 percent of the time despite making the worst possible base rate prediction. In fact, in the Dawes *et al.* (1977) study subjects were *very* poor at predicting who would and who would not cooperate.

Moralizing

Noting that the subjects in the Dawes *et al.* (1977) study often raised moral issues in the discussion and commitment groups, Dawes *et al.* (unpublished manuscript) ran two experiments in which the experimenters themselves moralized at the subjects. These two studies, one conducted at Santa Barbara, California, and one conducted at Eugene, Oregon, contrasted a no-communication condition with a no-communication condition in which the experimenter delivered a 938 word sermon about group benefit, exploitation, whales, ethics, and so on. At both locations the sermon worked, yielding rates of cooperation comparable to those found in the discussion and commitment groups of the earlier experiments.

CONCLUSION

The question most asked by social theorists in social dilemma situations is whether the incentive structure provided by a particular institution or pattern of social organization works to a socially optimal or socially suboptimal end. The question is being asked in contemporary work in constitutional choice (Orbell and Wilson, 1978a, 1978b; Romer and Rosenthal, 1978) where various rules of collective decision-making are analysed in the context of social dilemmas with different cost–benefit parameters. But it can also be asked of normative and religious systems, as Campbell (1975) has shown. Generally, human societies can organize themselves in an infinite variety of ways, but all such patterns have implications for the incentives individual members are confronted with. Which patterns work most efficiently to bring individual incentives into line with achievement of social optima?

Notice that there is a temptation to assume that 'institutional evolution' works to socially optimal ends, but that this is not *necessarily* the case. Constitutional conventions can make mistakes (for example), and dominant institutional patterns can reflect the interests of some subset to the detriment of the whole. Moreover, the environmental situation can change (e.g. with overpopulation) so that a previously optimal system is so no longer. Before we leap to the conclusion that 'what is, is justified' we must understand the process through which 'what is' came to be. Such normatively loaded questions do, however, seem susceptible to both formal and empirical research.

How far has the empirical research reviewed in the previous section taken us? Although this work does report a considerable incidence of cooperative behaviour under various experimental conditions, it is not always clear which of the mechanisms discussed in the theoretical section of this paper are operating. Communication works, for example, but does it work because it brings with it interpersonal pressures (normative rewards and punishments) or because it triggers conscience — because talking about the dilemma of choice makes people aware of it and, thereby, 'activates an internalized reward-punishment system'? Similarly, does moralizing work because it activates conscience or because it increases the expectation of others' cooperating and therefore decreases the likelihood of individuals' playing the sucker role?

Possible interactions among legal systems, normative systems, conscience and more fundamental motivational considerations need exploration. Brubaker (1975) has suggested one most interesting such interaction. If individuals were assumed to be (selfishly) more interested in avoiding the sucker's role than in reaching the free rider's role, a modest change in the rules of the game could well ensure high levels of cooperation. Models of collective good provision usually assume that contributions, once made, are not retrievable if sufficient contributions from others are not forthcoming. But if they *were* retrievable, if an intermediary simply did not purchase the good until sufficient contributions were in hand, the possibility of being a lone sucker would be eliminated. Players might be expected to operate under a 'golden rule of revelation' by which they contribute in the expectation that others will do the same (a more optimistic view of human motivation than the standard free-rider assumption, as Brubaker points out). Critically, however, neither the motivational change nor the rule change could be expected to have the desired result by themselves. Brubaker cites empirical studies (Bohm, 1971, 1973) supporting his hypothesis. What other such interactions are possible?

There is a fundamental problem in generalizing the experimental results to the real-world circumstances (the environment, population, resource depletion, etc.) that generate much interest in social dilemma logic. We argued earlier that the extensive research on two-person prisoners' dilemmas was not applicable to such problems, in part because in two-person groups individuals have considerable capacity to manipulate the behaviour of their partner. The research we have discussed involves larger groups, but not large *enough* to eliminate the problem. Buchanan (1965) pointed out that in *small* groups, the individual's choice of the 'moral' alternative could be seen as having a measurable impact on the group outcome. In a five-person group, for example, the individual is one-fifth of the whole and his or her 'moral' choice will ensure that the 'all defect' outcome is not reached. Similarly, the individual in a small group can reasonably expect to influence the choices of others.

But in a *large* group — certainly one the size of a whole society — the choices of others are simply part of the environment to which the individual must react in a passive manner, and there is no possibility of his or her behaviour influencing the general outcome. What is the threshold between *large* and *small*? Buchanan does not provide any *a priori* answer; nor does Olson (1965) who argues along similar lines. But it does seem that the groups whose behaviour has been studied in the laboratory are closer to *small* than *large* and, therefore, that the findings should be generalized to society-wide dilemmas only with very great caution. The mechanisms that have been shown to support cooperative behaviour in the laboratory setting *might* have the same result at the level of whole societies, but the logic of choice for individuals is quite different at the latter level and they might have no impact at all. Generally, the results of experimental research to date can be said to suggest some hypotheses for the resolution of small-group dilemmas — clearly an important subject. But the resolution of large-group dilemmas remains the province of theoretical work and is largely untouched by empirical findings.

ACKNOWLEDGEMENTS

The authors wish to thank Rebecca Goodrich of the Institute for Social Science Research, University of Oregon for her careful reading and preparation of the manuscript.

NOTES

1. Ideology can be understood as working in the same way as conscience. Margaret Levi (1979) has argued that Marxists avoid the free-rider problem by the use of ideology:

> . . . However, to do this requires a notion of ideology. On the one hand, the hold of ruling class ideology helps the state maintain its stability despite pressures which, from the Marxist point of view, should produce class struggle. On the other hand, the dominated class must have an ideology that enables its members to organize as a class.

In our terms, ideology provides supplementary payoffs sufficient to ensure group-oriented (class-oriented) behaviour in the face of pressures to the contrary.

2. The game could equally well be phrased in terms of the chooser of the red chip taking $1.00 from each of the other players. Having the defectors' harm (externality) shared by all players including the defector results, however, in a much more mathematically coherent structure for analysing all dilemmas.

3. Properties A and B do not imply property C unless $c_1 = c_2$ because it is possible that payoffs for cooperation and defection are linear but do not have equal slopes. On the other hand, properties A and C not only imply property B, but that c_1 is equal to c_2 as well. Properties B and C yield the same implication. Property C by itself has no implication other than condition no.1 because it does not specify that the payoff functions need be straight lines.

4. These results require qualification. The communication that was effective in the

Rapoport *et al.* (1962) study was unintended; it occurred during a break between two 3-4 hour sessions, and because the experiment's 'main interest was in the distribution of *choices* in the absence of communication', the results after the break were ignored except for noting the high degree of cooperation. The game in the Bixentine *et al.* (1966) study was not strictly a dilemma, because there were some points at which defection did not dominate cooperation.

5. Interestingly, there *is* an optimal solution for harvesting animals in their natural environment. Determine the maximal population size were there no harvesting, and then keep the population at precisely half that size. See Dawes *et al.* (1974), who reached this conclusion through a crude algebra and Anderson (1974) who reached it through differential equations.

REFERENCES

Alexander, R. D. (1980) *Darwinism and Human Affairs*, University of Washington Press, Seattle.

Anderson, J. M. (1974) 'A model for the "Tragedy of the Commons"', *IEEE Transactions on Systems, Man, and Cybernetics*, **1974**, 103-5.

Bixentine, V. E., Levitt, C. A., and Wilson, K. R. (1966) 'Collaboration among six persons in a prisoner's dilemma game', *Journal of Conflict Resolution*, **10**, 488-96.

Blaney, P. H. (1976) 'Genetic basis of behavior — especially of altruism', *American Psychologist*, **31**, 358.

Bohm, Peter (1971) 'An approach to the problem of estimating demand for public goods', *Swedish Journal of Economics*, **1**, 55-65.

Bohm, Peter (1973) 'Estimating demand for public goods: An experiment', *European Economic Review*, **3**, 111-30.

Bonacich, P. (1972) 'Norms and cohesion as adaptive responses to political conflict: An experimental study', *Sociometry*, **35**, 357-75.

Bonacich, P. (1976) 'Secrecy and solidarity', *Sociometry*, **39**, 200-8.

Bonacich, P., Shure, G. H., Kahan, J. P., and Meeker, R. J. (1976) 'Cooperation and group size in the *N*-person prisoner's dilemma', *Journal of Conflict Resolution*, **20**, 687-705.

Brechner, K. C. (1977) 'An experimental analysis of social traps', *Journal of Experimental Social Psychology*, **13**, 552-64.

Brubaker, Earl R. (1975) 'Free Ride, Free Revelation, or Golden Rule?', *The Journal of Law and Economics*, **17**, 147-61.

Buchanan, James M. (1965) 'Ethical rules, expected values, and large numbers', *Ethics*, **76**, 1-13.

Buchanan, James M. (1968) *The Demand and Supply of Public Goods*, Rand McNally and Co., Chicago.

Buchanan, James M. (1971) 'The bases for collective action', *General Learning Corporation*, **1971**, 1-18.

Buchanan, James M. (1975) *The Limits of Liberty*, The University of Chicago Press, Chicago.

Caldwell, M. D. (1976) 'Communication and sex effects in a five-person prisoner's dilemma', *Journal of Personality and Social Psychology*, **33**, 273-81.

Campbell, Donald T. (1975) 'On the conflict between biological and social evolution and between psychology and moral tradition', *American Psychologist*, **December**, 1103-26.

Coase, R. H. (1960) 'The problem of social cost', *The Journal of Law and Economics*, **3**, 1-44.

Cooke, Alistair (1955) *The Essential Mencken*, Vantage Books, New York.

Coombs, C. H. (1973) 'A reparameterization of the prisoner's dilemma game', *Behavioral Science*, **18**, 424–28.

Dawes, R. M. (1975) 'Formal models of dilemmas in social decision-making', in *Human Judgment and Decision Processes* (Eds. M. F. Kaplan and S. Schwartz), Academic Press, New York, 88–107.

Dawes, R. M., Delay, J., and Chaplin, W. (1974) 'The decision to pollute', *Environment and Planning*, **1974**, 3–10.

Dawes, R. M., McTavish, J., and Shaklee, H. (1977) 'Behavior, communication, and assumptions about other people's behavior in a commons dilemma situation', *Journal of Personality and Social Psychology*, **35**, 1–11.

Dawes, R. M., Shaklee, H., and Talarowski, F. 'On getting people to cooperate when facing a social dilemma: Moralizing helps', unpublished manuscript.

Demsetz, Harold (1966) 'Some aspects of property rights', *The Journal of Law and Economics*, **9**, 61–70.

Demsetz, Harold (1967) 'Toward a theory of property rights', *American Economic Review, Proceedings Issue*, **May**, 347–60.

Edney, J. J. and Harper, C. S. (1978) 'The effects of information in a resource management problem: A social trap analog', *Human Ecology*, **6**, 387–95.

Edney, J. J. and Harper, C. S. (1980) 'Heroism in a resource crisis: A simulation study', *Environmental Management*, in press.

Fox, J. and Guyer, M. (1978) ' "public" choice and cooperation in *N*-person prisoner's dilemma', *Journal of Conflict Resolution*, **22**, 468–81.

Frohlich, Norman, Oppenheimer, J. A., and Young, O. R. (1971) *Political Leadership and Collective Goods*, Princeton University Press, Princeton.

Goodman, G. (1972) 'Welfare recipients getting photo I.D.', *New York Times, 8 April*, p.1.

Hamburger, H. (1973) '*N*-persons prisoners' dilemmas', *Journal of Mathematical Sociology*, **3**, 27–48.

Hardin, Garrett (1968) 'The tragedy of the commons', *Science*, **162**, 1243–48.

Harper, C. S. (1977) 'Competition and cooperation in a resource management task: A social trap analogue', in *Priorities for Environmental Design Research* (Eds. S. Weidman and J. R. Anderson), Environmental Research Associates, Washington, D.C., 305–12.

Harper, C. S., Gregory, W. L., Lindner, D., and Edney, J. J. 'Group size effects in a simulated commons dilemma', unpublished manuscript.

Heilbroner, Robert (1974) *An Inquiry into the Human Prospect*, Norton, New York.

Hobbes, Thomas (1947) *Leviathan*, Kent (1651), London.

Jerdee, T. H. and Rosen, B. (1974) 'Effects of opportunity to communicate and visibility of individual decisions on behavior in the common interest', *Journal of Applied Psychology*, **59**, 712–16.

Kahan, J. P. (1973) 'Noninteraction in an anonymous three person prisoner's dilemma game', *Behavioral Science*, **18**, 124–27.

Levi, Margaret (1979) 'On the Marxist theory of the state', paper presented to the 1979 Annual Meeting of the Public Choice Society, Charleston, SC, 17–19 March, and the 1979 Annual Meeting of the Western Political Science Association, Portland, OR, 22–24 March.

Luce, R. D. and Raiffa, H. (1957) *Games and Decision: Introduction and Critical Survey*, John Wiley, London.

Marwell, G. and Schmidt, D. R. (1972) 'Cooperation in a three-person prisoner's dilemma', *Journal of Personality and Social Psychology*, **31**, 376–83.

Niskanen, William A., Jr. (1971) *Bureaucracy and Representative Government*, Aldine-Atherton, Chicago.

North, Douglass C. and Thomas, Robert Paul (1973) *The Rise of the Western World*, Cambridge University Press.

Olson, Mancur (1965) *The Logic of Collective Action*, Harvard University Press, Cambridge.

Ophuls, William (1973) 'Leviathan or oblivion?', in Herman E. Daly (ed.), *Toward a Steady State Economy* (Ed. Herman E. Daly), Freeman, San Francisco.

Ophuls, William (1977) *Ecology and the Politics of Scarcity*, Freeman, San Francisco.

Orbell, John M and Rutherford, Brent (1974) 'Social peace as a collective good', *British Journal of Political Science*, **4**, 501–10.

Orbell, John M. and Wilson II, L. A. (1978a) 'Institutional solutions to the N-prisoners' dilemma', *The American Political Science Review*, **72**, 2, 411–21.

Orbell, John M. and Wilson II, L.A. (1978b) 'The uses of expanded majorities', *The American Political Science Review*, **72**, 4, 1366–68.

Rapoport, Amnon (1967) 'Optimal policies for the prisoner's dilemma', *Psychological review*, **74**, 136–48.

Rapoport, Amnon, Chammah, A., Dwyer, J., and Gyr, J. (1962) 'Three-person non-zero-sum nonnegotiable games', *Behavioral Science*, **7**, 30–58.

Romer, Thomas and Rosenthal, Howard (1978) 'The N-prisoners' dilemma: A bureaucrat-setter solution', *The American Political Science Review*, **72**, 4, 1364–65.

Samuelson, Paul A. (1954) 'The pure theory of public expenditure', *Review of Economics and Statistics*, **36**, 387–89.

Samuelson, Paul A. (1955) 'Diagrammatic exposition of a theory of public expenditure,' *Review of Economics and Statistics*, **37**, 350–56.

Schelling, Thomas C. (1973) 'Hockey helmets, concealed weapons, and daylight saving: A study of binary choices with externalities', *Journal of Conflict Resolution*, **17**, 381–428.

Schmid, A. Allan (1978) *Property, Power, and Public Choice*, Praeger Publishers, London.

Sharpe, L. J. (1973) 'American democracy reconsidered: Part II and conclusions', *British Journal of Political Science*, **3**, 133.

Shils, Edward and Janowitz, Morris (1953) 'Cohesion and desintegration in the Wehrmacht', in *Reader in Public Opinion and Communication* (Eds. Bernard Berelson and Morris Janowitz), The Free Press, Glencoe. 407–22.

Smith, Adam (1976) *The Wealth of Nations*, The University of Chicago Press (1776), Chicago.

Stern, Paul C. (1978) 'When do people act to maintain common resources? A reformulated psychological question of our times', *International Journal of Psychology*, **13**, 2, 149–58.

Taylor, Michael (1976) *Anarchy and Cooperation*, John Wiley, London.

Trivers, R. L. (1971) 'The evolution of reciprocal altruism', *Quarterly Review of Biology*, **46**, 4, 35–57.

Tullock, Gordon (1974) *The Social Dilemma*, University Publications, Blacksburg.

Tyszka, T. and Grezlak, J. L. (1976) 'Criteria of choice in non-constant zero-sum games', *Journal of Conflict Resolution*, **20**, 357–76.

Progress in Applied Social Psychology, Volume 1
Edited by G. M. Stephenson and J. M. Davis
© 1981 John Wiley & Sons, Ltd.

3

Understanding Criminal Sentencing: Views from Law and Social Psychology

SHARI SEIDMAN DIAMOND and CAROLE J. HERHOLD

INTRODUCTION

Social psychologists examine the way in which people attribute responsibility to others. They explore the consistency of behaviour across situations. They are intrigued by the effect of examples or 'modeling' on observers' behaviours. All of these interests are represented in one of the most frequent activities of the criminal justice system: the sentencing of a criminal defendant. The purpose of this chapter is to examine theories and empirical findings that can contribute to an understanding of general patterns in sentencing,[1] and to identify points at which contributions can be made through research by social psychologists. The general approach will be to examine legal statutes and sentencing practices in the light of social psychological theory and research, making explicit the connection between the presumed goals of sentencing and the existing of judgement.

Five purposes are traditionally associated with the sentencing of criminal offenders. The first four are utilitarian goals aimed at the reduction of crime. The *rehabilitation* goal views the sentence as a vehicle to change and reform the offender. Punishment is also presumed to lead to *specific deterrence*, i.e. to discourage the offender from repeating his criminal behaviour, and to *general deterrence*, in which the punishment example warns others against engaging in illegal activity. Prison and jail sentences function to *incapacitate* offenders so that while serving their sentences they cannot commit additional crimes, at least against the civilian public. Finally, sentences are justified simply as expressions of *retribution*, society's obligation and opportunity to punish those who violate its norms.

Each of these purposes requires a different kind of judgement to be made about a particular offender and his offence. For example, clinical psychologists are often involved in judgements about rehabilitation. Presentence reports may contain psychiatric information provided by a psychologist that suggests how an offender is likely to respond to supervision or incarceration, and what kind of attention is likely to lead him to change. The other goals of sentencing involve similarly difficult judgement tasks: e.g. the culpability of the offender for the offence may provide a clue to the likelihood that he will repeat his activity; an assessment of the damage produced by the offence may influence the level of punishment perceived consistent with just retribution.

These examples point to the complexity of the sentencing decision. Not only are such judgements difficult, but in addition conflicting goals must be melded in the construction of the sentence. Some legislative standards are provided, but judges are generally given wide discretion on the assumption that such latitude will permit them to use the available information and strike the appropriate balance among the potentially conflicting goals of the sentence.

The accuracy of the resulting sentence cannot easily be assessed because there is no direct standard against which the sentence can be measured. It is possible, however, to examine the ways in which the pieces of information available to the sentencer are likely to be used, and the extent to which such items of information predict the future behaviour in the offender. The purpose of this chapter then is to examine the formation and predictive validity of sentencing judgements.

RETRIBUTIVE SENTENCING

The tension among the different sentencing goals is evident in two of the dichotomies used to categorize sentencing criteria. The first, which provides the framework for Thomas's (1970;1979) analysis of English sentencing practices, is whether the sentence will be designed to reflect society's evaluation of the offence and its circumstances (the so-called tariff), or whether it will be designed to deal with the needs of the offender (the individualized sentence). While retribution and, secondarily, general deterrence and incapacitation are reflected in the tariff, rehabilitation and specific deterrence are the primary goals of individualized sentencing. Because the tariff stresses equality in sentencing, it is endemically in conflict with the attempt to fit the sentence to the offender's particular needs (Hood, 1972).

A second set of categories, the framework we will rely on here, focuses on the contrast between retributive and utilitarian sentencing purposes. Retribution stresses payment by the offender for what he has done, while the utilitarian approach justifies punishment because of its presumed impact on crime reduction (Cross, 1975). The primary focus of social psychologists has been on retribution. Judged culpability, attributions of intent, and determinations of responsibility and blameworthiness are the major dependent variables in this literature. This concentration of attention is particularly interesting in view of the ambivalence expressed by the criminal justice system toward retribution. While Kant (translation, 1965) argued that members of an isolated island society deciding to disband and disperse would have to first execute all murderers remaining in prison or else 'be regarded as accomplices in the public violation of legal justice' (p.102), more recent perspectives view punishment as justified only if it promotes crime reduction (e.g. Cross, 1975; Walker, 1969).

Yet some patterns of sanctioning appear to reflect a retributive goal. Thomas (1979), in his review of the sentencing decisions made in cases appealed from the Crown Court in England, describes sentences as based either on tariff or on the needs of the offender. The application of the tariff

> requires the sentencer to find the sentence that most accurately reflects the offender's culpability, a process which involves relating the gravity of the offence to the established pattern of sentences for offences of that kind, and then making allowance for such mitigating factors as may be present which tend to reduce the offender's culpability (p.9).

While sometimes used in part to achieve general deterrence or some other purpose, the tariff has as its major principle proportionality between the offence and the sentence, suggesting that equitable retribution is a guiding force. Cross (1975) too, in discussing retributive theories of punishment, refers to the gravity of the offence as a major basis for determining how much punishment should be inflicted. In this he includes proportionality to the moral deserts of the offender as well as to the amount of harm done by the offender. Psychologists would translate these two phases into assessments of responsibility-as-culpability[2] and severity of outcome or consequences.

Responsibility — Just Deserts

A major element in most criminal action is intentionality, although some offences do hold the actor strictly liable for the consequences of unintended events presumably under his control. The law also mandates punishment for the individual who inflicts injury as a result of negligence, but more severe penalties are entailed when an offence involves a planned injury. Thus, a drunken speeding motorist who kills a pedestrian will be charged with reckless homicide, and will be eligible for less punishment than an individual who successfully plans and carries out the murder of his spouse. Because both offences result in the death of the victim, the differing punishment levels cannot be motivated by varying severity of the offence consequences. Furthermore, the motorist is probably more likely to repeat his offence than the spouse murderer (Bluebeard excepted), so that incapacitation or need for rehabilitation to reduce future damage cannot adequately justify the difference. The remaining plausible explanation is society's interest in approaching punishment according to desert.

A variety of cues may be used to infer intent and to assign responsibility. Much of the recent literature on attribution theory in social psychology has focused on the way observers use information about an act and an actor in making such attributions (e.g. Jones and Davis, 1965). In reviewing this literature we will be asking: What evidence do we have that legislators mandate and judges utilize these cues in determining criminal sentences?

Built into most criminal statutes is the requirement that the offender must be able to distinguish between right and wrong and to make his behaviour conform to the laws of society. Blame is generally confined to those who, it is presumed, could have behaved properly but did not. Assessments of offender abilities and the dispositional nature of the offence should therefore play a major role in attributions of culpability.

Offender Position and the Standard of Conduct

Stricter adherence to the law is expected for individuals in certain professions. This higher expectation may make them liable to more severe punishment than the average citizen. Thus, there are special provisions for sentencing postal employees who delay or destroy mail, steal mail matter, or misappropriate postal funds.[3] In Canada, where sentence appeals often bring out elements of the sentencing purpose that are left unspecified in U.S. sentencing decisions, several cases clearly express the greater perceived culpability of certain violators. In a hit-and-run auto accident that resulted in the death of a young girl, the offender was a police officer with an unblemished record. The appellate court noted, 'The trial court quite properly considered that a greater degree of moral fault rested upon J as a member of a police force sworn to uphold the law. J not only disobeyed the law but aggravated the offence and further breached his police duty by attempting to conceal his complicity and mislead the investigators. In many ways, it is difficult to conceive of a more serious case.'[4] In another case in which a lawyer of excellent reputation converted client monies to his own use, the court noted, 'It is not wrong to sentence a person more severely just because he is a lawyer. The penalty imposed varies according to the circumstances, and one of those circumstances is that O breached his duty as a trustee and as a lawyer. The court will not allow the very reputation which was depended upon to perpetrate the fraud to be used as a mitigating factor in sentencing.'[5]

One explanation for the increased culpability assigned in these examples is a motivation for control. Since people try to achieve control in their lives, they learn to trust those who are most reliable. When an object of this trust is shown to be untrustworthy, this poses a greater threat to the observer's control than if the violator was not initially trusted. Moreover, since the mail employee, attorney, and police officer in our examples are in a particularly good position to cause harm, it is therefore potentially more damaging when they decide to violate the law. This explanation is also consistent with Thomas's (1979) observation that sentence discounts for general good character are not likely to occur if acts of indecency with children are committed by a person in whose care they have been entrusted.

On the surface these results appear inconsistent with the finding that attractiveness and liking generally reduce attributions of responsibility and temper the assignment of blame. Numerous studies by psychologists (e.g. Landy and Aronson, 1969; Sigall and Landy, 1972) have shown this effect. If high status people are more attractive, they are blamed less. Attractiveness, however, may turn to a disadvantage under certain circumstances. In Sigall and Ostrove (1975) there was a trend toward punishing an offender who had used her attractiveness to facilitate a swindle more than an unattractive offender involved in an identical offence. When attractiveness did not increase the ability of the offender to carry out the offence (a burglary), the familiar significant attractiveness advantage resulted. The offenders in the earlier legislative and judicial examples also appeared to evoke greater blame because they took advantage of their special opportunities.

At the same time, there is also some evidence from legal decisions that such penalties may not occur when the offence is unrelated to a position of trust. Thomas (1979) reports that '[w]here a police officer commits offences which are wholly unrelated to his duties and do not involve any abuse of authority or position, his position should be ignored in assessing the appropriate sentence' (p.15, note 4).

Sociologists have been concerned with the role of 'offender social advantage' in sentencing. Based primarily on a conflict perspective, they assume that higher status offenders will receive better treatment from middle-class judges who cannot identify with the poor (Chambliss and Seidman, 1971). Evidence for this proposition, however, has been mixed (e.g. Black, 1971; Bordua, 1967; Chiricos and Waldo, 1975; Hagan, 1974), and one possible reason is that culpability assessments are mediated by the trust and opportunity considerations outlined above. A close examination of offence circumstances, an approach not generally typical of sociological work, might provide an appropriate way to extend the investigations begun in the laboratory.

Level of Psychological Functioning

The law recognizes that some individuals who lack ordinary levels of psychological functioning cannot be found guilty of offences that require *mens rea*, the guilty mind. These individuals do not enter consideration for sentencing since they are found 'not guilty by reason of insanity'.[6] Leniency in sentence, however, is often urged in presentence reports on convicted offenders in the light of less severe forms of psychological disturbance. There is little evidence on the extent to which such data actually affect the outcomes for such offenders since the research on sentencing by sociologists has not included this variable. There has, however, been some experimental work by psychologists that points to such an impact. Jones, Hester, Farina, and Davis (1959) found that a verbal attack by a maladjusted person with a traumatic mental history resulted in more favourable evaluations of the derogator than when the attack was made by an apparently well-adjusted individual. It is not clear from this result that reduced punishment would also follow, but a recent study by Monahan and Hood (1976) suggests it would. Subjects in that study judged an offender with a history of prior psychological disorder as less morally responsible, less blameworthy, and less deserving of punishment than an offender who had no psychiatric history. The mentally disordered offender was also perceived as having less free will, and this finding points to the centrality of attributions about volition in assessments of culpability.

Level of Intellectual Functioning

The abilities to distinguish right from wrong and to control one's behaviour may be influenced by the offender's level of intellectual functioning. Although not explicitly recognized by statute, there is some evidence that low intelligence may mitigate culpability judgements. Cross (1975) describes the case in England of a father who was convicted of incest with his 18- and 12-year-old daughters. He reports that although the Court of Appeal 'would not have dreamt of interfering with the sentences if Smith had been a man of ordinary intelligence, they made the sentences concurrent on account of his low IQ' (p.142). A similar reduction, apparently stimulated by the offender's 'childlike level of understanding', contributed to a sentence reduction in Massachusetts at a session of the Sentence Review Division.[7]

The analogy of lower intelligence and youthful understanding in the Massachusetts judge's comment suggests that age may affect assignment of responsibility. In this area there has been substantial work. A separate juvenile court system is predicated on the assumption that youthful offenders should be handled differently from adults. Special sentencing provisions are also available for the youthful offender in some adult systems (e.g. Youth Corrections Act).[8] A primary reason for this difference is to arrange better opportunities for the reform of offenders who are not yet to be held fully responsible for their activity (Fox, 1977). As many have observed, however, there is no clear evidence that juvenile justice does systematically result in greater leniency for youthful offenders.[9]

Studies of the determinants of sentencing have examined age as a predictor of sentence level within adult offender populations. Here the evidence has been mixed. Age had no effect in studies by Clarke and Koch (1976),

Diamond (1981), and Landes (1974), but there was some evidence for leniency toward younger bank robbers with no criminal record in research by Tiffany, Avichai, and Peters (1975), and Thomas (1979) found a number of cases in which an offender's youth was given as the reason for a sentence reduction.[10] The available work does not specifically examine the role of age (or intelligence) in affecting culpability judgements alone. Even if culpability were judged to be lower, the expectation of more likely future criminal activity by a young or mentally deficient individual might cancel the benefits of moderated blame.

Liquor or Drug Involvement

There is some suggestion that intoxication and drug-use may make a defendant incapable of forming requisite specific intent,[11] but there is also case law concluding that *voluntary* drug intoxication cannot be considered to demonstrate lack of capacity to form the specific intent required for conviction in many offences.[12] Research on the sentencing of offenders under the influence of drugs shows no evidence for sentencing alterations. The Federal Judicial Center (Partridge and Eldridge, 1974) submitted offender and offence descriptions to a series of federal judges. For half of the judges one of the offenders convicted on a drug charge was a former addict and for the other half he was currently an addict. In both instances he was in a drug treatment programme at the time of the offence and was believed to be drug-free. The median sentence for both offenders was the same. In a second case involving mail theft, for half the judges the offender was an addict, addicted at the time of the offence, and for the other half the offender had no record of addiction. Again the sentence distributions did not differ.

We have seen evidence for sentence reduction in response to reduced control associated with low IQ and deficiencies in psychological functioning. However, reduced control associated with drugs does not appear to evoke this response. Such a response might have been expected from a review of work on Heider's (1958) levels of responsibility. Shaw and his associates (Shaw and Reitan, 1969; Shaw and Sulzer, 1964) found that attributed responsibility increased from extended commission (contingent but non-foreseeable consequences) to careless commission (foreseeable consequences) and again to purposive commission (intended consequences). If the addict offender is guilty of careless commission (his drug-use leads to a predictable need for money), his responsibility (and perceived blameworthiness) should be less than the non-addict for whom the attribution is purposive commission. Part of the answer may lie in the length of the causal chain involved in the attribution. Brickman, Ryan, and Wortman (1975) point out that 'Causes . . . have causes. Furthermore, the prior causes may or may not be of the same type as the immediate cause' (p.1060). Whereas a mental ability is generally not attributed to voluntary activity, drug and alcohol addiction are frequently perceived as initiated by the addict. Thus, if the causal chain is viewed as beginning with the drug- or alcohol-use, the offender may be held fully responsible for criminal offences that apparently follow from that action. There is some evidence that judges are more likely to disagree about the appropriate sentence when drug addiction is involved (Diamond, 1981), and this may reflect judicial variation in the construction of causal chains.

Thus far we have discussed how relatively enduring characteristics of individuals affect culpability judgements. There is another less stable class of internal characteristics that may also affect assignment of blame. To the extent that the offender has put forth effort and planning, his perceived culpability is likely to increase.

Effort and Planning

An act is premeditated if some planning is involved, and such acts may be subject to increased sentences. Thomas (1979, p.95) notes: 'Evidence of any significant degree of deliberation, such as the acquisition or possession of a dangerous weapon, may justify a sentence at the upper extreme of the bracket.' The prior determination involved need not exist for any particular period, but 'Premeditation differs essentially from will, which constitutes the crime; because it supposes, besides an actual will a deliberation, and a continued persistence' (Black, 1957, p.1343).

The role of effort in culpability assessments is suggested by the results of a study by Joseph, Kane, Gaes, and Tedeschi (1976). Subjects perceived an actor who drove a great distance to inflict injury as more desiring of harm and more aggressive than an actor who did not exert as much effort. A similar analysis can be applied to the finding of Harvey and Enzle (1978). Subjects in their study observed a person retaliate after being insulted. The retaliator was blamed less when he acted immediately. Furthermore, subjects judged the delayed reaction to be more premeditated, but not more intentional, than the swift response. The reason that perceived culpability increases when there is evidence of planned aggression is not clear. One possibility is that when an action is considered, the individual is expected to exert control over his impulse to aggress and then to refrain from committing the illegal act. Actions taken impulsively are not subject to this rational review. Implicit in this explanation is the presumption that the unplanned act might not have taken place if the actor had an opportunity to reconsider his potential behaviour or to rectify the situation before its discovery.

The actor's reaction to external as well as internal pressures can also affect culpability judgements.

Motive

Motive, as distinguished from intent, is the reason that stimulates an intentional act (Black, 1957). This distinction is often lost in psychological research on responsibility (e.g. Shaw and Reitan, 1969). Two individuals may both intend to rob a grocery store, but if one does so to pay for a needed operation and the other is motivated by a desire to purchase new clothes, attributions of culpability are likely to differ. Motives that are apparently externally stimulated may be perceived differently than motives that have no apparent outside source. Moreover, the specific nature of the motive is likely to affect evaluation of the actor. Although the perception of differently motivated criminal actions has not been directly examined in the laboratory, early work by Pepitone and Sherberg (1957) suggests that different effects are likely. When their subjects saw a positive motive in an insult, the insultor was viewed as more attractive than when the same insult was motivated by an attempt at personal gain.

Presentence reports in the United States and social inquiry reports in England often reflect an interest in the motivational base for the offence, at least by the probation officer who prepares the report. For example, in a case of attempted robbery[13] the offender was described as in a desperate financial state: 'He was overdrawn at the bank, unable to pay his own National Insurance contributions and behind in his mortgage payments. He acted in an impulsive and uncharacteristic way because he felt he was in a desperate crisis.'

It is of course impossible from this evidence to assess whether such considerations actually decrease criminal sentence, although Thomas's (1979) analysis suggests that the English Court of Appeal considers motive a possible mitigating circumstance. Even if sentence is affected, however, it is difficult to tell whether reduced culpability is the mediator. If the motive is based on a temporary need, the act may be attributed to an unstable external force. The observer may therefore recommend a lower penalty because a repeat offence is unlikely. A similar ambiguity between effects on culpability and prognosis may occur when more proximal stimuli appear to evoke criminal behaviour.

Provocation

Heider's original work (1958) on the naive psychology of attribution distinguished between two forces that control action, personal force, and environmental force. Later researchers (e.g. Jones, Davis, and Gergen, 1961) have suggested that personal or dispositional attributions may be reduced to the extent that situational explanations for behaviour are available. Although some recent work has questioned the interdependence of dispositional and situational attribution (e.g. Solomon, 1978), the bulk of the evidence indicates that perceived culpability tends to be lower when there is evidence of provocation or other environmental triggers (e.g. Brown and Tedeschi, 1976; Harvey and Enzle, 1978). In Heider's framework, justifiable action is perceived when the act is viewed as something that most people would have done in similar circumstances. As Horai (1977) has suggested, if estimates about the behaviour of others do not lead the observer to an environmental attribution, responsibility may not be reduced.

Legal distinctions reflect some of these considerations. Indeed, one of the primary legal distinctions of voluntary manslaughter, a class 2 felony in Illinois, as opposed to murder, a class 1 felony, involves the discounting stimulus of provocation. 'A person who kills an individual without lawful justification commits voluntary manslaughter if at the time of the killing he is acting under a sudden and intense passion resulting from serious provocation . . . . Serious provocation is conduct sufficient to excite an intense passion in a reasonable person.'[14] There is a substantial amount of case law which attempts to specify what constitutes sufficient provocation, but significant ambiguity remains. For example, ' "provocation" is usually restricted to physical assaults, mutual quarrel or combat, adultery, and similar situations; however, a general rule that mere words, no matter how aggressive or abusive, cannot constitute adequate provocation for offense of voluntary manslaughter is not absolute'.[15]

The 'reasonable man' standard in this case may be compared with the environmental attribution (others would have acted the same) required for justification in psychological research. Thus, psychologists may be in a favourable position for testing the circumstances that evoke perceptions of reasonableness.

Harm Done — Severity of Consequences

Piaget (1932), in his studies of moral development in children, distinguished between two stages in the attribution of responsibility. Very young children use objective reasoning, apportioning blame according to the amount of damage produced. Later on, subjective attribution develops and intention and motive are considered in the assignment of culpability. There is some evidence that both legal and lay observers maintain some measure of objective damage-controlled attribution.

Criminal statutes often distinguish between offences solely on the level of injury or damage they produce. Theft penalties, for example, are generally influenced by the value of the stolen goods. While it may be argued that more effort is generally involved in the theft of costly as opposed to inexpensive items, other penalty correlations with danger level cannot be explained in this fashion.

The Illinois Criminal Statutes, like many others, consider each attempted offence category as one felony class level below that of the actual offence.[16]

Thus, attempted unarmed robbery is a class 3 felony while unarmed robbery itself is a class 2 felony.[17] The difference between a murder and an attempted murder may be solely an accident of interruption or the work of a skilful surgeon. The justifications in such cases for distinguishing between offenders who succeed and those who fail would appear to rest solely on the particular outcome of the act.

While legislative provisions support the role of damage as a factor in determining sentence, it is difficult to assess the extent to which judges weigh damage in their sentencing decisions. In the case of attempts, plea bargaining often reduces robbery to attempted robbery and thus it is inappropriate to compare overall sentence levels for robbery and attempted robbery in the hope of assessing a damage tariff. Moreover, a reduced sentence for a foiled attempt may not always produce credit simply because damage is absent. A would-be murderer may fail because he is inept and therefore less likely to pose a future threat. He may also fail because he is not sufficiently motivated to succeed or he has second thoughts at the last minute and thus his level of intent is lower than the successful offender.

One study of legal decision-makers does suggest the importance of damage in sentencing. Hood (1972) asked English magistrates to make sentence recommendations in a case of drunken driving in which no accident had occurred. The magistrates were then asked what their sentences would have been if an accident had occurred in the same case and minor injuries had resulted (bruised ribs for the other driver), and what it would have been if an accident had occurred which led to serious injury (permanent disablement for the other driver). The serious injury led to significantly greater increases in sentence than did the slight injury.

Psychological research in this area suggests the interdependence of some of these attributions. For example, Horai and Bartek (1978) manipulated the amount of harm done in the process of a criminal assault. They found that the level of intent attributed to the offender increased with the amount of harm done. Amount of harm done was also manipulated in this study, and the attributed intent increased with the amount of harm done.

The interdependence of perceived intent, foreseeability, injury, and expected future behaviour may be partially responsible for the inconsistent findings of social psychologists on severity of consequences and attributions of responsibility. While Walster's (1966) study showed increased blame attributed to the owner of a car when it caused serious as opposed to minor damage, later research has not consistently supported this result. Brewer (1977) has suggested that subjects react to the expected outcome of the actor's behaviour rather than to the actual outcome itself. Therefore, outcome severity should only increase attributions of blame 'when there is some basis for assuming congruence between an action taken (or not taken) and the ultimate outcome' (p.62). Some legal support for this approach can be found in the American Law Institute's Model Penal Code (1962). The Code proposes that judges consider in mitigation that the defendant did not think his criminal conduct would cause or threaten serious bodily harm.[18] Despite this suggestion, criminal offences are in fact defined partially by their outcomes, and questions remain on the extent to which outcomes alone affect judgements of blame and punishment.

Equity and Retribution

Retribution sounds deceptively simple in the phrase 'let the punishment fit the crime'. Except in simple property offences there is rarely a clear standard for a fair punishment level that will be equivalent to the original offence. In the sentencer's search for a standard, therefore, a consideration of equality may contribute to the judgement. One source for comparison is what similar offenders in a similar (or the same) offence have received.

There is no statute or sentencing guideline known to these authors that directs punishment to be contingent upon the outcome of co-defendants. In fact, under Illinois law there is an explicit statement in the elements of the offence of conspiracy that: 'It shall not be a defense to conspiracy that the person or persons with whom the accused is alleged to have conspired (1) has not been prosecuted or convicted.'[19] While conspiracy by definition involves more than one person, this statute indicates that avoidance of punishment by one must not inhibit punishment of the remaining partner. Yet there is clear evidence that concern with equal treatment of co-defendants may enter into sentencing decisions. In a study of sentence review in Massachusetts and Connecticut (Zeisel and Diamond, 1977) reasons for sentence reductions were examined in Connecticut and inferred in Massachusetts where stated reasons are not required. Twenty-nine percent of the cases in Connecticut and 25 percent of the inferred reasons in Massachusetts involved the reduction of sentences that were seen as out of line with the sentences of co-defendants. Thomas (1979) suggests that sentence reductions in England may occur when an appellant claims that his sentence is disproportionate to that of his co-defendants, but that such adjustment rarely occurs solely because of disparity. The Court of Appeal's practice is to reduce a sentence 'only if there is "such a glaring difference between the treatment of one man as compared with another that a real sense of grievance would be engendered"' (p.72). These equity concerns were also reflected in the results of a laboratory study by DeJong, Morris, and Hastorf (1976). A shorter prison term was recommended by subjects when the robber's accomplice successfully escaped (thereby avoiding punishment) than when the accomplice attempted escape but was captured.

UTILITARIAN SENTENCING

The utilitarian goal for sentencing is the reduction of criminal activity. Under this rubric are two assessments of interest to the social psychologist that may enter the sentencing decision. The first involves the prediction of future behaviour. If further criminal activity by the convicted offender is anticipated, crime may be reduced by incapacitating him through incarceration. The second assessment of social psychological relevance reflecting a utilitarian goal is the expected general deterrent value of the sentence, i.e. its anticipated ability to affect the behaviour of other potential offenders.[20]

Unlike retributive judgements, both prediction- and deterrence-motivated decisions can be tested against their presumed effects. While culpability is in the eye of the beholder, and thus may vary across observers, predictive and deterrent values constitute outcomes capable of objective evaluation. If punishment is a means to an explicit goal, i.e. crime reduction by the offender or others, success in achieving that goal can, in principle, be assessed. Of course there may be great difficulty in obtaining adequate data on which to base this assessment, but the reference point is fact rather than a potentially shifting value consensus. For this reason our discussion of utilitarian sentencing will be concerned with the ability of the sentencer to predict the future behaviour of the offender, and the ability of the sentence to affect criminal behaviour in the community at large.

Prediction

The task of predicting behaviour has a long history in both psychology (e.g. Allport, 1937) and criminal justice (e.g. Warner, 1923). Yet predicting specific behaviours is extremely difficult and many researchers would not share the implicit optimism expressed in a recent United States Supreme Court opinion. In holding that it was not unconstitutional for a state to use a prediction of future violent activity as the basis for imposition of the death penalty, the Court in Jurek v. Texas (1976)[21] noted, 'It is, of course, not easy to predict future behavior. The fact that such a determination is difficult, however, does not mean that it cannot be made' (p.2950).

An examination of sentencing decisions suggests that such predictions are made daily by the sentencing judge. Whether the penalty is designed for the purpose of incapacitation or rehabilitation or special deterrence, the expectation of further criminal activity will mediate the decision to incarcerate. In our discussion of prediction, we will consider some of the specific cues that appear to be used as predictors in sentencing (amount, recency, and nature of past criminal behaviour). We will also examine more general classes of attributions (dispositional versus situational) that are believed to facilitate predictions.

Criminal History

The offender's record of criminal activity is generally a major predictor of sentence (e.g. Diamond, 1981; Hagan, 1974; van Alstyne and Gottfredson, 1978). Only the seriousness of the particular offence tends to correlate more highly with the sentence, and even this variable may only overtake prior criminal history when the offence is extremely serious (Wilkins, Kress, Gottfredson, Calpin, and Gelman, 1976). There are two types of potential explanations for the attention to criminal record. First, a prior conviction suggests that the offender has rejected a warning and engaged in further criminal activity; such behaviour may lead to an attribution of increased culpability. Secondly, the recidivist offender is perceived as more likely to continue his criminal career than the first offender. The prior conviction indicates that previous punishment and rehabilitation efforts, whether probation or incarceration, have been unsuccessful. Moreover, since recidivists appear to be responsible for a significant portion of criminal actions (e.g. Petersilia, Greenwood, and Lavin, 1977; Wolfgang, Figlio, and Sellin, 1972), increased penalties may be justified as a means of reducing crime through incapacitation.

Habitual offender statutes in many states and in Canada authorize extended terms for recidivists. The language of these statutes indicates clearly a concern with incapacitation and is reflected in the American Bar Association Standards for Sentencing Alternatives and Procedures (1968): 'An additional term (on grounds of habitual criminality) should only be permitted if the court finds that such a term is necessary in order to protect the public from further criminal conduct by the defendant . . .' (section 3.3 (b)). The Canadian Criminal Code (section 660, cited in Mewett, 1961) allows an extended sentence of preventive detention if '(a) the accused is found to be an habitual criminal, and (b) the court is of the opinion that because the accused is an habitual criminal, it is expedient for the protection of the public to sentence him to preventive detention'. In most instances habitual offender statutes further specify that prior criminal activity must amount to at least two felony convictions, and in some states (e.g. New Jersey, 1966) four prior convictions are required.

The decision to grant parole shares much with the original sentencing decision. In particular, when indeterminate sentences are the common practice, the major determination of the length of a prison term may actually rest with the parole board. The United States Parole Commission uses a series of guidelines that were designed to suggest sentence levels consistent with two criteria. Release is to be granted when '(1) that release would not depreciate the seriousness of his [the offender's] offense or promote disrespect for the law; and (2) that release would not jeopardize the public welfare'.[22] Thus, a prediction of future criminal activity partially guides parole decisions and is explicitly included in determining the guideline sentence through the 'salient factor score', a scale that measures parole prognosis.[23] Five of the eleven possible points on this scale are determined by the number of prior convictions and incarcerations.

A second aspect of the offender's record that has been used in prognosis is the nature of the offence involved. The salient factor score predicts a worse prognosis for offenders convicted of auto theft and cheque offences than for federal offenders serving sentences for other crimes, since such offences tend to be repeated. Many prediction studies have been concerned with recidivism rates for different offences. For example, Warner found in 1923 that sex offenders had lower recidivism rates than offenders convicted of breaking and entering. It is difficult to know the extent to which such prognostic cues are regularly used in determining sentence.

The timing of prior convictions may play a role in sentencing. The American Bar Association Standards (1968) suggest that offenders should not be sentenced under habitual offender standards unless '(ii) Less than five years have lapsed between the commission of the present offense and either the commission of the last prior felony or the offender's release [from prison]' (section 3.3). Similarly, the U.S. Parole Commission guidelines mention that a 'substantial crime free period since his last offense' may be viewed as a mitigating factor that improves parole prognosis. Hood (1972) found that the magistrates in his sample recommended lower sentences for drunken driving when a previous conviction had been 10 years earlier than when it had occurred 2½ or 5 years before the present offence. Further, in Hogarth's (1971) study of Canadian magistrates he found that 'Magistrates who rely often upon the prevention of crime through incapacitation . . . respond primarily to the recency of the offender's last conviction' (p.298).

The prominent role of prior record in prognosis in generally consistent with the logic of attribution theory reflected in the work of Kelley (1967; 1971). According to his notion of co-variation, effects are attributed to causes with which they co-vary. Consistent behaviour by the same individual across different situations is attributed to some personal disposition. Thus, in observing multiple different instances of criminal behaviour, the judge is likely to conclude that the offender has a relatively enduring propensity to criminal activity.

Despite a general agreement with the attribution framework, some specifics in the evaluation of prior offences do not necessarily mesh with logical implications of Kelley's work. For example, evidence for a wide range of criminal behaviours would seem to indicate a generalized law-breaking career that is maintained across a range of environmental stimuli; the robbery offender with a history of assault and damage to property would seem to suggest a more dispositional attribution toward crime than the individual with a consistent background in robbery. Apart from types of offences that show career patterns (e.g. cheque offences), the focus on consistent choice of violation behaviour evident in some sentencing standards may be unwarranted. For example, Morris (1951) looked at the criminal patterns of 270 confirmed recidivists in England who had each been convicted of at least six offences punishable by two or more years and had been imprisoned on at least four occasions. He found that only four had been consistently convicted of the same type of offence (offences were classified in sixteen categories). Almost one-third of the sample had committed at least four different types of offences. Similarly, in an analysis of a juvenile cohort, Wolfgang *et al.* (1972) found no evidence of specialization among juvenile offenders. This is an instance in which two kinds of research would probably be profitable. The first would examine the extent to which decision-makers attend to the generality of crime career patterns. The second would involve close scrutiny of these cues as valid predictors of future behaviour. Different relationships or links with other characteristics might underlie surface correlations.

Research on predictions has had relatively little to say about the recency of prior activity, but attention to this variable appears to be consistent with an extension of attribution theory, in that a 'discounting effect' may occur when prior activity is not recent. The discounting principle (Kelley, 1971) assumes that a given cause is discounted as producing a given effect if other plausible causes are also present. When substantial time has passed since the earlier criminal activity, the observer may be more likely to attribute the early history of prior offences to environmental and personal characteristics that have changed in the interval. Furthermore, a recent crime-free period (or at least one in which crime has been undetected) may itself represent information that reduces a criminal dispositional attribution.

Dispositional Attributions

The primary focus of efforts to predict future criminal behaviour appears to be on dispositional as opposed to situational cues. In the U.S. parole guidelines a history of drug dependence leads to a more unfavourable prognosis. Moreover, the younger the age of first commitment, controlling for the length of criminal record, the less favourable the prognosis (e.g. Elder and Cohen, 1977). Hogarth's (1971) Canadian magistrates, interested in reducing crime through incapacitation, ascribed great importance to perceived pathology in the offender.

A focus on dispositional attribution is particularly evident in legal efforts to predict dangerousness. 'Dangerousness' is generally used to refer to a propensity to engage in dangerous behaviour (Shah, 1978). Although its application to criminal action has sometimes been extended to any criminal act (cheque-writing in Overholser v. Russell, 1960),[24] predictions of dangerousness relevant to sentencing have more recently been identified with 'significant physical or psychological injury to persons or substantial destruction of property' (State v. Krol, 1975).[25] Shah (1978) suggests that a sample of dangerous behaviour often produces a conceptual short cut leading the observer to view and label the individual himself as dangerous. This dispositional conceptualization of behaviour, according to Shah, is typical of most judges and lawyers, as well as mental health workers. Moreover, work by Carroll and Payne (1977a, 1977b) indicates that the release decisions of parole officers are determined in large part by their attributions about the dispositions of offenders.

The predictive value of type-of-person explanations also receives support from some attribution theorists. For example, Shaver (1975, p.31) argues that 'going beyond a personal disposition to its presumed source may enhance our understanding, but it will not materially affect our ability to predict what a particular actor is apt to do in the future'. Not all psychologists share this confidence in the predictive value of dispositional explanations. Citing the low correlations of cross-situational behaviour (Mischel, 1968) and the poor hit-rate for dangerousness predictions (Monahan, 1978), these researchers argue that environmental or situational conditions are critical for the improvement of prediction.

Environmental Attributions

The controversy over the trait conception of behaviour has a long history (Bem and Allen, 1974). Recent literature suggests that $+0.30$ may be the ceiling on cross-situational correlation coefficients (Mischel, 1968). Mischel argues that this is due not to limitations in method, but to the situational specificity of most behaviour. Thus, if we are to improve behavioural predictions, we must focus on environmental determinants as well as personal dispositions.

In crime, as well as in other areas, situation-based prediction entails several methodological difficulties. Most important of these is the likely variability over time of environmental conditions. An ex-offender may live with his parents and work for an uncle one day, and leave home and lose his job the next. Thus, some environmental-based predictions will be endemically unreliable. As Gottfredson, Wilkins, and Hoffman (1978) have pointed out, however, potentially variable qualities can be included in predictions by using conditional probability statements. Predictions would then take the form, for example, $P \; r/a =$ if an offender goes to his old address, his chance of reconviction is $x\%$. While these predictions may require a more elaborate data base, they are in principle possible.

Indeed, the criminal justice system itself has some history of attention to situation variables. Parole conditions, for example, may include such provisions as a requirement that the parolee 'refrain from frequenting unlawful or disreputable places or consorting with disreputable persons' and 'have in his possession no firearm or other dangerous weapon unless granted written permission' (Model Penal Code, 1962, section 301.1). Although such actions in themselves may not violate the law, they may create an environmental condition in which an offence is more likely to occur.

Attention to the situational determinants of behaviour can be found in early social psychology (Lewin, Lippitt, and White, 1939). Some of the recent research on crime has also focused specifically on environmental influences (Moos, 1975; Newman, 1972). The potential value of multi-dimensional approaches in this area is clearly indicated by the results of a study of federal prisoners by Edinger and Auerbach (1978). They found that both self-reported willingness to engage in prohibited behaviour in prison and actual infractions varied with situation characteristics, and that the effect of situation on both measures of violation varied with offender personality type. This kind of research may offer the most promising avenue for improving predictions of criminal activity. Moreover, it is one area of study for which social psychologists are particularly well-suited.

General Deterrence

A criminal sentence motivated by utilitarian concerns may take into account more than the likelihood of further criminal activity by the offender being sentenced. It may also represent an attempt at crime reduction through its presumed impact on other potential offenders. The severity of a sentence may be expected to pose a sufficient threat to would-be offenders that they will be deterred from exposing themselves to the chance of similar punishment.

General deterrence-motivated sentencing has been criticized (e.g. Bittner and Platt, 1966) because it requires no necessary connection between the punishment and the needs or deserts of the individual offender. There is clear evidence, however, that at least some sanctions are administered with this focus in mind. For example, when the offender convicted of income-tax evasion is a middle-class first offender for whom indictment and conviction represent major punishments, there is no need for incarceration to avoid a repeat offence by this individual. Yet many federal judges (e.g. Hoffman, 1971) have noted that such tax offenders are frequently sentenced to some period of incarceration specifically so that others will be deterred from committing similar violations. At a Sentencing Institute for federal judges, Hoffman (1971) reports that the consensus was for commitment as a rule with probation as the exception 'because imprisonment would be a deterrent — and a needed deterrent — to others' (p.317).

Similarly, there are instances when penalties are increased for particular crimes with the express purpose of reducing their frequency. Wooton (1963) cites an English case in 1958 when nine young boys were sentenced to four years of imprisonment as a result of their participation in race riots in London.

These sentences were more severe than those in earlier similar cases, and were handed out as a warning to others.

Gauging the effectiveness of deterrence is fraught with difficulties, some of which may be reduced by social psychological theory and research. Thus far the application of psychological research to deterrence questions can be characterized most gently as rather limited. Early work by psychologists was done primarily on direct punishment with non-human subjects. For example, Skinner (1938) trained rats to press a bar for food. He then punished them by a short slap on the paw for this response. The punishment only temporarily suppressed the bar pressing and Skinner concluded that punishment was not effective for eliminating behaviour. Other researchers reported that the effectiveness of punishment was dependent upon its immediate proximity to the punishment response (e.g. Brown, 1948), and on its intensity (e.g. Azrin and Holz, 1961).

Some authors have attempted to apply the results of this research to the legal system. Jeffery (1965), for example, argued that the immediacy of punishment is critical to its effectiveness. Appel and Peterson (1965) concluded that the conditions required for effective punishment simply could not be met by the criminal justice system. More recently such applications have been criticized by jurisprudential scholars (Andenaes, 1974) and by sociologists (Gibbs, 1975). As we evaluate these criticisms, we will discuss some present and potential contributions of work by social psychologists on the deterrent effects of punishment. In reviewing our research suggestions, the reader should be aware that these proposals represent only one of several possible lines of research on the problems of deterrence. We focus on this particular path in our discussion because we believe that its potential has been mistakenly rejected or simply ignored by many researchers in deterrence, and because we hope to encourage social psychologists to direct their attention to some of the variables involved in deterrence theory predictions. Moreover, the bulk of research on deterrence consists of correlational studies based on official crime and arrest rates (notable exceptions include Chambliss, 1966; Ross, 1973; Schwartz and Orleans, 1967). The correlational studies are clearly high in external validity in that they focus on the criminal activity that deterrence attempts seek to affect. While they have contributed to our understanding of deterrence, however, correlational studies using official statistics are weakened by a number of threats to internal validity that limit their ability to identify causal relationships (*for a similar view, see Farrington, 1979*).

Present Deterrence Research

The correlational studies that comprise the bulk of the empirical deterrence research have been done by sociologists and economists who compare variations in crime rates across jurisdictions that differ in severity and certainty of punishment (see Nagin, 1978, for an excellent review of this literature). As correlational studies, they are subject to the usual spuriousness questions that arise when a significant relationship is detected (see Campbell and Stanley, 1963, for a discussion of correlational designs and causal inference). Moreover, in this instance there are plausible candidates for the third variable that generates the correlation. For example, suppose that police forces vary in their motivation or in the external pressure placed on them to perform well. Two indicators often used to reflect police effectiveness are high clearance rates (the ratio of crimes 'solved' to reported crimes) and low crime rates. Police have considerable control over both. Thus, a suspect may be promised leniency if he admits to additional unsolved crimes, thereby increasing the clearance rate. Similarly, offences may not be recorded at all or their severity may be reduced in official records so that crime statistics are kept low. If these manipulations are responses to the same pressures, a spurious negative relationship between clearance rates and crime rates will result.

Note that this example of spuriousness may not stem from an effect on actual crime and sanctioning rates, but rather produces the relationship by influencing only the measured versions of these constructs. Other official sources of data outside of law enforcement agencies can also produce distortions that lead to apparent support for deterrence effects (e.g. court statistics on convictions resulting from plea-bargained offence categories). Gibbs (1975) has suggested several improvements for measuring crime rates. While worthy of attention, they are expensive and still do not address the problem of adequately assessing sanctioning levels and probabilities.

Even if some causal connection between punishment and crime rates is assumed, a major flaw in the correlational deterrence research remains. Many have argued (e.g. Cook, 1977) that the direction of causality may be two-way, so that sanctioning both affects and is affected by crime rates. The correlational research must therefore admit a system of simultaneous influence in which both variables represent causes and effects. Economists (e.g. Ehrlich, 1973; Forst, 1967) have attempted to identify crime functions by excluding various demographic variables, but there appears to be little justification for many of their decisions. As Nagin (1978) has pointed out, incorrect identification can lead to entirely erroneous conclusions.

These problems in the present deterrence literature provide a background for our discussion of social psychology's potential in the study of deterrence. Both laboratory and field experiments as well as time-series quasi-experiments can be designed to test many aspects of the deterrence question. While some of the strategies suggested may be criticized for their relatively weaker external validity, we will argue that many of the specific criticisms voiced by deterrence researchers can be overcome, and that the greater control possible in experimental analysis contribute a fresh perspective, and can provide an important supplement to the correlational research that dominates this field.

Social Psychology and Deterrence

Two of the major reservations about the relevance of psychological research on punishment can easily be addressed. First, Andenaes (1974) points out that much of this research has focused on punishment as a means of causing the subject to produce a particular behaviour, what Solomon (1964) called 'active avoidance learning' and Woodworth and Schlosberg (1954) called 'punishment for inaction'. Punishment as a motivator for law-abiding behaviour aims at the reverse: it is directed at reducing forbidden activity, Solomon's 'passive avoidance learning' and Woodworth and Schlosberg's 'punishment for action'. To the extent that these two kinds of activities are governed by different stimuli, research aimed at increasing knowledge about deterrence should certainly concentrate on the latter. Although some psychologists argue for the 'unifying position' (Solomon, 1964), Andenaes (1974) may be correct in his uneasiness about consistent behaviour across punishment goals.

In the second criticism, both Gibbs (1975) and Andenaes (1974) draw attention to the wide use of non-human subjects in much punishment research. One major reason they dismiss much of this research is that they are interested in general deterrence, in which the individual is deterred not by his direct experience with punishment, but by the threat of such experience. With their superior cognitive skills, humans may react to threats while animals are insensitive to such cues.

Social psychology has provided a significant response to both of these criticisms. Research primarily conducted by Bandura and his colleagues (e.g. Bandura, 1965; Bandura, Ross, and Ross, 1963; Walters and Parke, 1964) has investigated the impact of vicarious punishment on the rule-abiding behaviour of children. The general paradigm has a child view the behaviour of a model who is punished, rewarded, or receives no reaction from the experimenter for his actions. The experimenter then leaves the child alone and the child has the opportunity to engage in the forbidden behaviour in the experimenter's absence. The results of such studies suggest that vicarious punishment may indeed reduce the production of forbidden behaviour. Children who viewed a model punished for his aggressive behaviour were less aggressive immediately following that experience (Bandura, 1965). They were also more likely to share after viewing a model punished for not sharing (Morris, Marshall, and Miller, 1973), and less likely to play with forbidden attractive toys 'belonging to another boy' after a model had been punished for engaging in such play (Walters and Parke, 1964).[26]

This research paradigm clearly meets two of the major criticisms of psychological research on punishment made by deterrence theorists. First, these studies investigate the effects of threatened punishment on humans and, secondly, both the Bandura (1965) and Walters and Parke (1964) studies examined the effects of the punishment on forbidden activity. The consistent results showing effectiveness of viracious punishment on behaviour provide some of the best available evidence for deterrence. Despite this contribution, such studies could be extended much further and their relevance to deterrence improved in other respects.

Gibbs (1975) has correctly labelled the typical experimental source of punishment information as 'direct and immediate' as contrasted with the criminal punishment threat which is 'indirect or second-hand'. The child in a Bandura study learns about punishment by viewing the punishment of another. Apart from the public execution system, now out of fashion, direct observation of the punishment of others for legal violation is rare.[27] While it is not clear that reactions to directly and indirectly obtained information about punishment contingencies will lead to different results, this is a testable hypothesis. The television news report would inform the experimental subject of the penalties attached to behaviours children generally prefer (e.g. playing with particular desirable toys), or could report on the penalties presumably given to children who engaged in such behaviours. These two variations, i.e. presentation of the penalty rule versus information on specific instances of punishment, would also offer some opportunity to evaluate Andenaes's (1974) concern over the abstract and impersonal nature of legal threat as opposed to the usual concrete stimulus in psychological experiments.

Further elaborations of this design might also investigate the most effective punishment models and sources of punishment information. For example, there is evidence that subject-model similarity (Rosekrans, 1967) and model status (Flanders, 1968; Lefkowitz, Blake, and Mouton, 1955) increase imitation. A reasonable prediction might be that these model characteristics are also particularly effective in reducing unwanted behaviour when the models are punished (e.g. If even he was punished, I'll surely be punished severely), but there is at present no research that directly investigates these possibilities.

'The objective certainty of punishment in the penal system does not remotely approach the objective certainty realized in virtually all experimental studies' (Gibbs, 1975, p.24). This observation is clearly correct, and it may be that at low probabilities of punishment, deterrence effects are nearly non-existent. The 1968 Federal Bureau of Investigation Uniform Crime Reports (1969) showed that only one-quarter of all robberies resulted in arrest and less than one-fifth of all burglaries. If victimization survey results are used instead of crimes reported to the police, the probabilities may drop to one-sixth and one-eighth (Biderman, 1967). If conviction rather than arrest were used as the indicator of punishment, the probability of punishment would drop even further.

Studies of vicarious punishment by psychologists have not generally been concerned with variations in certainty, but it would certainly be possible to vary the frequency with which a model is punished for a particular behaviour. Rosekrans and Hartup (1967) used this approach to compare the aggressive responses of children who viewed a model who was consistently punished for aggressive behaviour with the responses of children who saw a model punished for half of his aggressive behaviours and rewarded for half of them. Consistent punishment in this case resulted in less imitation than inconsistent punishment.

Certainty of punishment may have different effects if the same model is punished for only a portion of his deviant acts, and if only some of a number of different models are punished for a forbidden behaviour. In the latter case the observer may believe he is more similar to the punished (or unpunished) models and determine his behaviour on that basis. In the former, he may or may not believe he can discriminate situational factors that determine when the model's behaviour leads to punishment. A comparison of these two versions of certainty of punishment would be useful.

Theorists as far back as Beccaria in 1770 (translation, 1880) have argued that the celerity of punishment affects its deterrent value. This view received substantial support from early studies on direct punishment in non-human subjects. Dramatic decreases in the effectiveness of punishment have been shown with delays of a few seconds (Solomon, 1964). The presumed explanation for this result, however, suggests that time lags may not have the same impact on humans, particularly in affecting general deterrence. Punishment contiguity presumably facilitates the connection between the act and the punishment so that the punished individual makes the association between the two. Walters and Grusec (1977) have argued that this immediacy may be unnecessary in humans. Discussing the limitations of the experimental psychology results for studies of child development, they point out: 'Children, . . . because of their capacity for language, are capable of spanning long periods between a response and punishment contingent on, although not continuous with, that response' (p.224).

An additional problem in generalizing from the experimental literature on punishment delay is that there are two possible types of delay in vicarious punishment situations. The first, actual delay, is the time between the model's act and his punishment, and the second, perceived delay, between when observer learns of the model's act and when he learns of the model's punishment. Concern over the criminal justice system's ability to reduce delay for purposes of general deterrence focuses on the first of these two. Yet the contiguity leads-to-association-and-punishment-effectiveness hypotheses only requires proximity of the latter two. If the newspaper informs us that Sam Johnson was arrested (or convicted) yesterday for an assault, our connection between those events should not be affected by when the assault took place.

There is a second hypothesis about delay that would predict a decrease in the effectiveness of vicarious punishment if it does not immediately follow the behaviour, even when the observer learns about both behaviour and punishment simultaneously. If a burglar's arrest immediately follows his offence, he is likely to get little pleasure from the profits of his crime; if he is captured only months later after he has enjoyed the fruits of his labour, the net cost of the punishment may appear to be reduced. This hypothesis, if correct, would suggest that the delay of a punishment only affects its deterrent value for those offences that involve delayed benefits: burglary but not vandalism, robbery but not assault. Again, these questions can be addressed by social psychologists. For example, manipulations of duration between crime and punishment would be expected to affect assessment only for specific types of crime if the second hypothesis is correct. In addition, Bandura's procedures can be adapted to test both forms of delay. The model who takes forbidden candy can be punished immediately, or only after he has eaten some of his booty. Similarly, delay between act and punishment can be manipulated in the information from a video news reporter. With somewhat greater effort, by holding more than one experimental session, delay between information on the model's act and information on his punishment can be varied.

The final criticism of past psychological experimentation in tightly controlled settings poses the greatest problem for potential research in this mode. Both Gibbs (1975) and Andenaes (1974) argue that the character of most criminal penalties differs dramatically from the punishments that can be manipulated at experimenter discretion. Criminal penalties can be long-lasting, and can have an intensity that may be qualitatively different from other punishments.

While there are constraints against introducing severe penalties solely for experimental purposes, there are two aspects of the question that facilitate the study of severity effects. First, since the concern is with the impact of vicarious punishment, there may be no need that actual punishment take place either inside or outside the confines of the laboratory. Tittle and Rowe (1973) examined the effect of the threat of sanction on cheating in sociology courses. In one of their manipulations some classes were informed that a cheater had been identified and would be penalized. Although Tittle and Rowe (1973) did not specify what penalty the offender would receive, such information could have been presented and its severity level varied across classes (discretion of the judge–instructor). In this case, since the punished cheater did not actually exist, it would have been possible to 'impose' a punishment as severe as removal from school.[28]

The second quality of sentence severity as a deterrent that facilitates its study is that it is the only one of the three independent variables assumed to affect deterrence (severity, certainty, and celerity) that can be directly affected by legislative or judicial decision. It is extremely difficult to make even small changes in the objective certainty of crime detection, and most observers of the legal system are pessimistic about the possibility of dramatically influencing actual celerity. The severity of the penalty attached to particular offences may, in principle, be altered[29] and its effect on crime rates assessed in a time-series quasi-experimental analysis. Thus far such designs have met with limited success (for a review of these efforts see Zimring, 1978), but those instances of success (e.g. Ross, 1973) provide exciting examples of what can be done to test causal questions in complex field settings.

Some deterrence quasi-experiments have apparently been implemented in that penalty severity (or certainty) has been altered, but closer examination discloses a missing element in implementation. For example, Shover and Bankston (1973) studied the impact of legislation in Tennessee that provided for mandatory jail sentences of at least 48 hours for anyone convicted of driving while intoxicated. The absence of reduction in traffic fatalities appeared to supply evidence against the deterrent effects of increased penalties. The authors, however, supplemented their analysis of traffic fatalities with a telephone survey of Tennessee licensed drivers. Only 41 percent of the respondents knew the change in the law. Less than one-quarter were able to identify a single provision of the law and only 5 percent of all drivers mentioned the mandatory jail sentence. This example points to the remaining element of the deterrence doctrine that could profit from investigation by social psychologists: the perceived characteristics of penalty structures.

There has been relatively little research done in this area. In nearly all of the relevant studies reviewed for this chapter (Bailey and Lott, 1976; Claster, 1967; Jensen, 1969; Teevan, 1976; Waldo and Chiricos, 1972) subjects were asked how likely (or severe) punishment would be if they (Claster, 1967) or someone like themselves (Waldo and Chiricos, 1972) or persons in general (Jensen, 1969) engaged in criminal activity. In some cases a particular type of offence was specified (e.g. shoplifting and marijuana use, Teevan, 1976) and in others it was not (e.g. 'people who break the law', Jensen, 1969). Self-reported violations, reported willingness to violate, or official records of criminal activity were then correlated with these responses.

Like the correlational studies of objective punishment levels and violation rates, there is a serious question about the causal structure that produces, for example, a negative correlation between reported marijuana use and perceived likelihood of being caught by the police (Waldo and Chiricos, 1972). Does perceived certainty of punishment lead to a reduction in marijuana use, or are both punishment perceptions and violation behaviour products of conventional norm-acceptance? Cross-sectional correlational analyses cannot distinguish between the two causal models.

There are also other important perceptual issues that these studies have not addressed. While several investigations (e.g. California Assembly Committee, 1968) have shown that the public is generally misinformed about actual penalty structures and that estimates of certainty tend to be inflated, there has been little research attempting to trace the development of this misinformation.

Thus, little is known about the translation between objective and subjective qualities of punishment. Moreover, the possible interrelation between punishment qualities has generally been ignored. Not only may severity and certainty interact in their effects upon offence rates, but they may also affect perceptions of one another. The observer considering a criminal action may assume that if a serious penalty is potentially involved, the police will be more diligent in pursuing him, or he may defensively discount the probability of getting caught more as the level of possible punishment increases.[30] The perceived delay in punishment may cause the observer to view the penalty as less severe. Studies that examine such effects could be done either in the laboratory or in field settings. The crucial factor in both cases is that the various objective qualities of punishment must be manipulated independently.

Some relatively crude attempts in this direction have been made. Rettig and Rawson (1963) manipulated certainty and severity of punishment in a study of ethical risk. They had students predict how likely it was that an individual would steal some money in each of a number of conditions. This type of design also can be used to get a subject to assess severity and certainty of punishment, as well as to predict behaviour (e.g. Diamond and Seals, 1980).

Crime and other forbidden activity

Some of the research suggestions we have made focus on activities that are not legally prohibited (e.g. cheating). An objection may be made that deterrence research should focus on crime, and not simply on behaviours open to punishment. The best response to this criticism comes from a closer examination of what a crime represents. It is an act forbidden by societal rules whose violation subjects the violator to potential punishment (according to Black, 1957, an act in violation of penal law; an offence against the state). To the extent that a rule system subjects an individual to its control in, for example, a school, and has the ability to punish those who do not adhere to its rules, the parallel with criminal law is strong. We suggest that the correspondence is great enough to recommend the study of such behaviours as a means of improving our understanding of social control in general, and deterrence in particular. Such research should proceed alongside more heroic attempts to evaluate the impact of large-scale changes in penalty policy.

THE FUTURE RELATIONSHIP
BETWEEN SENTENCING AND SOCIAL PSYCHOLOGY

This chapter has focused on three aspects of sentencing judgements: retribution, prediction, and general deterrence. We have summarized research done by social psychologists that bears on each of these decisions and pointed to weaknesses in the available literature. We conclude with a brief general discussion of research directions likely to improve understanding of this difficult judgement task.

Field Studies using Social Psychological Variables

Sentencing field studies have been done primarily by sociologists. Thus, the focus has been on demographic characteristics rather than on more social psychological variables. Field research has generally ignored such variables as provocation and motive which may loom large in both culpability and prediction judgements. While data collection becomes more difficult due to missing and less reliable data, some jurisdictions do record information on presentence investigations that should permit such analysis.

Heterogeneous and Judicial Samples for Culpability Studies

Experimental research on culpability judgements has been done almost entirely with samples of college students. To the extent that sentencing is expected to reflect community standards and if blaming behaviours vary across persons, a more heterogeneous subject population is needed to evaluate those standards. A specialized population should also be considered if the researcher is interested specifically in criminal sentencing behaviours: judges in nearly all instances are the final sentence-givers and their construction of culpability as well as their perceptions of community retributive requirements are an almost completely untapped source of information (exceptions are Hogarth, 1971; Partridge and Eldridge, 1974; Thomas, 1979; Hood, 1972).

Prediction Studies with Judges

Prediction studies, apart from those involving mentally ill or 'dangerous' individuals, have almost uniformly examined the ability of demographic and case characteristics to predict success on parole. While some research has been done with parole officers, we know very little about the way in which judges formulate predictions about the offenders they sentence. Predictions are not made independently of sentences, and the field studies and experimental work needed on this topic would require the interest and support of the judges supplying these predictions. While it is naive to assume uniform support for such research, judges who are concerned about the outcome of their sentencing decisions and who recognize the difficulty of the sentencing task may have an interest in exploring questions of prediction. Researchers who can provide the judges with information that appears to have some value may find themselves rewarded with thoughtful and experienced respondents.

Environmental Analysis in Prediction Studies

In both descriptive and normative studies of prediction the major potential contribution of social psychologists is an appreciation of situational influences on behaviour. Studies of the availability of situational cues in sentencing and parole decisions, thorough examinations of environmental characteristics for samples of released offenders, and comparisons of the environments of successful and unsuccessful probationers and parolees are missing from the research literature. All represent messy types of research that offer some promise for understanding and improving prediction.

Basic Research on Threat of Punishment

Research on deterrence is at an earlier stage than research on retribution and prediction, for basic questions remain about the general deterrent value of punishment. For this reason, some of the research likely to contribute most is basic research on the way in which people respond to the threat of punishment. Laboratory and field experiments that separately manipulate certainty, severity, and celerity of punishment are needed to explore the power and interaction of these classic deterrence doctrine variables.

Time-series Quasi-experiments on Deterrence

At the same time, policy research on deterrence of crime can be improved. Time-series quasi-experiments can be used to test the effects of legal change in penalty structures; simple before–after studies are particularly weak in deterrence research because penalty increases and enforcement crackdowns are most likely to occur in response to crime rates at their peak. The results of the quasi-experiments will be clearest when multiple measures are employed to trace public awareness of the penalty changes, and when independent measures of crime and enforcement can reduce the likelihood that those with a vested interest in the results have influenced the outcome measures. Such research is not cheap, but it has been done (Ross, 1973) and the Law Enforcement Assistance Administration earmarked substantial funds in both 1978 and 1979 for 'policy experiments on general deterrence'.

Subjective Qualities of Punishment

Converting objective to perceived penalty characteristics is a translation process in need of research. Diamond and Seals (1980) found that manipulating severity of punishment affected its perceived certainty, while variations in manipulated certainty did not affect perceived severity. The potential interactions of severity, certainty, and celerity in affecting the subjective evaluation of punishment require exploration in order to understand which penalty properties are actually being responded to.

Combining Information and Goals

The discussions of retribution, prediction, and deterrence have focused on a variety of different pieces and levels of information available to the sentencer, and on a set of potentially conflicting goals of the sentence. In putting together these bits of reality and value the judge is involved in a Herculean task. If he is interested in retribution, he must gauge community standards as well as offender's abilities and motives; if he is concerned with prediction, he must consider the offender's dispositional and environmental characteristics; and if deterrence is on his mind, he must anticipate how the sentence will affect others he will never see.

Hogarth (1971) in his study of Canadian magistrates showed that self-reported sentencing philosophy correlated with the actual sentencing behaviour of the magistrates. His research and that of others (e.g. Wheeler, Bonachich, Cramer, and Zola, 1968) suggests that studies of variations in the behaviour of judges may shed light on the determinants of these decisions.

A further complication for the sentencing decision is that the goals of sentencing may overlap and conflict. For example, the evidence may indicate much damage (e.g. the death of a spouse), but a low probability of future criminal activity. The judge may conclude that the offender has been punished enough by his conviction, yet the deterrence of others argues for a prison term. Combining pieces of information and reaching decisions under conditions of uncertainty is the subject of research on behavioural decision theory (Slovic, Fischoff, and Lichtenstein, 1977) This theoretical framework has thus far not been applied to the study of criminal sentencing, but the prospects for its usefulness are great. Studies of the difficulties in coping with intercorrelated cues (Lindell and Stewart, 1974), the 'law of small numbers' (Tversky and Kahneman, 1971), and judgement by availability (Tversky and Kahneman, 1973) all have the potential for explaining judicial decisions.

The specific aim of our discussion of sentencing has been an increased understanding of criminal sentences. Yet the payoff of such research can extend beyond this territory. A thorough examination of a criminal code discloses a variety of assumptions about violation, intent, motivation, and control. Earlier we looked at some of the felony classes associated with different forms of homicide. Conspiracy laws and the rules of evidence, too, suggest a multitude of hypotheses about behaviour and social influence with implications for culpability assessments. Social psychologists who read court opinions and other legal documents will find that the legal system was grappling with attributions about causality long before social scientists turned their attention to them, and legal insights and inconsistencies may be sources of theoretical development as well as applied research domain.

NOTES

1. There is much evidence for, and interest in, disparity in sentencing, the extent to which similar offenders convicted of similar offences receive different sentences. Some research on disparity has revealed systematic differences in judicial attitudes and backgrounds that can be used to predict differences in sentencing behaviours (Hogarth, 1971). In the present chapter, however, our focus is on explanations for shared (across-judge) patterns in sentencing rather than on explanations for variations among sentencers.

2. As distinguished from responsibility-as-causality, responsibility-as-culpability is a kind of moral evaluation referring to the extent to which an individual deserves blame. It frequently (but not always) results in legal accountability (see Shaver, 1975, and Harvey and Rule, 1978).

3. 18 U.S. Code, §§1970, 1709, and 1711 respectively.

4. R. v. Jackson (N.S.S.C. App. Div.), MacKergan, C. J. N. S., Coffin and MacDonald, J. J. A., 3 June, 1977 (reported in *Criminal Law Quarterly*, **20**, 1977, pp.22–23).

5. R. v. Oliver (B.C.C.A.), Farris, C. J. B. C., Branca and Seaton, JJ.A., 27 June, 1977 (reported in *Criminal Law Quarterly*, **20**, 1977, pp.20, 25).

6. Of course, there is evidence that such persons are often incarcerated in the name of treatment for periods longer than would have been likely had their disposition been a guilty verdict.

7. The comment of a Sentence Review Division judge at a session observed by one of the present authors (S.S.D.).

8. 18 U.S. Code, §5010.

9. For example, in re Winship, 1970, 397U.S.358, 90 S.Ct. 1068, 25 L.Ed. 2d 368; this case deals with a twelve-year-old New York boy who had entered a locker and stolen $112 from a woman's pocketbook. As a juvenile he could receive as much as six years of incarceration; as an adult the sentence would have been six months.

10. Thomas's (1979) study of the appellate decisions on sentence provides a rich analysis of reasons given by the Court of Appeals for reducing or refusing to reduce sentences. In many cases the Court's opinion appears to provide a clear explanation for the level of sentence it has sanctioned. To assess the strength of these apparent explanations, however, it would be important to know whether, for example, offenders under 20 were more likely to receive lenient sentences than offenders over 20 convicted of similar offences.

11. U.S. v. Scott, 1975, 529 F. 2d 338, 174 U.S. App. D.C. 96.

12. U.S. v. Hartfield, C.A. Cal. 1975, 513 F. 2d 254.

13. An English case from the files of Professor David Thomas, University of Cambridge.

14. *Illinois Criminal Law and Procedure*, 1978, Chapter 38, Section 9-2.

15. People v. Curwick, 1975, 33 Ill. App. 3d 757, 338 N.E. 2d 468.

16. *Illinois Criminal Law and Procedure*, 1978, Chapter 38, Section 8-4.

17. *Illinois Criminal Law and Procedure*, 1978, Chapter 38, Sections 8-4 and 18-1.

18. *Model Penal Code*, Proposed Official Draft, 1962, Section 7.01 (2) (l).

19. *Illinois Criminal Law and Procedure*, 1978, Chapter 38, Section 8-2 (b). Note that Illinois law with regard to conspiracy is typical of common U.S. practice.

20. A third major utilitarian focus in sentencing is on rehabilitation. We will not discuss rehabilitation in this chapter for several reasons. First, it is more the province of clinical rather than social psychology. More importantly, there is substantial agreement that 'The available research on the impact of various treatment strategies both in and out of prison seems to indicate that, after controlling for initial selection differences, there are generally no statistically significant differences between the subsequent recidivism of offenders, regardless of the form of treatment (Blumstein, Cohen, and Nagin, 1978, p.66). Finally, the trend in sentencing, partially as a result of rehabilitation's perceived failure, is away from the indeterminate sentencing patterns that mandated release only when the offender was 'cured'.

21. Jurek v. Texas, 96 S.Ct. 2950 (1976).

22. 18 U.S. Code, §4206(a).

23. This scale was developed by Leslie Wilkins and his colleagues by combining parole practices with available information on valid predictors of parole success.

24. Overholser v. Russell, 283 F. 2d 195 (1960).

25. State v. Krol, 344 A. 2d 289 (1975).

26. There is, moreover, some limited evidence that vicarious and direct punishments do not differ in their impact on performance of a forbidden activity. Benton (1966) found that children punished for their own actions and children who watched a model punished for the same behaviour were equally likely to repeat or perform the behaviour.

27. One can, however, think of instances. Passing auto drivers may see the speeding motorist receive a ticket.

28. The perceived severity of this penalty, at least by students, may be quite high. In one of the only studies to find that severity of punishment may affect behaviour more than certainty of punishment, Rettig and Rawson (1963) used two levels of severity. Under high severity the student offender was expelled, while under low severity the matter was settled privately. Even though the two levels of perceived certainty of punishment were nearly zero versus total certainty, respondents predicted that severity level would affect offence rates more than would certainty level. Of course the minor nature of the low severity condition, handling the matter privately, may have been responsible for the severity effect as well as major perceived severity of the high severity condition, i.e. expulsion.

29. Even severity is difficult to affect. Gibbs (1975) has distinguished between (1) prescribed severity, i.e. the legislatively implied sentence, and (2) the sentence a convicted offender receives. These both may differ substantially from the sentence an offender actually serves. Each of the three is under the control of a different actor or set of actors who may adjust for actions taken by other decision-makers. For example, if legislatively mandated penalties are increased, prosecutors may be more willing to allow the offender to plead guilty to a lesser offence.

30. In fact the negative relationship between certainty and severity may have some objective validity. If probability of conviction is used as the measure of certainty, there is some historical evidence that increasing the severity of the legislatively mandated penalty decreases the willingness of juries to convict (Kalven and Zeisel, 1966).

REFERENCES

Allport, G. W. (1937) *Personality: A Psychological Interpretation*, Holt, New York.

American Bar Association (1968) *Standards for Sentencing Alternatives and Procedures*, Institute of Judicial Administration, New York.

American Law Institute (1962) *Model Penal Code*, Philadelphia.

Adenaes, J. (1974) *Punishment and Deterrence*, University of Michigan Press, Ann Arbor, Michigan.

Appel, J. B. and Peterson, N. J. (1965) 'What's wrong with punishment?', *Journal of Criminal Law, Criminology, and Police Science*, **56**, 450-53.

Azrin, N. H. and Holz, W. C. (1961) 'Punishment during fixed-interval reinforcement', *Journal of the Experimental Analysis of Behavior*, **4**, 343-47.

Bailey, W. C. and Lott, R. P. (1976) 'Crime, punishment and personality: An examination of the deterrence question', *Journal of Criminal Law and Criminology*, **67**, 99-109.

Bandura, A. (1965) 'Influence of models' reinforcement contingencies on the acquisition of imitative responses', *Journal of Personality and Social Psychology*, **1**, 589-95.

Bandura, A., Ross, D., and Ross, S. A. (1963) 'Vicarious reinforcement and imitative learning', *Journal of Abnormal and Social Psychology*, **67**, 601-7.

Beccaria, C. B. (1880) *An Essay on Crimes and Punishment* (J. A. Farrar, Trans.), Chatto and Windus, London.

Bem, D. and Allen, A. (1974) 'On predicting some of the people some of the time, *Psychological Review*, **81**, 6, 506-20.

Benton, A. (1966) 'Effects of the timing of negative response consequences on the observational learning of resistance to temptation', Paper delivered to the Western Psychological Association.

Biderman, A. D. (1967) 'Surveys of population samples for estimating crime incidence', *Annals of the American Academy of Political and Social Science*, **374**, 16-33.

Bittner, E. and Platt, A. M. (1966) 'The meaning of punishment', *Issues in Criminology*, **2**, 79-99.

Black, D. J. (1971) 'The social organization of arrest', *Stanford Law Review*, **23**, 1087-111.

Black, H. C. (1957) *Black's Law Dictionary* (Fourth Edition with guide to Pronunciation), West, St Paul, Minnesota.

Blumstein, A., Cohen, J., and Nagin, D. (1978) *Deterrence and Incapacitation: Estimating the Effects of Criminal Sanctions on Crime Rates*, National Academy of Sciences, Washington, D.C.

Bordua, D. J. (1967) 'Recent trends: Deviant behavior and social control', *Annals of the American Academy of Political and Social Science*, **369**, 149-63.

Brewer, M. B. (1977) 'An information-processing approach to attribution of responsibility', *Journal of Experimental Social Psychology*, **13**, 1, 58-69.

Brickman, P., Ryan, K., and Wortman, C. B. (1975) 'Causal chains: Attribution of responsibility as a function of immediate and prior causes', *Journal of Personality and Social Psychology*, **32**, 1060-67.

Brown, J. S. (1948) 'Gradients of approach and avoidance and their relation to level of motivation', *Journal of Comparative and Physiological Psychology*, **41**, 450-65.

Brown, R. C., Jr. and Tedeschi, J. T. (1976) 'Determinants of perceived aggression', *Journal of Social Psychology*, **100**, 77-87.

California Assembly Committee on Criminal Procedure (1968) *Deterrent Effects of Criminal Sanctions*, Assembly of the State of California, Sacramento, California.

Campbell, D. T. and Stanley, J. (1963) *Experimental and Quasi-Experimental Designs for Research*, Rand McNally, Chicago.

Carroll, J. S. and Payne, J. W. (1977a) 'Crime seriousness, recidivism risk, and causal attributions in judgments of prison term by students and experts', *Journal of Applied Psychology*, **62**, 595-602.

Carroll, J. S. and Payne, J. W. (1977b) 'Judgments about crime and the criminal: A model and a method for investigating parole decisions', in *Perspectives in Law and Psychology, Vol. I: Criminal Justice System* (Ed. B. D. Sales), Plenum, New York, 191-240.

Chambliss, W. J. (1966) 'The deterrent influence of punishment', *Crime and Delinquency*, **12**, 70-75.

Chambliss, W. J. and Seidman, R. B. (1971) *Law, Order and Power*, Addison-Wesley, Reading.

Chiricos, T. G. and Waldo, G. P. (1975) 'Socioeconomic status and criminal sentencing: An empirical assessment of a conflict proposition', *American Sociological Review*, **40**, 753–72.

Clarke, S. H. and Koch, G. G. (1976) 'The influence of income and other factors on whether criminal defendants go to prison', *Law and Society Review*, **11**, 57–92.

Claster, D. (1967) 'Comparison of risk perception between delinquents and non-delinquents', *Journal of Criminal Law, Criminology and Police Science*, **58**, 80–86.

Cook, P. J. (1977) 'Punishment and Crime: A critique of current findings concerning the preventive effect of criminal sanction', *Law and Contemporary Problems*, **41**, 1, 164–204.

Cross, Sir Rupert (1975) *The English Sentencing System*, 2nd edn, Butterworths, London.

DeJong, W., Morris, W. N., and Hastorf, A. H. (1976) 'Effect of an escaped accomplice on the punishment assigned to a criminal defendant', *Journal of Personality and Social Psychology*, **33**, 192–98.

Diamond, S. S. (1980) 'Exploring patterns in sentence disparity', in *Perspectives in Law and Psychology, Vol. II: The Trial Process* (Ed. B. D. Sales), Plenum, New York.

Diamond, S. S. and Seals, E. (1981) 'The effects of objective certainty and severity of penalty on perceived certainty and severity', Unpublished manuscript, University of Illinois, Chicago.

Edinger, J. D. and Auerbach, S. M. (1978) 'Development and validation of a multi-dimensional multivariate model for accounting for infractions in a correctional setting', *Journal of Personality and Society Psychology*, **36**, 12, 1472–89.

Ehrlich, I. (1973) 'Participation in illegitimate activities: A theoretical and empirical investigation', *Journal of Political Economy*, **81**, 3, 521–65.

Elder, J. and Cohen, S. (1977) 'Prediction of work release success with youthful, non-violent, male offenders', *Criminal Justice and Behavior*, **5**, 2, 181–92.

Farrington, D. P. (1979) 'Experiments on deviance with special reference to dishonesty', in Advances in Experimental Social Psychology, **12**, (Ed. L. Berkowitz), Academic Press, New York, 207–52.

Federal Bureau of Investigation (1969) Uniform Crime Reports, 1968, U.S. Government Printing Office, Washington, D.C.

Flanders, J. P. (1968) 'A review of research on imitative behavior', *Psychological Bulletin*, **69**, 316–37.

Forst, B. (1967) 'Participation in illegitimate activities: Further empirical findings', *Policy Analysis*, **2**, 3, 477–92.

Fox, J. (1977) *The Law of Juvenile Courts*, West, St Paul, Minnesota.

Gibbs, J. (1975) *Crime, Punishment, and Deterrence*, Elsevier, New York.

Gottfredson, D., Wilkins, L., and Hoffman, P. (1978) *Guidelines for Parole and Sentencing*, Lexington, Massachusetts.

Hagan, J. (1974) 'Parameters of criminal prosecution: An application of path analysis to a problem of criminal justice', *Journal of Criminal Law and Criminology*, **65**, 4, 536–44.

Harvey, D. and Enzle, M. E. (1978) 'Effects of retaliation latency and provocation level on judged blameworthiness for retaliatory aggression', *Personality and Social Psychology Bulletin*, **4**, 579–582.

Harvey, M. D. and Rule, B. G. (1978) 'Moral evaluations and judgments of responsibility', *Personality and Social Psychology Bulletin*, **4**, 583–88.

Heider, F. (1958) *The Psychology of Interpersonal Relations*, Wiley, New York.

Hoffman, Hon. W. E. (1971) 'Purposes and philosophy of sentencing', Seminars for newly appointed judges, 1970–71, Federal Judicial Center, Washington, D.C., 286–346.

Hogarth, J. (1971) *Sentencing as a Human Process*, University of Toronto Press, Toronto.

Hood, R. (1972) *Sentencing the Motoring Offender*, Heinemann, London.

Horai, J. (1977) 'Attributional conflict', *Journal of Social Issues*, 33, 88–100.

Horai, J. and Bartek, M. (1978). 'Recommended publishment as a function of injurious intent, actual harm done, and intended consequences', *Personality and Social Psychology Bulletin*, 4, 575–78.

Jeffery, C. R. (1965) 'Criminal behavior and learning theory', *Journal of Criminal Law, Criminology, and Police Science*, 56, 294–300.

Jensen, G. F. (1969) ' "Crime doesn't pay": Correlates of a shared misunderstanding', *Social Problems*, 17, 189–201.

Jones, E. E., Davis, K. E., and Gergen, K. J. (1961) 'Role playing variations and their informational value for person perception', *Journal of Abnormal and Social Psychology*, 63, 302–10.

Jones, E. E. and Davis, K. E. (1965) 'From acts to dispositions', in *Advances in Experimental Social Psychology, Vol. 2* (Ed. L. Berkowitz), Academic Press, New York, 219–66.

Jones, E. E., Hester, S. L., Farina, A., and Davis, K. E. (1959) 'Reactions to unfavorable personal evaluations as a function of the evaluator's perceived adjustment', *Journal of Abnormal and Social Psychology*, 59, 363–70.

Joseph, J. M., Kane, T. R., Gaes, G. G., and Tedeschi, J. T. (1976) 'Effects of effort on attributed intent and perceived aggressiveness', *Perceptual and Motor Skills*, 42, 706–11.

Kalven, H. and Zeisel, H. (1966) *The American Jury*, Little, Brown, Boston.

Kant, I. (1965) *The Metaphysical Elements of Justice* (J. Ladd, Trans.), Bobbs-Merrill, Indianapolis, Indiana.

Kelley, H. (1967) 'Attribution Theory in Social Psychology, in *Nebraska Symposium on Motivation* (Ed. David Levine), University of Nebraska Press, Lincoln, Nebraska, 192–238.

Kelley, H. (1971) 'Attribution in social interaction', in *Attribution: Perceiving the Causes of Behavior* (Eds. E. E. Jones, D. Kanouse, H. Kelley, R. Nisbett, S. Valins, and B. Weiner), General Learning Press, New Jersey, 1–26.

Landes, W. (1974) 'Legality and reality: Some evidence on criminal procedure', *Journal of Legal Studies*, 3, 287–337.

Landy, D. and Aronson, E. (1969) 'The influence of the character of the criminal and his victim on the decisions of simulated jurors, *Journal of Experimental Social Psychology*, 5, 141–52.

Lefkowitz, M., Blake, R. R., and Mouton, J. S. (1955) 'Status factors in pedestrian violation of traffic signals', *Journal of Abnormal and Social Psychology*, 51, 704–5.

Lewin, K., Lippitt, R., and White, R. (1939) 'Patterns of aggressive behavior in experimentally created "social climates" ', *Journal of Social Psychology*, 10, 271–99.

Lindell, M. K. and Stewart, T. R. (1974) 'The effect of redundancy in multiple cue probability learning', *American Journal of Psychology*, 87, 393–98.

Mewett, A. W. (1961) 'Habitual criminal legislation under the criminal code', *Canadian Bar Review*, 39, 43–58.

Mischel, W. (1968) *Personality and Assessment*, Wiley, New York.

Monahan, J. and Hood, G. (1976) 'Psychologically disordered and criminal offenders', *Criminal Justice and Behavior*, 3, 2, 123–34.

Monahan, J. (1978) 'The prediction of violent criminal behavior: A methodological critique and prospectus', in *Deterrence and Incapacitation: Estimating the Effects of Criminal Sanctions on Crime Rates* (Eds. A. Blumstein, J. Cohen, and D. Nagin), National Academy of Sciences, Washington, D.C., 244–69.

Moos, R. H. (1975) *Evaluating Correctional and Community Settings*, Wiley, New York.

Morris, N. (1951) *The Habitual Criminal*, Longmans, Green and Company, London.

Morris, W. N., Marshall, H. M., and Miller, R. S. (1973) 'The effect of vicarious punishment on prosocial behavior in children', *Journal of Experimental Child Psychology*, **15**, 222–36.

Nagin, D. (1978) 'General deterrence: A review of the empirical evidence', in *Deterrence and Incapacitation: Estimating the Effects of Criminal Sanctions on Crime Rates* (Eds. A. Blumstein, J. Cohen, and D. Nagin), National Academy of Sciences, Washington, D.C., 95–139.

Newman, O. (1972) *Defensible Space*, Macmillan, New York.

Partridge, A. and Eldridge, W. (1974) *Second Circuit Sentencing Study: Report to the Judges of the Second Circuit*, Federal Judicial Center Report no. 74-4, U.S. Government Printing Office, Washington, D.C.

Pepitone, A. and Sherberg, J. (1957) 'Intentionality, responsibility, and interpersonal attraction', *Journal of Personality*, **25**, 757–66.

Petersilia, J., Greenwood, P. W., and Lavin, M. (1977) *Criminal Careers of Habitual Felons*, Rand Corporation, Santa Monica, California.

Piaget, J (1932) *The Moral Judgment of the Child*, Kegan Paul, Trench, Trubner, New York.

Rettig, S. and Rawson, H. E. (1963) 'The risk hypothesis in predictive judgments of unethical behavior', *Journal of Abnormal and Social Psychology*, **66**, 243–48.

Rosekrans, M. A. (1967) 'Imitation in children as a function of perceived similarity to a social model and vicarious reinforcement', *Journal of Personality and Social Psychology*, **7**, 307–15.

Rosekrans, M. A. and Hartup, W. W. (1967) 'Imitative influences of consistent and inconsistent response consequences to a model on aggressive behavior in children', *Journal of Personality and Social Psychology*, **7**, 429–34.

Ross, H. L. (1973) 'Law, science and accidents: The British Road Safety Act of 1967', *Journal of Legal Studies*, **2**, 1–78.

Schwartz, R. D. and Orleans, S. (1967) 'On legal sanctions', *University of Chicago Law Review*, **34**, 274–300.

Shah, S. (1978) 'Dangerousness: A paradigm for exploring some issues in law and psychology', *American Psychologist*, **33**, 224–38.

Shaver, K. G. (1975) *An Introduction to Attribution Processes*, Winthrop, Cambridge, Massachusetts.

Shaw, M. E. and Reitan, H. T. (1969) 'Attribution of responsibility as a basis for sanctioning behaviour' *British Journal of Social and Clinical Psychology*, **8**, 217–26.

Shaw, M. E. and Sulzer, J. L. (1964) 'An empirical test of Heider's levels in attribution of responsibility', *Journal of Abnormal and Social Psychology*, **69**, 39–46.

Shover, N. and Bankston, W. (1973) 'Some behavioral effects of new legislation', Unpublished, University of Tennessee (described in Zimring, 1978).

Sigall, H. and Ostrove, N. (1975) 'Beautiful but dangerous: Effects of offender attractiveness and nature of the crime on juridic judgment', *Journal of Personality and Social Psychology*, **31**, 410–14.

Sigall, H. and Landy, D. (1972) 'Effects of the defendant's character and suffering on juridic judgment: A replication and clarification', *Journal of Social Psychology*, **88**, 149–50.

Skinner, B. F. (1938) *The Behavior of Organisms*, Appleton-Century, New York.

Slovic, P., Fischoff, B., and Lichtenstein, S. (1977) 'Behavioral decision theory', *Annual Review of Psychology*, **28**, 1–39.

Solomon, R. L. (1964) 'Punishment', *American Psychologist*, **19**, 239–53.

Solomon, S. (1978) 'Measuring dispositional and situational attributions', *Personality and Social Psychology Bulletin*, **4**, 589-94.

Teevan, J. J. (1976) 'Subjective perception of deterrence (continued)', *Journal of Research in Crime and Delinquency*, **13**, 2, 155-64.

Thomas, D. A. (1979) *Principles of Sentencing*, Heinemann, London (2nd edn; 1st edn, 1970).

Tiffany, L., Avichai, Y., and Peters, G. (1975) 'A statistical analysis of sentencing in federal courts', *Journal of Legal Studies*, **4**, 369-90.

Tittle, C. R., and Rowe, A. R. (1973) 'Moral appeal, sanction threat, and deviance: An experimental test', *Social Problems*, **20**, 488-98.

Tversky, A. and Kahneman, D. (1971) 'The belief in the "law of small numbers"', *Psychological Bulletin*, **76**, 105-10.

Tversky, A. and Kahneman, D. (1973) 'Availability: A heuristic for judging frequency and probability', *Cognitive Psychology*, **5**, 207-32.

U.S. Parole Commission (1978) *Parole Commission Guideline Application Manual*, Appendix 4, Federal Prison System, 1 May, 1978.

van Alstyne, D. and Gottfredson, M. (1978) 'A multidimensional contingency table analysis of parole outcome', *Journal of Research in Crime and Delinquency*, **15**, 2, 172-93.

Waldo, G. P. and Chiricos, T. G. (1972) 'Perceived penal sanction and self-reported criminality: A neglected approach to deterrence research', *Social Problems*, **19**, 522-40.

Walker, N. (1969) *Sentencing in a Rational Society*, Basic Books, New York.

Walster, E. (1966) 'Assignment of responsibility for an accident', *Journal of Personality and Social Psychology*, **3**, 73-79.

Walters, G. and Grusec, J. (1977) *Punishment*, Freeman, San Francisco.

Walters, R. H. and Parke, R. D. (1964) 'Influence of the response consequences to a social model on resistance to deviation', *Journal of Experimental Child Psychology*, **1**, 269-280.

Warner, F. B. (1923) 'Factors determining parole from the Massachusetts reformatory', *Journal of Criminal Law and Criminology*, **14**, 172-207.

Wheeler, S., Bonachich, E., Cramer, M. R., and Zola, I. K. (1968) 'Agents of delinquency control: 'A comparative analysis', in *Controlling Delinquents* (Ed. S. Wheeler), Wiley, New York, 31-60.

Wilkins, L. T., Kress, J. M., Gottfredson, D. M., Calpin, J. C., and Gelman, A. M. (1976) *Sentencing Guidelines: Structuring Judicial Discretion*, U.S. Government Printing Office, Washington, D.C.

Wolfgang, M., Figlio, R., and Sellin, T. (1972) *Delinquency in a Birth Cohort*, University of Chicago Press, Chicago, Illinois.

Woodworth, R. S. and Schlosberg, H. (1954) *Experimental Psychology*, Holt, New York.

Wooton, B. (1963) *Crime and the Criminal Law*, Stevens and Sons, London.

Zeisel, H. and Diamond, S. S. (1977) 'The search for sentencing equity: Sentence review in Massachusetts and Connecticut', *American Bar Foundation Research Journal*, **4**, 883-940.

Zimring, F. (1978) 'Policy experiments in general deterrence: 1970-1975', in *Deterrence and Incapacitation: Estimating the Effects of Criminal Sanctions on Crime Rates* (Eds. A. Blumstein, J. Cohen, and D. Nagin), National Academy of Sciences, Washington, D. C., 140-86.

Progress in Applied Social Psychology, Volume 1
Edited by G. M. Stephenson and J. M. Davis
© 1981 John Wiley & Sons Ltd.

4

A Critical Evaluation of Fiedler's Contingency Hypothesis

DIAN-MARIE HOSKING

INTRODUCTION

It is now fifteen years since Fiedler published his contingency model of leadership effectiveness (Fiedler, 1964). Since then, many tests of his central hypothesis have been conducted, these studies being reviewed in a number of papers published in the early 1970s. The reviewers failed to agree on the implications of the aggregated data: authors such as Mitchell *et al.* (1970), Fiedler (1971) and Rice and Chemers (1973) concluded that Fiedler's hypothesis had empirical support, whilst others such as Graen *et al.* (1970) and Ashour (1973a, 1973b) disagreed.

The validity of Fiedler's hypothesis continues to be questioned. In addition, criticisms have been levelled against his *model* (i.e. his interpretation of his hypothesis) and his methodology (see, for example, McMahon, 1972; Shiflett, 1973; Schriesheim and Kerr, 1977; and Hosking, 1978). Despite these controversies, new general texts appear and describe the model as though only minor problems (if any) attend it (see, for example, Hardy, 1976; Herbert, 1976; Raven and Rubin, 1976). Furthermore, Fiedler and his colleagues have marketed a leadership training program which they claim is based on 'one of the most researched and best validated leadership theories' (Fiedler, Chemers, and Mahar, 1976, p.3).

These observations suggest that it is time to reassess Fiedler's contingency hypothesis. The purpose of this chapter is to determine whether Fiedler's hypothesis has sufficient empirical support to warrant further attention. This will be achieved by *detailed* description and analysis of the relevant literature —something which previous reviews have not done. Given the diversity of procedures used to test the hypothesis, plus the different ways in which authors have assessed the significance of the results, detailed analysis of the available studies is essential.

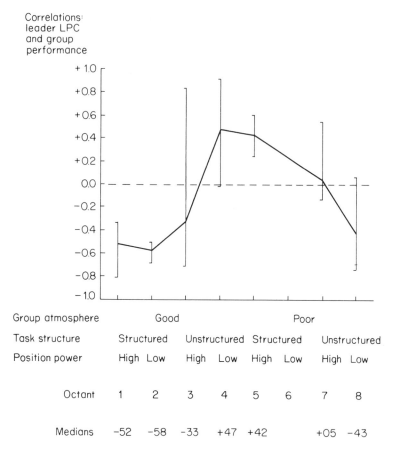

Figure 1. Fiedler's contingency model of leadership effectiveness.. *Source:* Fiedler (1967, Tables 9-1 and 9-2). (Reproduced by permission of McGraw-Hill Book Co.)

FIEDLER'S CONTINGENCY HYPOTHESIS DEFINED

In his 1971 review, Fiedler made a formal distinction between *two* contingency hypotheses. His central hypothesis (hereon referred to as CF) is tied to the methodology of his early work and is defined by the pattern of correlations shown in Figure 1. In other words, only when leadership situations are defined in terms of group atmosphere (GA), task structure (TS), and position power (PP) as operationalized by Fiedler (1967) does he regard the CF as having been tested. Furthermore, by definition, the CF can only be tested by obtaining correlations between leaders' scores on the Least Preferred Co-worker Questionnaire (LPC scores) and group performance data: 'studies that do not conform to the explicit methodology of the earlier work cannot be used as exact tests of model' (Fiedler, 1971, p.132). However, when reviewing support for his CF, Fiedler cited studies which did depart from his methodology (for example, Shima, 1968; Hill, 1969; Fiedler, O'Brien, and Ilgen, 1969). In fact, when Fiedler wrote his review, not one study had utilized all the necessary measures: in other words, *the CF had never been tested!*

Fiedler regards GA, TS, and PP as important determinants of the leader's influence over group activities — what he calls 'situational favourableness' (SF). Situations are deemed to be 'very favourable' when they are characterized by good group atmosphere, a structured task, and high position power; poor group atmosphere, an unstructured task and low position power reflect a 'very unfavourable' situation. Fiedler argues that factors other than GA, TS, and PP might determine degrees of SF, for example: stress (Fiedler *et al.*, 1969), or linguistic homogeneity of the work group (Fiedler, 1966). The second, or 'more general hypothesis' referred to by Fiedler (1971) refers to relationships between SF (however measured) and leader LPC scores.

Low LPC leaders are suggested to be more effective (than high LPC leaders) in 'very favourable' and 'very unfavourable' situations. The reverse is predicted in situations of 'moderate favourableness'. Unfortunately, no adequate theory of situational favourableness exists; nor does a 'universal' metric for defining different levels. Until such are available, *the general hypothesis is untestable.*

PROCEDURES USED TO TEST FIEDLER'S CF: DESCRIPTION AND EVALUATION

Examination of studies claimed (by the authors or by Fiedler) to constitute tests of the CF reveals a tremendous diversity of testing procedures. These variations make it extremely difficult to determine what the combined weight of evidence 'adds up to', and provide one major reason why reviewers have failed to agree on this matter. These variations in procedure will be described as will their implications for attempted validation studies. This will provide the basis for a critique of the relevant literature.

Subjects Studied

Student subjects (usually American) have been employed in over half the studies. It seems reasonable to assume that few of them would have had leadership experience. It is possible that Fiedler's CF is only supported by, for example, experienced leaders; furthermore, it seems unwise to assume that experienced and inexperienced subjects obtain the same results for the same reasons. These comments suggest that combining these sources of data may obscure certain effects; indeed, indirect evidence has been obtained in support of this line of reasoning (Hosking, 1978). Another related variation concerns the manner in which a 'leader' is identified. Fiedler defined the leader as the person who performs the job of 'directing and co-ordinating task-relevant group activities' (Fiedler, 1967, p.8). In practice, leaders have been assumed to be those who have been formally appointed to a leadership role by their employers (as, for example, in the study by Nealey and Blood, 1967); or have been identified using sociometric techniques (see, for example, Fiedler *et al.*, 1969).

These variations characterize validation studies and studies from which the model was derived. The limitations of these operational differences should be recognized: the appointed leader may or may not be the person who actually performs the leadership function. Furthermore, different methods of identifying 'informal' or 'emergent' leaders may lead to different findings (Cattell and Stice, 1954).

Types of Group

Contingency model investigations have dealt with groups which vary on a number of dimensions. These include whether the groups were 'ongoing' or 'ad hoc'; size of group; composition: culturally and linguistically homogeneous or heterogeneous, all male or male and female, 'compatible' or 'incompatible' group members; and 'interacting relations' between group members or some other form of relation.

Ad hoc versus Ongoing Groups

Few studies have involved leaders and their existing work-groups (i.e. ongoing groups). Most have dealt with ad hoc collections of strangers or acquaintances assembled specially for the investigation. Whilst the use of ad hoc groups may allow controlled manipulation of the experimental variables, this may be at the cost of reduced external validity. Groups are more than mere collections of individuals (Herbst, 1970), they have recognizable structures, norms, etc. Aggregating data from ad hoc and ongoing groups (as Fiedler does) may obscure real differences and increase the amount of error variance in LPC/group performance relationships.

Group Size

In the development and testing of Fiedler's model, the size of work-groups has ranged from 3 to 23. Fiedler attaches no significance to such variations, although there is presumably a maximum number that he would accept as a small group. Clearly, whether the size of the group influences leadership effectiveness is an empirical question—and one about which we have little information. It seems reasonable to speculate that certain critical group sizes might influence 'situational favourableness' but this possibility is not formally built-in the model.

Linguistic and Cultural Composition

Fiedler commented that his CF is based upon, and can therefore only be tested by, groups which are homogeneous in this respect (Fiedler, 1971, p.135). Only one validation study varied this aspect of group composition (Fiedler, 1966). However, it should be noted that few authors ever mention the ethnic backgrounds of their subjects—presumably Fiedler is arguing that within a given group all subjects should have the same cultural background and first language. This may not have been true in some validation studies (see, for example, Fiedler, O'Brien, and Ilgen, 1969).

Group Composition: Males, Mixed Sex, or Females

Most of the studies from which the CF was derived involved groups of male subjects only. This has also been true of the validation studies. Fiedler has aggregated studies which vary in this aspect of composition, again possibly increasing the proportion of unexplained variance.

Group Composition: Variations in Liking, Compatability, etc.

Authors, including Fiedler, have sometimes effected *situational* manipulations by selecting group members against some sociometric criterion (for example, Hardy *et al.*, 1973; Vecchio, 1977). Motivational and ability criteria have also been used: O'Brien (1969) constructed compatible and incompatible groups using scores on Shutz's FIRO-B scales; Shiflett and Nealey (1972) assigned individuals to groups according to their verbal ability and LPC score. It is difficult to determine the effects of these variations on the validity of studies claimed to test the CF. Manipulations of relations defined by sociometric data seem acceptable since these reflect the ways in which GA is assessed. Varying group composition such that it is heterogeneous or homogeneous in terms of members' abilities or motivations seems less acceptable: such procedures do not characterize the pre-validation studies. Furthermore, they may well influence the relationship between leader LPC scores and group productivity.

Work Relations: Interacting, Counteracting, or Co-acting

Fiedler distinguished between different types of intragroup relations and limited the range of the CF's application to 'interacting work groups' (Fiedler, 1967, p.18.) The defining features of such groups are that the members are interdependent—'Each man must do his part if the team is to be successful'

(Fiedler, 1967, p.19), and the group as a whole is usually rewarded. Some authors have explicitly set out to study co-acting groups (for example, Hunt, 1967), and others may have done so unwittingly (for example, Shima, 1968). Such investigations cannot be regarded as legitimate tests of the CF. Unfortunately it is often difficult to judge whether groups are truly interacting or not. Authors typically give little information regarding the tasks they have employed, and seldom present data which would validate their claims for interacting relations.

Operational Definitions of SF

These have varied in four main ways.

Dimensions of Favourableness: GA, TS, and PP or others

Some authors conceptualize favourableness in terms of Fiedler's three components: GA, TS and PP; others do not. Similarly, they use different scales to measure the situational variables. For instance, Fiedler and his colleagues studied the effects of variables such as 'environmental stress' on LPC/performance correlations (Fiedler *et al.*, 1969). Others have measured 'precedence relations between sub-tasks' and claim their results support Fiedler's CF. Furthermore, some of the so-called situational variables have in fact been aspects of the *leader* (for example, Csoka and Fiedler, 1972: leader intelligence and experience).

Ordering of GA, TS, and PP in Terms of Their Relative Contributions to Situational Favourableness

Figure 1 portrays Fiedler's assumptions regarding the relative importance of these three variables. When investigators have measured these variables, they have usually ordered them in the manner specified by Fiedler (1967). One exception can be found in Fiedler's post-hoc classification of the Belgian Navy data (see Fiedler, 1966, Figures 5 and 6).

Source of Descriptions of Situational Variables: Leader's Ratings versus Other Persons

Fiedler (1967) conceptualized GA, TS, and PP as situational variables which are independent of the leader. In the studies from which the model was derived, TS and PP were usually measured by obtaining data from independent judges. GA has been measured in one of two ways depending on whether the groups being investigated were ad hoc or ongoing (see above). In the case of ad hoc groups, the leader's rating of GA has been employed, whereas in ongoing groups, sociometric preference ratings have been obtained from group members. Clearly, when leader descriptions of situational variables are employed, the independence of the situation from the leader is in doubt. Most attempted validation studies have conformed to Fiedler's procedures; however, in one study, leaders described all three situational dimensions (Kretzschmar and Luecke, 1969).

Method of Stratifying Situational Dimensions: Critical Values or Median 'Splits'

Fiedler combined GA, TS, and PP by stratifying each into two levels and combining each with each to obtain eight cells (see Figure 1). Use of this technique raises the question of the criterion levels at which the variables were dichotomized. As Korman (1973) noted, contingency theories should include a specification of criterion levels or 'critical values'. Whilst critical values have been made available (Posthuma, 1970, unpublished), few researchers (including Fiedler) have employed them. Instead, sample medians have been calculated and used to stratify the sample distributions. Since distributions of scores are likely to vary in different studies, definitions of the levels of the situational variables are also likely to vary. Such variations may have a critical effect on whether or not particular cells are validated.

Predictor Measures of Leadership Effectiveness

Leadership Style Measured by ASo or LPC Scores

Fiedler's early investigations involved correlations between group performance data and leader's scores on a measure of 'assumed similarity between opposites' (ASo). Approximately one-third of the correlations which define the CF reflect relationships between *ASo scores* and performance. Since 1963 he has used LPC scores (one component of ASo) as a convenient substitute. Most of the validation studies have also used LPC: indeed, the study by Shima (1968) seems the only exception.

Leader Behaviour as a Predictor of Style/Performance Relationships

Considerable controversy surrounds the meaning of LPC/ASo scores. One of Fiedler's early interpretations was that low LPC leaders act in a task-oriented manner, whilst high LPC leaders' behaviour is relationships oriented. The available evidence does not support this view, but does suggest relationships of a very complex nature between LPC scores and leader behaviour (Hosking, 1978). Some authors have claimed to test Fiedler's CF by manipulating leaders' behaviours assuming this would result in predictable variations in leader LPC scores (e.g. Shaw and Blum, 1966). In view of the previous comment, this seems unlikely to be the case.

The data describing relationships between leader LPC scores and behaviour suggest that tests of the CF should avoid manipulations of leader behaviour. Such manipulations merely make LPC/performance correlations uninterpretable. For example, O'Brien (1969) manipulated leaders' behaviour in order to effect different leadership situations. This procedure inevitably confounds the individual-difference dimension with the situational metric.

Methods of Measuring Group Performance

Ratings or Objective Measures

Fiedler defined leadership effectiveness in terms of the *group*'s performance on its 'primary assigned task' (Fiedler, 1967, p.9). He has measured performance in one of two ways depending on whether the groups were ongoing or ad hoc, and on the level of task structure. Examination of the studies from which the model was induced shows that ratings were usually obtained in the case of ad hoc groups doing unstructured tasks, whereas ongoing groups working on structured tasks have usually been assessed using 'objective' measures (see Fiedler, 1967).

Source and Object of Performance Measures

As has already been noted, Fiedler measured the leader's effectiveness in terms of the group's performance. Conventionally, this has been achieved by obtaining data from persons other than the leader. Validation studies have usually followed these procedures. Exceptions include the studies by Hill (1969), who obtained ratings of the leader's performance, and Kretzschmar and Luecke (1969), who had the leaders describe their own performance.

Conclusions: Variations in Procedure and Their Effects on Validation Attempts

The preceding review demonstrates the wide variety of procedures employed in tests of the CF. Many of these differences characterize the research from which the hypothesis was induced, and for this reason cannot be said to render a study unacceptable as a test of the CF. Others result in an inadequate test of the contingency hypothesis. Three categories of variation having this effect have been described and may be summarized as follows. First, measures or procedures were employed which represent substantial departures from Fiedler's methodology: either SF was defined using variables other than GA, TS, and PP, or these were employed but ordered in a manner differing from that specified by the contingency hypothesis (CF). Secondly, certain limiting conditions specified by Fiedler (1967) were contravened in that group members (a) had work relations that were not 'interacting'; (b) differed in their linguistic and/or cultural backgrounds; or (c) were selected to be similar to each other in certain personal characteristics (for example, ability). Thirdly, measures and procedures were employed which confounded the situational and individual-difference dimensions: group leaders described the situation and/or their performance; the leader's characteristics were included in the definition of SF; or leaders' behaviour was manipulated.

Consequently, if a researcher has employed any of the above mentioned practices, this is sufficient to render the study irrelevant to an assessment of the empirical validity of Fiedler's CF. Even so, it is still extraordinarily difficult to determine the impact that a given study has on the contingency hypothesis. The acceptable studies are characterized by a wide variety of procedures employed at different research sites. This makes interpretation of the aggregate data difficult, since the hypothesis may hold under some, but not all, of the conditions involved. For this reason, studies in which all eight cells (octants) were tested using the same procedures are particularly valuable.

PROCEDURES USED TO EVALUATE THE SIGNIFICANCE OF LPC/PERFORMANCE RELATIONSHIPS

Having judged a study to constitute an adequate test of the CF, it is next necessary to evaluate the implications of the findings. This is done by locating the groups in the appropriate octants and examining the relationship between leader LPC (or ASo) scores and some measure of the productivity of their work-groups. Linear correlations have usually been used to calculate the nature of the relationship. In practice, the number of groups in each cell is usually small, and in consequence statistically significant correlations are hard to obtain (Sashkin, 1972). As a result, a variety of procedures have been advocated to provide a more sensitive test of the CF. Unfortunately, some of these procedures are grossly misleading when used in this context; others are perfectly acceptable in principle but have been used in a misleading manner; one is acceptable but of limited utility; and another, whilst powerful, strictly speaking does not test the CF at all. These variations provide a further reason why critics fail to agree about the validity of the CF: data are misrepresented, and if a particular summary statistic is inappropriate, the data are seldom presented in sufficient detail to allow a revised evaluation. These points must be borne in mind when evaluating the findings of validation studies. For this reason these techniques will be outlined and briefly commented upon.

Analyses Based on Data Combined Within Octants/Across Studies

One such technique involves comparison of the *median correlations* obtained in validation studies with the direction (+ or -) of those found in studies on which the model was based (see, for example, Fiedler, 1971). This method is acceptable in principle but is extremely misleading when consistency in the size and direction of correlations is missing.

A second technique of this sort involves analysis of correlations obtained in validation studies using the method of joint probabilities (Fisher, 1976). Again, this method seems acceptable but statistically significant results should be expected in every octant (see Ashour, 1973a). Failure to find statistically significant results cannot be excused on the groups of sample size (or any other grounds) and should be regarded as casting doubt on the validity of the CF.

Analyses Performed on Data Aggregated Across Octants and Studies

Three techniques of this sort have been employed, as follows.

(a) The median correlations which define the CF are taken as *point predictions*. This set of median values is then compared with the set of medians obtained in validation studies and an overall correlation coefficient calculated.

(b) The *binomial distribution*, i.e. the probability ($p(x)$) of obtaining x correlations in the predicted direction is calculated using the formula provided by Spiegel (1961, p.122).

(c) Stouffer's method, where individual correlations are converted into Z scores; these scores are summed, and the probability of $Z/N^{1/2}$ is calculated (see Fiedler, 1973, p.358).

Each of these techniques is open to one serious criticism when used in the context of Fiedler's model, namely that they are applied to data *aggregated across octants* and therefore obscure the differential predictive power of the CF in the various cells. That is to say, variations in the size and statistical significance of correlations implies that we can be more confident about some than others. To the extent that large correlations are not uniformly distributed across octants, the results of one or two cells will bias the total picture and lead to the conclusion that the CF is valid. For this reason, techniques which combine data across octants are inappropriate and misleading.

Analysis of Variance

Analysis of variance has been employed by treating the observed correlations as data points, and looking for significant effects due to variations in GA, TS, and PP (see, for example, Graen *et al.*, 1970, p.292). This method seems acceptable but fails to provide detailed information on the size of observed differences, and cannot comment on interactions between LPC (or ASo) and the situational variables.

As alternative use of ANOVA involves analysis of the effects of variations in LPC scores, GA, TS, and PP on group performance data (see, for example,

Hardy, 1975). Strictly speaking, this does not provide a direct test of the CF since this is operationally defined in terms of LPC/performance *correlations* (see Figure 1). Having said this, it would clearly be absurd to regard such results as irrelevant to an assessment of the CF. Furthermore, this technique has the advantage of assessing the relative contribution of each of Fiedler's variables. Its main drawback seems to be that it should not be applied to performance data obtained using a variety of procedures. However, this is also true of other techniques described.

Conclusions: Statistical Techniques for Evaluating Fiedler's CF

These comments suggest that particular care should be taken when evaluating the summary statistics and significance tests reported by researchers. Methods which combine data from the various octants are totally unacceptable, and the practice of combining data within octants is permissible but may be grossly misleading (see above). Analysis of variance performed on group performance scores may be the most sensitive test since it combines the necessary criterion of statistical reliability with the desirable feature of being able to test the interactions implied by Fiedler's CF (for a more detailed analysis, see Hosking, 1978, Appendix B.)

A FORMAL CLASSIFICATION OF VALIDATION STUDIES

It should by now be clear that any careful assessment of the validity of Fiedler's CF involves an exercise of considerable complexity. Relevant studies have been conducted using a wide variety of procedures and evaluation techniques. Some formal classification of the methods involved is therefore a prerequisite for any serious discussion of the evidence.

It would be possible to organize the literature using any (or all) of the variations in the procedure described. Use of all these dimensions of difference would provide an unwieldy and unhelpful taxonomy. Consequently, some selection of the more important variations is necessary. In view of Fiedler's comments regarding the manner in which the CF must be tested (see above), it seems appropriate to distinguish between studies in terms of the way SF is (a) conceptualized and (b) measured. Such a scheme is useful because it demonstrates the assumptions required to regard each study as a test of the CF (see Table 1).

Studies of type 1 conceptualize situational favourableness in terms of GA, TS, and PP, and at least two of the situational factors are measured using Fiedler's scales. The results of such studies are relatively easy to evaluate since, all other things being equal, Fiedler's hypothesis can be seen to be tested. However, moving in sequence from studies of type 1 to studies of type 5, more and more assumptions are required in order to relate the study concerned to Fiedler's CF. In the most extreme case, studies of type 5 extend Fiedler's

Table 1   Typology of validation studies

	Conceptual level			
	GA	TS	PP	Other
Fiedler's measures		1		X
Other measures		2		4
Operational level				
No measures:				5
Manipulations		3A		
A priori assumptions		3B		

Table 2   Validation studies classified according to type

	Conceptual level			
	GA	TS	PP	Others
Fiedler's measures	Hardy (1971) Hardy et al. (1973) Csoka (1975) Schneier (1978)	1		X
Other measures	Hill (1969) Hunt (1967)	2		Fiedler, O'Brien, and Ilgen (1969) Kretzschmar and Luecke (1969) Csoka (1974) 4 O'Brien (1969) Hewett et al. (1974)
Operational level				
No measures — manipulation only	Fiedler (1966) Graen et al. (1970) Chemers and Skryzpek (1972) Shima (1968) Hardy (1975) Vecchio (1977) Sashkin (1972) Shiflett and Nealey (1972) Johnson and Ryan (1976)	3A		
— a priori assumptions only	Shaw and Blum (1966) Hovey (1974) Reavis and Derlega (1976) Rice and Chemers (1973) Michaelsen (1973)	3B		Nealey and Blood (1968) Hardy and Bohren (1975) 5

(1967) definition of SF, assume that it is affected by certain experimental manipulations, but make no measurements of the range of variation involved. Any claim that such studies constitute adequate tests of the CF rests on numerous assumptions of unknown validity.

Studies claimed as tests of the CF are classified according to type in Table 2. Some of those cited by Fiedler (1971) have been omitted because they are unpublished and have proved to be unobtainable. Other studies cited by Fiedler (1971) have also been omitted because Fiedler performed his own post-hoc analyses on data not presented in the published articles. There seems little point in attempting a thorough critique on studies and data which are not available for detailed appraisal.

DESCRIPTION AND ANALYSIS OF TYPE 1 STUDIES

Studies which conceptualize and measure the leader's situation in the manner described by Fiedler (1967) constitute 'public' tests of CF. Studies of this type are therefore particularly valuable in assessing its validity. Until 1971, no such test had been conducted. Since then, four have appeared (Hardy, 1971; Hardy *et al.*, 1973; Csoka, 1975; and Schneier, 1978).

These studies differ in a number of respects. The investigations by Hardy and his colleagues were laboratory studies of ad hoc collections of male and female acquaintances. The dimensions of SF were typically manipulated and measured. In contrast, Csoka conducted a field study of army stewards and their (ongoing) work-groups, and simply measured the situational variables. The authors of each of the studies are vague about the actual measures used: only by process of inference is it concluded that their measures are *probably* Fiedler's (and therefore that the studies are type 1). Furthermore, it seems doubtful that TS was measured in any of these investigations. Finally, these authors used different methods to examine relations between the variables: Hardy and his colleagues used ANOVA techniques and tested main effects plus interactions, whilst Csoka and Schneier employed linear correlation coefficients.

Hardy (1971)

Hardy's groups were led by high LPC ($\bar{X}$ LPC score $= 92$) and low LPC leaders ($\bar{X} = 40$) assigned by the experimenter. GA was assessed using post-performance measures which showed it to be good. TS was manipulated by the use of two tasks (repeated measures design) but the manipulations do not appear to have been checked. The supposedly unstructured task required opinions to be expressed on what to do about a problem student, whereas the structured task was an objective test. These manipulations have reasonable face validity. PP was manipulated by instructions to the groups; members' ratings suggest that 'high' and 'low' manipulations were seen as *different*; however, the high PP condition was in fact only moderate (see Hardy p.370).

This investigation seems an adequate test of CF: Hardy's definition of the situations seems valid and 'high' and 'low' LPC leaders were clearly observed. However, whether or not the groups were interacting seems questionable (see Hardy p.6). Data were obtained in octants 1, 2, 3 and 4 and showed mean differences (between high and low LPC-led groups) in the predicted direction in three of the four octants (no significant different in octant 2). It seems that the possible range of performance scores was from 3 to 150 (see pp.369–70), in which case the mean differences were extremely small (minimum = 3 scale points, maximum = 9). Thus, this study provides weak support for octants 1, 3, and 4 of the CF.

Hardy, Sack, and Harpine (1973)

The authors followed similar procedures to those employed by Hardy (1971). One difference is that GA was manipulated on the basis of sociometric choices and rejections, and validated after task performance. TS was manipulated as before, and again does not seem to have been validated. PP was manipulated by obtaining group members' perceptions after the experiment. Factorial analyses of variance were performed on the performance data, providing tests of the model in octants 2, 4, 6, and 8. In comparisons between octants 2 and 6, an interaction between GA and LPC scores was predicted. None was found. Instead, a main effect was observed for LPC, high LPC leaders being more effective in octant 6 (no significant difference in octant 2). An interaction was also predicted between LPC and GA in octants 4 and 8: this was found, but the data only provide convincing support for differences in octant 4 ($\bar{X}$ difference = 6 scale points: high LPC leaders more effective).

In conclusion, this seems a reasonably adequate test of the CF. Again, whether or not the groups were truly interactive seems questionable, and the 'poor' GA groups were not particularly poor. The results are somewhat mixed; of the four octants tested, only two were supported by the data and the mean differences were small.

Csoka (1975)

Csoka's primary purpose was to investigate relationships between SF and organization climate (House and Rizzo, 1971). Whilst GA, TS, and PP were measured, this was achieved by obtaining the leader's ratings. Furthermore, the measure of TS combined Fiedler's traditional method with a calculation designed to take account of modifications to task structure caused by training (Csoka and Fiedler, 1972). These departures from the methodology described by Fiedler (1967) are seen as grounds for rejecting this study as a valid test of

Fiedler's CF (see above). However, the fact that sizeable relationships were observed between LPC scores and group performance (–66, –80, –69, and + 80) suggests that the LPC scale may have some utility, given a valid situational metric.

Schneier (1978)

Schneier placed American undergraduates in five-person groups who then worked together on a variety of experiential learning exercises. At the end of fifteen weeks leaders were identified by asking group members to nominate who had the most influence and who most often had their suggestions accepted. GA and TS were measured following Fiedler (1967). PP was assumed to be low on the grounds that the leaders had no formal authority; this assumption was validated using the scales developed by Hunt (1967).

Performance ratings were correlated with leader LPC scores resulting in a coefficient of -0.55 ($N = 42$, $p < 0.001$). Whether or not this result supports Fiedler's CF depends upon the adequacy of the study and the octant to which it should appropriately be assigned. The only doubt is with respect to TS: whilst the judges rated the tasks as structured, Schneier's description suggests otherwise (the tasks included case-study analyses, critiques and designs of a personnel programme, and role-plays). Despite this concern, this study is taken to constitute an adequate and supportive test of Fiedler's CF in octant 2.

Conclusions: Type 1 Studies

Relatively few assumptions need to be made in concluding that the studies by Hardy (1971) and Hardy et al. (1973) constitute valid tests of the CF. Between them, they tested six of Fiedler's eight cells (excluding octants 5 and 7). Examination of the mean performance scores shows significant differences in octants 1, 3, 4, and 6. Whilst each of these differences was in the direction predicted, they were small. Furthermore, octants 2 and 8 were not validated. Consequently, these two studies provide only weak support for Fiedler's CF.

Whilst Csoka's results show sizeable relationships between leader LPC and group performance, his methodology was such that they cannot be viewed as relevant to an empirical assessment of the CF. Schneier's results provide substantial support for octant 2 inasmuch as 30 percent of the total variance was accounted for by the relationship between LPC scores and group performance.

DESCRIPTION AND ANALYSIS OF TYPE 2 STUDIES

Two studies of this type have been conducted: Hunt (1967) and Hill (1969). These researchers *formally measured every variable* (individual and situational) referred to in Fiedler's CF. However, the measures of GA, TS, and PP were developed by Hunt being *based* on those described by Fiedler (1967). Consequently, if these studies are to be regarded as valid tests of CF, it must be assumed that Hunt's and Fiedler's measures are appropriately correlated. Neither Hunt nor Hill provide any evidence of this. Therefore the only means of assessing this assumption is in terms of the similarity in the content of the scales. Whilst they seem sufficiently similar to warrant acceptance of these studies as valid tests of the CF, it is unfortunate that the relevant correlational data are not available.

A second point which requires comment is that the researchers used sample statistics (medians, percentiles, etc.) to define different levels of the situational variables. If these studies are to be regarded as tests of Fiedler's CF, it must also be assumed that similar levels of GA, TS, and PP were measured, or that the variation in the levels was small and not critical.

Hunt (1967)

This was a field study involving five sets of work-groups in three American organisations. Hunt obtained data from co-acting and interacting work groups; in view of earlier comments only the latter data are discussed. Leader LPC scores were obtained but no information was given as to what constituted high and low. Group performance was assessed using company measures, i.e. objective scores and ratings; as in most field studies, the measure used depended on the work-group concerned.

Correlations between LPC scores and the performance measures were calculated for octants 1, 3, 5, and 7. Individually, the correlations did not differ significantly from zero (Table 4); however, when the probabilities for each separate sample were *combined with octants* the combined probability was significant.

Hill (1969)

This study was conducted in a large electronics firm in the United States. The subjects were engineering groups and their supervisors. Leader LPC scores were obtained but, as in the Hunt study, no information was provided on what constituted high or low LPC. Leadership effectiveness was measured using managers' ratings of the *leader's* job performance. This procedure has already been commented on as undesirable, but as far as one can judge, not sufficient grounds for rejecting a study as a valid test of the CF.

Correlations were computed between leader LPC scores and effectiveness in octants 2, 3, 6, and 7. None of the coefficients was statistically significant (see Table 4). Despite this, Hill concluded that this data supported the CF: presumably because three of the four correlations were in the predicted direction. However, the correlations in octants 2 and 3 were small (−0.10, −0.29) and the correlation in octant 7, whilst positive (as predicted), differed considerably from the point prediction based on the pre-validation data. To regard the obtained correlation as supportive of the CF simply because it is in the predicted direction, is generous to say the least.

Conclusions: Type 2 Studies

It seems that the studies by Hunt and Hill constitute valid tests of Fiedler's CF but provide it with little empirical support. The correlations are typically small and non-significant. Furthermore, where more than one correlation was calculated in a given octant, the r values varied from positive to negative. Only in octant 1 are the correlations large *and* in the predicted direction (but statistically unreliable).

These data do not support the CF; however, Hunt's findings suggest *a* contingency between LPC, situational variables, and effectiveness since high and low LPC persons appear to differ in octant 1 but not in the remaining situations.

DESCRIPTION OF TYPE 3 STUDIES

Examination of Table 2 shows that most validation studies are of this type: the situations are conceptualized in terms of GA, TS, and PP, but measures of these variables are seldom obtained. One major type of variation in procedure also occurs *within* this category: authors either manipulated the situational variables or simply made *a priori* assumptions regarding their status. These distinctions are preserved by labelling such studies as types 3A and 3B, respectively. These are discussed and evaluated separately.

DESCRIPTION AND ANALYSIS OF TYPE 3A STUDIES

Nine studies of this type have been conducted: Fiedler (1966); Chemers and Skryzpek (1972); Graen, Orris, and Alvares (1970); Vecchio (1977); Shima (1968); Hardy (1975); Sashkin (1972); Shiflett and Nealey (1972); and Johnson and Ryan (1976). The first four tested all eight cells of the CF. These studies are characterized by the fact that all three of the situational variables were usually manipulated. This was done in a number of ways. In general, position power was manipulated by the use of different instructions to groups and leaders, whilst task structure was varied by the assignment of different tasks. Group atmosphere was either manipulated by constructing groups on the basis of sociometric data (Chemers and Skryzpek; Hardy; and Vecchio) or simply measured. Sashkin's methodology was unique in that he assumed the situational variables to be manipulated by the use of role-play materials.

Three of the investigations were experimental field studies involving various sections of the armed forces (Fiedler, 1966—Belgian Navy; Chemers and Skryzpek, 1972—Army Cadets; Vecchio, 1977—Air Force Personnel), the remainder were laboratory studies of students. All groups consisted of ad hoc collections of acquaintances or strangers.

Fiedler 1966—The Belgian Navy Study

Fiedler constructed three-man groups of French and Dutch-speaking petty officers ($N = 48$) and recruits ($N = 240$). Individuals were assigned such that half the groups were culturally and linguistically homogeneous, whilst the remainder were not. As already noted, data from heterogeneous groups of this kind cannot be used to test the CF, therefore these data will be ignored. GA was not manipulated but measured after task performance: leaders and group members completed questionnaires which included Fiedler's GA scale. Position-power was manipulated by the assignments of petty officers (high PP) or recent recruits (low PP) as group leaders. The face validity of the manipulation seems reasonably high, although it is important to note that it confounds the effects of position-power with the effects of leadership experience.

Two tasks defined *a priori* as 'structured' plus one supposedly 'unstructured' task were used to manipulate TS. Fiedler found performance on the two structured tasks to be uncorrelated and therefore chose to calculate separate correlations, one for each. This resulted in two correlations in the structured octants (1, 2, 5, and 6) and one in each unstructured octant (3, 4, 7, and 8). Fiedler also calculated LPC/performance correlations for each of two orders of task presentation, resulting in four correlations in each of the structured octants and two in each unstructured octant. Examination of these data shows them to be randomly distributed; consequently, they do not support Fiedler's CF (see Fiedler, 1966, p.255, Table 6).

Having cited the above mentioned correlations, Fiedler did not evaluate them in terms of their implications for the CF. Instead, he argued that data from the first structured task (ST1) should be rejected because the groups made many errors by failing to follow instructions, and because nine of the groups obtained a perfect score. He therefore dropped the ST1 data from his analyses, leaving two correlations (one for each order of presentation) in each structured octant. He then calculated the mid-position and presented a graph linking these mid-points (see Fiedler, 1966, Table 6 and Figure 5). Whilst these practices resulted in an appreciable reduction of the variance, the resulting graph did not support the CF. Accepting this to be the case, Fiedler continued by performing two post-hoc analyses using two entirely novel definitions of SF. In terms of the taxonomy presented above, these analyses are type 5. However, they will be presented here for the sake of convenience.

These post-hoc analyses included factors such as homogeneity/heterogeneity and learning effects as situational variables (see Fiedler, 1966, Figures 5 and 6). Fiedler seems to regard these analyses of tests of, and providing support for, his CF. However, given the novel definitions of SF, the specific hypothesis cannot be regarded as having been tested. It is concluded that the post-hoc analyses do not test the CF, but that the data reported earlier (ignoring ST1) when classified in the manner described by Fiedler (1967), may be used to assess the CF's validity. However, since the hypothesis makes no reference to task order effects, the *raw data* for the two task sequences should be combined. Unfortunately, only the correlations (not the raw data) are available; they fail to support the CF (see Table 4, p.136).

Chemers and Skryzpek (1972)

This investigation involved four-man groups of American cadets attending a military academy. High and low LPC persons were identified and assigned as leaders but, as is often the case in validation studies, sample-based definitions were employed and the critical values not given. GA was manipulated and checked by obtaining leaders' ratings of group atmosphere (Fiedler, 1967). Comparison of GA scores in the two conditions showed them to be significantly different; however, neither the size nor region of the difference was cited.

PP was manipulated by informing the high PP groups that their performance would be evaluated by their leaders, and that this would contribute to their training grades. Low PP groups were told that the experimenter would evaluate their performance, but that this would have no effect on their training grades. This manipulation may not have been successful. Personal experience suggests that trainees find it difficult to believe that their performance has no bearing on their final grade. If this was the case, the differences between high and low PP groups would have been less than supposed. TS was manipulated by the use of two tasks and no formal measurements were taken.

Correlations between leader LPC scores and group performance were calculated, as were relationships between these and the median correlations which define the CF. The latter procedure resulted in a large, positive, and statistically significant relationship (rho $+$ 0.86, $p<0.05$; $r+0.89$, $p<0.01$). This method has been strongly criticized (see earlier); consequently only the correlations within each octant will be considered.

Three of these coefficients were around 0.10 and the largest was 0.43 (see Table 4). In other words, the largest proportion of the variance accounted for was approximately 18 percent. Fiedler claimed that this study constitutes 'the methodologically most adequate test of the entire model' (Fiedler, 1971). If this is the case, the results are particularly disturbing since they suggest the CF has little predictive power.

Vecchio 1977

This study shares certain features of that performed by Chemers and Skryzpek: an experimental field study; American forces personnel allocated to ad hoc groups of acquaintances; and manipulation of all the situational variables. Seven tasks were employed, five of which were selected according to the criteria specified by Fiedler (1971). Group atmosphere was manipulated on the basis of sociometric data (details not given) such that Poor GA was characterized by unfavourably ranked persons rated as relatively 'cold' on a warm/cold scale, whilst Good GA was the reverse. PP was manipulated by informing some groups that their leader had the power to recommend extra duty (or relief from duty), whilst in low power groups no such instructions were given.

Leaders were selected and assigned to groups on the basis of the LPC scores (levels of high and low being similar to those specified by Posthuma). After the groups had performed their tasks they completed a variety of measures including the GA scale. Only if the leaders' ratings of GA endorsed the manipulations were the data included in the LPC/performance analyses. (N.B. 27 different measures of performance were used.) Vecchio conducted six analyses of variance on the data from structured and unstructured tasks (session 1, session 2 and both sessions combined). Of the 308 F-values obtained, eight reached conventional levels of significance ($p<0.05$) and a further eleven attained marginal levels ($p<0.10$). Acknowledging that the ANOVA results produced little support for the CF, Vecchio calculated Spearman correlations within each cell and applied the binomial formula (see earlier discussion). He noted that the results showed a 'consistent trend in the wrong direction', indicating that 'the predictions derived from the contingency model are invalid' (Vecchio, 1977, p.29).

Vecchio's investigation seems an adequate test of the contingency hypothesis. In many respects it is a very careful study, attention being paid to critical values and the validity of situational manipulations. Only the position-power manipulation seems questionable—the difference between high and low PP does not seem sufficient. Unfortunately, no data are available with which to evaluate this suspicion. In conclusion, Vecchio's study seems to test, but fails to support, Fiedler's CF.

Graen, Orris, and Alvares (1970)

These authors conducted two laboratory experiments, the second being a replication but with different tasks. These studies have been strongly criticized by Fiedler (1971a) who claimed that their procedures did not provide an adequate test of the CF. He used three arguments to support his position.

(a) It is difficult to produce high PP in a laboratory context. Fiedler argued that Graen *et al.*'s manipulations were inadequate; in particular, they did not result in fate control in the high PP condition. Furthermore, he argued that their practice of demoting a leader after one task session and promoting a member to leader status was likely to diminish PP. In sum, he claimed that no high PP situation was tested.

Graen *et al.* replied by citing the results of an indirect measure of PP. Leaders' reports of how much influence they felt themselves to have had. They concluded that their results 'though weak' were 'generally in the right direction' (p.207). This is true of the trends *within* each experiment, but comparison of the means across experiments does not support their claims (Hosking, 1978, p.41). Thus, the PP manipulation is open to question.

(b) Task structure was not adequately manipulated: the tasks did not differ sufficiently from each other. Graen *et al.* replied that their tasks were above and below the critical value quoted by Fiedler (1967), and that the mean ratings of those tasks (pre-existing data used for selection) were representative of those employed in previous studies. This is undoubtedly true (see, for example, Godfrey *et al.*, 1959; Meuwese and Fiedler, 1964).

(c) The distribution of LPC scores across octants was biased as a result of the random assignment procedure. To support this criticism Fiedler performed a one-way ANOVA on the LPC scores, with the octants as cells in the design. A significant F-ratio ($F = 3.1$, $p<0.01$) was obtained in the case of data from experiment 1. Graen and his colleagues investigated the issue further by conducting Scheffé analyses (Winer, 1962) to test all pairwise differences between the octant means. They found no significant comparisons at the 0.05 level. However, if the F-ratio was significant at 0.01, at least one comparison of the octant means should have produced a statistically reliable difference at the same level of significance (Keppel, 1973, p.89). It therefore seems that a fault was made either in the calculation of the F-ratio or in the Scheffé tests.

Examination of Fiedler's criticisms and Graen *et al.*'s 'defense' suggests that only his criticism of the position-power manipulation can be substantiated. As a result, the LPC/performance correlations should be reclassified into low PP octants. These data, regardless of whether they are classified by Graen *et al.* or reclassified into low PP octants, fail to support Fiedler's CF (see Table 4).

Hardy 1975

This is a slightly unusual test of the CF in that it was conducted with nine- and ten-year-old American *school children*. They were given a 'modified version' of the LPC scale to complete and persons were identified as being high (>87) or low (<44) LPC scorers. Groups of acquaintances were constructed on the basis of sociometric data. Poor GA was assumed to exist when the leader was working with those he identified as persons he would least like to work with, or when members had identified the leader as the one with whom they would least like to work (note the difference between these operational definitions). No good GA conditions were created.

Two tasks were selected as being either high or low TS (Hardy is not clear as to whether the choice was based on pre-existing data from Shaw, 1971). The supposedly structured task involved dot-to-dot line completion — whether or not this involved interacting relations seems doubtful. The position-power manipulations were similar to those employed in many laboratory studies: in the high PP condition, groups were told their leaders 'should be a real help' and would tell the teacher if anyone was slacking. In low PP conditions, groups were told their leader was 'no better than anyone else' and next time they could choose another.

Performance on the unstructured task was rated by three judges on three criteria; the scales were from 1 to 50. An objective score key was used for the structured task (maximum possible score = 40). Two ANOVAs were performed: one on the structured and the other on the unstructured task data. A main effect of LPC was hypothesized in comparisons of octants 5 and 6: this was found ($F = 1'7.3$, $p < 0.001$). Interactions between LPC and PP were hypothesized when comparing cells 7 and 8: mixed support was obtained depending on the criterion (three criteria and a total score were calculated). In particular, cell 8 received little support.

Whether or not this study constitutes an adequate test of the CF seems particularly difficult to determine. The age of the subjects, the fact that the LPC scale was modified, and the nature of the structured task (interacting?) all constitute departures from Fiedler's methodology. These departures are tentatively concluded to warrant rejection of this study as a valid test of Fiedler's hypothesis.

Shima (1968)

Shima used a variety of procedures to create/identify different leadership situations. These variations make it difficult to classify the study in the taxonomy currently being used. Having said this, type 3 seems the most accurate description.

The situational definitions were effected as follows: GA was measured using leader GA scores obtained after task performance. TS was supposedly manipulated by the use of different tasks; however, the criteria which guided their selection was not reported, and one of the tasks (the 'Unusual Uses Test') has been suggested to require co-action rather than interaction (Fiedler, 1967, p.128). The status of PP was described *a priori* as being high on the grounds that the leader was elected by his group. However, since the groups were ad hoc, this assumption seems dubious.

Leader ASo scores were correlated with group performance data on the structured and unstructured tasks. Correlations of -26 and $+71$ were obtained. The implications of these data depend on the octant to which they should correctly be assigned. This seems problematic. Ignoring for the moment the dubious nature of one of the structured tasks, and assuming that TS was manipulated, considerable doubt still remains regarding the octants tested. If, as Shima originally stated, (p.15) GA was 'moderate' (i.e. not poor?), PP was 'moderately strong' and TS varied from structured to unstructured, then octants 1 and 3 were tested. If, as he later stated (p.19) GA was moderately good in the structured task situation and moderately bad in the other task situation (deemed to be unstructured), then octants 1 and 7 were tested. If, as Fiedler (1971a, p.136) suggested, PP was in fact low, then octants 2 and 4 or 2 and 8 were tested (depending upon which of Shima's statements is accepted).

It is concluded that the results of this study are uninterpretable and therefore irrelevant to an empirical assessment of the CF.

Sashkin (1972)

American undergraduates acted as subjects for two experiments: one involving sixty, four-person groups of females, the second employing twenty-six groups of mixed sex. In the first experiment, leaders were assigned on the basis of their LPC score (values not given); they took the position of foreman in a role-play exercise where a decision has to be reached on the future working arrangements of three subordinates. Sashkin claimed that GA, TS, and PP were clearly defined and manipulated by the role-play materials, their effect being to create an octant 3 situation.

Whether or not Sashkin succeeded in testing octant 3 depends on the subjects' perceptions and acting-out of the play. In the first experiment, indirect evidence was obtained which suggested that GA was good, but no other validation data were collected. The status of the position-power manipulation seems particularly problematic: Fiedler has argued that high PP situations are difficult to contrive in a laboratory context — the leader seldom has fate control over his group (Fiedler, 1971a). Only if the subjects behaved *as if* the leader had such authority could the situation be described as high PP.

These doubts do not seem sufficient justification for dismissing Sashkin's data. Consequently, his correlations of -0.29 ($N = 53$, $p<0.05$), -19 ($N = 22$, ns), and -26 (combined, $N = 75$, $p<0.05$) have a bearing on Fiedler's CF. Whilst they are in the predicted direction and two of the three are significantly different from zero, their size suggests that the CF has little predictive strength in octant 3.

Shiflett and Nealey (1972)

These authors attempted a laboratory test of Fiedler's situational engineering hypothesis (Fiedler, 1965) using male undergraduates as subjects. Three-man groups were constructed to be homogeneous (high or low) on verbal ability and LPC scores (all moderate). The authors manipulated GA by informing the subjects that they were compatible with their fellow group members. This manipulation was validated by obtaining leader GA scores after task performance. TS was manipulated by selecting two unstructured tasks. Although this manipulation was not evaluated, similar tasks (writing TAT stories) have been found to be unstructured (Fiedler, 1967). Low and high PP conditions were contrived by the use of different instructions, but no validity checks were carried out.

These manipulations were designed to test octants 3 and 4 of Fiedler's CF. The results provided little support: analysis of variance failed to show a significant interaction between LPC and PP ($F<1$); and the LPC/performance correlations did not differ significantly from zero ($r = 16$, $r\,0.05$; $n = 16$).

Shiflett and Nealey manipulated the leadership situations in a number of ways not specified by Fiedler's specific hypothesis (see above). Consequently, the data have little bearing on the CF. However, since the data were consistent with contingency model predictions in the low ability groups, they suggest the CF may have predictive ability once other influential situational variables are added.

Johnson and Ryan (1976)

These researchers attempted to test the CF by manipulating leadership style and situational variables. One hundred and sixty students were assembled in four-man groups and a randomly selected person was instructed to act as a 'directive' or 'non-directive' leader. GA was assumed to be good (and was validated); TS was varied by the use of two tasks employed by Shaw and Blum (see below); and PP was manipulated by giving the leader more (or the same) information about the task, and authority (or more) to distribute financial rewards.

Leader LPC scores were correlated with group performance data in octants 1, 2, 3, and 4. In order, the coefficients were 0.01, 0.16, 0.15, and -0.30. Unfortunately, since leader behaviour was manipulated, these coefficients are uninterpretable and the CF was not tested.

Discussion of Type 3A Studies

The common feature of studies in cell 3A is (by definition) the use of experimental variations and a general absence of formal measurements. Consequently, the only way of assessing whether Fiedler's CF was tested is by examining the experimental procedures and the face validity of the manipulations. The studies by Fiedler (1966), Chemers and Skryzpek (1972), Vecchio (1977),

Graen *et al.* (1971), and Sashkin (1972) proved to be adequate when judged against the criteria established earlier in this chapter. The results of these investigations suggest that LPC/performance relationships account for a very small porportion of the total variation in group productivity. A few large correlations were obtained (for example 0.77, 0.72, and 0.60), these being found at the extremes of the SF dimension. More usually, the correlations are small and unreliable, and range from positive to negative in all but two of the octants (1 and 5). Only in octant 1 are the correlations large *and* in the direction predicted by the CF. Consequently, these results provide little support for Fiedler's contingency hypothesis.

DESCRIPTION AND ANALYSIS OF TYPE 3B STUDIES

Five studies are of this type: Rice and Chemers (1973); Hovey (1974); Reavis and Derlega (1976); Shaw and Blum (1966); and Michaelsen (1973). Two of the investigations involved emergent leaders (as did, for example, the study by Fiedler, 1966), whilst the remainder manipulated the behaviour of appointed leaders. The first four described all examined ad hoc groups whilst Michaelsen studied supervisors and their work-groups.

Rice and Chemers (1973)

This study was designed to test predictions regarding the leadership style (LPC score of emergent leaders. Eighteen four-man groups of equal numbers of high and low LPC scorers (critical values not given) were assembled. Nine groups were assigned a task assumed to be structured (as task similar to that employed by Chemers and Skryzpek, 1972); the remainder composed stories based upon a TAT card (similar tasks have been classified as unstructured in other studies).

It was assumed that group members would be competing for leadership, and that group atmosphere would therefore be poor. Presumably the authors are arguing that group structures were still in the process of development and role-differentiation had not yet stabilized. However, 'leaders' were identified after task performance by asking members to indicate who had emerged as 'the leader'. Thus, the logic underlying their assumption that GA was necessarily poor, seems contradicted.

A related point concerns the questions they asked in identifying group leaders. Simply asking 'who emerged as the leader?' seems likely to result in different nominations depending on the ways in which the group members construed the term 'leader'. Furthermore, whether or not they adopted the definition of leader given by Fiedler (1967) seems problematic. PP was assumed to be low on the grounds that emergent leaders have no formal authority. This seems a reasonable assumption.

In sum, the author's conclusions regarding the status of TS and PP have acceptable face validity. That GA was poor seems more dubious, as does their method of identifying the leader. However, in the absence of firm evidence to the contrary, this study is tentatively accepted as a valid test of the CF. Consequently, the correlations of $+0.3$ and -0.4 may be assigned to the appropriate octants (6 and 8, respectively) and examined in terms of their implications for the CF. Neither are statistically reliable, but the correlation of -0.4 is in the direction predicted by the CF (no prediction for octant 6).

Hovey (1974)

Hovey attempted a validation study involving sixteen self-selected groups working on a 'highly unstructured, complex' research project lasting approximately six weeks. At the end of this time a leader was identified by asking the group members (students) who was the most influential member, and whom they considered the definite leader. Prior to the project, subjects' LPC scores had been obtained using one of Fiedler's scales, but with clarifying instructions. No information was given on the operational definitions of high and low LPC.

Group members rated GA on a number of measures which were then combined and stratified to produce classifications of good and poor GA. PP was assumed to be low and the task was assumed to be unstructured. A variety of dependent variables were measured including members' ratings of the effort they put into the project, their ratings of the quality of their report, and the instructor's ratings of the report. Only the latter are considered since they provide a source of data most similar to that reported by Fiedler (1967).

If Hovey's categorization of the situational variables was valid, octants 4 and 8 were tested, the correlations between leader LPC scores and group performance being -36 and -59, respectively. Since the face validity of the situational classifications seems reasonably high, this study is tentatively concluded as a valid test of Fiedler's contingency hypothesis. Neither correlation was statistically reliable, and only one was in the direction predicted by the CF (-59, octant 8).

Reavis and Derlega (1976)

These authors set out to test hypotheses 'derived from Fiedler's contingency model' (Reavis and Derlega, 1976, p.221). They attempted to do so by studying eight classroom groups each consisting of twenty-three male pupils. Their methodology departed from that described by Fiedler (1967) in a number of significant ways: the groups were considerably larger than those normally studied; group relations were said to be (and seemed to be) co-acting rather than interacting; leader behaviour was manipulated; and no LPC scores were obtained. These procedural differences justify rejection of this study as a valid test of Fiedler's CF (see above).

Shaw and Blum (1966)

Fiedler (1971) defined this study as a test of the 'more general hypothesis' and concluded that the results 'conform[ed] to the general expectations of the model' (p.141). However, not one of the operational dimensions of Fiedler's CF was measured, including LPC. Instead, Shaw and Blum made *a priori* assumptions about the status of situational variables, and assumed that they had manipulated LPC scores by manipulating leader behaviour. As has already been noted, manipulations of leader behaviour cannot be assumed to result in predictable variations in LPC scores.

It is concluded that this study is irrelevant to an assessment of Fiedler's CF.

Michaelsen (1973)

The methodology of this study was similar to that performed by Shaw and Blum. The status of two situational variables was assumed *a priori*, and the third, group atmosphere, was measured using items quite different from those employed by Fiedler (1967). Leaders described their own behaviour on a 'human relations' and a 'theory X' index, and these scores were used to predict effectiveness in situations of low, moderate, and high SF. Whilst Michaelsen regarded his results as providing support for Fiedler's CF, it is concluded that his procedures render the study inadequate as a test of the CF.

Conclusions: Type 3B Studies

The studies by Shaw and Blum, Reavis and Derlega, and Michaelsen were regarded as inadequate tests of the CF, largely because the authors manipulated (or measured) leader behaviour and failed to obtain LPC scores. The validity of Rice and Chemers' and Hovey's investigations was more difficult to assess, but they are tentatively concluded to be adequate tests; consequently, the resulting correlations may be used to evaluate the CF. None of the four correlations was statistically significant, although two were 0.4 or larger. These data will be considered along with those from other adequate studies when drawing conclusions about the combined weight of evidence for or against the contingency hypothesis.

DISCUSSION AND ANALYSIS OF TYPE 4 STUDIES

Three of the studies discussed by Fiedler (1971) were of this type: Fiedler, O'Brien, and Ilgen (1969); O'Brien (1969); and Kretzschmar and Luecke (1969).

To these may be added three studies which have appeared since 1971: Csoka and Fiedler (1972); Csoka (1974); and Hewett, O'Brien, and Hornik (1974).

The two investigations by O'Brien and his colleagues were laboratory experiments involving ad hoc groups of male and female students. The remainder were field studies: three dealt with formally appointed leaders (military personnel or managers) whilst Fiedler *et al.* (1969) identified emergent leaders. The situational variables were typically measured, but operational definitions of the levels of these variables were seldom provided.

Fiedler, O'Brien, and Ilgen (1969)

These authors studied volunteer public health and community development teams working for three weeks in Honduras. Leaders were identified at the end of the project by asking group members to state which of their team-mates they would prefer as a leader in a similar situation. Leader GA scores (Fiedler, 1967) were obtained at the end of the project. TS was not measured owing to the wide variety of tasks performed by the group, and PP was judged to be irrelevant on the grounds that the leaders were emergent. SF was therefore measured by the use of GA scores and ratings of 'environmental stress' provided by the project director. Group performance ratings (six criteria) were obtained from various personnel on the project.

Both the authors and Fiedler (1971) judged this study to provide support for the CF. However, it is impossible to determine the relationship between SF as defined in this study and SF as defined by Fiedler (1967). Claims that this study tested Fiedler's hypothesis rest on numerous assumptions of unknown validity. Consequently, this study is regarded as having no bearing on Fiedler's CF. However, a number of sizeable correlations were obtained between leader LPC scores and group performance, suggesting that these variables are related.

Kretzschmar and Luecke (1969)

Fiedler (1971) cited this study but judged it to be unclassifiable and consequently ignored it when evaluating empirical support for the CF. He gave two reasons for adopting this line: leaders' ratings of the situational variables were obtained, and leaders rated their own performance. This line of reasoning seems perfectly valid: when leaders rate the situational variables, the definition of SF is not independent of the leader.

Csoka and Fiedler (1972)

Members of the American armed forces acted as subjects for this study. Army sergeants, petty officers, and unit commanders completed the following scales: LPC (Fiedler, 1967), GA (Fiedler, 1967), the Henmon–Nelson Tests of Mental

Ability, and a questionnaire assessing the length of their leadership experience (no details given). Their performance was rated by two or three of their superiors (no details given).

SF was defined in terms of three variables, each being stratified into two levels, and each level combined with each to produce eight cells. The variables were defined and ordered as follows: group atmosphere, leadership experience, and leader intelligence. These eight cells were then argued to be equivalent to octants 1, 3, 5, and 8 of the original contingency graph.

The results of this study are irrelevant to an empirical assessment of Fiedler's CF: two of the so-called situational variables are in fact attributes of the leader and should therefore be treated as predictor variables, not situational moderators; the authors' ordering of their 'situational' variables is complete speculation, as is their labelling of the situations thus identified as equivalent to certain octants in the original contingency graph (see Figure 1). These assumptions and procedures render Csoka and Fiedler's study an inadequate test of the CF. However, the LPC/performance correlations suggest that leader LPC scores are related to productivity (fourteen of the twenty correlations were larger than 0.5, and nine of them were reliable).

Csoka (1974)

The measures, definitions, and procedures employed in this study are identical to those reported by Csoka and Fiedler (1972). Similar subjects were also studied with the addition of a sample of fifty-two mess-unit sergeants. This being the case, the same criticisms apply and the study is irrelevant to an empirical assessment of Fiedler's CF. However, as with Csoka and Fiedler, the size and reliability of the correlations suggests that leader LPC scores and performance are related.

O'Brien (1969)

This experiment was designed to test Fiedler's CF using the techniques of structural role theory. SF was defined in terms of the leader's 'potential influence'. This in turn was defined as 'the ratio between the number of paths connecting (the leader) to the task system and the total number of paths between persons and tasks' (O'Brien, 1969, p.282). It was assumed that SF would be more favourable the 'greater the amount of access he has to elements of the task system' (p.282).

The relationships between three elements (persons, positions, and tasks) were respectively defined as 'interpersonal relations', 'legitimate power', and 'precedence relations between sub-tasks'. These relations were manipulated in order to achieve different levels of SF: low, medium, and high. O'Brien obtained a large, highly significant correlation between LPC and group effectiveness in the medium SF condition ($r = 0.77$, $p < 0.01$) but small, non-significant correlations when SF was high ($r = 0.08$) or low ($r = 0.13$). O'Brien commented that these data were 'consistent with predictions derived from the contingency model' (p.288).

There are at least two reasons why O'Brien's conclusion cannot be accepted. First, the manipulation of potential influence also manipulated leader behaviour. Secondly, it is not at all clear how O'Brien's definition of potential influence corresponds with Fiedler's definition of situational favourableness. Consequently, O'Brien's data cannot be used to test the CF.

Hewett, O'Brien, and Hornik (1974)

Thirty-two, three-person groups of American undergraduates (male and female) were required to construct as many molecular models as possible in 40 minutes. Their method of work organization was manipulated by instruction, such that one of four types was employed (two levels of coordination and two of collaboration). The 'interpersonal compatability' of the group members was manipulated such that half the groups were compatible and half incompatible (Shutz, 1958). Groups were also assigned either a high LPC ($\bar{X} = 83$) or low LPC leader ($\bar{X} = 34$).

Group performance was assessed in terms of quantity and quality of output. Each set of scores was analysed using a four-way, fixed effects ANOVA (coordination × collaboration × LPC × compatibility). No significant effects were observed for quality and when quantity was taken as the dependent variable, no significant effects were observed for LPC. Unfortunately the implications of these findings for the meaning/utility of LPC scores are obscure since the behaviour of group leaders was manipulated.

Conclusions: Type 4 Studies

Not one of these studies constitutes an adequate test of the CF: the relationship between the authors' definitions of SF and those which define the contingency hypothesis are impossible to determine. Furthermore, in a number of the studies the individual-difference metric was confounded with the situational metric: a conceptual and methodological error which renders LPC/performance relationships meaningless. Consequently, the only value of these studies, or rather those in which leader behaviour was not manipulated (i.e. Fiedler, O'Brien, and Ilgen, 1969; Csoka and Fiedler, 1972; and Csoka, 1974) is to demonstrate that LPC scores and group performance are significantly associated. These findings in turn suggest that, given a valid situational metric, LPC may be a useful predictor of leadership effectiveness.

DISCUSSION AND ANALYSIS OF TYPE 5 STUDIES

Studies of this type are characterized by a general absence of situational measures, and by a conceptualization of favourableness in terms other than GA, TS, and PP. Fiedler (1971) cited one such study—by Nealey and Blood (1967)—to which may be added the investigation by Hardy and Bohren (1975). Both suffer from severe deficiencies which render them inadequate as tests of the CF.

Nealey and Blood (1968)

This was a field study designed to investigate variations in leadership demands from one organizational level to another. LPC scores were obtained from first and second level hospital supervisors, their performance being rated by their immediate superiors. The resultant LPC/performance correlations were -22 (first level supervisors, $N = 21$) and $+0.79$ ($N = 8$, $p<0.01$). Fiedler (1971) argued that the *major difference* between two levels of supervision was in the extent to which their subordinates' tasks were structured. Such arguments led him to conclude support for the CF. Clearly this post-hoc interpretation depends on numerous assumptions which are not even face valid. It also relies upon a novel distinction (as far as Fiedler's model is concerned) between the structure of the leaders's task and the structure of the subordinate's task. Consequently, this study has no bearing on the validity of the CF but the data suggest that leader LPC and group performance may be related.

Hardy and Bohren (1975)

University lecturers and their students were the subjects of this study. Students rated their lecturers' ('leaders') effectiveness (note that *leader*, not group performance is being measured here) on a 'student reaction to courses' scale. The authors proposed a revised sixteen-cell version of Fiedler's model, having organizational complexity (seemingly size) as the most important variable. Simple/complex situations were viewed as being more or less favourable depending on the experience of the leaders. They claimed to have tested cells 9 and 15 of the revised model, and obtained results supportive of cell 15. The relevance of this study to Fiedler's CF seems obscure since it is impossible to deduce the relationship between the author's definition of SF and Fiedler's. Furthermore, it seems likely that one of Fiedler's limiting conditions was contravened: the groups were study groups and probably did not have interacting relations (see, for example, Reavis and Derlega, 1976, p.221: 'the typical classroom represents a co-acting group').

Discussion of Type 5 Studies

These studies are of little value with respect to Fiedler's CF. At best they may suggest LPC scores and group performance are correlated. The authors' claims that certain situational variables moderate these relationships rest on a very high level of inference, as do their unsubstantiated assumptions that the results reflect on the CF.

CLASSIFICATION OF VALIDATION STUDIES IN TERMS OF PROCEDURAL VARIATIONS AND THEIR IMPLICATIONS

During the years 1970–73, a number of reviews of Fiedler's model were published. Even when they examined the same studies, the reviewers disagreed about the implications of the data (see earlier). Furthermore, some reviewers cited studies as tests of the CF simply because the author(s) or Fiedler said they were. In this chapter it has been argued that a distinction should be drawn between adequate and inadequate tests of Fiedler's hypothesis. The grounds on which this distinction should be made have already been described. In addition, a further distinction may be drawn between inadequate studies which produce uninterpretable results, and those which test contingencies other than Fiedler's (see Table 3).

Table 3   Classification of studies according to their judged adequacy as test of Fiedler's contingency hypothesis

Type	Adequate	Uninterpretable	Test of other contingencies
1	Hardy (1971) Hardy *et al.* (1973) Schneier (1978)		Csoka (1975)
2	Hunt (1969) Hill (1967)		
3A	Fiedler (1966) Chemers and Skryzpek (1972) Vecchio (1977) Graen *et al.* (1970) Sashkin (1972)	Shima (1968) Johnson and Ryan (1976) Hardy (1975)	Shiflett and Nealey (1972)
B	Rice and Chemers (1973) Hovey (1974)	Reavis and Derlega (1976) Michaelsen (1973)	Shaw and Blum (1966)
4		O'Brien (1969) Hewett *et al.* (1974) Kretzschmar and Luecke (1969)	Fiedler *et al.* (1969) Csoka and Fiedler (1972) Csoka (1974)
5		Hardy and Bohren (1975) Nealey and Blood (1967)	

Classification of Studies: Adequate, Uninterpretable, or Tests of Other Contingencies

To summarize the earlier discussion, certain procedures render LPC/performance relationships *uninterpretable*.

(a) Manipulations of leader behaviours: since complex relationships exist between LPC scores and leader behaviour such manipulations confound the LPC/performance relationships (see O'Brien, 1969; Hewett *et al.*, 1974; Reavis and Derlega, 1976; Johnson and Ryan, 1976).

(b) Leaders or groups rate their own performance: their performance descriptions may reflect many different sources of variation (see Kretzschmar and Luecke, 1969): thus, relationships with LPC scores are unintelligible.

Studies characterized by these procedures provide correlations which tell us nothing about the validity of the contingency graph, and fail to provide data from which it can be concluded that LPC scores and group performance are related. Other studies provide data which are uninterpretable with respect to Fiedler's CF, but may provide results which suggest significant relationships between LPC scores and group performance. This is the case when:

(c) the data cannot be classified in definable situations (see, for example, Shima, 1968; Nealey and Blood, 1967); and

(d) doubt exists as to whether or not Fiedler's limiting conditions were met (for example, Hardy, 1975).

Other contingencies are tested when the following conditions are met.

(a) When leader behaviour scores are correlated with group performance (ignoring LPC) and the results can be described according to the situation in which they were obtained (Shaw and Blum, 1966).

(b) When LPC/performance relationships are examined in defined situations which cannot be interpreted in terms of SF (see, for example, Fiedler, O'Brien, and Ilgen, 1969). Note that each defined situation should be treated separately from each other (i.e. each is a separate hypothesis); strictly speaking no dimension can be induced.

(c) When some aspects of the 'situation' are measured by *leader* characteristics (see, for example, Csoka and Fiedler, 1972; Csoka, 1974). Whilst this is conceptually unsatisfactory, and implies a very different contingency from that proposed by Fiedler, the results do have implications for contingency theories in general.

(d) When leaders describe their own situations. Again, such procedures produce a very different contingency from that described by Fiedler (1967). The results of such studies simply show that leaders who vary in their *perceptions* of certain situations also vary in respect of the relationship between their LPC score and group productivity (see Csoka, 1975).

The results of such studies provide evidence of contingencies; however, the reliability of this evidence must be assessed. If large, reliable

LPC/performance correlations are obtained, these suggest that LPC scores *may* be useful predictors of group performance.

VALIDATION STUDIES: ANALYSIS OF RESULTS

Having identified those studies which constitute adequate tests of the CF, it becomes possible to assess the extent to which they provide it with empirical support. Most of the data consists of correlation coefficients (see Table 4) which, strictly speaking, provide the only valid means of testing the CF.

Table 4   Correlations obtained in adequate tests of the CF

Type	Authors	Octants							
		1	2	3	4	5	6	7	8
1	Schneier (1978)		−0.55[c]						
2	Hill (1967)		−0.10	−0.29			−0.24	+0.62[a]	
	Hunt (1969)	−0.64		+0.60		+0.21		+0.30	
		−0.51		−0.80				−0.30	
3A	Fiedler (1966)	−0.72	+0.50	−0.16	+0.13	+0.16	+0.14	+0.26	+0.60
		−0.77	+0.37	−0.54	+0.08	+0.03	+0.07	−0.27	−0.37
	Chemers and Skryzpek (1972)	−0.43	−0.32	+0.10	+0.35	+0.28	+0.13	+0.08	−0.33
	Graen *et al.* (1971)		+0.18		+0.33		+0.39		+0.44
			−0.41		−0.08		−0.43		−0.33
	(reclassified)		+0.47		+0.46		+0.25		+0.45
			−0.13		+0.02		−0.52		+0.43
	Sashkin (1972)			−0.26[b]					
3B	Rice and Chemers (1973)						+0.30		−0.40
	Hovey (1974)				−0.36				−0.59

[a]$p<0.10$.
[b]$p<0.05$.
[c]$p<0.001$.

Earlier in this chapter it was noted that few validation coefficients are reliably different from zero, and that this is attributable, at least in part, to the small samples on which they are based. Other means of assessment were reviewed and it was argued that sizeable coefficients, consistent in size and direction, should be looked for within each octant of the contingency graph. The validation coefficients will now be examined against these criteria.

Size of Correlations

The size of LPC/performance correlations is of significance inasmuch as sizeable *r*-values are a minimum requirement for LPC scores to have predictive utility. Of the 56 correlations on which the contingency was based, 53 percent were larger than 0.4. Fewer sizeable correlations were obtained in the adequate validation studies: 22/57 were equal to, or more than, 0.4 (i.e. approximately 38 percent). In addition, there was considerable variation between octants. For example, in octant 1, all five r-values were greater than 0.4, whilst in octant 5 none of them was. The larger correlations appear at the extremes of the contingency graph; in addition the only median r larger than 0.4 occurs in octant 1. This was in the predicted direction.

Sign of Correlations

Fiedler evaluates support for his CF by the number of correlations in the predicted direction. His prediction for each octant is indicated by the sign (+ or -) of the median r which defines the CF. Taking this as the criterion, 71 percent were in the direction predicted (41/57). Again, there were considerable differences between octants: four of the nine correlations in octant 8 were contrary to prediction (note: two were reclassified from the Graen *et al.* study), whilst in octant 1 none of them was (see Table 4).

Range of Correlations

The variation about the medians should be taken into account when determining the validity of the CF. For example, if all the validation study medians were as predicted, but the r-values within each octant varied from positive to negative, this would indicate little support. The data shown in Figure 2 shows substantial variation about the medians, particularly in octants 2, 3, 6, 7, and 8. Of even greater concern is the fact that the variation extends from positive to negative in all but two of the octants. When compared with the correlations upon which the CF was based, the validation data show more variation in octants 2, 7, and 8.

Results of Analyses of Variance

Three of the 'adequate' studies employed analysis of variance. The studies by Hardy (1971) and Hardy *et al.* (1973) produced cell means which show significant differences between high and low LPC leaders in octants 1, 3, 4, and 6, but not in 2 and 8. These mean differences are small, but since they are statistically significant they provide some support for the CF. Vecchio presented his results in a way that cannot easily be summarized with precision. However, very few significant findings were obtained and Fiedler's CF was not validated.

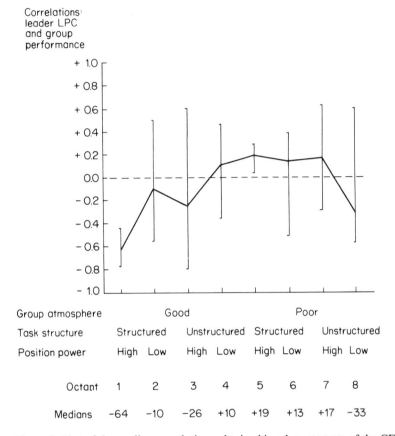

Figure 2. Plot of the median correlations obtained in adequate tests of the CF

IMPLICATIONS OF THE VALIDATION DATA

In the first Carbondale Leadership Symposium, Ralph Stogdill commented that 'Fiedler's LPC measure appears to be the one leadership variable that is consistently *related* to performance' (Stogdill, 1973, p.103; emphasis added). Whether or not these variables are associated can be judged by the size and statistical significance of LPC/performance correlations.

As has already been noted, just over a third of the correlations from the adequate studies are equal to, or greater than, 0.4 (see Table 4). To these may be added the results of studies which failed to test the CF, but obtained interpretable LPC/performance correlations. Six investigations are of this type: Shaw and Blum (1966), Fiedler *et al.* (1969), Shiflett and Nealey (1972), Csoka and Fiedler (1972), Csoka (1974), and Csoka (1975). Together they obtained fifty-three correlations of which 75 percent (40/53) were at least as big as 0.4. Furthermore, 41 percent (22/53) were statistically significant ($p<0.05$).

These results seem exceptional on the grounds that it is unusual to find sizeable relationships between individual-difference variables and group performance (Morley and Stephenson, 1977). However, the situation is similar to that faced by Fiedler over twenty years ago, and a valid interpretation of the data is yet to be found. Later in this chapter it will be argued that this situation is unlikely to change.

Stogdill's conclusion that leader LPC scores and group performance are related has empirical support; however, whether any causal relationship exists is quite another matter. Furthermore, it is one about which we have little information since relationships between LPC scores and group performance have usually been indicated by static correlation coefficients. Despite this, theorists have made causal inferences, arguing that variations in LPC scores cause variations in group performance. For example, Fiedler has for many years recommended that leaders should be placed in situations that match their LPC score, or should 'engineer' their job so that a match is achieved (Fiedler, 1965). Such recommendations ignore the possibility that variations in group performance might affect changes in leader LPC scores, or that reciprocal causation might characterize the relationships. Consideration of *how* variations in leader LPC scores might affect group performance (that is, the linkage) render such possibilities highly likely. Presumably leader LPC scores must be related (however obscure the relationship) with leader behaviour, and the effects of group performance on leader behaviour have been known for some time (see, for example, Lowin and Craig, 1968; Greene, 1975).

The primary purpose of this chapter is to establish whether or not leader LPC scores and group performance are reliably associated in the manner predicted by Fiedler's contingency hypothesis. Analysis of the sign, size, and variation of correlations within octants shows that his CF has little empirical support. Whilst the sign of the coefficients is usually as predicted, the median 'curve' differs considerably from that which defines the CF and there is substantial variation within most octants. Only in octant 1 is there a sizeable median comparable to Fiedler's and every correlation in the predicted direction (see Figure 2). The only possible conclusion seems to be that LPC scores do not predict group performance except in octant 1 of the contingency graph. Whilst there will undoubtedly be those who will argue that these data show sufficient consistency to demand an explanation—whether or not it is Fiedler's—this position is untenable. This is because it relies on two assumptions: that leader LPC scores are reliable, and that Fiedler's situational metric is of acceptable validity. In the next section it will be argued that neither of these views are valid.

FIEDLER'S CONTINGENCY MODEL:
SUMMARY AND CONCLUSIONS

The results of this critique suggest that LPC scores correlate with group performance; however, sometimes the relationships are positive and sometimes they are negative. Whilst Fiedler has hypothesized that the direction of the correlations depends on interactions between group atmosphere, task structure, an position-power, the weight of evidence does not support his claim. This conclusion raises the question as to whether or not Fiedler's contingency model should be abandoned in favour of some other approach. A satisfactory answer requires consideration of more than just the weight of empirical support for the CF—some basic methodological and theoretical issues also require comment.

Methodological Problems Associated with Fiedler's CF

As was noted at the beginning of this chapter, Fiedler's measures of his situational variables have been subjected to severe and valid criticisms (see, for example, McMahon, 1972; Ashour, 1973a). In particular, one of the methods he used to measure GA is not independent of the leader—yet his 'situational favourableness' is conceptualized as an independent dimension. His method of combining GA, TS, and PP has also received criticism: no sufficient logic exists for the manner in which the variables are combined and ordered; critical values for stratifying the variables have seldom been employed; and dichotomized variables are interpreted as a *dimension* of favourableness. In addition, Korman and Tanofsky (1975) have detailed a number of problems associated with contingency theorizing which seem particularly relevant to Fiedler's model. Furthermore, it seems that the methods Fiedler uses to identify the *leader* may cause LPC scores to be obtained from persons who do not actually perform the leadership function. One consequence of this is that Fiedler's conceptual and operational definitions of the model differ.

Having identified the leader, Fiedler has used at least four different sets of scales to obtain an LPC score. These measures may correlate in different ways with group performance, and may do so for different reasons; in other words scores derived from different LPC scales may mean different things. A further problem with LPC scores is their questionable test–retest reliability—the coefficients are variable and often unacceptably low (see reviews by Hosking, 1978; and Schriesheim and Kerr, 1977). If LPC scores are unstable, so will be their relationships with other variables. Low stability coefficients also suggest that LPC scores do not reflect any stable, underlying characteristic of leaders.

Once LPC scores are obtained, Fiedler correlates these with group performance. He has used a variety of techniques for assessing the significance of these data, but has denied the legitimacy of the conventional criteria of *statistical significance*. These practices lead to a number of weighty problems, not the least of which concerns the criteria by which the CF can legitimately be evaluated. These methodological problems are evident both in the studies from which the hypothesis (CF) was derived and in the validation attempts. Their only solution lies in the development of new measures and procedures, in other words in the development of a new contingency model.

Theoretical Shortcomings of Fiedler's Model

Fiedler argues that a leader's effectiveness is contingent upon the relationship between his (or her) LPC score and 'situational favourableness'. His explanation of this contingency is incomplete and, as far as it goes, is entirely speculative. First, the meaning of LPC scores is obscure. One of his earliest interpretations was that high and low LPC scorers behave in different and predictable ways (Fiedler, 1958). This interpretation lacks empirical support, as do subsequent 'explanations' in terms of goal-hierarchies and 'differentiation matching' (Hosking, 1979a, 1979b). Investigations of LPC scores in terms of more general information-processing dimensions have also failed to cast light on their meaning (Hosking, 1978). In sum, no satisfactory interpretation of LPC scores exists. Whilst they appear to reflect complex differences in leader behaviour, these differences cannot be described with any precision owing to the absence of a valid metric for describing leadership situations.

Not knowing what LPC scores mean also implies not knowing why they should be expected to correlate with group performance. Furthermore, not only are we unaware of what high and low LPC leaders do, but we are also ignorant of group members' reactions to the leader, and how group members behave in the (supposedly) different situations. Models of leadership effectiveness are incomplete when they fail to specify these linkages (see Schriesheim *et al.*, 1978; Child and Hosking, 1978).

As was pointed out by Korman (1973), Fiedler's model, like many others, assumes that the situation in which the leader and his group are operating is reasonably unchanging. This static view of leadership situations may constitute a gross misrepresentation of reality. The relative dearth of longitudinal studies makes it difficult to evaluate Fiedler's assumption, but indirect evidence exists which casts serious doubt on its validity (see, for example, McCall, 1977). These various shortcomings all reduce the theoretical adequacy of Fiedler's model.

Implications of These Inadequacies

Empirically-based models are presumably intended to have practical utility (e.g. for selection and training), and provide fruitful directions for future research. The theoretical and methodological shortcomings of Fiedler's model, when taken with the fact that it lacks empirical support, suggest that it is unable to serve either of the above purposes.

Practical Utility

Shortly after his model was first published, Fiedler suggested it could be used to 'engineer the job to fit the manager' (Fiedler, 1965). At the time it was a relatively novel suggestion. Since then he and his colleagues have produced a self-instruction manual, based on the contingency model, designed to provide a valid means for selection, placement, and 'job engineering' (Fiedler, Chemers, and Mahar, 1976). It appears that this manual is being widely used for just these purposes (see the Foreword to Fiedler, Chemers, and Mahar, 1976). The preceding discussion suggests that Fiedler's model is incapable of providing a valid base for such practices, and indeed may do more harm than good (see Hosking and Schriesheim, 1978).

Fiedler's Model as a Guide for Future Research

Considerable effort has been devoted to testing the various aspects of Fiedler's model. To use Argyris's expression, the results of these efforts have not been 'additive' (Argyris, 1978). Twenty years of investigations into the meaning of ASo/LPC scores have failed to produce a valid interpretation, and fifteen years of research into the validity of the CF has left reviewers still arguing over its support. Given the methodological and theoretical shortcomings of the model, there seems little reason to suppose that this will change.

WHAT SHOULD A THEORY OF LEADERSHIP EFFECTIVENESS LOOK LIKE?

Having concluded that Fiedler's model has outlived its usefulness, the question arises as to what should take its place. Answers will be sought by examining past and current approaches and the criticisms that have been levelled against them. This will indicate the sorts of decisions that are involved in theory construction.

Factors requiring Consideration

Whatever the theorist's particular area of interest or objectives, decisions must be made: first about how to conceptualize the variables; secondly, the level of analysis at which the theory should be focused; thirdly, how to conceptualize and explain the relations between the variables; and fourthly, how to make the theory operational.

Identifying the 'Leader'

This term has been employed in a great many ways, often with such a lack of precision that it is difficult to determine who would be excluded by the definition. Gibb (1969) identified eight *varieties* of definition which differ in a number of important ways. For example, some exclude the possibility that more than one leader may exist within a particular group at a given time, whilst others do not (compare Bales, 1955, with Fiedler, 1967). Leaders may be identified by the behaviours they employ (e.g. Hemphill, 1956); by the consequences of those behaviours in terms of influence (Hollander, 1978); or by changes in group performance (Cattell, 1951). Otherwise they may be observed by the functions they perform or by the fact that they have been formally appointed to a particular role position with 'legitimate' authority (Fiedler, 1967).

Empirical research into leadership and leadership effectiveness has often been conducted with lower levels of management in organizations. Supervisors have been deemed to be leaders, either by definition — because they have been formally appointed in charge of other people's job performance — or the researcher has assumed that the supervisor is a leader in some other sense (e.g. they perform certain functions or influence group performance). This practice has resulted in the neglect of certain definitions and has led to comments of the sort that lower-level managers may only be leaders in a very restricted sense. For example, they may have relatively few leadership functions to perform (see McCall, 1977) or may have relatively little influence when compared with, say, the shop-steward.

A variety of possibilities exist if a functional definition of leadership is adopted. These functions may be found to be distributed amongst a number of persons within a group (see Katz and Kahn, 1978), none of whom was formally appointed to perform such functions. Furthermore, some may be performed not by people but by, for example, payment systems, job design, or performance appraisal procedures. Kerr's discussion of 'substitutes for leadership' reflects this viewpoint (Kerr, 1976); however, like other theorists, Kerr retains the concept of a leader as a person. It may be that certain leadership functions can only be performed by a person (e.g. handling inter-personal conflict within a group), but this is a matter for research and theory development.

Leaders and Leadership

Some do not distinguish between these terms whilst others define them quite differently. Hollander (1978) adopts the latter viewpoint by viewing *leaders* as people who influence others, whilst *leadership* is seen as a *process* of which the leader is only a part. Returning to the view of leaders as persons who perform specified functions, if certain procedures and aspects of organization design also enact these functions, the terms 'leader' and 'leadership' have very different meanings.

Leadership Effectiveness

Some theorists have chosen to distinguish between leadership and leadership effectiveness. For example, *leadership* may be defined in terms of the performance of certain behaviours, and *effectiveness* may be assessed in terms of the consequences of those behaviours (Reddin, 1970; Fleishman, 1973). Others define leadership in terms of its consequences, in which case leadership and leadership effectiveness are synonymous (see, for example, Cattell, 1951). Researchers have usually attempted to measure leadership effectiveness by examining the relationship between certain leader behaviours and selected aspects of group performance. Criterion measures have included quantity and quality of production, scrap levels, and quality of decision-making. Factors such as subordinate job satisfaction, satisfaction with supervision, and labour turnover have also been employed. It is important to appreciate that when aspects of group performance are measured as indicators of leadership effectiveness, the researchers' concern has been to understand and predict leadership effectiveness, not develop a more general theory of group performance.

The Level of Analysis at Which the Theory Operates

Early research and theory development was conducted at the level of the individual. The personal characteristics of 'leaders' and 'non-leaders' (their personality traits, intelligence, physical strength, etc.) were investigated without reference to the situations in which they were operating. In the late 1940s researchers turned their attention to leader behaviour, and in particular to its effects on the satisfaction and performance of individuals and groups. They also came to recognize the effects of group and task characteristics on leadership effectiveness. These findings encouraged the development of theories which root the concept of leadership in a work-group (for example, Cattell, 1951; Fiedler, 1967; Schriesheim, Mowday, and Stogdill, 1978). Indeed, there are theorists who believe that leadership and leadership effectiveness cannot be understood until an adequate theory of groups has been developed (see, for example, Fiedler, 1967, p.16; Thibaut and Kelley, 1959, p.290).

Whether or not the group is an appropriate level of analysis depends on a number of factors including the way in which leaders and leadership are conceptualized. It seems to have become fashionable to criticize this focus on leader–group interactions on the grounds that managers (who are also, in some sense, leaders) spend relatively small proportions of time with their work-group (see, for example, McCall, 1977, p.379). This criticism is not necessarily valid, for the reasons noted earlier. Furthermore, if *managerial* effectiveness is the object of prediction (as McCall implies), the observation that managers spend relatively little time with their subordinates simply implies that their leadership effectiveness may be relatively unimportant. A further criticism of this focus on leader–group interactions is that many work-groups may not be 'groups' at all but collections of individuals (see Herbst, 1970, for a distinction). Again, this is not a fundamental attack on the validity of such theories, but simply implies that they may have only a limited scope for application.

A number of authors have suggested that theories of leadership effectiveness conceptualize the context of leadership in too restricted a fashion. They have argued that environmental variables such as organization structure and control systems should be included as part of the conceptual framework (see, for example, Child and Hosking, 1978). Such arguments do not necessarily imply a shift in the level of analysis of the theories. They may only indicate the author's conviction that the addition of such variables would increase the ability of a theory to predict variations in leadership effectiveness. In other words, the type of theory being advocated could look like Fiedler's, but with the addition of environmental (as compared with situational) variables.

Some writers have clearly indicated their desire for theories of leadership effectiveness which have as their level of analysis not leader–group interactions, but leader–system interactions (see, for example, McCall, 1977, p.379). Theories of this sort would clearly look very different from the contingency theories which continue to dominate the literature (such as Fiedler, 1967; Vroom and Yetton, 1973; House, 1973). For example, whilst the leader could be identified using one of a number of current definitions (such as formal appointment), a wider range of variables and a greater variety of possible interrelations would be considered. A possible problem with this level of analysis is that it becomes difficult to distinguish between theories of leadership, managerial, and organizational effectiveness. Focusing at the level of leader-system interactions would also increase the number of possible mechanisms of leadership and leadership effectiveness. These issues—relations between variables, and mechanisms of cause and effect—represent fundamental decisions in theory development and will be considered next.

Relations between Leader Characteristics and Effectiveness— Issues of Cause and Effect

Specified characteristics of the leader have usually been conceptualized as independent variables which influence subordinate satisfaction and/or aspects of group performance in different ways depending on the status of situational moderators (group cohesion, clarity of task–role requirements, the position-power of the leader, etc.). The contingency models devised by Fiedler (1967) and House (1973) provide well-known examples of this approach.

Different theoretical frameworks are clearly possible. For example, situational factors could be viewed as dependent variables, some of which may be susceptible to influence by the leader. The degree to which leaders manipulate situations in certain ways may be viewed as one indicator of their effectiveness, or could represent a defining characteristic of leadership (see, for example, Batstone *et al.*, 1977).

Another possibility would be to treat certain situational and environmental factors as *independent* variables which may influence not only the consequences of specified leader behaviours, but also the behavioural repertoire from which the leader can choose. For example, a leader whose subordinates are on 'payment by results' may have a more restricted range of behavioural choices than a leader whose subordinates are on 'measured daywork'.

Aspects of group performance have typically been conceptualized as dependent on leader behaviour or leader–group interactions. Again, the reverse may be predicted. Lowin and Craig (1968) are amongst those who have demonstrated such relationships. These then are some of the choices available to those attempting to construct a theory of leadership or leadership effectiveness. The choices made will depend, in part, on the objectives set for the theory, but must also reflect the empirical findings already available.

Explanations of Relations between Variables

One requirement of an adequate theory is that it should provide explanations of why variables are expected to interrelate in specified ways (Ashour, 1973). Leadership theorists have been slow to provide such explanations; however, this situation is gradually changing. For example, House (1973) uses expectancy theories of motivation to explain why various types of leader behaviour have different effects on subordinate satisfaction. Schriesheim and his colleagues have attempted to specify the linkages between leader behaviours and group performance in germs of the leader's influence on group drive and cohesion (Schriesheim *et al.*, 1978). Others have attempted to provide explanations of relationships predicted by theories which are deficient in terms of mechanism. For example, Foa, Mitchell, and Fiedler (1971) argue for an information-processing interpretation of Fiedler's contingency model. Attempts to understand the impact of different leader behaviours in terms of their reinforcement properties are also gaining popularity (see, for example, Sims, 1977).

As can be seen, most of these explanations are concerned with the reasons why leader behaviours have certain effects on subordinate satisfaction or group performance outcomes. Theories which, for example, attempt to explain why some behaviours are selected rather than others, or why certain environmental conditions appear to influence the 'effectiveness' of given behaviours, will need to consider additional mechanisms or linkages.

Making the Theory Operational — Sources of Description

In the last twenty-five years researchers have tended to use paper and pencil measures of leader behaviour, and have then classified these behaviours into a few, often only two, categories. They have also concentrated on the frequency with which these behaviours have been employed, rather than, for example, their timing. These trends have been encouraged by the use of factor analysis to identify clusters of behaviours (see, for example, Fleishman, 1953). Certain unresolved debates have resulted from these practices, e.g. whether a sufficient range of behaviours has been identified and from what source the data should be obtained.

The problem of data source is one of a number of important, general issues. It can be illustrated as follows. When measuring leader behaviour, researchers have used a number of different sources of data: the leaders' own descriptions; some average of the subordinates' descriptions; or the observations of an independent party. It turns out that there is little correspondence between these data sources, i.e. they reflect different 'things' (Mitchell, 1970; Ilgen and Fugii, 1976).

These findings suggest that theorists should choose how to measure behaviour in a way that accords with the internal logic and purpose of their theory. For example, if leaders' behaviours are hypothesized to influence subordinates' work behaviours, presumably the variable of concern is 'leader behaviour as perceived by subordinates' and not as intended by the leader. This observation seems likely to be true of other variables. For example, leaders' perceptions of their organization climate might influence some of their behavioural choices, whereas subordinates' perceptions (of what has in the past been treated as the same variable) might influence their reactions to those behaviours. It seems likely that those involved in theory development will need to build such recognitions into their theories.

Where do we go from here?

This discussion has indicated the range and complexity of decisions involved in producing an adequate theory of leadership effectiveness. Some suggestions as to future direction now seem in order. However, as the Cheshire Cat said to Alice, 'that depends a good deal on where you want to get to'.

Some theorists have indicated their object to be to develop a valid base for the selection, training, and/or placement or those formally appointed to leadership positions (for example, Blake and Mouton, 1964; Reddin, 1970;

Fiedler, 1967). The theories they have developed share a number of characteristics which include: a focus on the office-holder as leader of a *group* (rather than, for example, a collection of individuals or an 'organization'); concentration on situational characteristics to the neglect of environmental ones; and the use of a contingency framework. They also share two key assumptions which are, first, that formal appointment guarantees there will be a leadership functions to perform, and secondly, that leaders have considerable freedom of choice in their activities. It appears that these assumptions are seldom justifiable.

With respect to the first mentioned assumption, it seems that many 'substitutes' for leadership may exist which render the leader role redundant (Schriesheim and Kerr, 1977). Consequently, to return to the question 'where do we go from here?', it seems one of the ways must involve increased recognition of this. What constitutes a 'substitute' will depend on the way the theorist has defined the concepts of leader and leadership. It will also depend on how leadership effectiveness has been defined, this because the notion of a substitute implies that some person(s), machine, procedure, etc. is doing the leader's job, i.e. helping him or her to meet the objectives by which they are judged. Those who seek to develop normative theories for the purposes of selection and training must seek to identify these substitutes — there seems little point in attempting the costly business of selection and training if a sufficient number exist (or can be developed) to render it unnecessary. A further requirement will be to develop measures which will distinguish between leaders who are 'effective' because they have developed adequate substitutes, or have recognized their presence and are monitoring and maintaining them, from leaders who are 'effective' (at least in the short term) 'by default'.

The second assumption noted above was that leaders have considerable freedom of choice in performing their various functions. Evidence suggestive of the contrary has been available for many years (see, for example, Dill, 1958). More recently, a great number of sources of constraint have been documented: constraints which limit the leader's influence (see, for example, Salancik and Pfeffer, 1977), and constraints which limit his 'behavioural repertoire' (see, for example, Bennis, 1976). Like substitutes for leadership, the nature (and possibly the number) of these constraints seems likely to vary depending on the leadership context. For example, Neustadt writes of how the President of the United States is 'checked and balanced by a set of rival chieftains' (Neustadt, 1976, p.26), whilst Ansoff describes how chief executives must be increasingly responsive to the pressures of 'external' agencies, consumer groups, trade-unions, legislation, etc. (Ansoff, 1979). the network of dependencies faced by a first line supervisor is likely to be somewhat different.

The object of theorists such as Selznick (1957) and Ansoff (1979) is to understand leadership at relatively senior levels in organizations. Selznick was primarily concerned with what he called 'institutional' as opposed to 'interpersonal' leadership, i.e. defining the mission of the organization, developing strategy, elaborating commitments, etc. It is Selznick's belief that an adequate theory of this kind rests upon an adequate theory of social organization (rather than a theory of groups, see earlier discussion). Ansoff (1979) and Bennis (1976), also writing of chief executives, make much of their need for political skills — skills in negotiating and persuasion. Whilst these skills may also be required by leaders occupying more lowly positions, they will probably be required for achieving rather different objectives.

So far this discussion has concentrated on appointed leaders — persons placed in charge of a particular constituency (which is not meant to imply that the constituency is necessarily easy to identify). There are many other conditions in which the concepts of leader and leadership are invoked, for example autonomous work groups. A theorist who wishes to develop a theory for this particular context would define a leader in terms other than a formal appointment. Less obvious choices might involve the selection of variables concerned with processes of role differentiation, small group dynamics, exchange, attribution, etc. In other words, theories of leadership effectiveness in autonomous work-groups would look quite different from the theories discussed earlier.

These observations suggest that the terms 'leader', 'leadership', and 'leadership effectiveness' take on different meanings depending on the context in which they occur, and the objectives set for the theory. Consequently, different theories — each having an explicit and limited range of application — will be more successful than a broad-brush approach. In other words, theories like Fiedler's, which attempt to predict the effectiveness of leaders of basket-ball teams, supervisors of shop-floor operators, and chairmen of boards of directors, *using the same set of variables*, may be doomed to failure. By implication, there will never be a 'unified and generally accepted paradigm' (McCall, 1977, p.376). Consequently, what is needed is the means by which any interested party can select a theory (and therefore a set of definitions, predictors, norms, etc.) from the available set. The development of decision tress, or a taxonomy having 'aspects of context' and 'purpose' as its principal axes will probably be required.

In sum, Fiedler produced a theory which was both pioneering and ambitious. It has been argued that the theory is incomplete, suffers from methodological and theoretical shortcomings, and lacks empirical support. Future attempts at theory development will achieve more by being more limited in scope and more precise in objectives.

REFERENCES

Ansoff, H. (1979) *Strategic Management*, MacMillan.

Argyris, C. (1978) 'How normal science methodology makes leadership research less additive and less applicable', Paper presented to the Fifth Biennial Leadership Symposium, Southern Illinois University.

Ashour, A. (1973a) 'The contingency model of leadership effectiveness: An evaluation', *Organisational Behaviour and Human Performance*, **9**, 339–55.

Ashour, A. (1973b) 'Further discussion of Fiedler's contingency model of Leadership Effectiveness', *Organizational Behaviour and Human Performance*, **9**, 369–76.

Bales, R. F. (1955) 'Role differentiation in small decision-making groups', in *Family, Socialization and Interaction Process* (Eds. T. Parsons *et al.*), Free Press, New York, 259–306.

Batstone, E., Boraston, I., and Frenkel, S. (1977) *Shop Stewards in Action*, Basil Blackwell, Oxford.

Blake, R. and Mouton, J. (1964) *The Managerial Grid*, Gulf Publishing Company.

Bennis, W. (1976) 'Leadership: A beleaguered species', *Organizational Dynamics*, **5**, 3–16.

Cattell, R. (1951) 'Concepts and methods for measuring leadership in terms of group syntality', *Human Relations*, **4**, 161–84.

Cattell, R. and Stice, G. (1954) 'Four Formulae for selecting leaders on the basis of personality', *Human Relations*, **7**, 493–507.

Chemers, M. and Skryzpek, F. (1972) 'An experimental test of the contingency model of leadership effectiveness', *Journal of Personality and Social Psychology*, **24**, 172–77.

Child, J. and Hosking, D. (1978) 'Crucial dimensions of leader–group interactions: Discussants commentary', Presented to the Fifth Biennial Leadership Symposium, Southern Illinois University.

Csoka, L. (1974) 'A relationship between leader intelligence and leader rated effectiveness', *Journal of Applied Psychology*, **59**, 1, 43–47.

Csoka, L. (1975) 'Relationship between organizational climate and the SF dimension of Fiedler's contingency model', *Journal of Applied Psychology*, **60**, 2, 273–77.

Csoka, L. and Fiedler, F. (1972) 'The effect of military leadership training: A test of the contingency model', *Organisational Behaviour and Human Performance*, **8**, 395–407.

Dill, W. (1958) 'Environment as an influence on managerial autonomy', *Administrative Science Quarterly*, **2**, 409–43.

Fiedler, F. (1958) *Leader Attitudes and Group Effectiveness*, University of Illinois Press, Urbana, Illinois.

Fiedler, F. (1965) 'Engineer the job to fit the manager', *Harvard Business Review*, **43**, 5, 115–22.

Fiedler, F. (1966) 'The effect of leadership and cultural heterogeneity on group performance: A test of the contingency model', *Journal of Experimental Social Psychology*, **2**, 237–64.

Fiedler, F. (1967) *A Theory of Leadership Effectiveness*, McGraw-Hill Book Co.

Fiedler, F. (1971) 'Validation and extension of the Contingency Model of leadership effectiveness: A review of empirical findings', *Psychological Bulletin*, **76**, 2, 128–48.

Fiedler, F. (1971a) 'Note on the methodology of the Graen, Orris & Alvares studies testing the contingency model', *Journal of Applied Psychology*, **55**, 3, 202–4.

Fiedler, F., Chemers, M., and Mahar, L. (1976) *Improving Leadership Effectiveness: The Leader Match Concept*, John Wiley & Sons, New York.

Fiedler, F., O'Brien, G., and Ilgen, D. (1969) 'The effect of leadership style upon the performance and adjustment of volunteer teams of oeprating in a stressful foreign environment', *Human Relations*, **22**, 503–14.

Fleishman, E. (1953) 'The description of supervisory behaviour', *Journal of Applied Psychology*, **37**, 1-6.

Fleishman, E. (1973) 'Twenty years of consideration and structure, in *Current Developments in the Study of Leadership* (Eds. E. Fleishman and J. Hunt), Southern Illinois University Press.

Fisher, R. (1976) *Statistical Methods for Research Workers*, 10th edn, Oliver & Boyd, London.

Foa, U., Mitchell, T. and Fiedler, F. (1971) 'Differentiating matching', *Behavioural Science*, **16**, 130-42.

Gibb, C. (1969) 'Leadership', in *The Handbook of Social Psychology* (Eds. G. Lindzey and E. Aronson), vol IV, Addison-Wesley, Reading, Mass.

Godfrey, E., Fiedler, F., and Hall, D. (1959) *Boards, Managers and Company Success*, Interstate Press, Danville, Ill.

Graen, G., Alvares, K., and Orris, J. (1970) 'Contingency model of leadership effectiveness: Antecedent and evidential results', *Psychological Bulletin*, **74**, 4, 285-96.

Graen, G., Orris, J., and Alvares, K. (1970) 'Contingency Model of leadership effectiveness: Some experimental restuls', *Journal of Applied Psychology*, **55**, 3, 196-201.

Greene, C. (1975) 'The reciprocal nature of influence between leader and subordinate', *Journal of Applied Psychology*, **60**, 2, 187-93.

Hardy, C. (1976) *Understanding Organisations*, Penguin, Harmondsworth.

Hardy, R. (1971) 'Effect of leadership style on the performance of small classroom groups: A test of the contingency model', *Journal of Personality and Social Psychology*, **19**, 3, 367-74.

Hardy, R. (1975) 'A test of the poor leader-member relations cell of the contingency model on elementary school children', *Child Development*, **46**, 4, 958-64.

Hardy, R. and Bohren, J. (1975) 'Effect of experience on teacher effectiveness — test of C.M.', *Journal of Psychology*, **89**, 1, 159.

Hardy, R., Sack, S. and Harpine, F. (1973) 'An experimental test of the contingency model on small classroom groups', *The Journal of Psychology*, **85**, 3-16.

Hemphill, J. (1956) *Group Dimensions: A Manual for their Measurement*, Bureau of Business Research, Ohio State University, Columbus.

Herbert, T. (1976) *Dimensions of Organizational Behaviour*, Macmillan Publishing Co. Ltd., New York.

Herbst, P. (1970) *Behavioural Worlds: The Study of Single Cases*, Tavistock, London.

Hewett, T., O'Brien, G., and Hornik, J. (1974) 'The effects of work organisation, leadership style, and member compatability upon the productivity of small groups working on a manipulative task', *Organizational Behaviour and Human Performance*, **11**, 283-301.

Hill, W. (1969) 'The validation and extension of Fiedler's theory of leadership effectiveness', *Academy of Management Journal*, **March**, 33-47.

Hollander, E. (1978) *Leadership Dynamics*, The Free Press.

House, R. (1973) 'A path goal theory of leader effectiveness', in (Eds). *Current developments in the study of leadership* (Eds. E. Fleishman and J. Hunt), Southern Illinois University Press.

House, R. and Rizzo, J. (1971) 'Toward the measurement of organizational practices: A scale development and validation', *Experimental Publication System*, **12**, Ms 481-1.

Hosking D. (1978) 'A critical evaluation of Fiedler's predictor measures of leadership effectiveness', Unpublished PhD Thesis, University of Warwick.

Hosking, D. and Schriesheim, C. (1978) Review essay: Improving leadership effectiveness: The leader match concept', *Administrative Science Quarterly*, **23** 3, 497–505.

Hosking, D. (1979a) *Differentiation Matching and Fiedler's Contingency Hypothesis: A Critique*, Working Paper Series, no.139, The University of Aston Management Centre.

Hosking, D. (1979b) *A Critical Evaluation of the Goal Hierarchy Interpretation of LPC Scores*, Working Paper Series, no.136, The University of Aston Management Centre.

Hovey, D. (1974) 'The low-powered leader confronts a messy problem: A test of Fiedler's theory', *Academy of Management Journal*, **17**, 2, 358–62.

Hunt, J. (1967) 'Fiedler's leadership contingency model: An empirical test in 3 organizations', *Organisational Behaviour and Human Performance*, **2**, 290–308.

Ilgen, D. and Fugii, D. (1976) 'An investigation of the validity of leader behaviour descriptions obtained from subordinates', *Journal of Applied Psychology*, **12**, 1–14.

Johnson, R. and Ryan, B. (1976) 'A test of the contingency model of leadership effectiveness', *Journal of Applied Social Psychology*, **6**, 2, 177–85.

Katz, D. and Kahn, R. (1978) *The Social Psychology of Organisations*, 2nd edn, John Wiley and Sons.

Keppel, G. (1973) *Design and Analysis: A Researcher's Handbook*, Prentice-Hall, Inc.

Kerr, S. (1976) 'Substitutes for leadership: Their meaning and measurement', in *American Institute of Decision Sciences Proceedings* (Ed. H. Schneider).

Korman, A. (1973) 'On the development of contingency theories of leadership: Some methodological considerations and a possible alternative', *Journal of Applied Psychology*, **58**, 3, 384–87.

Korman, A. and Tanofsky, R. (1975) 'Statistical problems of contingency models in organisational behaviour', Academy of Management Journal, **18**, 2, 393–97.

Kretzschmar, V. and Luecke, H. (1969) 'The Fiedler contingency model of leadership effectiveness', *Arbeit und Leistung*, **23**, 53–55.

Lowin, A. and Craig, J. (1968) 'The influence of level of performance on managerial style: An experimental object lesson in the ambiguity of correlational data', *Organizational Behaviour and Human Performance*, **3**, 440–58.

McMahon, J. 61972) 'The contingency theory: Logic and method revisited', *Personnel Psychology*, **25**, 697–710.

McCall, (1977) 'Leaders and leadership: Of substance and shadow', in *Perspectives on Behaviour in Organizations* (Ed. J. Hackman), McGraw-Hill, New York.

Meuwese, W. and Fiedler, F. (1964) *Leadership and Group Creativity Under Varying Conditions of Stress*, Group Effectiveness Research Laboratory, University of Illinois, Urbana, Ill.

Michaelson, L. K. (1973) 'Leader orientation, leader behaviour, group effectiveness and situational favourability: An empirical extension of the contingency model', *Organizational Behaviour and Human Performance*, **9**, 226–45.

Mitchell, T. (1970) 'The construct validity of three dimensions of leadership research', *Journal of Social Psychology*, **80**, 89–94.

Mitchell, T., Biglan, A., Onchen, G., and Fiedler, F. (1970) 'The contingency model: Criticism and suggestions', *Academy of Management Journal*, **18**, 253–267.

Morley, I. and Stephenson, G. (1977) *The Social Psychology of Bargaining*. George Allen & Unwin, London.

Nealey, S. and Blood, M. (1967) *Leadership Performance of Nursing Supervisors at Two Organizational Levels*, Technical Report no. 48, University of Illinois.

Neustadt, R. (1976) *Presidential Power: The Politics of Leadership*, 2nd edn, John Wiley and Sons, Inc.

O'Brien, G. (1969) 'Group structure and the measurement of potential leader influence', *Australian Journal of Psychology*, 21, 277–89.

Posthuma, A. (1970) *Normative Data on the Least Preferred Coworker Scale (LPC) and the Group Atmosphere Questionnaire (GA)*, Organisational Research Technical Report no. 70-8, University of Washington, Seattle.

Raven, R. and Rubin, L. (1976) *Social Psychology: People in Groups*, John Wiley and Sons, Inc.

Reavis, C. and Derlega, V. (1976). 'Test of a contingency model of leadership effectiveness', *Journal of Educational Research*, 69, 6, 221–25.

Reddin, W. (1970) *Managerial Effectiveness*, McGraw-Hill.

Rice, R. W. and Chemers, M. (1973) 'Predicting the emergence of leaders using Fiedler's contingency model of leadership effectiveness', *Journal of Applied Psychology*, 57, 281–87.

Salancik, G. and Pfeffer, J. (1977) 'Constraints on administrator discretion: The limited influence of mayors on city budgets', *Urban Affairs Quarterly*, 12, 475–96.

Sashkin, M. (1972) 'Leadership style and group decision effectiveness: Correlational and behavioural tests of Fiedler's Contingency Model', *Organisational Behaviour and Human Performance*, 8, 347–63.

Schneier, C. (1978) 'The Contingency Model of Leadership: An extension to emergent leadership and leader's sex', *Organizational Behaviour and Human Performance*, 21, 220–39.

Schriesheim, C. and Kerr, S. (1977) 'Theories and measures of leadership: A critical appraisal of current and future directions', in *Leadership The Cutting Edge* (Eds. J. G. Hunt and L. L. Larson, Southern Illinois University Press.

Schriesheim, C., Mowday, T., and Stogdill, R. (1978) 'Crucial dimensions of leader-group interactions', Paper presented to the Fifth Biennial Leadership Symposium, Southern Illinois University.

Selznick, P. 61957) *Leadership In Administration*, Row, Peterson, Evanston, Illinois.

Shaw, M. (1971) *Group Dynamics: The Psychology of Small-Group Behaviour*, McGraw-Hill, New York.

Shaw, M. and Blum, J. (1966) 'Effects of leadership style upon group performance as a function of task structure', *Journal of Personality and Social Psychology*, 3, 238–42.

Shiflett, S. (1973) 'Contingency model of leadership effectiveness: Some implications of its statistical and methodological properties', *Behavioural Science*, 18, 429.

Shiflett, S. and Nealey, S. (1972) 'The effects of changing leader power: A test of "situational engineering"', *Organizational Behaviour and Human Performance*, 7, 371–82.

Shima, H. (1968) 'The relationship between the leaders modes of interpersonal cognition and the performance of the group', *Japanese Psychological Research*, 10, 1, 13–30.

Sims, H. (1977) 'The leader as a manager of reinforcement contingencies: An empirical example and a model', in *Leadership The Cutting Edge* (Eds. J. Hunt and L. Larson), Southern Illinois University Press.

Spiegel, M. (1961) *Theory and Problems of Statistics*, Schavin Publ. Co., New York.

Stogdill, R. (1973) 'Discussents' comments', in *Current Developments in the Study of Leadership* (Eds. E. Fleishman and J. Hunt), Southern Illinois University Press.

Thibaut, J. and Kelley, H. (1959) *The Social Psychology of Groups*, John Wiley and Sons Inc.

Vecchio, R. (1977) 'An empirical examination of the validity of Fiedler's model of leadership effectiveness', *Organizational Behaviour and Human Performance*, 19, 180–206.

Vroom, V. and Yetton, P. (1973) *Leadership and Decision Making*, University of Pittsburgh Press.

Winer, B. (1962) *Statistical Principles in Experimental Designs*, McGraw-Hill, New York.

Progress in Applied Social Psychology, Volume 1
Edited by G. M. Stephenson and J. M. Davis
© 1981 John Wiley & Sons, Ltd.

5

Social Psychological Approaches to the Study of the Induction and Alleviation of Stress: Influences upon Health and Illness

J. M. INNES

Department of Psychology, University of Adelaide

INTRODUCTION

Psychologists have been concerned for many years with the study of stress and those factors which induce the reaction of stress. The literature on stress currently constitutes between 1 and 2 per cent of the research reported in psychological journals. While that proportion has not increased significantly over the past ten years, as indexed by the abstracts categorized as dealing with stress in *Psychological Abstracts*, since the total amount of psychological research reported has increased by 57 percent in that period, it is clear that the study of stress continues as an important theme in psychology.

The reasons why research on stress has been a popular feature of psychological research are complex, as for any scientific endeavour. It is possible to identify endogenous, or intrinsic, influences upon the development of a research tradition and also exogenous, or extrinsic, influences (e.g. Spengler, 1968). Among the former influences is the provision of an organizing theory which has as its accoutrements a variety of experimental methods and techniques. It is not necessary to adopt in its entirety Kuhn's (1962) version of the development of science to see this as a major factor guiding the direction of research. The identification by Selye (1952) of the General Adaptation Syndrome (GAS), with its stages of alarm, resistance, and exhaustion shown in the physiological response to a wide variety of environmental stimuli, gave the impetus to the study with animals and humans of behavioural responses which could be expected to be consequent upon and influenced by the elicitation of the physiological responses. The demonstration that physical and psychological threats to an organism elicited a common set of responses was an important factor in guiding the nature of research. The earlier realization by psychologists that high levels of motivation could lead to a decline in performance, the postulated Yerkes–Dodson law, was another factor intrinsic to psychology which could be linked quite easily and profitably to the demonstration of short- and long-term changes in physiological response under stimulation (Duffy, 1962).

The second set of factors to influence the direction of research includes various practical problems and social concerns that arise in contemporary society. The realization that quite clear relationships existed between the high levels of physical threat experienced in combat and behavioural and psychological breakdown, as revealed for example in the studies of the *American Soldier* (Stouffer, Lumsdaine, Williams, Smith, Janis, Star, and Cottrell, 1949) and in the analysis of the effects of strategic bombing (e.g. Janis, 1951), was an important impetus to the study of threat and its effect upon behaviour. While the study of behaviour in such natural settings could not achieve high levels of precision and give clear and consistent support to psychological and physiological models (e.g. Baker and Chapman, 1962; Jacobson, 1973; Strumpfer, 1970) the occurrence of disaster and the stress of war continued to add to the desire to understand the generalized effects of stressors. The study of the effect of unambiguously stressful experiences has continued in a variety of settings, much of it to do with military training situations (e.g. Berkun, Bialek, Kern, and Yagi, 1962; Ursin, Baade, and Levine, 1978). Other work has been done with closely related situations, such as sports parachuting (Epstein, 1967; Fenz, 1964, 1973) or with underwater diving training (Radloff and Helmreich, 1968). A lot has been learned about the nature of the attempts people make to deal with stress in such extreme conditions although there still remains considerable opportunity for debate over the nature of any adjustments people may make following stress in such conditions (Grearson, 1975). Indeed, why so many people fail to show the effects of stress is a major problem (Rachman, 1978).

At a less traumatic level, the belief that the technological developments in society and the press of life in modern urban society have characteristics which may evoke the stress response has led medical researchers and social scientists to the study of people in work and in general day-to-day settings to see to what extent we may be in a state of chronic stress as a result merely of living.

Research by psychologists into stress and those stimuli which evoke the response has been characterized by a concern with the impact of physical stimuli or the threat thereof, stimuli which exist quite normally in the environment but which may become stsressful when they attain high amplitudes or when they are of long duration. So stimuli such as noise (Kryter, 1970) or heat (Bursill, 1958; Poulton and Edwards, 1974) are examined for the detrimental and occasional beneficial effects they may have on behaviour, especially upon skilled performance and the components of that skill. While this work has been pursued for many years still it is possible for considerable controversy to exist as to whether, for example, noise has beneficial or detrimental effects upon performance over a fairly wide range of noise levels or at what stage in a sequence of behaviour the external stimuli are having their effect (e.g. Broadbent, 1978; Poulton, 1977, 1978).

Much of the controversy centres around the nature of the experimental tasks and on the way in which the external stimulus, for example noise, may interfere with the processes thought to underlie performance. Whether there is a simple masking effect (Poulton, 1977) or whether there is a narrowing of selective attention to critical external cues, this narrowing aiding or hindering performance depending upon the position of cues in the stimulus display (Easterbrook, 1959; Forster and Grierson, 1978; Hockey, 1970; Kahneman, 1973) or whether there is a biasing of the mechanism whereby responses are selected (Broadbent, 1971) remains to be worked out. There can be criticism of the range of stimulus magnitudes which have been, and indeed can be, manipulated in laboratory settings. There seems to be a considerable lack of fit between results obtained in laboratory and in field or applied settings (e.g. Rodda, 1967). This may be due to the attenuation of any effect when a lower level of stimulus is used in a laboratory (whether of lower magnitude or for a shorter duration). It may also be due to the fact that subjects in a laboratory setting have different expectancies about what can happen to them compared with people in a work situation and they have the knowledge that they may remove themselves from the stressor when they wish. Even such an apparently minimal factor as signing an 'informed consent' form to participate in an experiment has been shown to moderate the impact of noise upon behaviour (Gardner, 1978). The reasonably clear-cut effects of trauma upon behaviour observed in disaster or combat are not easily replicable with more moderate stimuli. This is not to say that in the extreme case the mechanisms mediating the relationships are clearly known.

Whatever the resolution of this problem, a major point to be drawn from what has been considered to date is that much of the work done by psychologists has been upon the effects of physical stimuli. The fact that a large proportion of a person's daily activity is taken up with interaction with other people in large numbers in a wide variety of social settings has not attracted the attention of too many psychologists. If engagement with stimuli to excess, either of numbers or over time, can be considered to result in a stress reaction, then the ubiquity of social interaction may be stressful. It would be over-simplifying matters to say that there has been *no* work on the impact of social stimuli upon stress by psychologists; the major point of the present chapter is to demonstrate what has been accomplished. But the work that has been done has been scattered and has often been done by workers in disciplines other than psychology. One paradoxical point to emerge is that even when social psychologists have turned to the study of stress as it exists in urban communities (e.g. Glass and Singer, 1972), the feature of urban society singled out for attention has been of a physical nature, namely noise.

MULTIDISCIPLINARY APPROACHES
TO THE STUDY OF SOCIAL STRESS

While social psychologists *per se* have not been very active in the study of the possible stressful effects of social events, researchers in other disciplines have. A concern with social stress takes the social psychologist to the borderlands with other disciplines, notably social epidemiology and psychosomatic medicine.

Epidemiology can be defined as 'the study of the distribution of diseases in the population and of the factors which affect this distribution' (Syme, 1974). As long as medical science was concerned with the prevention and cure of acute diseases and conditions, epidemiology had little relevance for psychology, concerned as it was with the identification and mapping of disease-carrying organisms and other pathogens. (We specifically exclude here the importance that epidemiology has played in the understanding of the aetiology of mental illness, cf. Hollingshead and Redlich, 1958.) The increasing incidence in Western society of chronic illnesses, such as cancer, cirrhosis of the liver, hypertension, and coronary heart disease, where no single pathogen can be identified, as led to increased activity in examining a wide variety of factors considered to be implicated in their aetiology.

From a concern with demonstrating a direct causal link between a microbial agent and a disease, epidemiology has turned more to the identification of the conditions whereby, as Dubos (cited in Wolf and Goodell, 1976) states '[the] equilibrium . . . which permits the different components of biological systems to live at peace together . . . is disturbed [and] one of the components of the system is favoured at the expense of the other . . . [resulting] in the processes of disease'.

Elsewhere Dubos (1965) states: 'the microbial diseases most common today arise from the activity of microorganisms that are ubiquitous in the environment, . . . and exert pathological effects only when the infected person is under *conditions of physiological stress*' (emphasis added).

Social relationships and the disruption of those relationships have been shown to have an effect upon susceptibility to acute infections such as tuberculosis (Wolf and Goodell, 1976). Somewhat minor infections such as herpes simplex ('cold sores') are apparently related to the arousal of emotional distress. Some researchers have found that even transient disruptions of social relationships in hospital wards have been shown to affect the excretion of metabolites known to be associated with stress (Schottstaedt, Jackman, McPhail, and Wolf, 1963) and hence possibly with disease susceptibility. The lead provided by such findings has stimulated the search for the identification of the role of more major social disruptions in the aetiology of illnesses for which no single infectious agent has been identified.

The study of epidemiology has broadened to the 'study of social factors as they affect distributions of disease . . . [the] ways in which *a person's position in the social structure* influences the likelihood that he will develop disease' (Syme, 1974, emphasis added). As Kasl (1977) points out, it is not possible to delineate very precisely what are epidemiologic methods, nor what are the defining methodological attributes of epidemiology which differentiate it from a discipline such a social psychology. What is important to point out here is that social psychologists have not been especially prominent in the field of relating social disruption to health and illness. Other disciplines have been doing the job without them.

Psychosomatic medicine is another field with common concerns which borders on to social psychology. For a long time identified as having a strongly psychodynamic orientation, the field is now somewhat difficult to distinguish from epidemiology, concerned as it is with psychological and social variables as they affect illness (and not just the small array of illnesses once identified as psychosomatic, such as peptic ulcer and ulcerative colitis) (Kasl, 1977). There may be differences in emphasis and, for example, in the nature of the subject populations studied, but essentially a belief that 'social stress' is related to the incidence of disease provides a common link.

Illness, is, of course, not the only consequent of social stress and epidemiology and psychosomatic medicine are not the only areas relevant to the study of social stress. Environmental psychology, for example, has much in common with social psychology. There has in fact been some debate in the literature as to whether the two fields can or should be separated (e.g. Altman, 1976; Proshansky, 1976). Environmental psychologists have contributed to an understanding of the effect of environmental stressors upon various categories of behaviour, including skilled performance referred to earlier, but also social behaviour such as aggression and altruism (c.f. Stokols, 1978). One particular stress which has been singled out for attention is crowding, indubitably a feature of *social* stress (Milgram, 1970). The effects of crowding on social behaviour have been studied (e.g. Freedman, 1975; Saegert, 1978), along with features of individuals likely to modify any stressful reactions (e.g. Langer and Saegert, 1977). Further consideration will be given to aspects of this work later in this chapter.

Sociologists also have long been interested in the social pathology which can be correlated with urban crowding, inner-city residence, and the alienation which is considered to follow. Crime, poverty, and child neglect and violence can all be shown to co-vary with variation in indices of over-population and urban decay (Park and Burgess, 1925; Sengel, 1978). For the social psychologist, however, concerned with the study of the response of an individual organism to present or past social relationships (e.g. Jones and Gerard, 1967), the sociological research is of less direct relevance.

What can the social psychologist contribute to this multi-disciplinary enterprise? In the main social psychologists have been trained to measure people's responses to social situations, their attitudes, emotions, cognitions and attributions, and their patterns of interaction; how a response may benefit or harm another person and how that person may retaliate. Such a training may be applied to the study of the precursors of health and illness by demonstrating that cognitions and attributions may mediate physiological processes and that behavioural adjustments may help a person to modify a physiological response. The patterns of social interaction that a person experiences and his capacity to deal with those interactions may also be shown to affect mediating physiological reactions. Both at the level of the consequent event—the behavioural and cognitive response—and of the antecedent event —the social interaction—the social psychologist can help sharpen and advance understanding of health and illness.

The social psychologist working in the field of social stress and health is faced with the need to understand that social and biological events are inextricably linked, but that any relationship between these events will only emerge through a clear conceptualization and precise measurement of social events. The social psychologist can contribute to the understanding and solution of a serious, applied problem by the use of his skills as a psychologist in collaboration with researchers from other fields.

The remainder of this chapter will be concerned with the role that social psychology can play in understanding the relationship between social stress and illness. Other co-variates of social stress, such as social pathology, will not be considered. What social psychology can offer in the way of concepts and methods to study the sources of stress and the modification of stress will be examined. As such the chapter will be examining research of a multi-disciplinary nature.

The work which is relevant to the topic comes from a wide variety of sources and very little of direct relevance comes from the core psychological journals such as the *Journal of Personality and Social Psychology*, although there are exceptions (e.g. Langer and Rodin, 1976; Langer, Janis and Wolfer, 1975). One feature is that little work is reported in the *Journal of Applied Social Psychology*. This may be due to the bias that applied social psychology has to do with social responses rather than with the effect of social relationships upon responses in a different category.

A major problem in considering research in the field is that it is essentially multi-disciplinary in nature and not interdisciplinary; that is to say, people working in different disciplines may be investigating (in parallel) similar problems but the amount of truly collaborative research, where the overlap between disciplines is used and where there is a *combination* of methods rather than the disciplinary use of mehods, is rather rare. Parochialism of method, reflected in the audience to which results are reported, is demonstrated by Hull (1977). She found that research workers in the various disciplines reported their research in different journals. Thus, for example, epidemiologists reported results in medical journals while psychologists reported theirs in those journals devoted to psychosomatic medicine. While Hull's work cannot be taken as definitive, for example her sample of the social psychological literature comprised the *Journal of Social Psychology* which social psychologists do not consider to be the central journal in the discipline, nevertheless it does demonstrate that the specialties are writing for different audiences. While other disciplines may read the papers and use the results of the research, there still remains a bias in the way results are reported. Since the manner in which results are reported may influence their understanding and the use to which they are put (Bauer, 1964), the present state of multi-disciplinary research leaves something to be desired. Any improvement upon the present state will only take place gradually.

CONCEPTUALIZATION OF SOCIAL STRESS

So far we have not attempted to define the terms 'stress' and 'social stress'. Kasl (1977) considers quite rightly that the term 'stress' has not been adequately defined and remains at best a 'pretheoretical term', i.e. open-ended and given to almost any interpretation one wishes to put on it. A large amount of empirical work is needed to enumerate the environmental (physical and social) events which elicit the stress response.

Selye (cited in Hinkle, 1973) regarded stress as the reaction of an organism to a noxious event. It was not to be regarded as an environmental event, which is better termed the 'stressor'. The work of Selye suggested that the three-stage response of the GAS was essentially the same for all classes of stressor. The initial emergency reaction, the release of the catecholamines epinephrine and norepinephrine from the adrenal medulla, was followed by the release of corticosteroids from the adrenal cortex, under the stimulus of adreno-cortico-trophic hormone (ACTH) from the anterior pituitary. This latter stage, the stage of resistance, appeared to be a response to utilize stored resources of energy for a rapid response to threatening stimuli. Most interesting from the point of view of illness as a possible consequence of stress is that during this stage there is an aggravation of the body's inflammatory reaction and a reduction of the immunological response. Thus, there is an enhanced response to any infection and a reduced resistance to that infection. Selye's work suggested that any threat—physiological, environmental, or psychological—resulted in the same stress response.

Stimuli do vary, however, in the response which they elicit. Epinephrine production has been shown to increase with increases in stimulation and with ratings of subjective stress (Frankenhaeuser, 1976), both for tasks which can be considered pleasant and unpleasant (e.g. Patkai, 1971). Noradrenaline excretion, however, has been shown to be less responsive, being maintained at an elevated level even when stress is lower and epinephrine excretion is shown to decline (Frankenhaeuser, 1976). The production of epinephrine seems to be a response associated with fear, while norepinephrine is associated more with anger and activity. Certainly Frankenhaeuser's data suggests that norepinephrine excretion remains high while the subjects in her study were attending to the stimuli and remaining active.

Work by Mason and his co-workers (e.g. Mason, Maher, Hartley, Mougey, Perlow, and Jones, 1976) also suggests that all stimuli do not have the same impact upon the response of the pituitary–adrenal complex. Laboratory investigations of the effect of exercise and heat, stimuli which are shown to elevate body temperature and oxygen consumption and the excretion of catecholamines, and which on the basis of previous work would be expected to elevate the secretion of the corticosteroids from the adrenal cortex, in fact do not show this last effect, provided that discomfort and subjective feelings of evaluation and competition are minimized. The crucial role of the corticosteroids in the stage of resistance seems to occur when psychological threat is present. Physical stressors may show diverse responses while psychological stressors present a common syndrome. Reviews of the various hormonal responses to stress can be found in Mason (1968) and in Henry and Ely (1976).

In the study of stress in society there is almost certainly some common factor of threat or the likelihood of evaluation or competition present and therefore the stress syndrome is almost certainly evoked. It may not be the case, however, that the study of the effects of physical stressors such as noise and heat will give clear guides as to the effect of social stressors. Further evidence that social stressors may not act in the same manner as physical ones comes from studies on crowding, where physiological adaptation, i.e. the apparent decline in arousal with continued exposure to a stimulus, is not apparent with the presence of people (D'Atri, 1975; Paulus, Cox, McCain, and Chandler, 1975). Other social stimuli have been shown to have measurable physiological effects (Kiritz and Moos, 1974) which are maintained at elevated levels.

If there is a common physiological response to psychological threat, then it seems unlikely that any specific illness will result from exposure to specific stressors (Cassel, 1976). What seems more likely is that the presence of social stressors, by altering the endocrine balance in the body, increases the susceptibility of the organism to any agent present. Rather than search for the relationship of *a* stressor to an illness, it is possible that exposure of a population to a wide range of stressors will increase the probability of illness, in many forms. While the adoption of such a view renders the hypothesis relating stress to illness virtually unfalsifiable, since *any* illness, however minor, can be made to relate to any life change and therefore give support to the hypothesis, the nature of the stress response as presently understood provides little alternative. Psychodynamic theorists, for example Bahnson (1974), suggest that the form of illness will be predictable at the individual level from a knowledge of that person, but no data have been produced to support that suggestion.

RESEARCH ON SOCIAL STRESSORS

While the work on physiological stress has continued, the bulk of the work which has been done on social stress and physical illness has been concerned with the measurement of 'life events'. These are changes in personal life which requires an adjustment by the individual to new circumstances. Thus, a new job, loss of a job, marriage, birth of a child, loss of a spouse, and emigration are life events which require a new set of responses and which are considered to enhance susceptibility to later illness. The research to date mainly requires subjects to recall the number of such events experienced over a set period of time and this figure is then related to the number of illnesses and doctor visits experienced by that subject. Typically there is no attempt to measure the internal physiological state which is presumed to mediate the appearance of illness.

Social psychologists and sociologists have much evidence to demonstrate the profound effects of traumatic events. Studies of concentration camp survivors (Eitinger, 1971) and of the effects of natural disasters or major accidents show evidence of increases in the incidence of physical illnesses over the short and long term. At a broader level, data on large populations show variation in the occurrence of illness, both physical (Bunn and Drane, 1975) and mental (Brenner, 1973), with variation in the 'health' of the economy. Unemployment is correlated with CHD; economic depression with mental depression. Loss of job can be implicated as a mediator of the relationship at the individual level.

It seems entirely plausible that an accumulation of minor events may have an eventual effect upon the well-being of an individual. A large amount of research has been carried out on the measurement of life events and several reviews are available (e.g. Dohrenwend and Dohrenwend, 1974; Masuda and Holmes, 1978). Most of the research has used the Holmes and Rahe (1967) Social Readjustment Rating Scale (SRRS). While there have been many studies that have demonstrated a relationship between number of events and illness, there are many which fail to show any clear-cut pattern (e.g. Goldberg and Comstock, 1976).

There has been considerable criticism of the nature of the scale and methodological criticisms of the research design typically used and the populations studied. Just what events are important to measure and what attributes of these events are crucial have all been the subject of debate. Is it the magnitude, the duration, unpredictability, or familiarity of the events that are important? Is subjective experience of the event an important mediator? No clear answers have been forthcoming. A major problem has been the nature of the research design used, typically a retrospective study in which people have to recall events. There is almost certainly a bias towards the recall of more recent events and towards salient ones (Horowitz, Schaefer, and Cooney, 1974). Many of the events are as likely to follow from illness as to precede it (Hudgens, 1974). Studies using the SRRS have very much used the same design and little opportunity has arisen to examine the effect of any such biases (cf. Rabkin and Streuning, 1976, for a clear review of the statistical and psychometric issues involved; see also Hurst, Jenkins, and Rose, 1978).

Research in this field generally seems to be ignorant of developments in research design and data analysis and of the destructive criticisms which are now available of many of the designs which are currently in use. Goldberg and Comstock (1976), for example, would surely have been hesitant in generalizing from their *post-facto* design had they been aware of Meehl's (1970) trenchant review. Research design can begin to take advantage of the developments in time-series analysis (Brenner, 1973; Glass, Willson, and Gottman, 1975) and more powerful statistical techniques can help to identify crucial interactions among variables which less sensitive analyses may mask. Andrews *et al.* (1978), for example, present analyses which suggest only main effects. A more powerful analysis of the same frequency data (Bishop, Fienberg, and Holland, 1975) does suggest, however, interesting interactions with important theoretical implications. Analyses of data are available (e.g. Jenkins, Zyzanski, Ryan, Flessas, and Tannenbaum, 1977), but are by no means generally known.

There have been numerous suggestions as to the future course of such research. One suggestion has been that, since it is already dead (Hudgens, 1974), it should be made to lie down (Wershow and Reinhart, 1974), an unlikely occurrence in social science where the availability of any scale has a multiplicative effect on the production of research (cf. Levy, 1961). There have been attempts to improve the quality of the scales (Dohrenwend, Krasnoff, Askenasy, and Dohrenwend, 1978; Hurst *et al.*, 1978; Masuda and Holmes, 1978), to categorize the type of events experienced more finely (Johnson and Sarason, 1978; Vinokur and Selzer, 1975), and to look at a variety of other factors likely to moderate any relationship (e.g. Andrews, Tennant, Hewson, and Vaillant, 1978).

In his elegant summary of research in this and closely related areas, Kasl (1977) concludes that the research requires to change direction and examine the effect of one social event at a time. His criticism is based upon the view that any event in a person's life is set in a network of other events. Only by examining the interaction between a life event and the expectations, coping mechanisms, family setting, etc. of the person can a clear picture emerge.

Work by Brown and his associates (Brown, Bhrolcháin, and Harris, 1975;

Brown, Harris, and Peto, 1973) points to the complexity of relationships which may be construed as life events. In the analysis of the effect of unpleasant life events upon psychiatric disorder a distinction must be drawn between events which may play a 'formative' role, increasing the predisposition to a breakdown, and those which have a 'trigger' function, accelerating the onset of a breakdown which would vary probably have occurred anyway. Such analysis can be of importance in the prediction of physical breakdown. A set of experiences within the family may increase the disposition of an individual to illness, whereas loss of employment or bereavement may act to trigger an illness. The social psychologist has a role to play in identifying the development of these factors and relating them to a stress response and illness.

THE CONTRIBUTION OF SOCIAL PSYCHOLOGY

It is possible to go beyond this criticism and suggest that the current work on life events and on social epidemiological studies in general has failed very frequently to analyse in sufficient depth the antecedent, mediating, and consequent factors in the relationships between social stress and illness. As already mentioned there has been a tendency to ignore the need for the assessment of intervening physiological stress responses in much of the work. This is an important link in the hypothesized causal chain and more attention needs to be paid to its analysis. The study of the effects of single events would facilitate such analysis. This improvement would not be within the purview of the social psychologist. What is possible for the social psychologist is to make a contribution to the analysis of other mediating factors.

Research on life events has encountered the problem of estimating the subjective value of a stressor as against measuring merely some objective attributes (Rabkin and Streuning, 1976). The effect of a stressor will be a function of magnitude and duration of the stimulus, but other social psychological research has shown the importance of other features. Glass and Singer (1972), for example, have clearly demonstrated that unpredictability of the occurrence of a stressor is a critical feature in any effect upon performance, even after the stressor has been removed. Such a feature has also been shown to affect social behaviour (e.g. Mathews and Canon, 1975). The effects of unpredictability have not yet really been investigated as a variable affecting stress.

The evaluation of a stimulus event as a stressor also seems to be a function of the target's belief that he can control it or somehow cope with it. The belief that a stimulus can eventually be avoided or controlled has been shown to influence the magnitude of the stress response (Averill, 1973). Predictability and controllability are factors which have been shown in animal studies to influence very clearly the physiological concomitants of a stimulus (Miller, 1979) and while not so clearly shown in human studies, certainly considerable debate surrounds the notion that learned 'helplessness' (Seligman, 1975) with health consequences, follows from unpredictability of feedback to a response. A person's anticipation of behaviour, of being able to respond effectively, will influence his perception of an event and therefore the psychologist can contribute to an understanding of stress by an analysis of what stimulus factors may heighten or undermine beliefs in controllability (Wortman, 1976; Wortman and Dintzer, 1978).

A clearer understanding of the effect of social stressors may be increased by an analysis of mediating factors at a more molar level than that of the physiological. A person experiencing stress brings to the situation a set of learned responses, which may be construed as fairly stable personality dispositions, and also a place in a social network, a set of relationships with other people, both positive and negative. Undoubtedly there are stable individual differences in coping skills and in the ability to learn them, making people more and less susceptible to stress. Many of the personality dimensions identified to date can be implicated as moderator variables in stress research (e.g. Garrity, Somes, and Marx, 1977). Many personality variables can quite readily be implicated in the mediation of stress. Only a few of these can be alluded to here. One which is closely related to the topics considered to date is locus of control (Rotter, 1966). The person who is characterized as 'internal', believing that he plays a role in determining the events which impinge upon him, will presumably be more likely than the 'external' individual to expect to cope with stressors, and hence perhaps will experience less stress. Such an individual difference variable has been shown to interact with stimulus manipulations (Hiroto, 1974) and perception of life events (Johnson and Sarason, 1978), a demonstration of the usefulness of the concept in predicting the onset of stress. The relationship between internal locus and response to a stressor may not always be positive, however. Such possibilities will be considered later in the chapter.

Other dimensions of personality which are likely to interact with stress include introversion–extraversion (Brebner and Cooper, 1978), especially as regards the extent to which the extrovert is 'geared to respond' and hence is likely to attempt a response when given the opportunity. The response to a stressor will be different from that of the introvert who is perhaps more likely to seek information and inhibit a response. A related predisposition is sensation-seeking (Zuckerman, 1974). A person with a low disinhibition score, and hence likely to be at a low level of arousal and with a tendency to 'dampen down' stimulation (Zuckerman, Murtaugh, and Siegel, 1974), is likely to be more severely affected by life events which when they occur will have a stronger effect than on the person at the other pole of the dimension (Smith, Johnson, and Sarason, 1978). Another possible dimension which should be mentioned is 'internality/externality' or the extent to which an individual is sensitive to internal or external cues. This postulated dimension has had some value in understanding obesity (Rodin, 1977), although there must be some doubts now about how generally valuable it may be (Nisbett and Temoshok, 1976).

It may also be noted that even if one takes the view that stable personality traits do not exist or are of little value to an understanding of behaviour (Mischel, 1976), one can still incorporate into an analysis of stressor/stress mediation the concept of a learned capacity and belief in control (Bandura, 1977).

A mediating factor at the interpersonal rather than the intrapersonal level which may modify the impact of a stressor is the social network of relationships a person maintains. The social network may act both to enhance any stress response and to form a buffer against it. Characteristically epidemiologists have pointed to the stress-reducing value of social networks (Cassel, 1976; Cobb, 1976; Kaplan, Cassel, and Gore, 1977; Kasl, 1977; Rabkin and Streuning, 1976; Wolf and Goodell, 1976). The value of family, friends, and neighbours has been noted in helping people to withstand change in life circumstances. De Araujo, van Arsdel, Holmes, and Dudley (1973), for example, found evidence that asthmatic patients who had evidence of considerable family support required less than one-quarter of the medication that patients without such support were administered, even when they had comparable life-change scores. And Nuckolls, Cassel, and Kaplan (1972) found up to three times the number of post-pregnancy complications in a group low on an index of social support compared with a group high on that index, again with comparable life changes. The observed low incidence of coronary disease in Roseto, even though other biological risk factors would indicate that incidence should be as high as that in neighbouring communities, has been attributed to the close family and friendship ties existing in that Italian-American community (e.g. Bruhn, 1965). The support of family has also been suggested as a major factor in maintaining the low level of CHD in Japan (Matsumoto, 1970). The more acculturated an ethnic Japanese man becomes in America, the more likely is he to suffer from CHD (Marmot and Syme, 1976), even when diet, blood-pressure, and other risk factors are controlled for.

That social support need not necessarily be a buffer against stress, however, is evidenced by a study by Gore (1978) where a parsimonious interpretation of her data is afforded by positing that lack of social support exacerbates stress rather than that social support reduces stress. Lack of social support could be conceived as a negative life-change event rather than support be considered as a stress reducer. The data showing that people who live alone have a higher incidence of chronic illness (Lynch, 1977; Rabkin and Streuning, 1976) does not offer clear support in either direction. Those people who are alone frequently are so because of divorce or bereavement or some other event characteristically perceived as stressful.

Brown's work referred to earlier (Brown, Bhrolcháin, and Harris, 1975) highlights the complexity of any relationships which may exist. Various groups in the population may have long-term difficulties which predispose them to illness (and these will probably not be distributed evenly across the population, a point made earlier by Dohrenwend and Dohrenwend, 1974, and by Innes, 1975, in another context), and the discrete life events will be imposed in addition to the long-term stressor, perhaps acting to trigger off the illness rather than cause it. The social psychologist has a role to play in helping to measure the distribution of such social predispositions as well as personal dispositions.

The epidemiological work has not clearly indicated what it is about social support that may act to reduce stress, although there has been speculation (Kaplan *et al.*, 1977). Social support is likely to interact with the personality of the individual and with the nature of the coping response demanded. It is not even clear whether the factor involved is not the personality of the person who is alone or without support. Certainly loneliness is partly correlated with aspects of personality and is not entirely a social phenomenon (Russell, Peplau, and Ferguson, 1978). Indeed, different investigators may code similar responses in different ways. While evidence of loneliness and shyness can be perceived as the result of social factors (Cobb, 1976), it is possible to perceive it as partly the result of personality factors (Jenkins *et al.*, 1977).

Even if interpersonal relationships are important in stress, how they act will depend upon the stressor and the response required. While being alone may not be especially advantageous in dealing with a stressor, it is not necessarily a disadvantage either. Experiencing some kinds of life changes may be helped by having family around, for example in coping with bereavement. But others may be exacerbated by having the responsibility for any effects upon others. The stress of taking on a large mortgage or of emigrating may be increased by the thought of what may happen to others as a result of one's behaviour. At the very least, before one may predict how social support may act with stress one needs to know the nature of the life event, whether there was the possibility of some control over its occurrence or whether it was essentially uncontrollable. Social support may help to bear the burden of fate, but may exacerbate the stress of taking decisions for oneself and for others. Research showing that controllability of a stressor reduces the stress response (Seligman, Maier, and Solomon, 1971) would suggest that stress will not be especially high in such conditions (as against the picture given by the early work by Brady, 1964, which suggested the opposite). But there is little work with humans where an individual has to work to decide upon courses of action knowing that they will affect others as well as himself. Any observed relationships will be complicated further by reason of the tendency for people to believe in the illusion of control even when they are operating in circumstances wholly dependent on chance (Langer, 1975). Also research on group decision-making, showing that the diffusion of responsibility may reduce stress, is not very relevant to this since most of the work has looked at the way the group may act to make a decision and not at the effect a decision has upon a person making it for the group.

The presence of others may act to define a situation as stressful or otherwise by creating a 'social' reality. If people about one are calm in the presence of some threatening stimulus, then this may act further to calm an individual (Epley, 1974). If on the other hand people are not calm then this may act to enhance a belief in an individual that he also is unlikely to cope. Stress may thus be exacerbated (Rachman, 1978). There are even data to suggest that people pay too little attention to how other people cope with a stressor (Nisbett, Borgida, Crandall, and Reed, 1976) and so may be uninfluenced by information about the behaviour of people around them. Laboratory data on stress and the presence of others certainly demonstrate complex relationships between the nature of the stressor and the effects of affiliation (Buck and Parke, 1972; Ellsworth, Friedman, Perlick, and Hoyt, 1978; Innes, 1980; Innes and Sambrooks, 1969; Morris et al., 1976; Schachter, 1959). Why relationships in complex social structures should be simpler is not clear. Those studies that have been done in applied settings (e.g. Lynch, Thomas, Paskewitz, Katcher, and Weir, 1977) have shown that human contact in stress settings has ameliorative effects, but it also shows every evidence of ignoring research in other disciplines which could be of value. The multi-disciplinary syndrome again?

Epidemiological research to date has also tended to ignore the possibly stressful consequences of social interaction itself. The mere presence of being with another person has been shown to induce physiological arousal (Zajonc, 1980), possibly owing to the need continually to monitor the other person's action for any possible consequences to oneself and this stressor has characteristics in common with other known stressors (Terris and Rahhal, 1969). People are likely to be unpredictable and they therefore possess some of the characteristics of a stress-inducing stimulus. The more people there are the more attention is consumed and thus more effort expended. Attention and social overload has been considered by environmental psychologists (Cohen, 1978; Saegert, 1976, 1978), with their consequences for social behaviour, but little has been done on any consequences for health and illness. Where there has been some research (Mettlin and Woelfel, 1974; Robbins, Meyersburg, and Tanck, 1974), too much reliance has been placed upon retrospective recall measures of interaction and symptoms for much reliance to be placed on the results.

Frankenhaeuser (1977) has shown that social information overload leads to epinephrine production, so much overload is arousing. Cohen and Lezak (1977) have shown a physical stressor to affect responsiveness to social cues. So social overload may lead to a reduction of attention to the very cues which are necessary for appropriate interaction and this in turn will lead to further overload and presumably stress (Singer, Lundberg, and Frankenhaeuser, 1978).

It has been suggested that behaviour in social organizations can help to reduce stress by providing the predictability of behaviour (e.g. Sengel, 1978). Behaviour in organizations, anyway, is not the same as the behaviour of organizing (Easterbrook, 1978; Sarason, 1972; Weick, 1969). Initiating new relationships and establishing forms of conduct is very different even from learning established conduct in an organization. There is in fact evidence of considerable stress experienced within organizations, although it is not uniform at all levels (Howard, Cunningham, and Rechnitzer, 1977; Sales, 1969; Saegert, 1976; Zaleznik, de Vries and Howard, 1977; Zyzanski, 1978). There will be a complex interplay between responsibility and predictability which will determine the degree of stress experienced by people engaged in social interaction within an organization. Those who can initiate action and are thus in some degree of control may suffer less from the stress which comes from the work overload commensurate with their position (Sales, 1969), while those who are in middle positions in an organization, with responsibility but without much control, may suffer more (Zaleznik *et al.*, 1977). Any effects will undoubtedly be further affected by the personality characteristics of the individuals in the roles (McClelland, 1976) and by the social skills which they bring to the position, as evidenced by Christenson and Hinkle's (1961) study of managers in Bell Telephone Laboratories.

In several ways therefore a social psychological approach can help to understand the epidemiology of illness. It is not possible to review all of the research on social psychological mediators of stressor/stress relationships or to consider what may be contributed in the future. Too many life events have been studied and too many illnesses have been implicated, from the common cold to cancer, for a brief review to be possible.

What it is proposed to do is to take a particular illness and review the work concerned with it, and to highlight the role of social psychology in understanding the aetiology. The illness to be considered is coronary heart disease (CHD). A great deal of research has been done on the identification of biological risk factors (Kuller, 1976) and longitudinal studies (e.g. the Framingham studies, Brand, Rosenman, Sholtz and Friedman, 1976) have enabled predictive equations to be written for disease incidence. The known risk factors only account for about half of any observed variance, however, and many have postulated that psychosocial variables may be important. There is in fact considerable agreement on this point although not about the mode of effect (Kasl, 1977). The case for the role of psycho-social factors in CHD is very different from that in, say, cancer, where there is still doubt that personality or social factors have much influence (Fox, 1978).

Work has been done by social psychologists and a number of models have been postulated to incorporate psychosocial risk factors. The contribution of social psychology to an understanding of how disease may occur can therefore be seen and assessed.

Knowledge of risk factors has prompted a number of studies into the prevention of CHD. Several studies have commenced by reducing known risk factors (cf. Breslow, 1978; Fielding, 1978). The modification of such risks as saturated fat intake and cigarette smoking appears to have had an effect upon the incidence of CHD, for example in the North Karelia project in Finland. In some of these programmes social psychological interventions have been attempted, as in the Stanford Heart Disease Prevention Program (McAlister' et al., 1976), so there is an opportunity to see to what extent interventionist applied psychology may pay dividends. Psychology may have something to contribute to the prevention of disease at a community level as well as at the more traditional level of the individual being helped by various forms of therapy (Suinn and Bloom, 1978).

In reviewing some of the work it is not the intention to present the view that social psychology has any dominant role to play in the understanding of the aetiology of CHD. Interdisciplinary studies seem to be the only avenue to understanding. But social psychology is one of the disciplines which may make a contribution.

BEHAVIOUR AND CORONARY HEART DISEASE

Elevated blood pressure, smoking habits, and serum cholesterol, among many other factors, have been shown to be correlated with the risk of CHD. Dietary factors and physiological indices, however, still only account for about half of the variance of CHD.

Since specific behavioural features, such as dietary habits and cigarette smoking, are associated with CHD, the suggestion has been made that aspects of personality or behaviour may be more generally associated with CHD. If individuals with a particular set of behavioural characteristics tend also to smoke or overeat, then such behavioural characteristics will clearly tend to contribute directly to the onset of illness. Alternatively, the effect of such characteristics may be mediated via quite distinct mechanisms (for example, increased stress overall); or it may be the combined, interactive effect of such characteristics with those of the smoking or eating habit that results in illness.

Several studies have been conducted in an attempt to relate the individual's more permanent behavioural features of personality to clinical CHD. Studies have used standard personality questionnaires, such as the Minnesota Multiphasic Personality Inventory (MMPI) or Cattell's 16PF, and have found relationships between certain personality characteristics and type of CHD (Jenkins, 1971). Much of the work using such devices has used a cross-sectional methodology, and hence has run foul of the criticism that personality differences are due to, rather than cause, the CHD.

A set of behavioural characteristics which have been implicated in the occurrence of clinical CHD has been termed the Type A overt behaviour pattern. The Type A pattern of behaviour is characterized by achievement striving, competitiveness, aggressiveness, and a strong sense of time urgency. The relationship of this Type A pattern, as against the Type B, more relaxed, pattern has been identified in a number of retrospective and also prospective studies (Jenkins, 1971, 1976, 1977).

A substantial degree of support for such a relationship comes from the Western Collaborative Group Study (WCGS), initiated in 1960–61 as a prospective epidemiological investigation of CHD incidence in over 3,000 men employed in ten companies (Rosenman, Friedman, and Strauss, 1964). In the most recent follow-up analysis, the death rate per 1,000 person-years for CHD was 2.92 for Type A and 1.32 for Type B (Rosenman, Brand, Jenkins, Friedman, Straus, and Wurm, 1975). CHD was significantly associated with such factors as blood pressure, serum level of cholesterol, smoking habits, etc. but the association with Type A still existed when these other risk factors were controlled for. Even with cholesterol levels low, or with systolic and diastolic blood pressure within normal levels, the rate of CHD for individuals categorized as Type A was at least twice that of those identified as Type B, in both the 39–49 year age group and in the 50–59 age group. These data seem to indicate that the overt behaviour pattern can be listed among the list of major risk factors. Cross validation of the WCGS study comes from a recent study in which Type A is independently associated with CHD prevalence in the Framingham study (Haynes, Feinleib, Levine, Scotch, and Kannel 1978).

MEASUREMENT OF TYPE A

Jenkins considers the Type A pattern to be a 'style of behaviour with which some persons habitually respond to circumstances that arouse them'. As such it does not seem to be possible to call it a personality *trait*. Jenkins, however, confuses matters somewhat by saying that the pattern is a 'deeply ingrained, enduring trait' (Jenkins, 1976).

Initial studies identified the Type A individual by use of a diagnostic interview. A classification is made by the interviewer on the basis of the content of the interviewee's answers to questions about behaviour and on non-verbal behaviour and speech characteristics. The judgement is a holistic one, but data suggest a good amount of inter- and intraobserver agreement (Jenkins *et al.*, 1978).

Recent studies have made use of questionnaires, typically the Jenkins Activity Survey (JAS) (e.g. Roseman and Friedman, 1974). The JAS was designed to maximize agreement with the interview-determined classification. Analysis of the JAS reveals three orthogonal factors: H, Hard driving and competitiveness; J, Job-involvement; and S, Speed and impatience. The individual factors do not appear to make any clear, independent contribution to the prediction of CHD, however; only the overall score is associated with incidence. Analysis of the interview responses reveals a wider, five-factor structure, with factors labelled as Competitive drive, Past achievements, Impatience, Non-job achievements, and Speed. In predicting later CHD, however, only the factors Competitive drive and Impatience showed significant relationships (Matthews, Glass, Rosenman, and Bortner, 1977).

Recent data suggest that the interview classification of the Type A pattern is superior to a JAS classification, at least in identifying near-future CHD cases (Brand *et al.*, in press; Shekelle, *et al.*, 1976). The JAS classification is made only on the basis of a respondent's answer *content*, i.e. on his subjective self-report and not upon his actual behaviour. While there are problems inherent in making holistic judgements, with clinicians often not being very good at combining information to make a overall judgement, the superiority of the interview classification may be due to the stressfulness of a face-to-face interview, especially one in which the interviewer challenges and hurries the respondent. Given that the Type A pattern is considered to be a pattern of response to stressful situations, the interview is more likely than is a self-report questionnaire to evoke the characteristic pattern. In response to a questionnaire a person has more time to think, to imagine unrepresentative hypothetical situations, and perhaps to censor his responses. Current concern with the measurement of personality characteristics and their relation to behaviour in different situations, would support the view that behaviour observed in one stressful situation would have a greater probability of predicting behaviour to other stressors than behaviour measured by questionnaire.

There is empirical evidence that the non-verbal aspect of behaviour in the interview is more important than the content of response in enabling a classification. Characteristics of speech in the interview, such as emphasis and speed of speaking correlated 0.72 with the classification made using the standard assessment procedure (Scherwitz, Berton, and Leventhal, 1977; Schucker and Jacobs, 1977). Emphasis alone accounted for 36 percent of the variance, whereas content accounted for only 4 percent. The correlation between the content of the interview answers and the content of the JAS responses was high, giving support to the validity of the behavioural dimensions being used. The weighting assigned to the non-verbal factors seems to be a crucial factor.

CONCEPTUALIZATION OF PATTERN A

Data from laboratory experiments have validated the components of the Type A syndrome, generally as these have emerged from analysis of the JAS. Type A subjects have been shown, for example, to work on a task at near maximum capacity, irrespective of whether or not there was a deadline, supporting the competitiveness/achievement motivation component of the syndrome. Type B subjects only exerted effort when there was an explicit deadline. The As and Bs did not differ in the proportion of items tried which were correctly solved, only in the number which were attempted when there was no explicit deadline provided. Differences between the two groups only emerge when external factors are taken into account (Burnam, Pennebaker, and Glass, 1975). Other work suggests that the Type A person reacts more strongly to the threat of evaluation than does the Type B, as indexed by greater increases in heart-rate and systolic blood pressure, although this susceptibility of arousal to evaluation is not reflected in better performance (Dembrowski, MacDougall, and Shields, 1977). The Type A pattern is significantly associated with norepinephrine production during competition, although not with epinephrine (Friedman, Byers, Diamant, and Rosenman, 1975).

A significant component of the Type A is the sense of time urgency. Type A subjects seem to have a distorted time sense. They judge the lapse of one minute sooner than do Type B individuals. That is, they perceive time as passing slower than do the Type Bs. The type A individual also performs more poorly than the Type B when he has to perform slowly in order to obtain a reward (Glass, Snyder, and Hollis, 1974). Observation of the subjects during the experimental session showed that four times as many of the Type A subjects demonstrated behaviour indicative of tension or hyperactivity.

Aggressiveness and hostility have also been implicated as a major characteristic of Type A and this has been shown to be a correlate of the sense of time urgency (Glass, Snyder, and Hollis, 1974). During a group discussion a confederate of the experimenter deliberately slowed down the discussion. The Type A subjects showed greater irritation in the slow-down experimental condition. This effect has been shown in a more recent study, with the Type A subjects reacting to frustration with significantly more aggression than Type B subjects, the aggression being directed towards individuals who had been responsible for the frustration, but also towards an individual who had merely been present during the frustrating experience although not responsible for it (Carver and Glass, 1978). Glass (1977) has suggested that the achievement striving, time urgency, and aggressiveness can be envisaged as a result of a need by Type A individuals to master the environment and avoid a loss of control. The Type A person is struggling to master the physical and social environment while the Type B is relatively free of such concerns. The achievement striving is certainly consistent with such a view, the aggressiveness which results from interference with attempts at mastery can also be seen as a learned mechanism to deal with loss of control, and the heightened sense of time urgency can be the result of an acceleration of pace to cope with the environmental demands which are continually met.

Such a view suggests that the Type A person will, when faced with frustration of his efforts to maintain control of events, first, make more persistent attempts to maintain control than will the Type B person. Secondly, when it becomes clear that control over events is not possible, then the Type A person will 'give-up', and this 'given-up' syndrome may persist longer than for the Type B person.

Krantz, Glass, and Snyder (1974) exposed subjects to noise with the expectation that the noise could be controlled. The Type As showed significantly more persistence in attempts to escape than did the Type Bs. But the presentation of noise was in fact uncontrollable, and initial repeated attempts to assert control led, more rapidly in the case of the Type A subject, to a perception of the non-contingency between response and outcome. The Type A subjects showed learned helplessness (i.e. they gave up efforts to escape after pre-treatment with an uncontrollable stressor) after a pre-treatment with a stressor of high intensity, but not after a pre-treatment with one of low intensity. Glass (1977) suggests that these data indicate the *salience* of the stimulus may be an important variable moderating the impact of the attempts to maintain control. Type As may only be more responsive than Bs when the uncontrollability cues are especially strong. The Type A characteristics can be viewed as manifestations of a need to exert control over events, especially when the events clearly threaten a belief in control. If the attempts at control are not successful then there will be subsequent helplessness and cessation of attempts to control. The Type B person, on the other hand, is less concerned with maintaining control and is less responsive to the salience of the cues in that they seem less prone to 'helplessness' under high stress.

Support for such a view of the role of behaviour patterns in the aetiology of CHD comes from a variety of sources. It has been shown that CHD is associated with the Type A pattern and also with depression. Kavanagh and Shephard (1975) found post-infarct patients to show either depression or hypomania on the MMPI. Given the problems of interpreting personality data following illness and inferring a causal relationship, one can see similarities between hypomania and the Type A pattern. Spicer (1978) has suggested that there may be two routes to CHD: either through a Type A pattern or via a series of experiences that lead to depression. Glass's (1977) view would suggest the possibility that the two are part of a larger pattern. The move to a learned helplessness state by Type A people when faced with loss of control is a move to a state of depression. As Spicer (1978) suggests, if the Type A individual moves regularly through such phases there may come a final irreversible shift to a depressive state.

Certainly helplessness has been identified as a possible factor as a precipitator of disease (Greene, Goldstein, and Moss, 1972). Sudden death due to CHD has been shown to have been preceded by depression for several months and there are parallels between clinical depression and helplessness (Engel, 1968; Seligman, 1975). The Type A person can be conceived to be especially prone to perceiving non-contingency since he will exert initially greater efforts to achieve control than a Type B. The realization of helplessness is therefore likely to be all the greater, provided of course that the cues are strong that control might be possible. If the cues are weak then the Type A person may be more immune to helplessness than the Type B since he will not attempt to exert control so strongly. In a like manner, it is conceivable that the person who is 'internally' oriented may be especially vulnerable to a series of events which demonstrate that he is in fact *not* in control. Glass (1977) does report evidence of a weak though significant correlation between Type A pattern and internal locus of control. The results of Johnson and Sarason (1978) may only be valid for exposure to events that enhance a person's sense of mastery. A reversal of effect could well be predicted. Problems with the locus of control concept are rife, however, and clear predictions are not easy to make (Ickes and Layden, 1978). Hopefully recent developments will help (Wallston, Wallston, and DeVillis, 1978).

SOME LIMITATIONS TO THE SCOPE OF RESEARCH ON THE TYPE A PATTERN

It may be suggested that we have to view those findings which suggest a relationship between cultural and social mobility and CHD, or between competition and CHD, i.e. work on the impact of a range of life events, as the result of a differential effect upon a subset of people, those demonstrating the Type A pattern. The Type A person will be the one most likely to be socially upwardly mobile (Zyzanski, 1978), or the one who will compete, and so will be especially prone, on the above grounds, to suffer from CHD. There will be individuals who are socially mobile for external rather than internal reasons and who will tend not to suffer from CHD because they do not have the predisposing behaviour pattern. It may be worthwhile re-examining the relationship between social incongruity, the inconsistency between one's social position and one's expectation, and similar life events, and CHD. Some work has suggested there is a link, although later research has failed to find a relationship (Shekelle, Ostfeld, and Paul, 1969; Horan and Gray, 1974). Since it has been shown, however, that social stress may influence CHD through the Type A behaviour pattern, failures to replicate studies may be due to different populations being used; a relationship may emerge or be masked depending upon the average disposition and the variability of the population being studied.

A clearer analysis of the Type A pattern is necessary if any advances are to occur in an understanding of the relationship between CHD and work setting. Stress at work has been implicated as a risk factor. Theorell and Floderus-Myrhed (1977), for example, find workload to be related to CHD. French and his co-workers (e.g. French, 1976; Caplan, Cobb, and French, 1975; Caplan and Jones, 1975) have often pointed to the effect of role overload upon health, and specifically the occurrence of CHD. The data on work overload is, however, very inconsistent (Kasl, 1977) and studies showing a positive relationship are likely to be matched by one showing no relationship. What may be important is job involvement associated with a degree of job dissatisfaction.

The picture is not clarified by recourse to the Type A pattern as a moderator. The factor of job involvement, which can be identified in the JAS, is not a significant predictor of CHD, although total JAS score has been shown to correlate with an independent measure of job involvement (Matthews and Saal, 1978). This did not hold for interview Type A score. Role overload, a function of a lack of 'fit' between a person's capacities and the demands of the job, does not seem to relate clearly to CHD via the Type A syndrome. The Type A person is likely to take on more work and this will contribute to a measure of role overload (Sales, 1969), but they may also have a picture of themselves as being capable of taking on more (Howard *et al.*, 1977). Any clear picture may only emerge when the four factors of personality, job involvement, job satisfaction, and workload are considered together.

The failure to discover a consistent relationship may also be due to a failure to differentiate between the demands of the job as a task and the requirements to interact socially and have responsibility for other people. Recent work does point to the importance of social factors in interaction with the Type A syndrome (Jenkins *et al.*, 1977). The Type A person appears to be uncomfortable in social relationships and feels insecure when in groups. The Type A individual also seems to prefer to be alone rather than with others when working on a task (Dembrowski and MacDougall, 1978). Such a preference to be alone when working would follow from the concern of the Type A person with achievement and avoidance of failure. The presence of others may exacerbate any sense of failure. It would also follow from a concern for personal control, since other people would be less amenable to influence than a physical task.

But a reluctance to work with others can place the Type A person in an especially difficult bind. Much of what has to be done in society requires the cooperation and direction of other people. The Type A person therefore will either have to accept the need to work with others, which will be stressful and which has been shown to increase lack of satisfaction in Type A people (Howard *et al.*, 1977), or will avoid it and take on too much individual responsibility, which also will increase stress. While the avoidance of contact with others in order to avoid risk of public failure may be attractive, it nevertheless remains the case that often only the feedback from other people will provide information as to how successful one has been. Other people are often necessary for comparison purposes and again the Type A person may be stressed, the stress arising from a conflict of needs. Heylen and Innes (1979) have found evidence that the Type A person, when performing a task under evaluative conditions, does engage in more attention to other people present. This was probably due, however, to a need to assess one's own performance, since further data (Innes and Herbertt, 1979) suggest that manipulations known to increase objective self-awareness (Duval and Wicklund, 1972; Innes and Young, 1975) especially affected Type A individuals, thereby inducing increased performance. Data from a recent study by Scherwitz, Berton, and Leventhal (1978) indeed suggests that what may truly identify the Type A pattern is a high degree of self-reference, as evidenced in conversation. Frequent referral to oneself, with Type A behaviour, was associated with greater physiological response under challenge, and this behaviour may well be indicative of a chronic state of objective self-awareness, leading to higher striving to meet standards and challenges. Data from the Innes and Herbertt study suggest, however, that the Type A person is not very open to cues about the appropriateness of social behaviour, as assessed by Snyder's (1974) self-monitoring scale. The Type A person may be responsive to information about the self, less so to information about others. This would in turn be consistent with Vallacher's (1978) data suggesting less social discrimination with objective self-awareness. In the Heylen and Innes study the greater attention was associated with better task performance, but in view of the overload implications of attention (Kahneman, 1973), and especially of social overload (Cohen, 1978) with the need for more monitoring, a downturn in performance could be expected. Social overload could thus lead to a loss of achievement — stressful for the Type A person — and could also lead to a loss of processing of social cues (Cohen and Lezak, 1977), with further loss of control and predictability — with stress implications.

One might think that the Type A person could be more immune to such effects, perhaps because of a greater capacity. There is the hint, however, that individuals with the Type A syndrome may be slower in processing information about their environment than are Type B persons. Several features of laboratory performance suggest that Type As and Bs do not differ in the amount of work achieved or the number of problems got right even though the former work harder (Burnam *et al.*, 1975; Friedman *et al.*, 1975), although there are exceptions (Stokols, Novaco, and Stokols, 1978). Abrahams and Birren (1973) have direct evidence of slower processing capacity among Type A people. Given the evidence that any cardiovascular pathology does reduce information processing capacity (Spieth, 1965; Szafran, 1966), once any kind of damage has begun to occur the limitations on capacity will be exacerbated, leading only to more stress.

It may well be that the Type A person will not meet stressful situations of the kind which lead to a belief in loss of control. If they are in managerial positions they will have control and may not receive much feedback that they are not succeeding. The role of an organization is partly to eliminate just such feedback. Managers need not have excess risk of CHD (Zaleznik *et al.*, 1977). Also, behaviour in an organization may be routine, 'mindless' (Langer, 1978), and therefore there is little need for monitoring the behaviour of others or for maintaining a wide repertoire of decision strategies (Saegert, 1976). In which case the risk of CHD will not be elevated. A prediction about CHD will not be possible unless an account is taken of the task and social requirements in any setting, and sampled accordingly.

An analysis of personality factors related to CHD which emphasizes the demands of social interaction is that by McClelland (1976). He argues very persuasively that people who have a high need for Power (n Power) are especially at risk, provided that they also have a strong inhibition of that need and use it in a socialized and not assertive manner. A high level of social Power need is correlated with production of epinephrine, i.e. with strong arousal. The idea of people with such dedicated, socialized drive for power reminds one of the description CHD-prone person as having job involvement 'without a sense of accomplishment, joy, or relief (the "Sisyphus reaction")' (Kasl, 1977). Perhaps only a particular kind of job involvement is predictive of CHD. There are similarities between the notions of the Type A pattern and that of the inhibited but high n Power individual that are clearly worth exploring. A problem resides in the apparently different hormonal basis of epinephrine with n Power and norepinephrine with Type A (Friedman *et al.*, 1975). Mathews and Saal (1978) have found no relationship between JAS score and n Power, but this study surely requires replication in view of the clear similarities between the constructs. Since Type A behaviour is posited to occur in response to particular tasks and n Power is elicited in social interaction any relationship may only occur when the setting is appropriate.

SOME PROBLEMS WITH THE CONCEPTION OF THE TYPE A PATTERN

However impressive the data may appear in support of a Type A pattern being implicated as a risk factor in CHD, there are problems. The first, alluded to in the earlier discussion of the nature of measurement of the pattern, concerns the question of whether Type A versus B is conceived as a dichotomy or as the ends of a continuum. Use of the JAS implicates a dimension. While the JAS has a factor structure suggesting at least three factors, the individual factors are not particularly useful in predicting CHD. A judgement about the cut-off point between those to be categorized as Type A and those as Type B has to be made. Depending upon the nature of the sample used in the study the difference in scores between the two categories may be small. Differences in sample means and variances may be a cause of the discrepancies found between the results of different studies.

The interview method of categorization has been found to be a more reliable predictor of CHD than the survey, perhaps partly because the interviewer is able to make a sharper distinction between the types than is possible with a self-report survey. The holistic judgement of the interview, subject to the biases which exist in such methods, may sharpen differences and create categorizations where continua exist. But the interview, based upon the observation of behaviour, may give a less equivocal categorization of the Type A individual.

A second problem is that several recent studies have shown that the personality structure of the coronary-prone person may be complex and they raise serious qualifications about making judgements which are too simplistic. A re-analysis of the MMPI data from the Western Electric Study, for example, using a principal components analysis, showed a multi-dimensional structure with different loading of variables on the factors for non-coronary, angina pectoris, and myocardial infarct groups (Lebovitz, Lichter, and Moses, 1975). One cannot put these three groups on a single dimension of 'Type A-ness'. In addition, it was found that, for the non-coronary group, personality scores derived from the MMPI and physiological measures, e.g. blood pressure, cholesterol, and smoking, were loaded on separate factors, whereas for the two CHD groups on the same factors there were loadings of *both* personality and physiological variables.

Recent analyses of data from the WCGS suggest differences in the responses to JAS items of people with angina, acute myocardial infarction, and silent myocardial infarction (the last group composed people with abnormalities in an electrocardiogram without clinical evidence of an infarction). The differences in response do separate the angina cases from the other two and from a group still healthy (Jenkins *et al.*, 1978). The analysis suggests that items may be able to identify subgroups of CHD cases with different behaviour patterns. The clinical descriptions of the classes of items identifying the various groups are, however, very subtle in their differences. In view of the reservations expressed earlier about the validity of questionnaire response to hypothetical situations, further data are needed before one can distinguish very confidently between behavour patterns associated with different forms of CHD. The Type A pattern has been show to predict *second* myocardial infarction, although a differential item analysis has not been done (Jenkins, Zyzanski, and Rosenman, 1976). It may be that a multi-dimensional analysis of behaviour patterns is possible and necessary, but more data are required.

A third problem, and one which may be very fundamental, relates to the genesis of the Type A syndrome. The work of Glass has validated the pattern as one which interacts with various stressors and gives a plausible account of how the pattern may increase CHD risk. But there is very little work which has attempted to examine the development of the pattern. One study has suggested a heritability component, but the effect is modest (Mathews and Krantz, 1976). The theoretical discussions have centred upon a social learning view of the development of the pattern, with certain features of contemporary society likely to reinforce behaviour concerned with control over the environment. This still leaves the possibility of some more fundamental difference between individuals underlying the growth of the behaviour pattern, perhaps processing capacity (Abrahams and Birren, 1973).

The role that culture plays in the aetiology of the Type A pattern has not been clearly established. Men are more clearly at risk from CHD than are women and have more clearly definable Type A patterns. Socialization practices may be more likely to shape behaviour of the Type A pattern in men. Where women do show a Type A pattern, however, it is associated with prevalence of CHD (Haynes *et al.*, 1978) and this is not mediated by elevated standard risk factors. Women in employment show higher incidence of Type A behaviour and greater prevalence of CHD. Whether the Type A behaviour leads women to employment or the situation shapes Type A behaviour remains to be seen. The evidence for genetic and cultural influences upon sex differences in Type A behaviour is as yet unclear (Waldron, 1978).

Evidence for the role of culture also comes from studies on Japanese-Americans, of the kind referred to above (Marmot and Syme, 1976). The Type A pattern is very infrequently found in Japanese samples. A new factor structure appeared in the Japanese-American sample (Cohen, 1978) and a factor defined as hard-working, separate from competitive items, was associated with CHD. So, even across cultures there may be a similarity of the relationship between behaviour and CHD. Cohen (1978) also found that when behaviour pattern and the degree to which Japanese had assimilated the American culture pattern were both taken into account, the risk of CHD was very similar to that of Americans.

TYPE A BEHAVIOUR AND CHANGE

Interventionist programmes appear to have had success in reducing the incidence of CHD; social psychology has contributed to this, demonstrating the role of interpersonal influence and the mass media in producing community change (McAlister *et al.*, 1976). It is not yet clear whether the Type A pattern mediates any change in health behaviour. Shekelle *et al.* (1976) found no evidence that Type A men complied more or less than Type B with medical regimens, although Caplan *et al.* (1975) did find evidence that people who gave up smoking tended to be Type B. As they point out, if this trend were to be maintained in the population there would be an increase in the relationship between smoking and CHD as a result of attempts at prevention. More work is required on the nature of the Type A person's response to persuasion and interpersonal influence.

There has of course been work done on behaviour modification techniques to change the Type A pattern (e.g. Suinn and Bloom, 1978). How successful this will be remains to be seen in the long term. Success could achieve much, in view of the evidence that Type A individuals have a higher risk of a secondary myocardial infarction (Jenkins *et al.*, 1976). In view of the impulsivity of the Type A person, however, and the lack of awareness of cues guiding behaviour, perhaps rational techniques will not be of great use. In view of the apparent insensitivity of the Type A person to the presence of physical symptoms during task performance (Weidner and Matthews, 1978), perhaps the Type A individual will be less likely to present himself for a physical examination when symptoms first appear, thus heightening risk, and may also be more difficult to train to monitor symptoms during any preventative or therapeutic regimen.

More work needs to be done to ascertain the value of teaching people various strategies to cope with stress (e.g. Lazarus, 1966), strategies which may be judged on the basis of their success and not on some value judgement about the degree of maturity involved (Andrews *et al.*, 1978). The role of attribution processes (e.g. Rodin, 1978) and of attention to and evaluation of symptoms (e.g. Pennebaker and Skelton, 1978) is likely to be important.

CONCLUSIONS

An attempt has been made to demonstrate social psychology's role in the understanding of social stress and illness. Much more has been done than has been reported here; the field of behavioural medicine is well on the way to becoming a 'boom' area. But much more needs to be done, hopefully work guided by a grounding in social psychological theory, both with respect to the cognitions and attributions of the individual and the social structure and interactions which shape those cognitions and add to the stress and ailments of people in society.

REFERENCES

Abrahams, J. P. and Birren, J. E. (1973) 'Reaction time as a function of age and behavioral predisposition to coronary heart disease', *J. Gerontology*, **28**, 471–78.

Altman, I. A. (1976) 'Environmental psychology and social psychology', *Pers. soc. Psychol. Bull.*, **2**, 96–113.

Andrews, G., Tennant, C., Hewson, D. M., and Vaillant, G. E. (1978) 'Life event stress, social support, coping style and risk of psychological impairment', *J. nerv. ment. Dis.*, **166**, 307–16.

Averill, JH. (1973) 'Personal control over aversive stimuli and its relationship to stress', *Psychol. Bull.*, **80**, 286–303.

Bahnson, C. B. (1974) 'Epistemological perspectives of physical disease from the psychodynamic point of view', *Am. J. Publ. Health.*, **64**, 1034–40.

Baker, G. W. and Chapman, D. W. (Eds.) (1962) *Man and Society in Disaster*, Basic Books, New York.

Bandura, A. (1977) 'Self-efficacy: Toward a unifying theory of behavioral change', *Psychol. Rev.*, **84**, 191–215.

Bauer, R. A. (1964) 'The communicator and the audience', in *People, Society and Mass Communications* (Eds.: L. A. Dexter and D. M. White), Collier-Macmillan, New York, 125–40.

Berkun, M. M., Bialek, H. M., Kern, R. P., and Yagi, K. 'Experimental studies of psychological stress in man', *Psychol. Monogr.*, **76**, (15, whole no. 534).

Bishop, Y. M. M., Fienberg, S. E., and Holland, F. W. (1975) *Discrete Multivariate Analysis*, M.I.T. Press, Cambridge, Mass.

Brady, J. V. (1965) 'Behavioral stress and physiological change: A comparative approach to the experimental analysis of some psychosomatic problems', *Trans. N.Y. Acad. Sci.*, **26**, 438–96.

Brand, R. J., Rosenman, R. H., Jenkins, C. D., Sholtz, R. I., and Zyzanski, S. J. (1980) 'Comparison of coronary heart disease prediction in the Western Collaborative Group Study using the structured interview and the Jenkins Activity Survey assessments of the coronary-prone Type A behavior pattern', *J. Chron. Dis.*, in press.

Brand, R. J., Rosenman, R. H., Sholtz, R. I., and Friedman, M. (1976) 'Multivariate prediction of coronary heart disease in the Western Collaborative Group Study compared to the findings of the Framingham study', *Circulation*, **53**, 348–55.

Brebner, J. and Cooper, C. (1978) 'Stimulus- or response-induced excitation: A comparison of the behaviour of introverts and extroverts', *J. res. Person.*, **12**, 306–11.

Brenner, M. H. (1973) *Mental Illness and the Economy*, Harvard University Press, Cambridge, Mass.

Breslow, L. (1978) 'Risk factor intervention for health maintenance', *Science*, **200**, 908–12.

Broadbent, D. E. (1971) *Decision and Stress*, Academic Press, New York.

Broadbent, D. E. (1978) The current state of noise research: Reply to Poulton', *Psychol. Bull.*, **85**, 1052–67.

Brown, G. W., Bhrolcháin, N. M., and Harris, T. (1975) 'Social class and psychiatric disturbance among women in an urban population', *Sociology*, **9**, 225–54.

Brown, G. W., Harris, T. O., and Peto, J. (1973) 'Life events and psychiatric disorders Part 2: Nature of causal link', *Psychol. Med.*, **3**, 159–76.

Bruhn, J. (1965) 'An epidemiological study of myocardial infarctions in an Italian-American community',*J. Chronic Dis.*, **18**, 353.

Buck, R. W. and Parke, R. D. (1972) 'Behavioural and physiological response to the presence of a friendly or neutral person in two types of stressful situation', *J. Pers. soc. Psychol.* **26**, 143–53.

Bunn, R. and Drane, N. (1975) 'Economic change as a factor in heart disease', *New Doctor*, **July**, no. 5.

Burnam, M. A., Pennebaker, J. W., and Glass, D. C. (1975) 'Time consciousness, achievement striving and the Type A coronary-prone behavior pattern', *J. abnorm. Psychol.*, **84**, 76–79.

Bursill, A. E. (1958) 'Restriction of peripheral vision during exposure to hot and humid conditions', *Quart. J. exp. Psychol.*, **10**, 113–29.

Caplan, R. D., Cobb, S., and French, J. R. P. (1975) 'Relationships of cessation of smoking with job stress, personality and social support', *J. appl. Psychol.*, **60**, 211–19.

Carver, C. S. and Glass, D. C. (1978) 'Coronary-prone behavior pattern and interpersonal aggression', *J. Pers. soc. Psychol.*, **38**, 361–66.

Cassel, J. (1976) 'The contribution of the social environment to host resistance', *Am. J. Epidemiol.*, **104**, 107–23.

Christenson, W. N. and Hinkle, L. E. (1961) 'Differences in illness and prognostic signs in two groups of young men', *J. Am. Med. Assoc.*, **177**, 247.

Cobb, S. (1976) 'Social support as a moderator of life stress', *Psychosom. Med.*, **38**, 300–14.

Cohen, J. B. (1978) 'The influence of culture on coronary-prone behavior', in *Coronary-prone Behavior* (Eds. T. M. Dembroski *et al.*) Springer-Verlag, New York, 191–198.

Cohen, S. (1978) 'Environmental load and the allocation of attention', in *Advances in Environmental Psychology*, (Eds. A. Baum, J. E. Singer, and S. Valins), vol. 1, Erlbaum, Hillsdale, N.J.

Cohen, S. and Lezak, A. (1977) 'noise and inattentiveness to social cues', *Environ. & Behav.*, **9**, 559–72.

D'Atri, D. (1975) 'Psychophysiological responses to crowding', *Environ. & Behav.*, **7**, 237-52.

De Araujo, G., van Arsdel, P. P., Holmes, T. H., and Dudley, D. L. (1973) 'Life change, coping ability and chronic intrinsic asthma', *J. Psychosom. Res.*, **17**, 359-63.

Dembrowski, T. M. and MacDougall, J. M. (1978) 'Stress effects on affiliation preferences among subjects possessing the Type A coronary-prone behavior pattern', *J. Pers. soc. Psychol.*, **36**, 23-33.

Dembrowski, T. M., MacDougall, J. M., and Shields, J. M. (1977) 'Physiologic reactions to social challenge in persons evidencing the Type A coronary-prone behavior pattern', *J. hum. Stress*, **3**, 2-9.

Dohrenwend, B. S. and Dohrenwend, B. P. (Eds.) (1974) *Stressful Life Events*, Wiley New York.

Dohrenwend, B. S., Krasnoff, L., Askenasy, A. R., and Dohrenwend, B. P. (1978) 'Exemplification of a method for scaling life events: The PERI life events scale', *J. Health. soc. Behav.*, **19**, 205-29.

Dubos, R. (1965) *Man Adapting*, Yale University Press, New Haven.

Duffy, E. (1962) *Activation and Behavior*, Wiley, New York.

Duval, S. and Wicklund, R. A. (1972) *A Theory of Objective Self-awareness*, Academic Press, New York.

Easterbrook, J. A. (1959) 'The effect of emotion on cue utilization and the organization of behavior', *Psychol. Rev.*, **66**, 183-201.

Easterbrook, J. A. (1978) *The Determinants of Free-will*, Academic Press, New York.

Eitinger, L. (1971) 'Acute and chronic psychiatric and psychosomatic reactions in concentration camp survivors', *Society, Stress and Disease* (Ed. L. Levi), Oxford University Press, London.

Ellsworth, P. C., Friedman, H. S., Perlick, D., and Hoyt, M. E. (1978) 'Some effects of gaze on subjects motivated to seek or to avoid social comparison', *J. exp. soc. Psychol.*, **14**, 69-87.

Engel, G. L. (1968) 'A life setting conducive to illness: The giving-up-given-up complex', *Ann. Intern. Med.*, **69**, 293-300.

Epley, S. W. (1974) 'Reduction of the behavioral effects of aversive stimulation by the presence of companions', *Psychol. Bull.*, **81**, 271-83.

Epstein, S. (1967) 'Toward a unified theory of anxiety', in *Progress in Experimental Personality Research* (Ed. B. Maher), vol. 4, Academic Press, New York, 2-87.

Fenz, W. D. (1964) 'Conflict and stress as related to physiological activation and sensory, perceptual and cognitive functioning', *Psychol. Monogr.*, **78**, 1-33.

Fenz, W. D. (1973) 'Stress and its mastery: Predicting from laboratory to real life', *Canad. J. Behav. Sci.*, **5**, 332-346.

Fielding, J. E. (1978) 'Successes of prevention', *Milbank Memorial Fund Quart.*, **50**, 274-302.

Forster, P. M. and Grierson, A. T. (1978) 'Noise and attentional selectivity: A reproducible phenomenon?', *Br. J. Psychol.*, **69**, 489-98.

Fox, B. H. (1978) 'Premorbid psychological factors as related to cancer incidence', *J. behav. Med.*, **1**, 45-134.

Frankenhaeuser, M. (1976) 'The role of peripheral catecholamines in adaptation to understimulation and overstimulation', in *Psychopathology of human adaptation* (Ed. G. Serban), Plenum Press, New York.

Frankenhaeuser, M. (1977) 'Quality of life: Criteria for behavioral adjustment', *Int. J. Psychol.*, **12**, 99-110.

Freedman, J. L. (1975) *Crowding and Behavior,*, Freeman, San Francisco.

French, J. R. P. (1976) 'Job demands and worker health: Introduction', Paper to 84th Annual Convention of A.P.A.

Friedman, M., Byers, S. O., Diamant, J., and Rosenman, R. H. (1975) 'Plasma catecholamine response of coronary-prone subjects (Type A) to a specific challenge', *Metabolism*, **24**, 205–10.

Gardner, G. T. (1978) 'Effects of Federal human subjects regulations on data obtained in environmental stressor research', *J. Pers. soc. Psychol.*, **36**, 628–34.

Garrity, T. F., Somes, G. W., and Marx, M. B. (1977) 'Personality factors in resistance to illness after recent life changes', *J. Psychosom. Res.*, **21**, 23–32.

Glass, D. C. (1977) *Behavior Patterns, Stress and Coronary Disease*, Erlbaum, Hillsdale, N.J.

Glass, D. C. and Singer, J. (1972) *Urban Stress*, Academic Press, New York.

Glass, D. C., Snyder, M. L., and Hollis, J. F. (1974) 'Time urgency and the type A coronary prone behavior pattern', *J. appl. soc. Psychol.*, **4**, 125–40.

Glass, G. V., Willson, V. L., and Gottman, J. M. (1975) *Design and Analysis of Time-Series Experiments*, University of Colorado Press, Boulder.

Goldberg, E. L. and Comstock, G. W. (1976) 'Life events and subsequent illness', *Am. J. Epidemiol.*, **104**, 146–58.

Gore, S. (1978) 'The effect of social support in moderating the health consequences of unemployment', *J. Health. soc. Behav.*, **19**, 157–65.

Grearson, A. T. (1975) 'Adaptation and motivation in sport parachuting, Unpublished Honours Thesis, Department of Psychology, University of Edinburgh. Presented at Social Psychology Conference of British Psychological Society, September, 1975.

Greene, W. A., Goldstein, S., and Moss, A. J. (1972) 'Psychosocial aspects of sudden death: A preliminary report', *Arch. Int. Med.*, **129**, 725–31.

Haynes, S. G., Feinleib, M., Levine, S., Scotch, N., and Kannel, W. B. (1978) 'The relationship of psychosocial factors to coronary heart disease in the Framingham study. II. Prevalence of coronary heart disease', *Am. J. Epidemiol.*, **107**, 384–401.

Henry, J. P. and Ely, D. L. (1976) 'Biologic correlates of psychosomatic illness', in *Biological Foundations of Psychiatry* (Eds. R. G. Grenell and S. Galay), Raven Press, New York.

Heylen, A. and Innes, J. M. (1979) 'Audience presence, evaluation apprehension and task performance as a function of the Type A coronary-prone behaviour pattern', Manuscript in preparation, Unversity of Adelaide.

Hinkle, L. E. (1973) 'The concept of "stress" in the biological and social sciences', *Sci. Med. and Man*, **1**, 31–48.

Hiroto, D. S. (1974) 'Locus of control and learned helplessness', *J. exp. Psychol.*, **102**, 187–93.

Hockey, G. R. (1970) 'Signal probability and spatial location as possible bases for increased selectivity in noise', *Quart. J. exp. Psychol.*, **22**, 37–42.

Hollingshead, A. B. and Redlich, F. C. (1958) *Social Class and Mental Illness*, Wiley, New York.

Holmes, T. H. and Rahe, R. H. (1967) 'The social readjustment rating scale', *J. Psychosom. Res.*, **11**, 213–18.

Horan, P. M. and Gray, B. H. (1974) 'Status inconsistency, mobility and coronary heart disease', *J. Health soc. Behav.*, **15**, 300–10.

Horowitz, M. J., Schaefer, C., and Cooney, P. (1974) 'Life event scaling for recency of experience', in *Life Stress and Illness* (Eds. E. K. E. Gunderson and R. H. Rahe), Thomas, Springfield, Ill.

Howard, J. H., Cunningham, D. A., and Rechnitzer, P. A. (1977) 'Work patterns associated with Type A behavior: A managerial population', *Hum. Relat.*, **30**, 825–36.

Hudgens, R. W. (1974) 'Personal catastrophe and depression: A consideration of the subject with respect to medically ill adolescents and a requiem for retrospective life events studies', in *Stressful life events* (Eds. B. P. Dohrenwend and B. S. Dohrenwend), Wiley, New York.

Hull, D. (1977) 'Life circumstances and physical illness: A cross disciplinary survey of research content and method for the decade 1965–1975', *J. Psychosom. Res.*, **21**, 115–39.

Hurst, M. W., Jenkins, C. D. and Rose, R. M. (1978) 'The assessment of life change stress: A comparative and methodological inquiry', *Psychosom. Med.*, **40**, 126–41.

Ickes, W. and Layden, M. A. (1978) 'Attributional styles', in *New Directions in Attribution Research* (Eds. J. H. Harvey *et al.*), vol. 2, Erlbaum, Hillsdale, N.J., 121–52.

Innes, J. M. (1975) 'Human behaviour under stress', *Fire*, **67**, 601–3.

Innes, J. M. (1980) 'Some problems with conceptual replications of studies of affiliative behavior: More than meets the eye', *Psychol. Rep.*, **47**, 943–946.

Innes, J. M. and Herbertt, R. M. (1979) 'Objective self-awareness and the Type A coronary-prone behaviour pattern', Manuscript in preparation, University of Adelaide.

Innes, J. M. and Sambrooks, J. S. (1969) 'Paired-associate learning as influenced by birth order and the presence of others', *Psychosom. Sci.*, **16**, 109–10.

Innes, J. M. and Young, R. F. (1975) 'The effect of presence of an audience, evaluative apprehension and objective self-awareness on learning', *J. exp. soc. Psychol.*, **11**, 35–42.

Janis, I. L. (1951) *Air War and Emotional Stress*, McGraw-Hill, New York.

Jacobson, S. R. (1973) 'Individual and group responses to confinement in a sky-jacked plane', *Am. J. Orthopsychiat.*, **43**, 459.

Jenkins, C. D. (1971) 'Psychologic and social precursors of coronary disease', *New Engl. J. Med.*, **284**, 244–55 and 307–17.

Jenkins, C. D. (1976) 'Recent evidence supporting psychologic and social risk factors for coronary disease', *New Engl. J. Med.*, **294**, 987–94 and 1033–38.

Jenkins, C. D. (1977) 'Epidemiological studies of the psychosomatic aspects of coronary heart disease', *Adv. Psychosom. Med.*, **9**, 1–19.

Jenkins, C. D., Zyzanski, S. J., and Rosenman, R. H. (1976) 'Risk of new myocardial infarction in middle-aged men with manifest coronary heart disease', *Circulation*, **53**, 342–47.

Jenkins, C. D., Zyzanski, S. J., and Rosenman, R. H. (1978) 'Coronary-prone behavior: One pattern or several?', *Psychosom. Med.*, **40**, 25–43.

Jenkins, C. D., Zyzanski, S. J., Ryan, T. J., Flessas, A., and Tannenbaum, S. I. (1977) 'Social insecurity and coronary-prone type A responses as identifiers of severe atherosclerosis', *J. consult. clin. Psychol.*, **45**, 1060–67.

Johnson, J. H. and Sarason, I. G. (1978) 'Life stress, depression and anxiety: Internal-external control as a moderator variable', *J. Psychosom. Res.*, **22**, 205–8.

Jones, E. E. and Gerard, H. B. (1967) *Foundations of Social Psychology*, Wiley, New York.

Kahneman, D. (1973) *Attention and Effort*, Prentice-Hall, Englewood Cliffs, N.J.

Kaplan, B. H., Cassel, J. C., and Gore, S. (1977) 'Social support and health', *Med. Care*, **15**, no. 5 supplement, 47–58.

Kasl, S. V. (1977) 'Contributions of social epidemiology to studies in psychosomatic medicine', *Adv. psychosom. Med.*, **9**, 160–223.

Kavanagh, T. and Shephard, R. J. (1975) 'Depression after myocardial infarction', *Can. Med. Ass.*, **113**, 23–28.

Kiritz, S. and Moos, R. H. (1974) 'Physiological effects of social environments', *Psycosom. Med.*, **36**, 96–114.

Krantz, D. S., Glass, D. C., and Snyder, M. L. (1974) 'Helplessness, stress level and the coronary-prone behavior pattern', *J. exp. soc. Psychol.*, **10**, 284–300.

Kryter, K. D. (1970) *The Effects of Noise on Man*, Academic Press, New York.

Kuhn, T. S. (1962) *The Structure of Scientific Revolutions*, University of Chicago Press, Chicago.

Kuller, L. H. (1976) 'Epidemiology of cardiovascular diseases: Current perspectives', *Am. J. Epidemiol.*, **104**, 425–56.

Langer, E. J. (1975) 'The illusion of control', *J. Pers. soc. Psychol.*, **32**, 311–28.

Langer, E. J. (1978) 'Role of thought in social interaction', in *New Directions in Attribution Research* (Eds. J. H. Harvey *et al.*), vol. 2. Erlbaum, Hillsdale, N.J. 35–58.

Langer, E. J., Janis, I. L., and Wolfer, J. (1975) 'Reduction of psychological stress in surgical patients', *J. exp. soc. Psychol.*, **11**, 155–65.

Langer, E. J. and Rodin, J. (1976) 'The effects of choice and enhanced personal responsibility: A field experiment in an institutional setting', *J. Pers. soc. Psychol.*, **34**, 191–98.

Langer, E. J. and Saegert, S. (1977) 'Crowding and cognitive control', *J. Pers. soc. Psychol.*, **35**, 175–82.

Lazarus, R. S. (1966) *Psychological Stress and the Coping Process*, McGraw-Hill, New York.

Lebovitz, B., Lichter, E., and Moses, V. K. (1975) 'Personality correlates of coronary heart disease: A re-examination of the MMPI data', *Soc. Sci. & Med.*, **9**, 207–19.

Levy, L. H. (1961) 'Anxiety and behavior scientists' behavior', *Am. Psychologist*, **16**, 66–68.

Lynch, J. J. (1977) *The Broken Heart: The Medical Consequences of Loneliness*, Basic Books, New York.

Lynch, J. J., Thomas, S. A., Paskewitz, D. A., Katcher, A. H., and Weir, L. O. (1977) 'Human contact and cardiac arrhythmia in a coronary care unit', *Psychosom. Med.*, **39**, 188–92.

McAlister, A. L., *et al.* (1976) 'Behavioral science applied to cardiovascular health', *Health, Educ. Monogr.*, **4**, 45–70.

McClelland, D. C. (1976) 'Sources of stress in the drive for power', in *Psychopathology of Human Adaptation* (Ed. G. Serban), Plenum, New York.

Marmot, M. G. and Syme, S. L. (1976) 'Acculturation and coronary heart disease in Japanese-Americans', *Am. J. Epidemiol.*, **104**, 225–46.

Mason, J. W. (1968) 'A review of psycho-endocrine research in the pituitary-adrenal cortical system', *Psychosom. Med.*, **30**, 567–607.

Mason, J. W., Maher, J. T., Hartley, L. H., Mougey, E. H., Perlow, M. J. and Jones, L. G. (1976) 'Selectivity of corticosteroid and catecholamine responses to various natural stimuli', in *Psychopathology of Human Adaptation* (Ed. G. Serban), Plenum Press, New York.

Masuda, M. and Holmes, T. H. (1978) 'Life events: Perceptions and frequencies', *Psychosom. Med.*, **40**, 236–61.

Mathews, K. A. and Krantz, D. S. (1976) 'Resemblances of twins and their parents in Pattern A behavior', *Psychosom. Med.*, **38**, 140–44.

Mathews, K. A. and Saal, F. E. (1978) 'Relationship of the Type A coronary-prone behavior pattern to achievement, power and affiliation motives', *Psychosom. Med.*, **40**, 631–36.

Mathews, K. E. and Canon, L. K. (1975) 'Environmental noise level as a determinant of helping behavior', *J. Pers. soc. Psychol.*, **32**, 571–77.

Matsumoto, Y. S. (1970) 'Social stress and coronary heart disease in Japan', *Milbank Memorial Fund Quarterly*, **1970**, 48.

Matthews, K. A., Glass, D. C., Rosenman, R. H., and Bortner, R. W. (1977) 'Competitive drive, Pattern A and coronary heart disease: A further analysis of some data from the Western Collaborative Group Study', *J. Chron. Dis.*, **30**, 489–98.

Meehl, P. E. (1970) 'Nuisance variables and the ex post facto design', in *Minnesota Studies in the Philosophy of Science* (Eds. M. Radner and S. Winokur), Vol. IV, University Minnesota Press, Minneapolis, 373–402.

Mettlin, C. and Woelfel, J (1974) Interpersonal influence and symptoms of stress', *J. Heal. soc. Behav.*, **15**, 311–19.

Miller, N. E. (1979) 'Effects of learning on physical symptoms produced by psychological stress', in *Guide to Stress Research* (Ed. H. Selye), Van Nostrand Reinhold, New York.

Mischel, W. (1976) *Introduction to Personality*, 2nd edn, Holt, Rinehart & Winston, New York.

Morris, W. N., Worchel, S., Bois, J. L., Pearson, J. A., Rountree, C. A., Samaha, G. M., Wachtler, J., and Wright, S. L. (1976) 'Collective coping with stress: Group reactions to fear, anxiety, and ambiguity', *J. Pers. soc. Psychol.*, **33**, 674–79.

Nisbett, R. E., Borgida, E., Crandall, R., and Reed, H. (1976) 'Popular induction: Information is not necessarily informative', in *Cognition and Social Behaviour* (Eds. J. S. Carroll and J. W. Payne), Erlbaum, Hillsdale, N.J.

Nisbett, R. E. and Temoshok, L. (1976) 'Is there an external cognitive style?', *J. Pers. soc. Psychol.*, **33**, 36–47.

Nuckolls, K. B., Cassel, J., and Kaplan, B. H. (1972) 'Psychosocial assets, life crisis and the prognosis of pregnancy', *Am. J. Epidemiol.*, **95**, 431–41.

Park, R. and Burgess, E. (Eds.) (1925) *The City*, University of Chicago Press, Chicago.

Patkai, P. (1971) 'Catecholamine excretion in pleasant and unpleasant situations', *Acta Psychol.*, **35**, 352–63.

Paulus, P., Cox, V., McCain, G., and Chandler, J. (1975) 'Some effects of crowding in a prison environment', *J. appl. soc. Psychol.*, **5**, 89–91.

Pennebaker, J. W. and Skelton, J. A. (1978) 'Psychological parameters of physical symptoms', *Pers. soc. Psychol. Bull.*, **4**, 524–30.

Poulton, E. C. (1977) 'Continuous intense noise masks auditory feedback and inner speech', *Psychol. Bull.*, **84**, 977–1001.

Poulton, E. C. (1978) 'A new look at the effects of noise: A rejoinder', *Psychol. Bull.*, **85**, 1068–79.

Poulton, E. C. and Edwards, R. S. (1974) 'Interactions and range effects in experiments on pairs of stresses: Mild heat and low-frequency noise', *J. exp. Psychol.*, **102**, 621–28.

Proshansky, H. M. (1976) 'Environmental psychology and the real world', *Am. Psychologist*, **31**, 303–10.

Rabkin, J. G. and Struening, E. L. (1976) 'Life events, stress and illness', *Science*, **194**, 1013–20.

Rachman, S. (1978) *Fear and Courage*, Freeman, San Francisco.

Radloff, R. and Helmreich, R. (1968) *Groups Under Stress*, Appleton-Century-Crofts, New York.

Robbins, P. R., Meyersburg, H. A., and Tanck, R. H. (1974) 'Interpersonal stress and physical complaints', *J. Pers. Ass.*, **38**, 578–85.

Rodda, M. (1967) *Noise and Society*, Oliver & Boyd, Edinburgh.

Rodin, J. (1977) 'Research on eating behavior and obesity: Where does it fit in personality and social psychology?', *Pers. soc. Psychol. Bull*, **3**, 333–55.

Rodin, J. (1978) 'Somatopsychics and attribution', *Pers. soc. Psychol. Bull.*, **4**, 531–40.

Rosenman, R. H., Brand, R. J., Jenkins, C. D., Friedman, M., Strauss, R., and

Wurm, M. (1975) 'Coronary heart disease in the Western Collaborative Group Study', *J. Am. Med. Assoc.*, **233**, 872–77.

Rosenman, R. H. and Friedman, M. (1974) 'Neurogenic factors in pathogenesis of coronary heart disease', *Med. Clin. North America*, **58**, 269–79.

Rosenman, R. H., Friedman, M., and Strauss, R. (1964) 'A predictive study of CHD', *J. Am. Med. Assoc.*, **189**, 15–22.

Rotter, J. B. (1966) 'Generalized expectancies for internal versus external control of reinforcement', *Psychol. Monogr.*, **80** (1, whole no. 609).

Russell, D., Peplau, L. A., and Ferguson, M. L. (1978) 'Developing a measure of loneliness', *J. Pers. Assess.*, **42**, 290–94.

Saegert, S. (1976) 'Stress inducing and stress-reducing qualities of environment', in *Environmental Psychology* (Eds. H. M. Proshansky *et al.*), 2nd edn, Holt, Rinehart & Winston, new York.

Saegert, S. (1978) 'High density environments: Their personal and social consequences' in *Human Responses to Crowding* (Eds. A. Baum and Y. Epstein), Erlbaum, Norwood, N.J.

Sales, S. M. (1969) 'Organization role as a risk factor in coronary disease', *Admin. Sci. Quart.*, **14**, 325–36.

Sarason, S. B. (1972) *The Creation of Settings and the Future Societies*, Jossey-Bass, San Francisco.

Schachter, S. (1959) *The Psychology of Affiliation*, Stanford Univ. Press.

Scherwitz, L., Berton, K., and Leventhal, H. (1977) 'Type A assessment and interaction in the behavior pattern interview', *Psychosom. Med.*, **39**, 229–40.

Scherwitz, L., Berton, K., and Leventhal, H. (1978) 'Type A behavior, self-involvement and cardiovascular response', *Psychosom. Med.*, **40**, 593–609.

Schottstaedt, W. W., Jackman, N. R., McPhail, C. S., and Wolf, S. (1963) 'Social interaction on a metabolic ward: The relation of problems of status to chemical balance', *J. Psychosom. Res.*, **7**, 83–95.

Schucker, B. and Jacobs, D. R. (1977) 'Assessment of behavioral risk for coronary disease by voice characteristics', *Psychosom. Med.*, **39**, 219–28.

Seligman, M. E. P. (1975) *Helplessness: On Development, Depression and Death*, Freeman, San Francisco.

Seligman, M. E. P., Maier, S. F., and Solomon, R. L. (1971) 'Unpredictable and uncontrollable aversive events', in *Aversive Conditioning and Learning* (Ed. F. R. Bush), Academic Press, New York.

Selye, H. (1952) *The Story of the Adaptation Syndrome*, Acta, Montreal.

Sengel, R. A. (1978) 'A graph analysis of the relationship between population density and social pathology', *Behav. Sci.*, **23**, 213–24.

Shekelle, R. B., Ostfeld, A. M., and Paul, O. (1969) 'Social status and incidence of coronary heart disease', *J. chron. Dis.*, **22**, 381–94.

Shekelle, R. B., Schoenberger, J. A., and Stamler, J. (1976) 'Correlates of the JAS Type A behavior pattern score', *J. chron. Dis.*, **29**, 381–94.

Singer, J. E., Lundberg, U., and Frankenhaeuser, M. (1978) 'Stress on the train: A study of urban commuting', in *Advances in Environmental Psychology* (Eds. A. Baum *et al.*), vol. 1, Erlbaum, Hillsdale, N.J.

Smith, R. E., Johnson, J. H., and Sarason, I. G. (1978) 'Life change, the sensation seeking motive and psychological distress', *J. consult. clin. Psychol.*, **46**, 348–49.

Snyder, M. (1974) 'The self-monitoring of expressive behavior', *J. Pers. soc. Psychol.*, **30**, 526–37.

Spengler, J. J. (1968) 'Exogenous and endogenous influences in the formation of post-1870 economic thought', in *Events, Ideology and Economic Theory* (Ed. R. V. Eagly), Wayne, State University Press, Detroit, 159–205.

Spicer, J. (1978) 'Dimensions of psychological predisposition to coronary heart disease', *Commun. Health Stud.*, **2**, 96–101.

Spieth, W. (1965) 'Slowness of task performance and cardiovascular diseases', in *Behavior Aging and the Nervous System* (Eds. A. T. Welford and J. E. Birren), C. C. Thomas, Springfield, Ill., 366–400.

Stokols, D., Novaco, R. W., and Stokols, J. (1978) 'Traffic congestion, Type A behavior and stress', *J. appl. Psychol.*, **63**, 467–80.

Stouffer, S., Lumsdaine, A., Williams, R., Smith, M., Janis, I., Star, S., and Cottrell, L. (1949) *The American Soldier, Vol. II: Combat and Its Aftermath*, Princeton University, Press, Princeton, N.J.

Strumpfer, D. J. W. (1970) 'Fear and affiliation during a disaster,' *J. soc. Psychol.*, **82**, 263–68.

Suinn, R. M. and Bloom, L. J. (1978) 'Anxiety management training for pattern A behavior', *J. behav. Med.*, **1**, 25–36.

Syme, S. L. (1974) 'Behavioral factors associated with the etiology of physical disease: A social epidemiological approach', *Am. J. publ. Health*, **64**, 1043–45.

Szafran, J. (1966) 'Age, cardiac output and choice reaction time', *Nature*, **209**, 836.

Terris, W. and Rahhal, D. K. (1969) 'Generalized resistance to the effects of psychological stressors', *J. Pers. soc. Psychol.*, **13**, 93–97.

Theorell, T. and Floderus-Myrhed, B. (1977) ' "Workload" and risk of myocardial infarction: A prospective psychosocial analysis', *Int. J. Epidemiol.*, **6**, 17–21.

Ursin, H., Baade, F., and Levine, S. (Eds.) (1978) *Psychobiology of Stress: A Study of Coping Men*, Academic Press, New York.

Vallacher, R. R. (1978) 'Objective self-awareness and the perception of others', *Pers. soc. Psychol. Bull.*, **4**, 63–67.

Vinokur, A. and Selzer, M. L. (1975) 'Desirable versus undesirable life events: Their relationship to stress and mental distress', *J. pers. soc. Psychol.*, **32**, 329–37.

Waldron, I. (1978) 'Sex differences in the coronary-prone behavior pattern', in *Coronary-prone Behavior* (Eds. T. M. Dembroski *et al.*), Springer-Verlag, New York, 199–205.

Weick, K. E. (1969) *The Social Psychology of Organizing*, Addison-Wesley, Reading, Mass.

Weidner, G. and Matthews, K. A. (1978) 'Reported physical symptoms elicited by unpredictable events and the Type A coronary-prone behavior pattern', *J. Pers. soc. Psychol.*, **36**, 1213–20.

Wershow, H. J. and Reinhart, G. (1974) 'Life change and hospitalization: A heretical view', *J. Psychosom. Res.*, **18**, 393–401.

Wolf, S. and Goodell, H. (1976) *Behavioral Science in Clinical Medicine*, C. C. Thomas, Springfield, Ill.

Wortman, C. B. (1976) 'Causal attributions and personal control', in *New Directions in Attribution Research* (Eds. J. H. Harvey *et al.*), vol. 1, Erlbaum, Hillside, N.J.

Wortman, C. B. and Dintzer, L. (1978) 'Is the attributional analysis of the learned helplessness phenomenon viable?: A critique of the Abramson–Seligman–Teasdale reformulation', *J. abnorm. Psychol.*, **87**, 75–90.

Zajonc, R. B. (1980) 'Compresence', in *Psychology of Group Influence* (Ed. P. B. Paulus), Erlbaum, Hillsdale, N.J.

Zaleznik, A., de Vries, M. F. R. K., and Howard, L. (1977) 'Stress reactions in organizations: Syndromes, causes and consequences', *Behav. Sci.*, **22**, 151–62.

Zuckerman, M. (1974) 'The sensation seeking motive', in *Progress in Experimental Personality Research* (Ed. B. A. Maher), vol. 7, Academic Press, New York, 80–148.

Zuckerman, M., Murtaugh, T., and Siegel, J. (1974) 'Sensation seeking and cortical augmenting—reducing', *Psychophysiology*, **11**, 535–42.

Zyzanski, S. J. (1978) 'Coronary-prone behavior pattern and coronary heart disease: Epidemiological evidence', in *Coronary-prone behavior* (Eds. T. M. Dembroski *et al.*), Springer-Verlag, New York, 25–40.

Progress in Applied Social Psychology, Volume 1
Edited by G. M. Stephenson and J. M. Davis
© 1981 John Wiley & Sons, Ltd.

6

Social and Interpersonal Factors in Driving

CHRISTOPHER K. KNAPPER
University of Waterloo, Canada

and

ARTHUR J. CROPLEY
University of Hamburg, Federal Republic of Germany

INTRODUCTION

In view of the far-reaching effects of the automobile on human behaviour and patterns of social interaction, it is surprising to find that the subject of cars and car-driving has been virtually ignored by social psychologists. Those writers who have commented on the social significance of the automobile have often done so in an impressionistic or largely speculative manner. The present chapter attempts to review some of the popular discussions of driving as a social skill, and then examines in more detail the more formal, empirical studies of driving behaviour that have been conducted within a social psychological framework. The general intention is to shed light on an aspect of behaviour that deserves to receive much more attention from social psychologists, as well as to suggest some fruitful areas for empirical inquiry in an area of everyday living that has crucial contemporary importance.

THE PLACE OF THE AUTOMOBILE IN WESTERN CULTURE

For most of this century the automobile has had a major influence on behaviour patterns and cultural attitudes, especially in the Western world. For example, in the early 1970s there were some 55 million cars registered in the countries of the E.E.C., and almost twice as many in the United States, despite its smaller population. In 1967 no fewer than 108 million Americans made 360 million trips by car that took them at least 100 miles from home and accounted for 312 billion passenger miles (Toffler, 1971). Automobiles are manufactured in North America at a rate of one every 3.5 seconds, and each year Americans spend about one-fifth of their earned income on the purchase and maintenance of motor vehicles. Indeed, there is one automobile for every 2.6 inhabitants of the U.S., and every sixth job in the nation is devoted to serving the needs of cars and drivers. In terms of driving itself, it is estimated that the average adult American male spends about 40 days a year—or one and a half years of his working life—inside a car. Hence, it is not surprising that road construction has proceeded at a rate of 200 miles a day during the past two decades (Schrank, 1976). As Hall (1969, p.75) puts it, 'the automobile is the greatest consumer of public and personal space yet created by man'.

One major by-product of this enormous personal and capital investment in cars has been an increasing toll from road accidents which, in the industrialized nations, constitutes one of today's major causes of suffering. In addition to the misery and human loss resulting from automobile deaths, the injured victims of accidents fill large numbers of sorely needed hospital beds, and add greatly to the cost of providing medical services. In fact the number of 'premature' deaths and injuries from motor vehicle accidents is surpassed only by casualty rates in war-time. For example, more than ten times as many Americans were killed on the roads between 1963 and 1970 as were killed in Vietnam (Cantor, 1970), and it is estimated that American children born in 1972 have a greater than even chance of being injured in a road accident during their lifetime. In Canada motor vehicle accidents are the leading cause of death among males between the ages of 15 and 35, and the number of fatalities on European roads also remains extremely high. The United Kingdom has an annual accident death toll of about 10,000, compared to a rate in West Germany of 15,000, in France 20,000, and a death rate in the U.S. of over 60,000 (American Safety Belt Council, 1974; Hauser, 1974). Thus, in addition to the economic importance of automobiles, both in terms of jobs and consumption of scarce resources, death and injuries from road accidents now constitute a public health problem of the first magnitude.

Not surprisingly, the automobile exerts a pervasive influence on contemporary society and popular consciousness, and a number of writers have focused attention on the motor vehicle as a phenomenon affecting the beliefs, habits, attitudes, and actions of everyday life. Although they have not for the most part gathered systematic empirical data, their contributions have considerable value for understanding the cultural significance of the motor car.

The anthropologist Hall (1969), for example, has described the relationship between the car and individual *personal space* requirements. According to him, the interiors of large American cars are arranged to prevent overlapping of personal space 'so that each passenger is only marginally involved with the others' (p.145). Lofland (1973) also described the ability of a car to surround its occupants in a 'cocoon of privacy', while Mehrabian (1975) argued that the automobile is an important mechanism used to counteract the negative effects of high population density by providing protection from interaction with other people.

On the other hand, some writers have argued that certain aspects of driving behaviour may actually facilitate (pro-) social behaviour. Ittelson, Proshansky, Rivlin, and Winkel (1974) pointed out that the automobile (in common with the telephone) has served to break down spatial boundaries for some groups of Americans, notably adolescents. In a similar vein, Goldberg (1969) argued that 'cruising' in the car serves a strong need for social gathering, and has become a device for meeting members of the opposite sex. Ashcraft and Scheflen (1976), in the context of a general discussion of the human tendency to seek out the company of others in many situations, have described the predilection of drivers to 'cluster', especially under adverse weather conditions, leaving extensive highway spaces vacant, even though this practice is known to be dangerous.

The motor car is also seen by some writers as *an extension of personality*. Vance Packard (1957) has commented on the psychological aspects of owning and buying cars, while Boorstin (1963, p.226) pointed out that advertising has made the automobile no longer merely a transportation machine, but 'something we wear and luxuriate in or something that gives us "that carefree feeling" and "that sense of indescribable luxury"'. A somewhat similar point is made by Toffler (1971) who writes that 'a car . . . is more than a conveyance. It is an expression of the personality of the user, a symbol of status' (p.69), a point echoed by Mehrabian (1975). Hence, automobiles are seen as 'a mass medium used by drivers to broadcast the state of their ego, opinions about the world and their feelings about the guy next door' (Schrank, 1976, p.66).

A third relevant theme is the relationship between driving and *arousal, excitement, and risk-taking behaviour*. Goffman (1967) quoted examples of advertisements for automobiles that clearly emphasize the vehicle's potential for action by the use of such phrases as 'blazing performance' or 'a piece of action that just won't quit'. He went on to comment that a good deal of pleasure from driving for many individuals involves risk-taking behaviour, with highways regarded as 'scenes of action, places where skills, impatience and costly equipment can be displayed under seriously chancy conditions' (p.192). Mehrabian (1975) is more ambivalent about the arousal potential of the automobile. On the one hand, fast driving is an arousing and exciting experience, but on the other hand, the arousal is to some extent offset by the comfort of the car's interior, so that riding in a car is usually less arousing than riding on public transport.

Mumford (1958) argued that the American way of life is founded on 'the religion of the motor car', and certainly there is little disagreement that the car has changed patterns of social behaviour, especially in North America. Jackson (1976), for instance, described the transformation of cities by motor vehicles, with the city centre being replaced as a focus of interest by strips of highway leading into the city. Schrank (1976) has gone even further in referring to what he calls 'the symbiotic relationship between auto and driver' (p.62). Thus it might be fairly stated that most people in Western nations live in a society shaped, to a greater or lesser extent, by cars. The degree of this influence is seen most clearly in the U.S., but the phenomenon obviously exists in other industrialized nations, even though there are disappointingly few cross-cultural comparisons in the available literature.

PSYCHOLOGICAL STUDIES OF DRIVING

In view of the central role of the automobile in contemporary Western society, it might be expected that driving would be a major issue for empirical research by social scientists, an area in which they could hope to make useful contributions both to practice and policy formation. Certainly there have been many studies of driving behaviour, the majority conducted by psychologists. However, as will shortly become apparent, these investigations have often been narrow and fragmented.

Traffic Accidents

As might be expected, a major focus of interest on the part of social scientists has been on road accidents. It has been common to identify three types of factor which may cause such accidents: (1) the vehicle, (2) the road or traffic environment, and (3) the driver of the vehicle. Vast sums of money have been spent in efforts to reduce accidents resulting from defects in the first two factors, for example, by improving the design of highways and traffic systems or by improving safety standards in vehicles. However, there has been a relative neglect of the third factor — the human operator.

As early as 1940 Ross pointed out that mechanical defects in the automobile and the road accounted for no more than 10 percent of all the motor vehicle accidents he studied. He concluded that the remaining 90 percent of accidents had to be explained in terms of driver characteristics. More recently Clayton and Mackay (1972) concluded that the environment alone or the vehicle alone accounted for a total of only 8.6 percent of traffic accidents in Britain, as opposed to a total of 44.7 percent attributed to the user (a further 31 percent of accidents was accounted for by interaction between the driver and the environment, with the remaining accidents attributed to other combinations of factors).

In the U.S., Treat and Joscelyn (1974) reported that human factors were the most frequent accident causes, with environmental factors ranking second, and vehicular factors third. Human beings were identified as 'definite or probable cause' in 96.7 percent of cases. Furthermore, in 57 percent of cases, human factors were the *only* cause of the accident which the investigating team could identify as being probable or definite. By contrast, environmental factors were definite causes in only 16.4 percent of accidents, the vehicle in a mere 4.2 percent and, in the case of both these categories, the majority of accidents involved contributions of other factors (primarily human) too.

Since so many investigators have identified *the driver* as the major variable in traffic accidents, it is understandable that there has been an increasing call for the involvement of psychologists in the study of driving behaviour. For example, Suchman (1960–61, p.43) urged that researchers 'approach accidents as behavior and apply the same explanatory models that the behavioral scientists have developed for understanding human behavior in general'. A number of other writers have also recently called for an increased emphasis on social and psychological factors in the whole transportation and traffic domain (e.g. Krampe, 1976; Leibbrand, 1976; Michon, 1976). Unfortunately, however, the efforts by traditional psychologists in the field of driver behaviour have been limited in scope. They have tended to regard automobile drivers as operators of a machine just like any other, and have concentrated on skilled performance in this role, often measuring variables which are of limited interest, such as reaction time (see McFarland, Tune, and Welford, 1964), or even trivial, such as the investigation of driving skill by Greenshields (1963) in which the dependent variable was the amount that the steering wheel was turned over a set course. Another approach has been to regard drivers as information processing systems (see Baker, 1963; Forbes, 1972; Perchonok, 1973; SWOV, 1971). But as Michon (1976) pointed out, this approach often overlooks the fact that people must process information about the social as well as the physical environment.

Finally, in discussing approaches to driving by experimental psychologists, mention should be made of behaviourism and the 'conditioning' of responses. Michon (1976) has written that the idea of using reinforcement to shape desirable driver behaviours is one that holds attractions for many psychologists working in the transportation domain. Unfortunately, however, it is by no means an easy matter to identify just what *are* the desirable driving behaviours. Furthermore, as Michon himself said, very little is known about the reinforcement system that motivates many drivers: for example, young drivers may well have quite different value systems from those of society at large, and hence may aspire to quite different driving behaviours from those the law encourages.

Personal Characteristics of Drivers

Some studies have looked at driving in terms of drivers' needs, motives, feelings, and the like. However, a number of problems have arisen. Research concentrating on what might be called 'personal factors' in the driving situation has tended to examine various characteristics of individual drivers and relate these to their driving behaviour. An important difficulty here however is that no one has yet come up with an adequate and complete description of the important variables in the driving situation—notwithstanding the attempts by behavioural psychologists to catalogue the different types of driving skills and their components.

One approach has been to correlate driver characteristics with a list of either 'good' driver behaviours or, more often, driver errors. Still more common are investigations that use the relatively more straightforward criteria of traffic violations or involvement in traffic accidents. Although this method has the attraction of providing a relatively clear-cut way of identifying 'bad' drivers, the very simplicity of the criterion often raises difficulties of its own. As Suchman (1960–61) pointed out, studying only those accidents and violations which are *reported* leaves out of consideration all those that took place but were never spotted, and fails to take account of all the errors made in driving that failed to have an obvious behavioural consequence.

A number of studies have looked at *experience* of driving, involving such factors as mileage driven, success in advanced driver training courses, enjoyment of driving, and even type of car driven (see, for example, Hoinville, Berthonol, and Mackie, 1972; Quenault and Parker, 1973). Of particular interest in this regard has been the effect of driver education and training programmes on subsequent performance. Harrington (1971) reviewed a large number of investigations in the U.S., and concluded that those who completed driver education or training programmes had better accident conviction records than those who did not. However, the attributes of those who opt for training programmes are such that the differences in subsequent driving performance may be merely a reflection of the 'superior personal characteristics' of this group. Among the general demographic traits to have been investigated are *sex* of the driver (e.g. Harrington, 1971; McGuire, 1969), *intelligence* (e.g. Egan, 1967) *education* (e.g. Boek, 1957), *socio-economic status* (e.g. Gutshall, Harper, and Burke, 1968) and *age*. The latter variable has been of considerable interest, especially as it relates to very old drivers and beginning drivers (for studies of the elderly driver see Baker and Spitz, 1970; Gianturco, Ramm and Erwin, 1974; McFarland, Tune, and Welford, 1964; and Planck, 1972; for studies of the newly licensed teenage driver see Carlson, 1973; Harrington, 1971; Henderson, 1971; Klein, 1972; and Waller, 1970).

Not surprisingly, there has also been considerable interest in the *personality* of good and bad drivers. Linares-Maza (1971) identified two basic types of study. The first type makes use of paper and pencil tests to measure a battery of personality variables, and then relates these to some index of driving such as accident rate or successful performance on a driving test (see, for example, the investigations of Benton, Mills, Hartman, and Crow, 1961; McGuire, 1969; Parry, 1968; and Undeutsch in Wagner and Wagner, 1968). Space precludes a full and detailed description of the results of this research, and it is difficult to generalize about the findings since most investigations made use of different sets of personality variables. However, a number of writers (e.g. Conger, Gaskill, Glad, Rainey, Sawrey, and Turrell, 1957) have summarized the evidence as indicating that—at least as far as involvement in accidents is concerned—poor driving is characterized by generally unsatisfactory adjustment to the social environment and a lack of conformity to institutionalized social patterns. This would seem to imply that driving behaviour is an extension of day-to-day social behaviour.

The second approach to personality and driving described by Linares-Maza has used more subjective, often psychoanalytic, techniques, and has tended to concentrate more on the personality structure and development of the chronically bad driver (see, for example, Alonso-Fernandez, 1966; Hamilton, 1967). Reviewing studies in this area, Linares-Maza (1971) suggested that investigations show the existence of three basic types of dangerous driver: the irresponsible driver, the arrogant driver, and the extra-punitive driver. An important concept stemming from this sort of approach to personality and driving is that of 'accident proneness', which derives from Freud's theory that unacceptable, suppressed impulses assert themselves in unconsciously motivated behaviour such as accidents, or that the victims of traffic accidents are people with unconscious suicidal or homicidal tendencies. It has also been suggested that some drivers take advantage of the anonymity of the car-driving situation to act out their own private fantasies, or that reckless driving may be indicative of emotions the driver does not feel free to express elsewhere, because they are socially unacceptable.

Disappointingly, this kind of research has failed to yield any definite conclusions about personality syndromes underlying good or bad driving. For example, Harrington (1971), reviewing dozens of studies in the area, found that what he called 'biographical variables' were poor predictors of accidents among young drivers, and Böcher (in Wagner and Wagner, 1968) reported that the correlations between actual driving performance and behaviour predicted on the basis of personality and demographic characteristics were usually quite low, and rarely more than 0.50 (the higher correlations being obtained only when batteries of psychological predictors were combined). Malik (1968) was able to relate the accident rate of a group of undergraduates to a number of disparate factors, ranging from family size to university grades, but the variables for which significant correlations were obtained were a small minority of those examined. A realistic conclusion from the personality studies in the area is that by Hoyos and von Klebelsberg (1965) that the best predictors of good and bad driving behaviour tend to be relatively superficial characteristics, such as years of driving experience, history of past court appearances, and so on.

This conclusion supports Ross's (1940) suggestion that the major influence on driver behaviour is the *attitude* of the average motorist. Some 25 years later, in their major work on accidents, Haddon, Suchman, and Klein (1964) echoed this conclusion and pointed out that 'by and large it appears that the behavioral scientist would have much more to contribute to accident research if he devoted relatively less attention to individual factors and more to social attitudes and behavior' (p.280). Even Malik, who herself employed a multi-variate approach, concluded that accidents are best viewed as social events to be explained primarily in terms of social and cultural (rather than personality) variables.

Attitudes and Opinions

Studies of individual attitude systems in drivers are relatively common in the literature. For example, Brown and Copeman (1969) investigated drivers' attitudes to the seriousness of road traffic offences in relation to the severity of penalties for committing them, Asai and Inayosh (1973) studied attitudes of high school students towards traffic safety, and Turrell (1957) showed that drivers who had had accidents had different scoring patterns on the Allport–Vernon–Lindzey scale of values compared to accident-free drivers.

It should be borne in mind, however, that an important consideration in studying attitudes is to determine if and how they are related to actual behaviour. In practice the easiest way to do this is to talk with drivers, rather than merely observe what they do. The reasons for this are twofold. Firstly, there are many practical difficulties involved in carrying out reliable and valid observations of driving behaviour. Even more crucial for any thorough understanding of driving is the need to go beyond what drivers actually do, and attempt to probe the underlying reasons for their actions. For example, it is well known that very few North Americans wear seat belts when driving. But it is a matter of considerably greater interest (and one that is more difficult to establish) to know *why* drivers fail to buckle up (see Knapper, Cropley, and Moore, 1976).

Studies employing interviews with drivers are on the whole rather rare, however, investigators generally preferring the type of inquiry described in the preceding section. Treat and Joscelyn (1974) conducted a series of careful interviews with drivers, while Goldstein and Mosel (1958) and Parry (1968) focused particularly on aggressiveness in the driving situation. Von Klebelsberg, Biehl, Fuhrmann, and Seydel (1970) and Zuercher, Sass, and Weiss (1971) used observers to rate and classify the performance of drivers in various situations. As might be expected, however, this procedure in each case yielded a classification system that leant heavily on skill and information processing variables, as opposed to the more subtle and subjective psychological factors mediating driver behaviour.

It is a striking fact about the few existing attitudinal studies of driving that they almost all tend to look at the driver as an isolated individual, rather than someone who is part of an ongoing system of social interactions. Malik (1968) pointed out that even when individuals are physically separated (as in the case of a single driver in the anonymity of the car), 'a mutually shared set of expectations operates with respect to the normative behavior required in any particular situation' (p.124). Later she went on to say that individuals' positions in the total social system largely determine the attitudes they bring with them to the situation of a potential accident, and that the social context may be a crucial factor in determining whether or not an accident actually takes place.

THE SOCIAL PSYCHOLOGY OF DRIVING

About twenty years ago Stewart (1958) had looked forward to the time when traffic research would become much more comprehensive, and would take into account the social interactions involved in traffic. Yet it is really only in the present decade that there has been a gradual realization of the fact that traffic behaviour does not take place in a social vacuum. Even so, Oeser was able to remark as recently as 1978 that 'studies that range over the whole social structures in which drivers are embedded are as yet very few indeed' (p.17). Wilde (1978a) went so far as to say that the failure of traffic safety researchers to study road user behaviour and accident causation from a social-interactive point of view is amazing. It is here that there seems to be a place for applied social psychology to make a contribution of a practical kind in an area of human behaviour which is of considerable real-life significance. Indeed, the process has begun, albeit in an incomplete and uncoordinated way.

Blumenthal (1970) is one researcher who has tried to relate driving behaviour to certain theoretical notions within social psychology. Protesting against the naive assumption that the driver is always capable of making rational decisions (a point of view often implied by the systems theory approach to driving), Blumenthal has outlined a conceptualization of the driving process in terms of Zajonc's (1966) theoretical model of social psychology, focusing particularly on this author's three basic paradigms of social behaviour. The first of these proposes that the presence of other people affects drive states and arousal levels and thereby influences learning and performance; the second sees the behaviour of other people as serving a cue function; the third regards the behaviour of other people as providing positive and negative reinforcement (sometimes, as in the case of driving, vicariously, in terms of modelling). A good deal of the existing research on social aspects of driving can be subsumed under one or more of these three paradigms. Other research has introduced additional concepts from social science, and the review that follows attempts to summarize relevant finding in terms of some key social psychological constructs, including the idea of social adjustment, social norms and conformity, imitation and modelling, social status, social perception and attribution theory, social interaction, and the more anthropological notion of personal space and territoriality.

Social Adjustment

Many studies have examined relationships between involvement in accidents, or convictions for traffic offences, and various social factors. Accident rates have been shown to be linked to socio-economic status (Borkenstein, Crowther, Shumate, Ziel, and Zylman, 1964; Gutshall, Harper, and Burke, 1968), social maturity (Sainchez-Jimeinez, 1967), and social inadequacy, as measured by scores on personality tests (Achtnich, 1967). The concept of social adjustment, especially in the family setting, has been shown to relate to involvement in both fatal and non-fatal accidents (Armstrong and Jamieson, 1973; Hagger and Dax, 1977; McFarland, 1957; Mayer and Treat, 1977; Ratilainen, 1968; Read, Bradley, Morison, Lewall, and Clarke, 1963; Sobel and Underhill, 1976; Williams and Malfetti, 1970), although there is some evidence that the relationship may be less strong, or even non-existent, in the case of females (Shaffer, Schmidt, Zlotowitz, and Fisher, 1977). If so, this might imply that there is a greater tendency for males than for females to 'drive as they live' in contemporary Western society—possibly because of cultural factors affecting sex role behaviour.

The related concepts of social conflict and social stress, brought about by disruptions in interpersonal relationships, have been shown to relate to accident involvement (Conger *et al.*, 1957; Selzer, Rogers, and Kern, 1968; Waller, Foley, and Jeffrey, 1972), especially where alcoholism or impaired driving is also involved (Brenner and Selzer, 1969; Selzer, 1969; Selzer and Vinokur, 1975; Selzer, Vinokur, and Wilson, 1977; Zelhart, 1972). Indeed, such social factors may play a crucial—and largely unrecognized—role in impaired driving and accident causation. For example, Sterling-Smith (1975), in discussing the relationship between responsibility for fatal car accidents and alcohol, has argued that it is over-simplistic to assume that those most responsible for such accidents are simply alcoholics. Rather, he maintains, they should be described as 'alcohol-influenced' at the time of the accident or 'without known alcohol-influence'. When Sterling-Smith categorized 267 accident-involved drivers in this way, he found that there were considerable differences between groups in social attitudes, interpersonal relationships, expressed anger, and hostility. The people in the alcohol-influenced group were more rebellious (i.e. anti-religious, anti-establishment), and were experiencing more family and marital conflicts. Along the same lines, Wilde (1975) has argued that since driving is usually a group activity, the law with regard to drinking and driving 'should be designed so as to address itself more to the patterns of human interaction in which drinking takes place' (p.821). He suggests as examples greater use of concepts like accessory to the act, and co-responsibility for driving after drinking.

Conformity Behaviour and Social Norms

In a formal sense, norms in the driving situation might be thought to involve official laws or codified 'rules of the road', such as are found in the British *Highway Code*, and in the North American state or provincial driving manuals. Human factors and systems theory approaches to the study of driving have tended to focus on normative behaviour defined in this narrow way. This had led in turn to an assumption that defective driving must result from either a failure on the part of the driver to conform to these norms because of weak signal detection skills, poor decision-making ability, and so on, or a failure on the part of authorities to communicate the norms effectively by means of such devices as traffic signals or road signs. Yet, as Michon (1978) comments, improvements in road signs and the like do not lead to increased road safety, because people still deviate from the new norms. As Williams and Malfetti (1970) put it (pp. vi–vii): 'Humans are not as easily or as well regulated as machines. Methods of traffic regulation and enforcement seem insignificant when human deviation from prescribed behavior is considered.'

Deehy (1968) and Lurie (1968) first drew attention to two different kinds of norms influencing driver behaviour that they labelled formal (i.e. legal rules) and informal (social norms). To cite a common example, most countries have a set of formal rules to regulate driving speed, but informal or social norms may dictate the speeds people actually drive at. Indeed, the informal norm may even be the basis for police enforcement and prosecution. The sociological concept of 'folk crime' has been used to describe some types of normative behaviour that conflict with formal traffic law. The term describes illegal acts that are not stigmatized by the public as criminal, but often perceived as purely 'technical' infringements. Many official driving offences are regarded in this way by large sections of the public, for example parking infractions, speeding (where no danger to human life exists), and even drinking and driving, in moderation. It is likely that many would agree with Ross's (1960–61) point that many traffic violators are not intent on being corrupt, despite the fact that their illegal acts are frequent and widespread.

Wilde (1978a) has pointed out that when different road users act on the basis of discrepant norms, conflict can arise that may ultimately lead to accidents. He cites Johnston's (1973) example of a woman who had four traffic accidents in four years but was not deemed to be legally at fault in any of them. It was found that she drove with a degree of caution—especially at yield and stop signs—which was within the legal norms but outside the bounds of the local informal norms.

Entering a new traffic environment might be thought to be particularly dangerous, in the sense that it may be difficult for drivers to recognize exactly what informal norm systems are at work. For example, Shor (1964) hypothesized that individuals who learned to drive in a highly competitive social climate (the instance he cited was Boston) will have different normative expectations from those who usually drive in an environment where courtesy is valued highly. When such drivers find themselves in an unfamiliar traffic environment, then conflicts can arise more easily — something that is frequently commented upon by people who drive for the first time in a large foreign city, such as Rome or Paris.

Certain driving situations seem to be inherently ambivalent in the sense that drivers bring to them slightly differing expectations about acceptable normative behaviour — sometimes with extremely dangerous consequences. For example, it is known that the installation of traffic lights at intersections generally fails to diminish the accident rate, and Wilde (1978a) has attributed this to the ambiguity of the amber period. Similarly, the frequency of accidents at North American railroad crossings might be attributed to the very different expectations about an appropriate speed of approach, or when it is 'too late' to cross (Wilde, 1978a). In both these cases there is no question about what the formal rules prescribe. Nonetheless, accidents persist.

Despite the inherent uncertainty that appears to exist in particular traffic environments, there are many cases where the informal rules of traffic behaviour are well known to local drivers. For example, Wilde (1978a) has distinguished between 'psychological right of way' and 'natural right of way', and von Klebelsberg (1963) and Gheri (1963) have observed that some streets have greater 'social status' than others (regardless of the legal situation), due to such factors as street width, amount of lighting, traffic volume, presence of shops, and so on.

A major effect of different informal norm expectations is on perceived level of risk in the traffic environment. Commenting on the short-term reduction in the accident rate in Sweden following the change-over from left-hand to right-hand driving in 1967, Wilde (1978b) pointed out that accident frequency returned to the general trend line within approximately two years. He attributed this to the fact that the change-over produced a sudden and definite increase in the level of perceived risk and, as a result, drivers used extreme caution, causing the accident rate to drop. After a time, however, drivers learned through the mass media and from their own experience that the roads were not as dangerous as they had originally feared. Wilde concluded that different levels of perceived risk stem from different driving experience, and speculated that the greatest danger in traffic may not simply be inexperienced drivers, but the mixture of road users with varying levels of experience, and hence different informal norm systems.

Despite the considerable evidence for the notion that much of driving involves conformity to a system of informal rules, rather than the formal laws of the land, most driver training and driver testing largely ignores this fact. For example, high school driver education programmes in North America have tended to concentrate almost exclusively on students' abilities to learn and recognize the formal rules, stressing such skills as knowledge of traffic laws, recognition of basic road signs, and so on, often in a classroom situation far removed from what would be experienced when actually handling a car. Yet if accidents could be explained purely in terms of rule breaking, then the frequency of collisions would be vastly greater than it is at present. Indeed, it is quite impossible to police more than a tiny portion of the infractions of rules of the road detailed in most driving manuals.

Social Facilitation and Modelling

In many situations the performance of an individual on a routine task is affected by the presence of spectators. In the case of driving behaviour, Black (1978) investigated the consequence of the presence or the absence of a passenger on driver behaviour in a medium sized Canadian city, including use of seat belts (compulsory in this jurisdiction), coming to a complete halt at a stop sign, correctly signalling a turn, coming to a full stop before making a right turn at a red light (such turns are legal in many North American cities), and driving within the speed limit. In all five cases the presence of a passenger was significantly associated with obedience to the traffic rule in question. Lawshe (1940) had earlier obtained a similar result in the case of driving speed, and Feest (1968) showed that accompanied drivers were twice as likely as unaccompanied drivers to stop properly at a stop sign, with the tendency especially marked at night. In the case of informal norms of driving behaviour, as opposed to formal rules, Ebbesen and Haney (1973) observed that drivers accompanied by passengers had a somewhat lesser tendency to take risks in terms of following behaviour, and Carlson and Cooper (1974) found that drivers with passengers took fewer risks when making a turn across two lanes of traffic.

Assuming that driving is a thoroughly practised and familiar activity, these findings support the notion that the presence of other people in the car improves driving performance, at least from the point of view of observation of norms. Commenting on the results from such studies, Wilde (1978a) has pointed out that because of the correlational nature of the observed association between passenger presence and drivers' compliance with formal and informal norms, it is not possible to say for certain that the passenger actually *causes* the driver to be more cautious or law-abiding. It is conceivable that some other factor is at work and that, for example, drivers who tend to be accompanied in their cars are inherently more cautious. Nonetheless, this does not in itself invalidate the theory of social facilitation, nor does it negate the importance of social influences on driving.

An interesting, but untried test of the theory would involve studying driving situations that might be expected to hamper, rather than facilitate, performance. For example, what would be the effects of passengers' presence on driving in dangerous situations, such as at high speed or on ice? Would there be differential effects of passengers upon experienced and inexperienced drivers? Previous research on social facilitation in other realms of behaviour would support the prediction that inexperienced drivers, especially under difficult driving circumstances, might tend to make more errors in the presence of passengers.

Closely linked to the notion of social facilitation is the idea that much driving behaviour involves modelling and imitation in the traffic environment. As Hutchinson, Cox, and Maffet (1969) put it: 'drivers follow each other like sheep'. Wilde (1978a) labelled this type of mutual imitation 'coaction' and cited a number of studies that have found the effect in different driving behaviours. For example, Herman and Gardels (1963) reported it with regard to car-following behaviour. Barch, Trumbo, and Nangle (1957) observed that signalling at an intersection was influenced by the behaviour of preceding vehicles, and various studies have shown a strong positive association between seat belts used by drivers and by passengers in the same vehicle (e.g. Anderson, 1971; Andreassend, 1972). In a different context, Clark (1976) demonstrated the effect of peer group pressure upon risk-taking behaviour among young, male Australian drivers. Such modelling and imitation in the traffic environment is not confined to drivers. The classic study by Lefkowitz, Blake, and Mouton (1955) showed that pedestrian violations at a light-controlled crossing were significantly increased when a well dressed model crossed against the light. Wilde (1973) reports that this study was repeated in Canada, and the modelling effect confirmed—although in this case the way the model was dressed had no measurable influence. The Canadian study also found that pedestrian behaviour was affected by the number of people waiting on the sidewalk for the light to turn green: the larger this number, the smaller the percentage who would follow the model.

On the basis of such observational and correlational studies, some investigators have attempted direct manipulation of driver behaviour by use of role models. For example, in France, Labadie, L'Hoste, and Wilde (1973) sent 4,000 people (out of a driving population of 150,000) letters inviting them to use their seat belts and to obtain a bumper sticker which read 'I use my seat belt—how about you?'. Observations of seat belt use in the area showed that the usage rate quickly rose from 6 to 12 percent. Additional evidence from questionnaires sent to the original sample led the research team to attribute this increase to modelling. Another somewhat similar study was conducted in Toronto by Wilson, Lonero, and Ish (1972) in which seat belt propaganda was given to about 4,000 seven- and eight-year-old children to see whether this had any effect upon their parents' use of belts. Significant increases of about 10 percent were observed in comparison with a control group of other parents. Despite these findings, Cropley, Knapper, and Moore (1977) recommended an alternative notion of social influence based upon obedience to some legitimate authority (such as the car driver or the law) in attempting to increase seat belt usage, and recent results of compulsory seat belt legislation in various countries seem to support their approach (see, for example, Foldvary and Lane, 1974; Robertson and Williams, 1978).

Social Status

One of the earliest studies of the effects of social status on driving behaviour was by Doob and Gross (1968). They arranged to have traffic lights blocked with either new or old cars, and observed how long it was before obstructed vehicles sounded their horns. They found that older cars provoked more horn honking behaviour, with female drivers being more tolerant, and young male drivers particularly quick to honk. A number of other studies have used variants of the same situation to investigate different characteristics of the car and driver — especially the sex of the frustrating motorist. Bochner (1971) used the blocking technique, but varied status by means of the presence or absence of a 'P' (for 'provisional') on the licence plates. He found that this had no effect on horn honking behaviour, but that female drivers in the obstructing vehicles provoked significantly fewer aggressive responses. Deaux (1971) also found a sex effect — but in the opposite direction: women drivers of the stalled vehicle provoked more horn honking than male drivers. In another replication of the Doob and Gross design, Chase and Mills (1973) found the opposite result with regard to status (newer cars provoked more honking), and failed to find any effects for sex. In explaining the discrepant results from different studies, these authors mentioned the possibility that social norms might change with time, and from region to region.

In Canada, Hankes-Drielsma (1974) used basically the same situation with the additional variable of the presence or absence of a clear ethnic identification on the blocking vehicle (a prominent Italian flag and decal). It was found that honking was significantly more rapid in the absence of the ethnic identification. Turner, Layton, and Simons (1975) used the blocked light technique to investigate the effects on frustrated drivers of a visible rifle in the blocking car, an aggressive bumper sticker ('Vengeance'), a non-visible driver (because of a curtain drawn across the rear window), and the usual sex and vehicle age variables. Results showed that the presence of the rifle in combination with the aggressive bumper sticker and driver invisibility (which the researchers related to dehumanization) provoked significantly more rapid horn honking. Using a different dependent variable, Heussenstamm (1975) found that California drivers bearing prominent 'Black Panther' stickers suddenly attracted large numbers of citations for traffic offences, though all the drivers had previously had clear driving records.

Some investigations have reflected the recent interest among social psychologists in altruistic behaviour, and have examined the factors that facilitate helping behaviour by road users. For example, Pomazal and Clore

(1973) examined the effects of dependency and sex on helping in three different situations. In the first, reactions of passing motorists were observed in relation to someone with a flat tyre, who could be either male or female, have a physical disability or not. Although the disability produced only slightly more helping behaviour, females were helped significantly more than males. In the second situation the same disability and sex variables were studied, but in a hitch-hiking context. Once again females were helped significantly more than males, but here the presence of a disability significantly reduced the numbers of offers of rides. A third situation involved a different sort of dependency cue in the hitch-hiking situation: the presence of a disabled vehicle. The latter significantly increased offers of help, and once again females were helped significantly more than males. Pomazal and Clore analyzed their results in terms of such factors as the perceived cost of helping, the attractiveness of those soliciting help, and whether or not the latter were perceived as being responsible for their state of dependency. The authors concluded that their results complemented findings of previous laboratory work on the same variables. Hurley and Allen (1974) used the 'flat tyre' situation to investigate the norms of diffusion of responsibility with respect to helping a stranger in need. They studied offers of help to a stranded motorist in two situations: a superhighway (high traffic density) and a country road (low density). As predicted, offers of help were greater in the low density condition, although average time between offers of help was less on the superhighway.

Simon (1976) arranged for a simulated stalled car with its hood up to be parked at the side of a very busy Kansas highway, near which either a male or female confederate was visible. Observations of how many drivers stopped to help each sex showed that females received almost nine times as many offers of aid as did males — although the total of such offers represented less than 5 percent of all cars passing by. Solomon and Herman (1977) studied the behaviour of male and female passers-by in a middle-class shopping centre in relation to a female struggling to load groceries into a car trunk. It was found that the target was much more likely to receive help when she was using a high status (i.e. new, large, clean) car than a low status vehicle. Penner, Dertke, and Achenbach (1973), in evaluating the effectiveness of an experimental automated highway help system for stranded motorists, found that direct and indirect helping behaviour was related to the race and sex of the supposedly stranded driver, with whites and females receiving more help.

In all four studies, most of the experimental effect was accounted for by male respondents (helpers), partially reflecting the fact that there were generally more male drivers in the situations studied.

Social Perception and Attribution Theory

Many of the studies described above presumably involve the attribution of certain characteristics by one driver to another on the basis of cues such as sex, ethnic identification, socio-economic status, and so on. In addition, a number of investigators have looked specifically and in depth at the personal attributions and perceptions generated in the driving situation. Shaw and McMartin (1975), for example, investigated attribution of responsibility in automobile accidents. Subjects read an account of an accident in which the driver and/or bystanders either suffered or did not, and were then required to rate the driver's responsibility for the accident and sentence the offender to a jail term. A major purpose of the study was to contrast three theoretical models: defensive attribution, moral salience, and equity. It was found that male subjects appeared to use an equity principle, in that they gave shorter jail sentences when the accident perpetrator himself suffered injury. On the other hand, female subjects were more inclined to act in terms of moral salience, increasing their sentences only when by-standers were injured. Of particular interest is the finding that, regardless of sex, subjects expressed a strong preference for information regarding personality characteristics of the accident-causing driver, as opposed to information about the environmental circumstances surrounding the collision. In other words they apparently reacted to accident situations in terms of what might be called 'interpersonal' factors.

Parry (1968) used extensive interviews with British drivers to investigate their perceptions of other road users, with particular reference to aggression in the driving situation. He distributed 382 questionnaires to motorists in the South of England to identify those with high levels of aggressive or anxious responses, and a further 55 respondents were subsequently interviewed in more depth, using a sentence completion task. Many of the drivers admitted to undergoing a change in attitude once behind the wheel of a car, with aggressive responses predominating. Aggression could be directed at oneself, at an inanimate object (a vehicle, a road obstruction, etc.) or at another driver, and the latter was by far the most common response. In addition, such aggression could be either reactive (in which a motorist responded to a particular situation) or 'endogenous', as when the motorist was aggressive for no apparent external or logical reason. In either case, Parry concluded, such responses were related to accidents. The extensive interview reports provided by the author provide some confirmation for the notion that many people appear to adopt exaggerated or irrational perceptions and attributions when driving, and this often appears to lead to aggressive or dangerous behaviour, especially with young male drivers. Just why this occurs is not clear.

A somewhat similar technique of investigation was used by Knapper and Cropley (1978) who interviewed Canadian road users in order to ascertain reactions to a number of common driving situations, such as involvement in a near collision. The behaviour of other drivers (and to a lesser extent passengers, pedestrians, and by-standers) was seen as a major cause of potential danger in traffic, and psychological reactions when driving appeared to be markedly affected by the behaviour of other road users. In this connection, drivers continually imputed motives, opinions, and values to other drivers, and it appeared that such inferences and perceptions were an important determinant of affective state and, ultimately, overt behaviour—including aggressive responses. Even more important, many of these kinds of inferences were ones that could not be made directly from observation of other drivers' behaviour, but only adduced from it indirectly. The authors found that there were basically three sets of characteristics of other drivers that influenced perception. The first set of factors involved what might be called 'fixed' traits such as age, sex, and physical appearance. The second involved perceived characteristics that could be inferred more or less directly from observation of fairly concrete aspects of other drivers' behaviour (e.g. attributions of carelessness or impatience). The third kind of characteristic involved perceived qualities of other drivers that could not be observed, but only inferred or adduced—such as arrogance.

Knapper and Cropley concluded that respondents regarded the driving situation as an extension of everyday social life, bound by the same rules as any other social intercourse among people. A somewhat similar conclusion was reached by Williams and Malfetti (1970), who conducted a series of studies in which they asked drivers to describe their perceptions of various elements in the traffic environment. The differences between good and bad drivers seemed to be related to a self-concept variable and the extent to which the individual identified with certain general social values. Drivers without accidents and violations had a self-view that was more compatible with safe and responsible driving, and yet which related to much broader social concepts such as courtesy and respect for the law.

The findings of Williams and Malfetti and of Knapper and Cropley reinforce some of the ideas of those who have argued for a relationship between personality and driving (reviewed earlier) to the effect that a person 'drives as he lives'. Accordingly, the act of driving is seen as being a microcosm 'in which the individual is likely to respond as he does in the larger milieu' (Williams and Malfetti, 1970, p.50). The same authors conclude that the driving situation is a 'special context in which to mete out social rewards for demonstrations of courtesy, responsibility, and social concern' (p.51). Unfortunately, however, as Williams and Malfetti point out, there are probably few extrinsic rewards for displaying such behaviour when driving (only punishment for extreme discourteous behaviour, under certain circumstances), and driver training programmes appear to have been fairly unsuccessful in cultivating in their students a notion of intrinsic reward for courteous behaviour on the road.

Social Interaction

A number of studies have examined the interaction between drivers and pedestrians at intersections or pedestrian crossings. For example, Ellsworth, Carlsmith, and Henson (1972) and Greenbaum and Rosenfeld (1978) studied reactions of drivers to being stared at by a by-stander when stopped at an intersection. Results showed that most drivers displayed avoidance behaviour, characterized by pulling up outside the normal stopping position, averting their gaze, and/or driving away at a faster speed (which might possibly have some implications for traffic safety). Observational studies by Herwig (1965) and Katz, Zaidel, and Algrishi (1973) indicated that drivers are more likely to slow down than stop at crossings when pedestrians cross as a group, rather than individually. The latter authors also examined the exchange of glances between pedestrians and drivers. The pedestrians were in fact confederates of the experimenters, and crossed the road either after attempting to make eye contact with the driver of the on-coming car or, alternatively, looked straight ahead when crossing. Observations of the speed of approaching vehicles showed that they were significantly lower when there was no eye contact, and the authors explained this by saying that the eye contact provided the driver with evidence that the pedestrian was aware of the vehicle, and thus in some sense shared the responsibility for any accident that might ensue. Where no evidence of awareness had been communicated, then a greater share of responsibility was passed on to the driver. Since eye contact and exchange of mutual gaze are known to be important mechanisms of interpersonal communication (see Argyle and Cook, 1976), it would appear once again that behaviour in the driving situation simply reflects more general patterns of social interaction.

One fascinating finding with regard to pedestrian behaviour at intersections was that of Fleig and Duffy (1967) that the installation of 'walk–don't walk' signals had little or no influence on accident rates in New York City. These authors also failed to observe any increase in unsafe acts after installation of the signals. It seems that pedestrians and drivers proceed and interact according to some subtle system of informal normative behaviour regardless of any formal rule system provided by traffic signals.

An ambitious and ingenious study by Hauber (1978) investigated drivers' aggressive reactions to last-minute walking by a pedestrian at various legal crossings in Holland, Denmark, and Switzerland. Hauber operationally defined driver aggression as a failure to stop, abusive gestures or comments, and horn honking. After such responses had been tabulated by observers, drivers were traced by means of licence plates, and another measure of aggression was obtained by means of reactions to two phone enquiries for a non-existent person. Finally, a subsample of drivers were interviewed in their homes. It was found that 25 percent of the drivers could be classified as aggressive, of whom a substantial proportion were younger men of lower socio-economic status. However, aggressive behaviour was also partly determined by the sex of the pedestrian, males provoking twice as many aggressive responses as females. A relationship was found between aggression in the telephone situation and on the road, but a much higher proportion of aggressive responses existed in the latter situation. This provides partial support for the notion that driving behaviour is just a special instance of general social behaviour, while suggesting that the automobile provides a special environment in which latent responses are more easily vented.

Another situation involving driver–pedestrian interaction is that of hitch-hiking. Encounters of this kind were studied by Alcorn and Condie (1975) in an attempt to test some of the similarity-attraction assumptions of balance theory. A confederate posing as a hitch-hiker dressed either conventionally or as a hippie, and the effect of this on being offered rides was observed. There was a general tendency for motorists to offer rides to the hitch-hiker who had an appearance similar to their own, which the investigators interpreted as implying a social attraction between the two individuals.

With respect to interaction between different drivers, a large amount of the material reviewed earlier, while not focusing specifically on such behaviour, implies that social interactions are indeed an important part of most driving situations. Investigators who have made interactions in driving a particular object of study include Leff and Gunn (1973), who showed that behaviour at British roundabouts could be explained in terms of the patterns of interactions between drivers of different vehicles. These patterns were greatly affected by variables such as the sex of the driver (all else being equal, females yielded the right of way twice as often as males), although the type of interaction had no relationship to roundabout accidents. Leff and Gunn's findings seem to have relevance for Wilde's (1976) notion of perceived level of risk, which may vary for different types of driver and may well be influenced by the sorts of inter-personal cue discussed in the section on attribution theory above. Indeed, the paper by Shor (1964) discussed earlier argues that social interaction in the driving situation can easily be observed, and such observations indicate that resident drivers in a particular locality communicate non-verbally in a 'dialect' not easily understood by occasional non-resident drivers. Expanding upon Shor's ideas, it might well be that to facilitate a more accurate estimation of risk, drivers need training in the recognition and correct interpretation of the different cues used by other drivers to signal their intentions.

Another factor affecting both risk taking and social interaction, according to Ebbesen and Haney (1973), is the frustration that can occur in certain common driving situations. They studied risk taking at intersections where a line-up of cars caused drivers to wait. In such circumstances risk taking increased markedly, although the presence of cars alongside or behind seemed to have no such effect. Finally, Bliersbach and Dellen (1978) carried out in-depth interviews with 230 drivers regarding their experience with driving in a large variety of different situations. The authors identified a number of different driving patterns, most of which implied the importance of interactions with others on the road. The factors were 'thrill' (seeing how fast the car would go), 'power display' (overtaking other vehicles), 'self-testing' (what the authors called 'snappy driving' and engaging in tricky manoeuvres), 'driving smoothly' (free of complications with other drivers), and 'piloting' (coping with traffic correctly, ably, and with poise). Bliersbach and Dellen commented that each of these patterns of driving has implications for interactions in traffic, but that most drivers are largely unaware of them. They went on to argue that one aim of driver education programmes should be to make motorists more aware of these patterns, the related psycho-social processes involved in driving, and the interaction effects that are caused by their behaviour on the road (i.e. the cues drivers provide for other drivers).

Personal Space and Territoriality

Personal space refers to the notion that there is an invisible boundary surrounding each individual, and that intrusions into this defined space or territory are resented and defended (see Sommer, 1969). The idea of personal space and the way it might relate to the driving situation has had attractions for many popular commentators on the role of the automobile and the motivation of drivers, and some of these ideas were discussed at the beginning of this chapter. Whitlock (1971) is one psychologist who has viewed the car as a 'private territory on the road', almost equivalent to the home. In terms of Sommer's concept of personal space, Whitlock points out that, in the case of a car, the boundaries are metallic, and hence relatively impermeable. He goes further and attempts to explain the more aggressive behaviour by male drivers in terms of the traditional role of the male as provider and defender of the home territory. The extremely aggressive behaviour of young males noted by many investigators is thought by Whitlock to be caused by the fact that the car may be all that they possess, and hence all their territorial instincts are focused there; the same might be said to apply to drivers from lower socio-economic status groups and those from poorer countries.

Richman (1972) attempted to test some notions of personal space in a real-life situation. He predicted that interactions between drivers and traffic wardens would be likely to provoke aggression on the grounds that personal territory had been threatened or invaded. In contrast to Whitlock's predictions, it was found that male drivers were rated as most aggressive in their behaviour by only 27 percent of the wardens, and young drivers by only 35 percent, whereas motorists of high socio-economic status were rated as most aggressive by 43 percent of the wardens. In a valiant attempt to support a personal space interpretation of his findings, Richman suggested that people of higher social status are accustomed to larger territories, and thus getting a parking ticket is a greater degradation and threat for them. The author did, however, admit that perhaps the best test of Whitlock's ideas might not be in the stationary situation involved in parking, but would be better exemplified when cars were in free motion. This idea has not yet been pursued in an experimental setting, although casual observation suggests that drivers do indeed differ in the amount of space they like to maintain in various traffic situations.

CONCLUSIONS

In practice, research on driver behaviour has been slow to acknowledge the importance of social psychological factors. McClintock (1972) is one writer who has criticized psychologists for concentrating too much on individual behaviour and on how various physical stimuli affect it, at the same time failing to remember that 'most human behavior occurs within a social matrix where all the participants mutually control their own and others' outcome'. The evidence reviewed above suggests persuasively that driving is a social situation in which interpersonal reactions are of great importance. Furthermore, these reactions appear to follow some general principles that are well established in the field of social psychology, involving concepts such as social norms, modelling, social status, interpersonal attraction, personal space, and the like. Not only does this have theoretical implications for fully understanding driver behaviour, but it also suggests some practical possibilities, for example in the field of driver training.

Oeser (1978, pp.16–17) has protested that

> the prevalent belief that one or two causes are responsible for any given accident — alcohol or speeding — is so limited as to be just plain silly. The causes are multiple, and form an interrelated system, which in turn is a subsystem of society . . . No substantial progress will be made in stopping the epidemic of deaths on the road unless and until research is done over a long period . . . each individual is the product of 20 and more years of learning his attitudes and social interactions.

(Spörli (1974) is another writer who has argued that a new approach in the form of a 'traffic psychology' is needed, and has commented on the disappointing progress to date in understanding driver behaviour. He attributes this partly to the very applied nature of the subject matter, which makes it a relatively unattractive field for most academic psychologists, who have consequently tended to leave the topic to a number of isolated specialists working on equally isolated aspects of the problem.

Although supporting an approach to the whole transportation domain that would stress psychological factors. Michon (1976) expressed a note of caution with regard to the burgeoning interest in a social science of driving. Agreeing that social interaction is an important aspect of the driving process, he argued that a plausible theory of social interaction on the road must account not just for the outputs (expressed opinions, observable driving behaviours, and the like), but must also be capable of explaining the processes which produce these outputs—in his own words, not just the 'taste of the cake', but also 'the recipe' for making it. For example, given a behaviour such as following too closely behind another vehicle or driving too hesitantly in heavy traffic, what processes need to be set in motion to ensure driving behaviour that is adequate in the sense that it will reduce rather than increase the risks involved? Even more fundamentally, what psychological processes or cognitive structures will achieve this end?

What both Spörli and Michon imply, as well as Oeser, Wilde, and others who have made the same plea, is that the current need is for a synthesis that will provide the basis for a new discipline. Certainly it seems sensible for future research into driving and other traffic behaviour to use insights from the full range of disciplines comprising the social sciences. Understanding of the social processes at work is, to this point, incomplete, scattered, and often not very profound. Nonetheless, the weight of the evidence does suggest that an approach to driving behaviour based on the concepts of social science could lead to important insights that have been neglected to date.

REFERENCES

Achtnich, M. (1967) 'Driver in the Szondi test', *Schweizerische Zeitschrift für Psychologie und ihre Anwendungen Supplement*, **51**, 80–81.

Alcorn, D. S. and Condie, S. J. (1975) 'Who picks up whom: The fleeting encounter between motorist and hitchhiker', *Humboldt Journal of Social Relations*, **3**, 56–61.

Alonso-Fernandez, F. (1966) 'Configuraciones psiquicas peligrosas del conductor tremulo', *Revista de Psicologia General y Aplicada*, **21**, 947–60.

American Safety Belt Council (1974) *Solution for Highway Carnage: Safety Belt Legislation*, American Safety Belt Council, Washington, D.C.

Anderson, T. W. (1971) *Shoulder Belt Utilization*, University of North Carolina Highway Safety Research Center, Chapel Hill, North Carolina.

Andreassend, D. C. (1972) 'The effects of compulsory seat belt wearing legislation in Victoria', paper presented at the National Road Safety Symposium, Canberra.

Argyle, M. and Cook, M. (1976) *Gaze and Mutual Gaze*, Cambridge University Press, Cambridge, England.

Armstrong, J. L. and Jamieson, D. G. (1973) *Sociology of Drivers: A Longitudinal Study of Drivers Involved in Serious Road Accidents*, New South Wales Department of Motor Transport, Sydney, Australia.

Asai, M. and Inayosh, H. (1973) *Some Determinants of Safety-Mindedness: The Attitude of High School Students toward Traffic Safety*, Mihon University Department of Psychology, Tokyo.

Ashcraft, N. and Scheflen, A. E. (1976) *People Space: The Making and Breaking of Human Boundaries*, Doubleday, New York.

Baker, J. S. (1963) *Traffic Accident Investigators Manual for Police*, Northwestern University Traffic Institute, Evanston, Illinois.

Baker, S. P. and Spitz, W. W. (1970) 'Age effects and autopsy evidence of disease in fatally injured drivers', *Journal of the American Medical Association*, 214, 1079–88.

Barch, A. M., Trumbo, D., and Nangle, J. (1957) 'Social setting and conformity to a legal requirement', *Journal of Abnormal and Social Psychology*, 55, 396–98.

Benton, J. L., Mills, L., Hartman, K. J., and Crow, J. T. (1961) 'Auto driver fitness: An evaluation of useful criteria', *Journal of the American Medical Association*, 176, 419–23.

Black, C. L. (1978) 'Driver's compliance with formal traffic regulations related to the presence of passengers', B.A. Thesis, Queen's University Department of Psychology, Kingston, Canada.

Bliersbach, G. and Dellen, R. G. (1978) 'Interaction conflicts and interaction patterns in traffic situations', paper presented at the International Congress of Applied Psychology, Munich.

Blumenthal, M. (1970) 'Traffic safety and the structure of a social problem', in *Highway and Stress*, University of North Carolina Highway Research Center, Chapel Hill, North Carolina.

Bochner, S. (1971) 'Inhibition of horn-sounding as a function of frustrator's status and sex: An Australian replication and extension of Doob and Gross (1968)', *Australian Psychologist*, 6, 194–99.

Boek, J. K. (1957) 'Driver behavior and accidents', *American Journal of Public Health*, 47, 546–52.

Borkenstein, R. F., Crowther, R. F., Shumate, R. P., Ziel, W. B., and Zylman, R. (1964) *The Role of the Drinking Driver in Traffic Accidents*, Indiana University Department of Police Administration, Bloomington.

Boorstin, D. J. (1963) *The Image—Or What Happened to the American Dream*, Penguin, Harmondsworth, England.

Brenner, B. and Selzer, M. L. (1969) 'Risk of causing a fatal accident associated with alcoholism, psychopathology, and stress: Further analysis of previous data', *Behavioral Science*, 14, 490–95.

Brown, I. D. and Copeman, A. K. (1969) *Drivers' Attitudes to the Seriousness of Road Traffic Offences Considered in Relation to the Design of Sanctions*, Medical Research Council Applied Psychology Research Unit, Cambridge, England.

Cantor, K. P. (1970) 'Warning—the automobile is dangerous to earth, air, fire, water, mind and body', in *The Environmental Handbook* (Ed. G. de Bell), Ballantine, New York, 197–213.

Carlson, K. and Cooper, R. E. (1974) 'A preliminary investigation of risk behavior in the real world', *Personality and Social Psychology Bulletin*, 1, 7–9.

Carlson, W. L. (1973) 'Age, exposure and alcohol involvement in night crashes', *Journal of Safety Research*, 5, 247–59.

Chase, L. J. and Mills, N. H. (1973) 'Status of frustrators as a facilitator of aggression: A brief note', *Journal of Psychology*, 84, 225–26.

Clark, A. W. (1976) 'A social role approach to driver behavior', *Perceptual and Motor Skills*, 42, 325–26.

Clayton, A. B. and Mackay, G. M. (1972) 'Aetiology of traffic accidents', *Health Bulletin*, 31, 277–80.

Conger, J. J., Gaskill, H. S., Glad, D. D., Rainey, R. V., Sawrey, W. L., and Turrell, E. S. (1957) 'Personal and interpersonal factors in motor vehicle accidents', *American Journal of Psychiatry*, 113, 1069–74.

Cropley, A. J., Knapper, C. K., and Moore, R. J. (1977) 'A clinical/quantitative analysis of public opinions about seat belts', *International Review of Applied Psychology*, **26**, 43–49.

Deaux, D. D. (1971) 'Honking at the intersection: A replication and extension', *Journal of Social Psychology*, **84**, 159–60.

Deehy, P. T. (1968) 'Sociology and road safety', paper presented at a seminar of the Engineering Institute of Canada Committee on Road Safety Research, Kingston, Canada.

Doob, A. N. and Gross, A. E. (1968) 'Status of frustrator as an inhibitor of horn-honking responses', *Journal of Social Psychology*, **76**, 213–18.

Ebbesen, E. B. and Haney, M. (1973) 'Flirting with death: Variables affecting risk-taking at intersections', *Journal of Applied Social Psychology*, **3**, 303–24.

Egan, R. (1967) 'Should the educable mentally retarded receive driver education?', *Exceptional Children*, **33**, 323.

Ellsworth, P. C., Carlsmith, J. M., and Henson, A. (1972) 'The stare as a stimulus to flight in human subjects', *Journal of Social and Personality Psychology*, **21**, 302–11.

Feest, S. (1968) 'Compliance with legal regulations: Observations of stop-sign behavior', *Law and Society Review*, **2**, 447–61.

Fleig, P. H. and Duffy, D. J. (1967) 'A study of pedestrian safety behaviour using activity sampling', *Traffic Safety Research Review*, **December**, 106-11.

Foldvary, L. A. and Lane, J. C. (1974) 'The effectiveness of compulsory seat belt wearing on casualty reduction', *Accident Analysis and Prevention*, **6**, 59–81.

Forbes, T. W. (1972) *Human Factors in Highway Safety Research*, Wiley, New York.

Gheri, M. F. (1963) *Über das Blickverhalten von Kraftfahrern an Kreuzungen*, Kuratorium für Verkehrssicherheit, Vienna.

Gianturco, D. T., Ramm, D., and Erwin, C. W. (1974) 'The elderly driver and the ex-driver', in *Normal Ageing* (Ed. E. Palmore), vol. II, Duke University Press, Durham, North Carolina, 173–79.

Goffman, E. (1967) *International Ritual: Essays on Face to Face Behavior*, Doubleday, New York.

Goldberg, T. (1969) 'The automobile: A social institution for adolescents', *Environment and Behavior*, **1**, 157–85.

Goldstein, L. G. and Mosel, J. N. (1958) *A Factor Study of Drivers' Attitudes with Further Study on Driver Aggression*, Highway Research Board, Washington, D.C.

Greenbaum, P. and Rosenfeld, H. M. (1978) 'Patterns of avoidance in response to interpersonal staring and proximity: Effects of by-standers on drivers at a traffic intersection', *Journal of Personality and Social Psychology*, **36**, 575–87.

Greenshields, B. D. (1963) *Driving Behavior and Related Problems*, University of Michigan Transportation Institute, Ann Arbor, Michigan.

Gutshall, R. W., Harper, C., and Burke, D. (1968) 'An exploratory study of the inter-relationships among driving ability, driving exposure, and socioeconomic status of low, average and high intelligence males', *Exceptional Children*, **35**, 43–47.

Haddon, W., Suchman, E. A., and Klein, D. (Eds.) (1964) *Accident Research: Methods and Approaches*, Harper & Row, New York.

Hagger, R. and Dax, E. C. (1977) 'The driving records of multiproblem families', *Social Science and Medicine*, **11**, 121–27.

Hall, E. T. (1969) *The Hidden Dimension*, Doubleday, New York.

Hamilton, J. W. (1967) 'The rear-end collision: A specific form of acting-out', *Journal of the Hillside Hospital*, **16**, 187–204.

Hankes-Drielsma, M. P. (1974) *Driver Aggression and Frustrator Identity*, Queen's University Department of Psychology, Kingston, Canada.

Harrington, D. M. (1971) *The Young Driver Follow-Up Study: An Evaluation of the*

Role of Human Factors in the First Four Years of Driving, California Department of Motor Vehicles Research and Statistics Section, Sacramento, California.

Hauber, A. R. (1978) 'The social psychology of driving behaviour and traffic environments: Research on aggressive behaviour in traffic', paper presented at the International Congress of Applied Psychology, Munich.

Hauser, D. J. (1974) 'Is freedom of choice worth 800 deaths a year?', *Canadian Medical Association Journal*, **110**, 1418–23.

Henderson, M. (1971) *Human Factors in Traffic Safety: A Reappraisal*, New South Wales Department of Motor Transport Traffic Accident Research Unit, Sydney, Australia.

Herman, R. and Gardels, K. (1963) 'Vehicular traffic flow', *Scientific American*, **209**, 6, 35–43.

Herwig, B. (1965) 'Verhalten von Kraftfahrern und Fussgängern an Zebrastreifen', *Zeitschrift für Verkehrssicherheit*, **11**, 189–202.

Heussenstamm, F. K. (1975) 'Bumper stickers and the cops', *Society*, **12**, 2, 32–33.

Hoinville, G., Berthanol, R., and Mackie, A. M. (1972). *A Study of Accident Rates amongst Motorists who Passed or Failed an Advanced Driving Test*, Ministry of Transport Road Research Laboratory, Crowthorne, England.

Hoyos, C. G. and von Klebelsberg, D. (with others) (1965) *Psychologie des Strassenverkehrs*, Huber, Bern.

Hurley, D. and Allen, B. P. (1974) 'The effect of the number of people present in a nonemergency situation', *Journal of Social Psychology*, **92**, 27–29.

Hutchinson, J. W., Cox, C. S., and Maffet, B. R. (1969) 'An evaluation of the effectiveness of televised socially oriented driver re-education', *Highway Research Record*, **292**, 51–63.

Ittelson, W. H., Proshansky, H. M., Rivlin, L. G., and Winkel, G. H. (1974) *An Introduction to Environmental Psychology*, Holt, Rinehart & Winston, New York.

Jackson, K. T. (1976) 'The effect of suburbanization on the cities', in *Suburbia: The American Dream and Dilemma* (Ed. P. C. Dolce), Doubleday, New York, 89–110.

Johnston, D. G. (1973) *Road Accident Causality: A Critique of the Literature and an Illustrative Case*, Hotel Dieu Hospital Department of Psychiatry, Kingston, Canada.

Katz, A., Zaidel, D., and Algrishi, A. (1973) 'Interactive behaviour of drivers and pedestrians at marked pedestrian crossings', paper presented at the First International Conference on Driver Behaviour, Zurich.

von Klebelsberg, D. (1963) *Eine Methode zur empirischen Ermittlung des 'psychologischen' Vorrangs an Strassenkreuzungen und -einmündungen*, Kuratorium für Verkehrssicherheit, Vienna.

von Klebelsberg, D., Biehl, B., Fuhrmann, J., and Seydel, U. (1970) 'Arbeiten aus dem Verkehrspsychologischen Institut: IV. Fahrverhalten: Beschreibung, Beurteilung und diagnostische Erfassung', *Kleine Fachbuchreihe Kuratorium für Verkehrssicherheit*, **8**, 5–84.

Klein, D. (1972) 'Adolescent driving as deviant behavior', *Journal of Safety Research*, **4**, 98–105.

Knapper, C. K., and Cropley, A. J. (1978) 'Towards a social psychology of the traffic environment', in *Environmental Assessment of Socioeconomic Systems* (Eds. D. F. Burkhardt and W. H. Ittelson), Plenum, New York, 263–78.

Knapper, C. K., Cropley, A. J., and Moore, R. J. (1976) 'Attitudinal factors in the non-use of seat belts', *Accident Analysis and Prevention*, **8**, 241–46.

Krampe, G. (1976) 'Cluster analysis of West German towns with special reference to personal rapid transit systems', in *Transportation Planning for a Better Environment* (Eds. P. Stringer and H. Wenzel), Plenum, New York, 149–60.

Labadie, M. J., L'Hoste, J., and Wilde, G. J. S. (1973) 'Conception et expérimentation d'une campagne d'incitation au porte de la ceinture de sécurité', paper presented at the first International Conference on Driver Behaviour, Zurich.

Lawshe, C. H. (1940) 'Studies in automobile speed on the highway', *Journal of Applied Psychology*, **24**, 297–307.

Leff, J. and Gunn, J. (1973) 'The interaction of male and female car drivers at roundabouts', *Accident Analysis and Prevention*, **5**, 253–59.

Lefkowitz, M., Blake, R. R., and Mouton, J. S. (1955) 'Status factors in pedestration violations of traffic signs', *Journal of Abnormal and Social Psychology*, **51**, 704–10.

Leibbrand, K. (1976) 'Recent changes in transportation and urban planning', in *Transportation Planning for a Better Environment* (Eds. P. Stringer and H. Wenzel), Plenum, New York, 13–22.

Linares-Maza, A. (1971) 'Psicologia clinica, psiquiatria y conduccion de automoviles', *Revista de Psicologia General y Aplicada*, **26**, 30–55.

Lofland, L. H. (1973) *A World of Strangers: Order and Action in Urban Public Space*, Basic Books, New York.

Lurie, L. H. (1968) 'Sociology and road safety: A review and discussion of available literature', paper presented at a seminar of the Engineering Institute of Canada Committee on Road Safety Research, Kingston, Canada.

McClintock, C. G. (1972) 'Social motivation: A set of propositions', *Behavioral Science*, **17**, 438–54.

McFarland, R. A. (1957) 'Psychological and psychiatric aspects of highway safety', *Journal of the American Medical Association*, **163**, 233–37.

McFarland, R. A., Tune, G. S., and Welford, A. T. (1964) 'On the driving of automobiles by older people', *Journal of Gerontology*, **19**, 30–55.

McGuire, F. L. (1969) *The Understanding and Prediction of Accident-Producing Behavior*, University of North Carolina Highway Research Center, Chapel Hill, North Carolina.

Malik, L. (1968) 'Social factors in accidents', unpublished doctoral dissertation, American University, Washington, D.C.

Mayer, R. E. and Treat, J. R. (1977) 'Psychological, social and cognitive characteristics of high-risk drivers: A pilot study', *Accident Analysis and Prevention*, **9**, 1–8.

Mehrabian, A. (1975) *Public Places and Private Spaces*, Basic Books, New York.

Michon, J. A. (1976) 'The mutual impacts of transportation and human behaviour', in *Transportation Planning for a Better Environment* (Eds. P. Stringer and H. Wenzel), Plenum, New York, 221–36.

Michon, J. A. (1978) 'Searching for stable parameters for the control of human mobility', paper presented at the Symposium of the International Association of Traffic Safety Sciences, Tokyo.

Mumford, L. (1958) *The Highway and the City*, Harcourt, Brace & World, New York.

Oeser, O. A. (1978) 'The ecology of driving behaviour and its implications for accident prevention', paper presented at the International Congress of Applied Psychology, Munich.

Packard, V. (1957) *The Hidden Persuaders*, David McKay, New York.

Parry, M. H. (1968) *Aggression on the Road*, Tavistock, London.

Penner, L. A., Dertke, M. C., and Achenbach, C. J. (1973) 'The "flash" system: A field study of altruism', *Journal of Applied Psychology*, **3**, 362–370.

Perchonok, K. (1973) *Accident Cause Analysis*, Cornell Aeronautical Laboratory, Ithaca, New York.

Planck, T. W. (1972) *The Ageing Driver in Today's Traffic: A Critical Review*, University of North Carolina Highway Research Center, Chapel Hill, North Carolina.

Pomazal, R. J. and Clore, G. L. (1973) 'Helping on the highway: The effects of dependency and sex', *Journal of Applied Social Psychology*, **3**, 150-64.

Quenault, S. W. and Parker, P. M. (1973) *Driver Behaviour: Newly Qualified Drivers*, Ministry of Transport Road Research Laboratory, Crowthorne, England.

Ratilainen, L. (1968) *Traffic Accidents Involving Children in Helsinki in 1965 and the Social Background of the Children Included*, TALJA, Helsinki.

Read, J. H., Bradley, E. J., Morison, J. D., Lewall, D., and Clarke, D. A. (1963) 'The epidemiology and prevention of traffic accidents involving child pedestrians', *Canadian Medical Association Journal*, **89**, 687-701.

Richman, J. (1972) 'The motor car and the territorial aggression thesis: Some aspects of the sociology of the street', *Sociology Review*, **20**, 5-27.

Robertson, L. S. and Williams, A. F. (1978) 'Some international comparisons of the effects of motor vehicle seat belt use and child restraint laws', paper presented at the Child Passenger Safety Conference, Nashville, Tennessee.

Ross, H. L. (1940) 'Traffic accidents: A product of social-psychological conditions', *Social Forces*, **18**, 569-76.

Ross, H. L. (1960-61). 'Traffic law violation: A folk crime', *Social Problems*, **8**, 231-41.

Sainchez-Jimeinez, J. (1967) 'Personality of the driver and accident causality', *Revista de Psicologia General y Aplicada*, **22**, 143-59.

Schrank, J. (1976) *Snap, Crackle, and Popular Taste: The Illusion of Free Choice in America*, Delta, New York.

Selzer, M. L. (1969) 'Alcoholism, mental illness and stress in drivers causing fatal accidents', *Behavioral Science*, **14**, 157-63.

Selzer, M. L. and Vinokur, A. (1975) 'Role of life events in accident causation', *Mental Health and Society*, **2**, 36-54.

Selzer, M. L., Rogers, J. E., and Kern, S. (1968) 'Fatal accidents: The role of psychopathology, social stress, and acute disturbance', *American Journal of Psychiatry*, **124**, 1028-36.

Selzer, M. L., Vinokur, A., and Wilson, T. D. (1977) 'A psychosocial comparison of drunken drivers and alcoholics', *Journal of Studies on Alcohol*, **38**, 1294-1312.

Shaffer, J. W., Schmidt, C. W., Zlotowitz, H. I., and Fisher, R. S (1977) 'Social adjustment profiles of female drivers involved in fatal and nonfatal accidents', *American Journal of Psychiatry*, **134**, 801-4.

Shaw, J. I. and McMartin, J. A. (1975) 'Perpetrator or victim? Effects of who suffers in an automobile accident on judgmental strictness', *Social Behavior and Personality*, **3**, 5-12.

Shor, R. E. (1964) 'Shared patterns of nonverbal normative expectations in automobile driving', *Journal of Social Psychology*, **62**, 155-63.

Simon, A. (1976) 'Chivalry on the road: Helping stalled drivers', *Psychological Reports*, **39**, 883-86.

Sobel, R. and Underhill, R. (1976) 'Family disorganization and teenage auto accidents', *Journal of Safety Research*, **8**, 8-18.

Solomon, H. and Herman, L. (1977) 'Status symbols and prosocial behavior: The effect of the victim's car on helping', *Journal of Psychology*, **97**, 271-73.

Sommer, R. (1969) *Personal Space*, Prentice-Hall, Englewood Cliffs, New Jersey.

Spörli, S. (1974) 'Entdifferenzierung als Feldeffekt des Systems Strassenverkehr: Gedanken zu einer pesonalen Systemtheorie', *Schweizerische Zeitschrift für Psychologie und Ihre Anwendungen*, **33**, 384-406.

Sterling-Smith, R. S. (1975) 'Alcohol, marijuana and other drug patterns among operators involved in fatal motor vehicle accidents', in *Alcohol, Drugs, and Traffic*

Safety (Eds. S. Israelstam and S. Lambert), Addiction Research Foundation of Ontario, Toronto, 93–105.

Stewart, R. G. (1958) 'Can psychologists measure driving attitudes?' *Educational and Psychological Measurement*, **18**, 63–73.

Suchman, E. A. (1960–61) 'A conceptual analysis of the accident phenomenon', *Social Problems*, **8**, 241–53.

Suchman, E. A. (1970) 'Accidents and social deviance', *Journal of Health and Social Behavior*, **11**, 241–243.

SWOV, Netherlands, Institute for Road Safety Research (1971) *Psychological Aspects of Driver Behaviour*, vols. I and II, Netherlands Institute for Road Safety Research, SWOV, Voorburg, Netherlands.

Toffler, A. (1971) *Future Shock*, Bantam, New York.

Treat, J. R. and Joscelyn, K. B. (1974) 'An investigation of the causes of accidents', paper presented at the meeting of the American Psychological Association, New Orleans.

Turner, C. W., Layton, J. F., and Simons, L. S. (1975) 'Naturalistic studies of aggressive behavior: Aggressive stimuli, victim visibility, and horn honking', *Journal of Personality and Social Psychology*, **31**, 1098–1107.

Turrell, E. S. (1957) 'Emotions: Personality's multiple facets', *Traffic Safety*, **51**, 6, 22–23, 53, 54.

Wagner, K. and Wagner, H. J. (Eds.) (1968) *Handbuch der Verkehrsmedizin*, Springer, Berlin.

Waller, P. F. (1970) *The Youthful Driver: Some Characteristics and Comparisons*, University of North Carolina Highway Safety Research Center, Chapel Hill, North Carolina.

Waller, P. F., Foley, J. P., and Jeffrey, D. W. (1972) *Stress and Driving: The Relationship between Life Crisis Experiences and a Sudden Deterioration in Driving Record*, University of North Carolina Highway Research Center, Chapel Hill, North Carolina.

Whitlock, F. A. (1971) *Death on the Roads: A Study in Social Violence*, Tavistock, London.

Wilde, G. J. S. (1973) 'Social psychological factors and use of mass publicity', *Canadian Psychologist*, **14**, 1–7.

Wilde, G. J. S. (1975) 'Evaluation of effectiveness of public education and information programmes related to alcohol, drugs and traffic safety', in *Alcohol, Drugs and Traffic Safety* (Eds. S. Israelstam and S. Lambert), Addiction Research Foundation of Ontario, Toronto, 813–24.

Wilde, G. J. S. (1976) 'Social interaction patterns in driver behaviour: An introductory review', *Human Factors*, **18**, 477–92.

Wilde, G. J. S. (1978a) 'Immediate and delayed social interaction in road user behaviour', paper presented at the International Congress of Applied Psychology, Munich.

Wilde, G. J. S. (1978b) 'Sozialverhalten von Verkehrsteilnehmern und Theorien der Unfallverursachung', *Gruppendynamik*, **4**, 263–82.

Williams, E. B. and Malfetti, J. L. (1970) *Driving and Connotative Meanings*, Teachers College Press, New York.

Wilson, W. T., Lonero, L., and Ish, D. M. (1972) 'Seat belt use and efforts to increase it', paper presented at the meeting of the American Association for Automotive Medicine, Chapel Hill, North Carolina.

Zajonc, R. B. (1966) *Social Psychology: An Experimental Approach*, Wadsworth, Belmont, California.

Zelhart, P. F. (1972) 'Types of alcoholics and their relationship to traffic violations', *Quarterly Journal of Studies in Alcohol*, **33**, 811–13.

Zuercher, J. D., Sass, E. J., and Weiss, J. M. (1971) 'Analysis of near accidents and accidents on the highway', *Behavioural Research in Highway Safety*, **2**, 98–106.

SECTION C

Research Reports

Progress in Applied Social Psychology, Volume 1
Edited by G. M. Stephenson and J. M. Davis
© 1981 John Wiley & Sons, Ltd.

7

Criminal Victimization of the Elderly: Validating the Policy Assumptions[1]

THOMAS D. COOK, JAMES FREMMING, and TOM R. TYLER
Northwestern University

INTRODUCTION

The claim is often made that crimes against the elderly are so 'special' that they deserve public attention and the heightened concern of public policy makers. This claim is usually based upon four premises: that the elderly are victimized more often than others by crime, that they suffer more serious consequences than others when they are victimized, that they live in greater fear of crime, and that this fear significantly restricts their daily mobility. This chapter considers the evidence relevant to these premises, and discusses the theoretical and policy implications of the research findings about crime and the elderly.

Many assertions have been made that the elderly are victimized more often than younger persons. Often, these assertions are global, specifying no particular type of crime or type of elderly victim. For instance, at a 1972 meeting of the Senate Subcommittee on Housing for the Elderly, Senator Harrison Williams said:

> Elderly tenants in private and public housing in many of our big cities are the most vulnerable victims of theft, violence, rowdyism, and outright terrorism . . . . Many older persons lock themselves within their apartments day and night and dread every knock on the door. Do we need any more proof that a crisis in crime exists? Do we need any more reason to act on an emergency basis?

In a widely reported 1975 message to Congress when he was still President, Gerald Ford said: 'Most of the victims of violent crimes are the poor, the old, the young, the disadvantaged minorities' (Ford, 1975). Social scientists have made the same general point about the high rate of crimes against older Americans with Carl Cunningham (1974) concluding that 'the elderly living in or near certain neighborhoods of Kansas City, Missouri, can be as much as eight times more vulnerable to serious crimes . . . than a young resident of a relatively safe suburb'. In a widely cited book which was awarded the Pulitzer Prize, Robert Butler, head of the National Institute on Aging, has claimed, 'Old people are victims of violent crime more than any other age group' (Butler, 1975). Finally, Goldsmith and Goldsmith (1976) have claimed that the elderly are more susceptible than others to being multiply victimized.

The claims in Goldsmith and Goldsmith are particularly interesting since they are not restricted to global issues of crime rate. Instead, some of the claims refer to specific kinds of crime from which the elderly are thought to suffer or to specific types of older Americans who are believed to be most vulnerable to crime. The differentiated claims most frequently made are that the elderly suffer more than others from purse snatching, confidence games, or the theft of checks from mailboxes and that the elderly persons most affected by such crimes are the poor, especially those living in public housing or in neighbourhoods that were once respectable but are now decaying.

Claims have also been made that, once victimized, the elderly suffer more serious financial, physical, and psychological consequences. A set of such claims were made in Congressional hearings in 1977 (U.S. Congress, 1977). There Clarence Kelly, the director of the Federal Bureau of Investigation, told the U.S. Subcommittee on Housing and Consumer Interests of the Select Committee on Aging that: 'Psychologically, financially, and physically, no group of citizens suffer more painful losses than our nation's elderly do at the hands of America's criminal predators.' Henry F. McQuade, Deputy Administrator for Policy Development at Law Enforcement Assistance Administration (LEAA) claimed at the same hearings: 'While there may be some uncertainty about criminal victimization among senior citizens, there is, I believe, little question about their vulnerability—physical, psychological, and financial.' An official of the National Retired Teachers Association/ American Association of Retired Persons stated:

Although the incidence of crime has risen throughout society in general, we are finding that crimes against older persons are becoming more prevalent and more frequent. This is particularly important to note because crime impacts most heavily on older persons, financially and physically; they are less able to cope with the loss or injury resulting from a criminal act.

Similarly, broad pictures of elderly victims of particular violent crimes are painted with great frequency in the media; and among social scientists Goldsmith and Goldsmith (1976) have made the point:

One major reason for focusing special attention on crime against the elderly is the differential impact of crime and increased vulnerability of the elderly. There are physical, economic, and environmental factors associated with aging that increase vulnerability to criminal attack and that magnify the impact of victimization.

The same point about the elderly suffering more from crime because they are on average poorer and frailer than younger persons can be found in two special issues devoted to crime and the elderly that appeared in *Police Chief*, a periodical aimed at senior law enforcement officials (*Police Chief*, **43**, 1976). Finally, there are the many heart-breaking newspaper, radio, and television stories about individual elderly persons who were beaten and robbed or murdered.

In addition to greater victimization, it is often asserted that the elderly live in greater fear of crime than younger persons. Such fear, it is believed, leads the elderly to stay in their homes, hence cutting them off from many community activities and increasing their sense of isolation.

Claims about the frequency and consequences of crimes against the elderly have been used to justify a high profile for the issue and to press for specific remedial actions. Indeed, the label 'crisis' is often used to refer to the current problem of crimes against older Americans, and we suspect that this label reflects a desire to see the problem attain and maintain a high level of public and political visibility. The previous quotations give some flavour of the claims for special status. In this respect one should also note the conclusion of Goldsmith and Tomas (1974) in the journal, *Aging*, a publication of the Administration of Aging of the Department of Health, Education, and Welfare: 'The elderly constitute a unique class of crime victim and . . . crimes against the elderly can be considered a distinct category of criminal activity.' Moreover, the National Council of Senior Citizens has a programme on Criminal Justice and the Elderly, and they are using information about the special consequences of crimes against the elderly to support a Federal law which would recompense all victims of violent crime and, for the elderly only, would waive the requirement that compensation should only be paid for losses above a predetermined level. The bill proposing such a law was narrowly defeated in the 95th Congress, but may fare better in the 96th. Victim recompense programmes with no requirements about a minimum loss may prove extremely expensive and in opposing them Congressman Wiggins asserted they might become 'the food stamp program of the Department of Justice', and he predicted that such programs would become 'the Snail Darters that bring the Department of Justice to a standstill'. The political implications are not trivial; the claims about the rates and consequences of crimes against the elderly therefore need careful examination.

As social scientists, we feel that it is important to examine public claims like those made about crimes against the elderly in order to test in which ways the best available evidence does and does not support the claims being made. If the evidence is largely supportive, then the policy positions being implicitly or explicitly advocated by the claimants deserve close consideration. But if the evidence is not supportive, then a case can be made that the social 'problem' in question deserves less emphasis than is being claimed and that other problems deserve closer scrutiny and perhaps action. We should not forget that action resources are limited and that devoting resources to elderly crime victims or to preventing crimes against the elderly can detract from helping those who might suffer more from crime. We are proposing, therefore, that the social scientist cast himself as the editor of claims which imply that a particular social problem deserves a high priority on the agenda of public attention. A high priority can lead to significant psychic and financial investments that are inevitably made at the expense of some other social issue.

Social scientists have rarely played such an editing role in the past since the data required were usually not available before the political agenda was set. Indeed, we suspect that the relevant evidence was often generated only because a particular issue was already on the political agenda and enjoyed a high priority rating. The opportunity for a more timely editing of public claims has increased considerably in the past decade as archives of economic, demographic, social, and subjective social indicators have been laid down, the data from which are often available to social science analysts (see Cook, Dintzer, and Mark, 1979, for a list of such archives).

In the case of criminal victimization of the elderly the relevant archive is provided by the Law Enforcement Assistance Administration (LEAA) of the U.S. Department of Justice. Because of technical problems with police reports of crimes, LEAA decided to ask the Census Bureau to conduct large-scale surveys of the nation that would have a sample size sufficient to investigate most, but not all, of the claims made. As a result, since 1973 data has been available each year concerning the rate, context, and consequences of crimes, including crimes against the elderly.

An understanding of how crime affects the elderly has theoretical implications as well as implications concerning policy options and a new role that social scientists might play. The principal theoretical implication relates to the origins and consequences of fear of crime. Many social-psychological theories deal with how individuals perceive the world and how their beliefs about the world are shaped by their experiences. It has generally been recognized that such beliefs can develop through personal experiences and through the experiences of others communicated via social networks (Skogan, 1977; Tyler, in press). Fear of crime among the elderly is one context within which we can explore the importance of these two sources of experience with the world. Such fear has generally been presented as the result of higher rates of personal experience with crime among the elderly. It may be, however, that the elderly do not differ from others in their first-hand contact with crime, but have higher levels of indirect experience with crime. This paper will examine the relative importance of direct and indirect experiences with crime upon fears among the elderly. In addition, it will test the conventional wisdom that there is something 'special' about the rate, context, and consequences of crimes against the elderly.

THE DATA SOURCES

The data to be reported come from two survey research programmes conducted by the Census Bureau with support from LEAA. One programme is oriented towards representative national samples of respondents, while the other is oriented towards representative samples in five major cities.

The National Data

Each month all persons 12 years of age or older in a national panel of 10,000 households are asked about their experiences with crime during the past six months, making for an annual total of about 375,000 interviews. The data we shall present are based on four years of such interviewing, and so a total sample of about 1,500,000 persons is involved. Though crime is a relatively rare event which necessitates large samples, 1,500,000 is larger than is needed for purposes of reliable estimation. Consequently, we drew a 10 percent subsample from the LEAA data set, leaving us with about 150,000 cases interviewed between 1973 and 1976.

During the interview respondents who have been victimized are asked about their experiences, and detailed information is collected about each incident of victimization. Although the survey collects data on household crimes (e.g. burglary) as well as personal crimes, we limit our attention in this study to personal crimes and their effects. These crime reports form the basis of this chapter, and they are very useful because they escape the limitations inevitably associated with using police records of reported crimes. However, the victimization surveys are not beyond methodological criticism (National Academy of Sciences, 1976), and they merely represent the best data currently available. A detailed description of the LEAA surveys is in Skogan (1976).

In the analysis to be presented we will collapse the data across the years in which the survey was conducted. Such presentation runs the risk of obscuring year-by-year differences in how crime affects the elderly. To avoid this problem, we first computed the analyses on a yearly basis and only summed across years once it was established that the relationship of crime to age was approximately equal across the years. Where possible, we shall also present the data broken down in such a way that we can examine age trends among the elderly. Consequently, we shall make distinctions among the following age groups: 60–64, 65–69, 70–74, and 75 + . In some cases the low sample size of victims of a particular crime does not permit such a fine differentiation and we are forced to resort to a single category of the elderly—persons 60 years of age and older.

The City Samples

The national data concentrate on reported crimes, the contexts in which such crimes occur, and the physical and financial consequences that are thought to have resulted from the victimization experiences. There is no stress on fear of crime. Fortunately, LEAA has funded large-scale surveys in five major U.S. cities that use the same basic methodology as the national survey but also include questions about fear of leaving the house by day and by night, and the reasons for such fear. Such surveys have the obvious disadvantage that they are not representative of the nation at large in that they do not include suburban and rural samples. Nonetheless, the most crucial issue is whether the relationship of victimization experiences to age is the same in the national and city samples. To judge by reports of the data published by LEAA this is indeed the case for those questions asked of both the city and national respondents. In the analyses of city data that follow we shall restrict ourselves to a 25 percent sample of the 1973 data obtained from 9,500 respondents in each of the five cities. Thus, the total number of cases analysed for our purposes was 11,752, with the cases weighted to produce a representative sample of the cities in question.

Rate of Victimization

The first question to be addressed is how the frequency of personal crimes against the elderly compares to the rate of crimes against members of other age groups. Table 1 gives the appropriate data for 1974, 1975, and 1976, as published by the Department of Justice (data for 1973 are not publicly available).[2] *Assault* (in which the object is to inflict physical harm upon the victim) was the most frequent personal crime reported. However, assault was most concentrated among younger persons, and elderly persons were the least frequent victims of such crimes. In 1976, for example, the victimization rate for the elderly was less than one-sixth that of the total sample and about one-third that of persons aged 16–19. *Robbery* (theft with the threat or use of force) was also concentrated among younger persons and was least likely to have an elderly person as its victim. By contrast, *personal larceny* (purse snatchings and picked pockets—simple theft involving personal contact), was not heavily concentrated in any particular age group. Finally, *rape* (carnal knowledge through the use of threat or force) was the least frequent personal crime to be reported, with an overall victimization rate of less than two victims per

Table 1a Victimization rates by type of personal crime and sex and age of victim, 1974–76

Age of victim:	(Rate per 1,000 persons in each age group)[a]							
	12–15	16–19	20–24	25–34	35–49	50–64	65 and older	All ages
Type of crime and sex of victim								
(1) Assault:								
Male	49.9	73.0	64.0	42.9	19.1	10.5	5.7	34.0
Female	31.0	34.4	30.3	21.0	11.6	5.6	3.1	16.8
(2) Robbery:								
Male	17.9	15.8	14.2	8.8	6.7	5.9	5.6	9.7
Female	4.6	5.2	7.2	4.5	3.5	2.9	1.3	4.1
(3) Personal larceny:								
Male	3.9	4.5	3.6	2.5	2.2	2.0	2.3	2.8
Female	1.6[b]	2.9	4.1	3.1	2.7	3.8	4.0	3.2
(4) Rape:								
Male	0.1[b]	0.1	0.4[b]	0.1[b]	0.0[b]	0.0[b]	0.0[b]	0.1[b]
Female	2.1	4.5	4.3	2.3	0.3[b]	0.4[b]	0.1[b]	1.6

[a]Rates shown are means of the annual rates for 1974, 1975, and 1976.
[b]Estimate, based on ten or fewer cases, is statistically unreliable.

Sources: U.S. Dept. of Justice (1975), (1977a), and (1977b).

Table 1b   Victimization rates by type of personal crime and age of victim, 1975 and 1976

(Rate per 1,000 persons in each age group)

Age of victim:	12–15	16–19	20–24	25–34	35–49	50–64	65 and older	All ages
Type of crime								
Assault:								
1975	42.5	51.2	45.9	31.8	15.7	9.0	3.4	25.2
1976	40.9	55.3	45.6	33.0	14.8	7.6	4.1	25.3
Robbery:								
1975	11.4	10.7	10.9	6.3	4.6	4.4	4.3	6.8
1976	10.0	9.4	10.3	6.4	5.1	4.5	3.4	6.5
Personal larceny:								
1975	3.0	3.3	4.4	2.9	2.8	2.7	3.3	3.1
1976	2.2	4.1	3.8	2.8	2.1	2.7	3.3	.9
Rape:								
1975	0.8	2.4	.26	1.2	0.3[a]	0.2[a]	0.1[a]	0.9
1976	1.1	2.1	2.6	1.2	(b)[a]	0.1[a]	0.1[a]	0.8

[a]Rate, based on ten or fewer cases, is statistically unreliable.

Source: U.S. Dept. of Justice (1977).

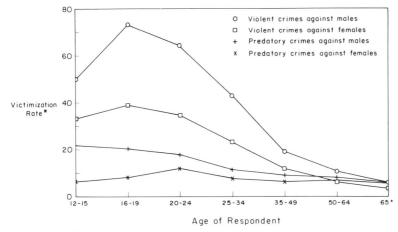

*Rate per 1,000 persons in each age group population. Rates shown are means of the annual rates of 1974, 75 and 76. Source: U.S. Dept. of Justice, 1977a and 1977b

Figure 1. Victimization rates: type of crime by sex and age of respondent

thousand females. Rape, like robbery and assault, is a crime suffered primarily by the young; almost none were reported by elderly respondents.

Figure 1 presents the same data grouped to represent crimes as 'violent' (rape and assault) or 'predatory' (robbery and personal larceny). The figure clearly shows lower victimization rates among the elderly, as compared to other age groups; and among females as compared to males. We may conclude from these data that the elderly are victimized less often than younger persons in all the categories that have been examined except perhaps for larceny–purse snatchings, where the rate is similar to that of other age groups.

Might there be something special about the types of crimes most prevalent *among elderly victims*? The data in Figure 2 (computed from the 1973–1976 survey results) show that, *when we focus on victims only*, victimization experiences of the aged are clearly different from those of adolescents and younger adults. When crimes are classified as 'violent' or 'predatory', the contrast is vivid. Elderly victims are more likely to be preyed upon than to be victimized with intent to do personal injury; younger victims are more likely to be treated violently than to be preyed upon. This contrast continues even *within* the elderly age group, with victimization among persons aged 75 or older proportionately more 'predatory' than among the relatively younger age categories.

Location and Time of Victimization

One hypothesis concerning the fear of crime is that different locations and times of day have considerable impact upon perceived vulnerability to crime.

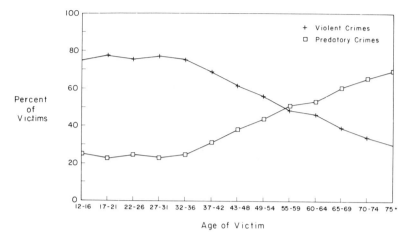

Figure 2. Type of crime committed against victims of different ages. *Source:* Computed by the authors from all regular and series incidents in National Crime Survey Data for 1973–76 (total *n* = 18,716)

For example, crimes committed in the home or near it (in doorways or elevators that are functionally part of the building in which the home is located) may be particularly distressing, for they represent threats to one's personal life space. Crimes committed during daylight hours may also be especially upsetting since they occur when many persons least expect to be victimized, and they disrupt one's daily routine.

Figure 3 shows the trends across age categories for violent and predatory crimes in various locations. The differences between the elderly and other adults in terms of the locations of violent crimes are noteworthy. While younger adults tend to suffer from violent crimes on the street or in other places (such as in stores, offices, or schools), older persons tend to suffer violent crimes in or near their homes. The location of predatory crimes shows less dramatic differences among age categories. Roughly half of all such offences occur in the street, regardless of the age of the victim.

We have found that the elderly appear to be less safe from crime during the daylight hours than are other persons. The relative proportion of both predatory and violent crimes committed during the daylight hours (6 a.m. to 6 p.m.) tends to increase with age for persons over 16. The proportions of crimes which occur during the daytime for adults under age 60 ranges from 33 to 55 percent; the range for persons over 60 is 61 to 79 percent.

Offender Characteristics

Certain offender variables may contribute to a fear-eliciting quality of the victimization experience for the elderly. Here we consider the extent to which

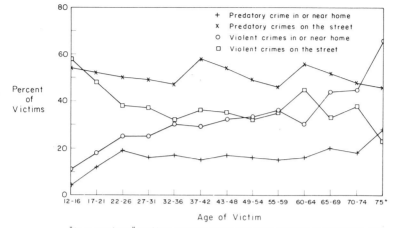

"In or near home" combines incidents which took place in houses or apartments, vacation homes, or residential rooms in hotels, and adjacent to the home in the yard, driveway, or hallway (in apartment buildings). "On the street" includes crimes which took place in parks, fields, or playgrounds, or on school grounds. Percentages of each crime type do not total to 100 percent, due to the occurrence of crimes in other places. Figures were computed from National Crime Survey incident data for 1973-76.

Figure 3. Location and type of crime by age of victim

Table 2   Percentage of crimes by age of victim and various offender variables

Age of victim	(1)	(2)	(3) % of	(4)	(5)	(6)
	% by youths[a]	% by strangers	whites by non-whites[c]	% by gangs[b]	% unarmed	% with gun
12–16	88	48	30	26	74	4
17–21	49	60	27	17	63	13
22–26	28	62	29	14	64	17
27–31	26	58	28	13	67	15
32–36	29	55	27	14	68	16
37–42	31	63	31	16	66	15
43–48	33	65	35	16	65	16
49–54	37	70	40	19	68	17
55–59	42	77	44	17	70	18
60–64	45	81	51	20	73	13
65–69	45	78	42	14	73	15
70–74	56	84	56	17	75	18
75 +	48	81	57	15	80	12
All age groups	47	60	31	18	68	17

[a]Under age 21.
[b]Groups of three or more offenders.
[c]Includes white victims of crimes committed by: (1) lone non-white offenders, or (2) groups of offenders, at least one of whom was reported to have been non-white.

Source: Computed by the authors from all regular and series incidents in the National Crime Survey data for 1972–76.

Table 3 Financial loss by age of victim

Age of victim	Median financial loss (dollars)	Median net loss as % of monthly family income[b]	% of victims who suffered catastrophic loss[c]	(N)[a]
		A. Robbery		
12–16	6.38	0.5	0	(301)
17–21	29.88	5.5	4.0	(305)
22–26	54.55	8.5	8.2	(257)
27–31	60.41	8.1	6.0	(140)
32–36	99.74	8.9	7.0	(74)
37–42	46.48	7.2	7.5	(93)
43–48	57.45	9.3	5.3	(131)
49–54	49.34	8.2	7.3	(96)
55–59	50.41	8.0	5.1	(99)
60–64	40.17	14.4	7.6	(66)
65–69	60.20	20.0	5.7	(53)
70–74	59.95	19.5	4.8	(42)
75 +	59.62	17.3	8.6	(58)
		B. Personal larceny		
12–16	6.03	0.5	0	(155)
17–21	24.95	4.2	1.0	(187)
22–26	29.65	4.7	2.0	(151)
27–31	37.96	6.7	1.1	(88)
32–36	61.26	7.1	4.8	(63)
37–42	55.35	9.2	6.0	(85)
43–48	39.88	4.5	0	(77)
49–54	49.27	8.0	0	(94)
55–59	38.32	6.5	4.1	(74)
60–64	30.54	4.8	3.3	(61)
65–69	30.52	7.6	7.4	(54)
70–74	36.67	11.5	7.0	(43)
75 +	24.85	7.2	0	(56)
		C. All personal crimes		
12–16	7.63	0.7	0.0	(2973)
17–21	24.64	4.0	3.0	(1020)
22–26	32.86	5.3	4.5	(776)
27–31	35.43	4.8	2.8	(497)
32–36	59.85	6.9	7.7	(260)
37–42	49.71	7.0	5.2	(290)
43–48	41.92	5.3	4.2	(333)
49–54	45.30	6.9	3.5	(289)
55–59	40.26	6.9	4.9	(247)
60–64	40.39	6.4	4.6	(196)
65–69	43.78	8.9	4.6	(153)
70–74	40.09	10.3	4.5	(112)
75 +	38.79	9.6	5.8	(154)

crimes against persons of different age groups are committed by young persons, by gangs, by offenders using weapons, by strangers, and by offenders who are non-whites (since non-whites seldom report being victimized by whites, this phenomenon is not considered).

The data for 1973–76 are presented in Table 2. Figure are for predatory and violent crimes combined since visual inspection showed no important differences in age trends according to the type of crime. The relationship of age to the probability of being victimized by youths is curvilinear. This is because the elderly are somewhat more likely than other adults to be victimized by youths, although the level of such crimes is less than for crimes by youths upon other youths. The table further suggests that the elderly are more likely to be victimized by strangers. Indeed, more than three-quarters of the crimes against the elderly were committed 'by persons the victim did not know'. The white elderly also tend to be attacked by non-whites relatively more frequently than their younger counterparts. The proportion of white persons aged 60 or older who are attacked by non-whites (51.5 percent) is considerably greater than for the sample as a whole (31 percent).

There are some respects in which crimes against the elderly might be less stressful than for younger victims. As the last three columns show, the elderly are among the least likely to be victimized by gangs, by persons with guns, or by persons with arms of any kinds. The perpertrators of crimes against them tend to be young strangers who act alone and without weapons and who typically steal women's purses in or near the victims' homes.

The Economic Consequences of Crimes Against the Elderly

Table 3 presents data on reported financial losses from personal crimes: robbery, personal larceny, and all personal crimes combined (predominantly assault). The first column gives measures of 'absolute' loss—the median amount lost in each age category. In all types of personal crime, teenagers and young adults tend to lose the least. The elderly lost less than most other adult age categories.

A more sensitive measure of financial loss involves net rather than total loss. Net loss is the amount lost minus the value of property or cash recovered or

---

Footnote to Table 3:
aIncludes only those respondents who reported some financial loss from a criminal incident.
bIn the National Crime Survey, income is categorized. We employ here the mid-point of each yearly family income category, divided by 12, as an estimate of monthly income. Net loss is the value of goods and money stolen plus the cost of any damages incurred, less the amount actually recovered by the police or on the basis of insurance claims.
cThese are losses totalling more than one month's family income.

Source: Computed by the authors from all regular and serious incidents in the National Crime Survey data for 1973–1976.

indemnified by insurance. An even more sensitive measure takes net loss as a percent of monthly income, the values for which are given in the second column of Table 3. Here we begin to see a trend of increasing economic impact with age.

The third column reports data on 'catastrophic' loss, operationally defined here as the net loss of more than a family's total monthly income. In this instance, teenagers (and their families) suffered the least severe impact. Among persons over 21, no marked relationship between age and catastrophic hardship appears.

In summary, the findings show that the elderly (1) lose the same or less than other adults when absolute loss measures are employed; (2) tend to lose more than other adults, when the net dollar loss is adjusted for monthly income; and (3) that the elderly are no more likely than others to suffer catastrophic financial losses.

Physical Consequences of Crimes Against the Elderly

The consequences of personal harm from victimization can be described in terms of a sequence of contingencies. The first is whether a victim is or is not attacked; the second is whether the attack does or does not lead to injury; the third is whether the injury is of a more or less serious type; the fourth is whether or not the injury warrants medical attention; and the fifth is whether that medical attention is or is not costly. We shall deal with all of these stages in the following analysis of victims of all ages.

Table 4 reports the relevant data. The first column of data shows that among adults the elderly are least likely to be attacked, are slightly more likely to be injured if attacked, and these injuries are even more likely than with other age groups to be bruises and cuts as opposed to broken bones, internal injuries, or a loss of consciousness. Moreover, the elderly are somewhat less likely to have had their wounds inflicted by a knife or a gun. Table 5 gives the medical consequences of these events. Among those injured, the elderly are slightly less likely than others to need medical care, and if they do need care it is equally likely to involve financial costs. However, when costs are involved, they are not likely to be higher for the elderly as an absolute sum though the net loss is probably a higher percentage of the elderly's monthly income than it is for other groups. (The difficulty with this last statement is that the survey measure of reimbursement refers to reimbursement by 'insurance or a health benefits programme'. It is therefore not clear that respondents recall Medicare or Medicaid benefits in response to this item.)

The preceding analysis of the physical consequences of personal crimes suggest that the elderly (1) tend to be attacked less often than others, (2) are among the more likely to be injured in the event they are attacked, (3) are relatively less likely than other groups to suffer knife or gun wounds but more

Table 4 Patterns of personal attack and injury

Age of victim	Base (N)	(1) % attacked	(2) % injured of those attacked	Type of injury: % who had			
				(3) Knife or gun wounds	(4) Internal injuries, unconscious	(5) Broken bones or teeth	(6) Bruises, cuts, black eyes, scratches
12–16	(3,701)	56.7	56.0	3.2	3.0	3.7	82.3
17–21	(4,205)	48.2	63.6	6.9	5.7	7.2	82.0
22–26	(3,053)	43.6	63.4	7.9	6.2	6.4	81.6
27–31	(2,027)	40.4	65.2	6.9	5.8	8.2	81.6
32–36	(1,101)	36.6	66.0	6.8	10.1	8.6	81.2
37–42	(1,060)	37.8	67.6	5.2	13.3	11.1	81.5
43–48	(963)	36.8	74.9	7.5	14.0	9.8	83.8
49–54	(773)	35.4	70.7	6.7	11.9	11.9	81.3
55–59	(560)	34.0	69.6	9.0	9.0	9.8	77.4
60–64	(444)	29.3	66.2	7.0	9.3	15.1	80.1
65–69	(347)	29.4	69.6	2.8	11.3	9.9	56.9
70–74	(209)	33.4	56.7	2.2	10.0	0.0	91.3
75 +	(274)	38.0	66.3	0.0	10.1	8.7	91.3
All victims	(18,716)	44.4	63.1	6.0	6.8	7.2	82.2

[a]Does not sum to 100 percent since victims could receive multiple injuries.

Source: Computed by the authors from all regular and series incidents in the National Crime Survey data for 1973–76.

Table 5   Medical consequences of injury

Age of victim	Base (N)	(1) % injured who needed medical care	(2) % of those who needed care who received same at some expense	(3) Median medical expense (dollars)	(4) Median medical expense as % of monthly income	(5) Median net medical expense as % of monthly income[a]	(N)
12–16	(1,174)	23.9	59.0	40.20	4.4	4.1	(165)
17–21	(1,289)	32.0	53.6	84.88	10.9	9.1	(221)
22–26	(844)	39.1	57.8	65.77	9.8	8.2	(190)
27–31	(534)	37.5	54.8	75.28	8.9	8.2	(110)
32–36	(266)	48.1	45.9	100.33	13.3	13.3	(59)
31–42	(271)	48.3	53.4	149.17	13.6	7.5	(70)
43–48	(265)	44.2	52.8	64.88	12.0	10.7	(62)
49–54	(193)	47.2	55.8	79.60	8.6	7.5	(51)
55–59	(133)	47.4	47.9	100.87	10.3	9.6	(30)
60–64	(86)	47.7	49.9	89.97	12.0	11.9	(20)
65–69	(71)	42.3	62.2	118.51	18.4	8.2	(19)
70–74	(46)	30.4	65.5	148.02	71.2	71.2	(9)
75 +	(69)	43.5	49.5	79.83	21.3	21.3	(15)

[a]Net medical expense, i.e. the total cost of medical care less any amount recovered by means of all types of medical insurance and benefit programmes.

Source: Computed by the authors from all regular and series incidents in the National Crime Survey data for 1973–76.

likely to suffer other, less serious kinds of injuries, (4) are no more likely than others to need medical care as a result of injuries, (5) may tend not to have outstandingly high medical bills from injuries, but (6) may have high medical costs relative to income.

Fear of Crime Among the Elderly

The first question of concern is whether the elderly are more fearful of victimization than younger individuals. The relevant data are in Figure 4.

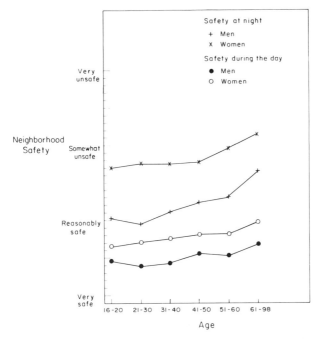

Figure 4. Perceptions of safety in own neighbourhood:
day and night by sex by age of respondent

The four trends in the figure are for men and women whose fear of crime by day and by night was assessed in terms of responses to the question: 'How safe do you feel or would you feel being out alone in your neighbourhood at night/ during the day?' Four response alternatives were given to respondents, and we have assigned a value of 4 to the response 'very unsafe', a value of 3 to the response 'somewhat unsafe', a 2 to 'somewhat safe', and a 1 to 'very safe'. These trends suggest that fear of crime increases with age, both for fear during the day (gamma = 0.15) and at night (gamma = 0.20). For all age and sex

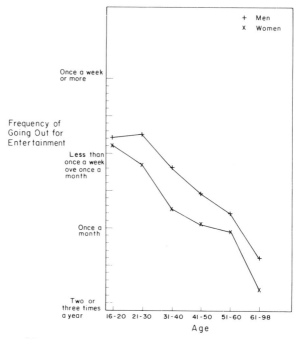

Figure 5. Frequency of going out for entertainment
by sex by age of respondent

groups fear of crime is greater during the night than the day. But for the elderly this increment is larger than for other groups, suggesting that the elderly are particularly distinguished by their fear of crimes at night.

The second issue is whether fears about crime lead to greater decreases in mobility among the elderly than in other age groups. Examination of the frequency with which the elderly report going out for entertainment, shown in Figure 5, suggests that the elderly do indeed go out less frequently than do members of other age groups. When asked if they had become more or less mobile in the past two years the elderly were no more likely to indicate less mobility, but they were less likely to indicate increases in mobility (Figure 6). The elderly seem clearly less mobile.

While the elderly are less mobile, responses to the question why they go out more or less frequently than in the past, shown in Figure 7, suggests two conclusions. First, among the elderly crime is the most frequently mentioned reason for staying home. However, crime is not mentioned by a majority of the elderly as the reason that they stay home. In fact, only 24 percent of the elderly mention crime as the reason for lessened mobility. A greater proportion of elderly persons indicate a restriction in activity due to age and health than to

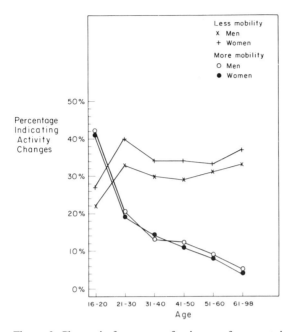

Figure 6. Change in frequency of going out for entertainment over the past year or two. (Question: Do you go out in the evening for entertainment more or less now than you did a year or two ago?) Frequency by sex by age

crime. Much of the lessened mobility of the elderly, therefore, is not related to concerns about crime.

In addition to being asked about their general mobility, respondents were asked to indicate whether they had changed their activities specifically because of a fear of crime. Figure 8 indicates the proportion of each age group indicating such a change. For both men and women there is an age trend, with older respondents more likely than younger ones to indicate that they have changed their activities due to concerns about crime. For the elderly, however, continuation of this trend is only observable among men. Among women, those aged 60 and above do not indicate more crime-related changes than do women in their fifties. Even among men, although the fear may restrict mobility, it does not appear to do so to an extent that is 'special', where 'special' is understood to mean deviating from the general age trend. In other words, although the elderly are less mobile than younger age groups (see Figure 5), only a small part of this reduced mobility may be due to fear of crime.

Further evidence that the decrease in mobility that occurs with age is independent of concerns about crime is provided by an examination of mobility rates among victims and non-victims of crime. As Figure 9 indicates,

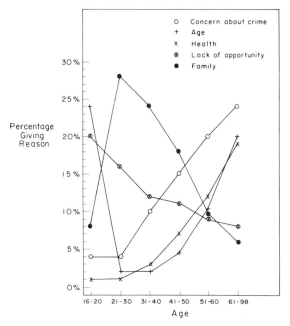

Figure 7. Reasons given for going out more or less than
in the past

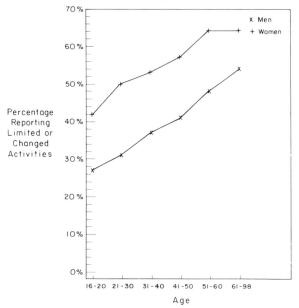

Figure 8. Changes in activity because of crime by sex
by age of respondent

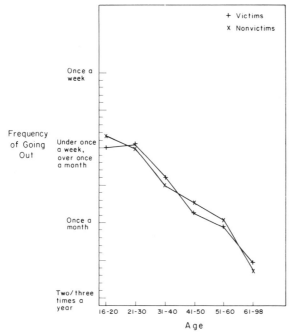

Figure 9. Frequency of going out by victim status by age of respondent

frequency of going out is unrelated to past victimization experience, both among the elderly and among other age groups.

The Origin of Fear

While first-hand experience with crime is generally seen to be a central source of crime-related fears, the elderly have higher levels of fear without suffering objectively greater rates of victimization. There are two possible explanations for this finding. First, objectively similar experiences with crime may have greater psychological consequences for the elderly. Secondly, the elderly may have greater indirect contact with crime.

Some of the higher levels of fear among the elderly may be attributed to the fact that a victimization experience does have a greater impact upon older victims. Comparison of fear levels among victims and non-victims, shown in Figure 10, suggests that victimization generally has more impact upon older individuals, a trend which appears to continue among the elderly. This increased impact of victimization with age is most pronounced in the case of judgements about neighbourhood safety during the day, but is also apparent

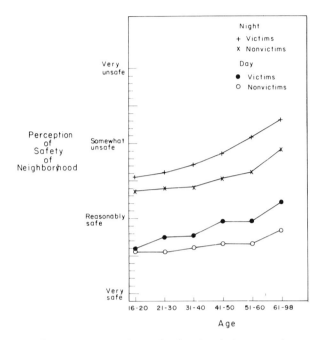

Figure 10. Perceptions of safety by victim status by age
of respondent

in judgements of safety at night. While, at any age, victims' judgements are influenced by victimization, the elderly are influenced to a greater degree.

In addition, however, fears about crime among the elderly are clearly influenced by indirect contacts with crime via social networks or the mass media. Changes in fear over time, shown in Table 6, suggests a dramatic increase in fear among the elderly between 1965 and 1974, a period during which crime among the elderly was not objectively greater than crime among other age cohorts. This increase suggests a strong indirect influence upon the fears of the elderly.

DISCUSSION

The Claims Revisited

The evidence we have reviewed allows us to reassess the claims made by commentators who are concerned about crime and the elderly. Contrary to a widespread belief, the elderly are not victimized more than younger persons when crime rates are examined. Indeed, in all but one of the crime categories

Table 6   Fear of crime among different age cohorts over time. Percentage 'afraid' (and N) by age cohorts in 1965, 1967, 1968, 1973, and 1974

Cohorts	1965	1967	1968	1973	1974
New:					
1965 (18–25)	35%	30%	37%	40%	43%
1967 (18–27)	(122)	(528)	(235)	(479)	(526)
1968 (18–28)					
1973 (18–33)					
1974 (18–34)					
Young:					
1965 (26–41)	36%	29%	29%	40%	40%
1967 (28–43)	(454)	(483)	(460)	(440)	(390)
1968 (29–44)					
1973 (34–49)					
1974 (35–50)					
Middle:					
1965 (42–58)	32%	33%	35%	42%	48%
1967 (43–60)	(488)	(528)	(465)	(393)	(363)
1968 (44–61)					
1973 (50–66)					
1974 (51–67)					
Old:					
1965 (59 +)	38%	33%	41%	46%	56%
1967 (61 +)	(335)	(356)	(297)	(171)	(187)
1968 (62 +)					
1973 (67 +)					
1974 (68 +)					

Source: Rebecca Adams and Tom W. Smith, Fear of Neighborhood, National Opinion Research Center Report 127C on the Social Change Project (NORC, Chicago, in press).

for which data exist the elderly are victimized less than others. The one known exception is for personal larceny. But even here the rates among the elderly are no higher than for other age groups.

Two qualifications need to be kept in mind about the above conclusions. The first is that no separate data exist about certain rarer types of crime that some commentators have claimed particularly affect the elderly. Thefts of Social Security cheques from mailboxes, and confidence games designed to rob victims of their savings, are foremost among the crimes mentioned. It should be noted, however, that such crimes are reported in the LEAA victimization surveys; they are simply not reported separately in published reports and are not available separately on computer tapes. We can confidently conclude, therefore, that if the elderly are specially victimized in any subcategory of crime, this is not to an extent which manifests itself as higher crime rates against the elderly in the crime category into which the subcategory data are aggregated.

The second point to note is that the crime rate data we have examined do not control for differences in the extent to which people from different age groups are exposed to situations where crime is a high risk. Consider the simplest such risk variable—being on the street. If the elderly go out less than others, the lower rate of crime against them may reflect reduced availability as targets, and the elderly might well be victimized more than others if they were more often on the street or in other situations of higher risk. We must be careful not to conclude from the crime rate data that criminals deliberately avoid the elderly as targets perhaps because they have less to steal or because the criminals fear stiffer penalities. Indeed, the possibility still exists that the elderly are preferred targets and that, under conditions of equal exposure to risk, criminals might tend to select elderly over younger targets.

The economic and physical consequences of crimes against the elderly seem, in general, also to be less special than commentators have claimed. In absolute dollar terms the elderly lose less than other adults and their medical expenses are no higher than those of younger persons. Indeed, they are less likely than others to need medical attention when they are attacked, which suggests that criminals use less force against them. It is only when economic expenses are expressed as a percentage of average monthly income that the loss of elderly victims exceeds that of other adults, though not that of teenagers and persons in their early twenties. But we cannot be so sure that their medical costs are higher relative to income since the availability to the elderly of Medicare, Medicaid, and private insurance may lead to higher reimbursements than is the case with younger persons who are not eligible for Medicare. The problem facing elderly crime victims seems, then, to be a problem of relative poverty rather than of the absolute magnitude of financial losses or physical injury.

This state of affairs may be explained by the special context of crimes against the elderly. When victimized, the elderly are more likely than others to be involved in incidents of property transfer without violence rather than acts of violence with or without intent to steal. Moreover, the perpetrators of these crimes—usually purse snatchings—are likely to be black unknown adolescents who act alone and without weapons, operating in or near where the victim lives. Such inexperienced young criminals are probably less dangerous than gangs or experienced older criminals with more developed and potentially more dangerous *modi operandi* than mere purse snatching.

It has frequently been maintained that crimes against the elderly increase fear among the elderly, and that this fear reduces the mobility of senior citizens, making them captives in their homes. It is true that the elderly fear crime more than others, and that their fear is not part of a more general syndrome such that older Americans are more fearful of everything rather than merely being more fearful of crime (Cook, Antunes, Cook, and Skogan, in preparation).

It seems likely, however, that the higher fear of crime among elderly

Americans is not the major force causing them to stay at home more than younger people. When asked why they stayed at home, crime was the single most frequently mentioned reason, but over three-quarters of the sample mentioned reasons other than crime—with health and age being the most important other reasons mentioned. If we assume that these other reasons do not mask a concern for crime, then crime is not the major force causing decreased mobility. Moreover, when asked whether they had changed their activities because of crime, women over 60 were not more likely to respond in the affirmative than were women in their fifties, although they were more likely to do so than were women under 50. Among men, elderly men were more likely to indicate that they had changed their activities because of crime, but elderly men were on the same trend line as men of all other ages. There were no signs of elderly males being an anomaly among males, although they were more likely to indicate changed activity than were younger males. While the data analysed here are not definitive, it seems likely that fear of crime among the elderly is not as important in keeping the elderly indoors as is commonly assumed.

Given the rate of direct experience with crime among the elderly, the high levels of fear among older Americans cannot be the result of direct victimization experiences. If the higher level of fear among elderly persons is not caused by direct experiences of crime and is not a part of a more general fear syndrome, to what then is it attributable? Our guess is that the fear is vicariously acquired, i.e. that it may be the result of indirect experiences.

Two modalities of indirect experience seem potentially important: informal social networks and the mass media. In our culture, crime may well be one of the favourite topics of mundane conversation among most age groups, and our guess is that this is especially the case with older Americans. Prior studies have suggested that such indirect communications about crime can have an important influence upon personal fears (Skogan, 1977; Tyler, 1980). In addition, the elderly are particularly likely to encounter vivid descriptions about crimes against their own age cohort through the mass media. Prior research has been unclear about the impact of media experience upon personal fears, with some studies suggesting such an impact (Gerbner and Gross, 1976a, 1976b) and others failing to find such influence (Doob and MacDonald, 1979; Tyler, 1980).

Obviously, we still need to learn a great deal about the roles that real and vicarious experience with crime play in mediating fear of crime among the elderly. An educated guess, based on the inconclusive data available at present, is that vicarious experience plays a major role nationally in instilling and maintaining high levels of fear among the elderly who—after all—go out less often than others and so are less likely to have their fear about the likelihood of victimization personally disconfirmed.

Policy Implications

The revisions we have made to the popular image of how crime affects the elderly have, we think, some important policy implications. The first concerns how the 'problem' of crime against the elderly should be defined. It is unclear whether there is any general problem of crime against the elderly. There may instead be a problem of fear of crime among the elderly and a problem of cushioning the economic losses that disproportionately affect the less affluent groups in society — primarily the very young and the very old. There may also be the need to do something about inexperienced young criminals who snatch purses from elderly women.

Secondly, the revised diagnosis implies more focused and less expensive interventions than have been advocated. A general need is informational, i.e. to let elderly people know that, according to the best knowledge at present available, they do not seem to be special targets. However, this message has to be given in such a way that they do not relax their vigil too much, for we do not yet have data about victimization with exposure to risk held constant. There would seem to be less need at this time for elaborate safety devices and preventative measures which themselves probably elevate and, by virtue of their visibility, help to maintain high levels of fear. Another informational need is to let elderly people know the role that the media and informal networks can play in causing fears which are not based upon accurately perceived dangers. A final informational need is to inform elderly women of how and when they should carry their purses so as to make themselves less vulnerable as targets of opportunity.

Thirdly, our revision of the prevailing image suggests that many current policies are overly expensive and of questionable worth because they are addressed to the wrong problem. Policies that call for more protective devices, more patrolling of areas where the elderly live, and greater publicity for the plight of the elderly, all serve to raise the salience of the issue of crime and the elderly. Yet the salience could profitably be reduced at this time, and scarce attention and resources could be devoted to more pressing issues. While keeping crime and the elderly high on the political agenda is good 'symbolic politics' (after all, politicians know that no one is against helping elderly victims) this high profile on the agenda of national problems may itself contribute to the elderly over-estimating the likelihood of being victimized and experiencing an unnecessarily high level of fear. It also probably justifies increased expenditures on crime and the elderly and may not be warranted.

Fourthly, since crime affects the poor disproportionately — both in terms of the frequency of crimes and the severity of their financial consequences — it might be useful to consider programmes of victim recompense for all poor persons, including the elderly. There are obvious difficulties in devising and implementing compensation programmes, but the experience of other nations, and even of the states in the US that already have such programmes, may help the Federal government avoid some of the pitfalls. But one thing is certain: it is not easy at this time to claim that criminal victimization of the elderly warrants the high political profile that it currently commands or that the problem deserves labelling as a 'crisis', as many political commentators have claimed.

A Role for Social Scientists

This chapter used survey data to validate public claims that responsible people have made to the effect that criminal victimization of the elderly is 'special' or warrants labelling as a 'crisis'. When confronted by the data most of the claims were seen to be wrong or over-generalized, and their very existence may well have contributed to assigning to criminal victimization of the elderly a higher profile on the agenda of national problems than it probably deserves. We functioned as scholars who defined their role in terms of using the best available data to edit claims.

This role is somewhat different from others that social scientists play in policy research. Some scholars use their theoretical knowledge and practical experience to help plan programmes; others use their methodological expertise to help evaluate projects and programmes in empirical fashion; and yet others use their analytical skills to help analyse the implicit logic behind individual programmes and even certain classes of programmes. The role we have played is perhaps more modest. One assesses the claims that are used to justify classifying some phenomenon as a 'new' social problem, and one then looks for secondary data sources that can be brought to bear quickly in order to assess the validity of these claims. The social scientist is thus cast in the role of someone who tries to influence the salience of issues on the social policy agenda by adding sources of input additional to those that currently determine the salience of issues.

The ability of social scientists to influence the political agenda in the manner we have described depends on a number of fairly obvious factors. One, critical to the timing of social scientific editing of social claims, is the easy availability of secondary data sources. The first correctives to the conventional wisdom that the elderly are victimized more often than others emerged about 1976, whereas newspaper reports about the problem started to appear with some frequency three or four years earlier, possibly as a result of the 1971 White House Conference on Aging. In part the tardiness of the corrective voice is due to the slow processing by the Census Bureau of the voluminous LEAA data and by the special tardiness with which data tapes were released to the scholarly world. But in part also the tardiness is endemic, since it is not possible to conduct responsible secondary analyses immediately after public claims begin to be made. The claims have first of all to be repeated to capture attention, and then time is required to obtain and analyse any relevant data that might be available. This said, it must also be acknowledged that the delay need not be so long as it was with criminal victimization of the elderly, and we suspect that, as the national store of objective and subjective indicators increases and as experience with such indicators grows, so too will the speed increase with which data are used to assess claims about the extent to which a given social problem should be taken seriously. But even with the growth of such indicators, it should not be thought that all claims about problems can be confronted. The archives will continue to be deficient in both comprehensiveness and quality, although not totally deficient.

A second obvious factor affecting the role of social science data analysts in editing claims about problems is the extent to which the 'problem' is embedded in a mesh of political and value concerns. We might anticipate that many problems will be resistant to redefinitions of priority, since important legislative, bureaucratic, and research constituencies support the establishment and maintenance of issues high on the political agenda. When this is the case, the data may well be ignored except in special instances where the data analysis is supported by legitimate authorities or where the analyst is persistent and insists on publishing his or her findings and succeeds in enlisting help. Sometimes, however, the very forces that impel some persons to define a phenomenon as a problem operate to maintain a rationale that militates against assigning any new status to the problem in question.

In our culture there are few persons outside of universities who can play the role of data-informed commentators on the jusification for defining something as a 'social problem'. Most social critics do not have the training or resources to comment on political agendas; their role is rather to put new things onto old agendas. Many social researchers in contract research agencies cannot afford the luxury of implicitly or explicitly criticizing the saliency assigned to a particular programme, largely because specific Federal agencies have vested interests in some phenomena being labelled as 'crises' and they may not welcome attempts to question their labelling, particularly if these attempts come from contract research agencies that depend on the Federal agency for new contracts. Only academics seem to us to have the freedom to play the 'editing' role we have described. We would very much like to see more social scientists responsibly playing this role, because it is socially important and no one else can do it as well, however imperfectly 'as well' may be.

NOTES

1. We would like to thank Fay Cook and Wesley Skogan for their comments on a draft of this chapter.

2. The published LEAA tables are used for the analysis of rates since they are based on the total sample of about 375,000 persons per year and our analysis would only re-create what LEAA has already done.

REFERENCES

In L. Bickman (Ed.) *Applied Social Psychology Annual*, 1, Sax Publications: Beverly Hills, pp.93–135.

Butler, R. (1975) *Why Survive? Being Old in America*, Harper & Row, New York.

Cook, F. L., Skogan, W. G., Cook, T.D., and Antunes, G. E., Setting and reformulating policy agendas: The case of criminal victimization of the elderly. Oxford University Press (in press).

Cook, T. D., Dintzer, L., and Mark, M. (1980) 'The analysis of concomitant time-series'. In L. Bickman (Ed.) *Applied Social Psychology Annual*, 1, Sage Publications, Beverly Hills, pp.93–135.

Cunningham, C. (1974) 'The pattern of crime against the aging: The Kansas City study, in Midwest Research Institute, *Crimes Against the Elderly*, Kansas City, MO: Midwest Research Institute.

Doob, A. N. and MacDonald, G. E. (1979) 'Television viewing and fear of victimization: Is the relationship causal?', *Journal of Personality and Social Psychology*, 37, 170–79.

Ford, G. (1975) 'Crime message to Congress', Office of the White House Press Secretary, Washington, D.C., 19 June.

Gerbner, G. and Gross, L. (1976a) 'Living with television: The violence profile', *Journal of Communication*, 26, 172–99.

Gerbner, G. and Gross, L. (1976b) 'The scary world of TV's heavy viewer', *Psychology Today*, April, 41–45, 89.

Goldsmith, J. and Goldsmith, S. (1976) *Crime and the Elderly*, Lexington Books, Lexington, MA.

Goldsmith, J. and Tomas, N. E. (1974) 'Crimes against the elderly: A continuing national crisis', *Aging*, 1974, no. 236–237 (June–July).

National Academy of Sciences (1976) *Surveying Crime*, Committee on National Statistics, National Academy of Sciences, Washington.

Skogan, W. G. (1976) *Sample Surveys of the Victims of Crime*, Ballinger, Cambridge, MA.

Skogan, W. G. (1977) 'Public policy and fear of crime in large American cities', in *Public Law and Public Policy* (Ed. J. A. Gardiner), Praeger, New York.

Tyler, T. R. (1980) 'The impact of directly and indirect experienced events: The origin of crime-related judgments and behaviors', *Journal of Personality and Social Psychology*, 1980, 39, 13–28.

U.S. Congress, House (1977) Select Committee of Aging, *In Search of Security: A National Perspective on Elderly Crime Victimization*, USGPO, Washington, D.C.

U.S. Department of Justice (1975) *Criminal Victimization in the United States, 1974: A National Crime Survey Report*, National Criminal Justice Information and Statistics Service, Law Enforcement Assistance Administration. Washington, D.C.

U.S. Department of Justice (1977a) *Criminal Victimization in the United States: A Comparison of 1975 and 1976 Findings*, National Criminal Justice Information and Statistics Service, Law Enforcement Assistance Administration, Washington, D.C.

U.S. Department of Justice (1977b) *Criminal Victimization in the United States, 1975: A National Crime Survey Report*, National Criminal Justice Information and Statistics Service, Law Enforcement Assistance Administration, Washington, D.C.

Progress in Applied Social Psychology, Volume 1
Edited by G. M. Stephenson and J. M. Davis
© 1981 John Wiley & Sons, Ltd.

8

Attitudes and Voting Behaviour: An Application of the Theory of Reasoned Action

MARTIN FISHBEIN
University of Illinois at Urbana-Champaign

and

ICEK AJZEN
University of Massachusetts at Amherst

INTRODUCTION

More than any other single act, voting provides the average citizen with an opportunity to become directly involved in the political process. Although the present chapter will focus primarily on voting behaviour within the United States, the theory and methods described herein are assumed to be applicable to the study of voting behaviour within any political system. We recognize that the particular alternatives confronting voters in different political systems and in different types of elections vary considerably, but we believe that the same processes underlie all voting decisions. By casting their votes, American citizens choose among candidates for various offices at all levels of government and influence policy in local or state-wide referenda. Because presidential elections involve and affect the nation as a whole, they have provided the context for most research on voting behaviour in the United States. In every presidential election since 1940, intensive efforts have been made to explain how a voter chooses among candidates. Early attempts to explain voting behaviour centred on the characteristics of the voter and on the role of social influence. Before long, however, explanations relying on variables of this kind were rejected as inadequate and emphasis shifted to the voters' attitudes toward what were assumed to be the major elements of a partisan election: the candidates, parties, and issues.

We will first provide a brief overview of the major approaches that have been taken in research on voting behaviour. Our discussion will then turn to the way in which partisan attitudes have been conceptualized and measured in the context of this research. We will compare use of the attitude concept in research on voting behaviour to our own view of the nature and measurement of political attitudes. This comparison will demonstrate that past research has often failed to obtain adequate measures of attitudes toward candidates, parties, and issues. We will try to show that our approach not only enables us to obtain more appropriate measures of political attitudes, but also identifies the major determinants of attitudes which can be used to predict and explain voting behaviour. We will argue that the utility of such attitudes is limited to the context of partisan elections involving a choice among candidates and that they cannot provide the basis for a general theory of voting behaviour. In the remainder of the chapter we will describe a general theory of human behaviour, the theory of reasoned action, and we will attempt to demonstrate its applicability to this domain. We will discuss how the theory of reasoned action can be used to predict and explain not only choice among candidates but also any other type of voting decision. Support for our theory will be provided by considering the results of empirical research in the context of a presidential election and a state-wide nuclear energy referendum.

PAST APPROACHES TO AMERICAN VOTING BEHAVIOUR

Until very recently, two schools of thought—the Columbia and Michigan schools—have dominated most research on American voting behaviour. Our overview will focus on the approaches adopted by these two schools.

The Columbia School

Systematic research on voting behaviour began with the pioneering work of Lazarsfeld, Berelson, and Gaudet (1944) at Columbia University's Bureau of Applied Social Research. In their attempt to explain voting decisions in the 1940 presidential election, these investigators interviewed a panel of respondents in Erie County, Ohio. Coming from a sociological tradition, they concentrated their efforts on demographic variables, the role of the mass media, and processes of interpersonal communication.

One of their main conclusions was that 'social characteristics determine political preference' (p.27). This conclusion was based on the finding that a small number of demographic variables permitted a fairly accurate prediction of voting behaviour. Specifically, they argued that high socio-economic status (SES), affiliation with the Protestant religion, and rural residence predisposed a person to vote for the Republican party, whereas the opposites of these factors (low SES, Catholic affiliation, urban residence) made for Democratic predispositions.

The second major conclusion they reached was that political campaigns have little or no effect on the election. Even before the nominating conventions, 64 percent of the voters had decided to vote for a given candidate. Forty-nine percent maintained that intention throughout the campaign, and voted in accordance with their intentions. According to Lazarsfeld *et al.* the campaign obviously had little effect on the 'opinions' of these constant voters. Since most of them voted in accordance with their predispositions (as determined by their demographic characteristics), it was concluded that the campaign merely reinforced their predispositions. The remaining 51 percent the 'changers', fell into three groups.

(a) Twenty-eight percent were called *chrystallizers*. These were people who 'didn't know' whom they were going to vote for in May, but eventually acquired a preference.

(b) Fifteen percent were called *waverers*. These were people who 'started out with a vote intention, then fell away from it [either to "Don't know" (11%) or to the other party (4%)] and later returned to their original choice'.

(c) Eight percent were *party changers*—people who started with a vote intention, changed to the other party, and eventually voted for that other party.

However, Lazarsfeld *et al.* noted that 'all the changes of the chrystallizers and most of the waverers involved only one of the parties; the other part of the change was a "Don't know" opinion'. Indeed, '88% of all the voters were limited to one party and the vote intentions of only 12% of the voters took in both parties, at one time or another' (p.66).

A third conclusion had to do with the image of the voter who, in the course of the campaign, switches his voting intention from one candidate to another. Prior to this study it had generally been assumed that these individuals are usually well-informed, thoughtful, and conscientious voters who are convinced by the issues of the election. According to Lazarsfeld *et al.*, this view 'is just plain wrong . . . These people . . . were: the least interested in the election; the least concerned about its outcome; the least attentive to political material in the formal media of communication; the last to settle upon a vote decision; and the most likely to be persuaded, finally, by a personal contact, not an "issue" of the election' (p.69).

In support of their view that the campaign has little effect on the voters, Lazarsfeld *et al.* discovered considerable self-selection in exposure to political communications. Rather than attending to all the arguments brought up in the campaign, people tended to expose themselves to campaign communications favouring the side associated with their own predispositions. The mass media's failure to influence voting behaviour suggested to the investigators that interpersonal influence plays a more important role in voting decisions than does exposure to the issues of a campaign.

A subsequent study of the 1948 presidential election (Berelson, Lazarsfeld, and Mcphee, 1954) provided support for this argument. Demographic characteristics were again found to be related to voting decisions, but Berelson *et al.* attributed their importance to the role they play in determining the people with whom an individual associates. The investigators found that a person tends to interact primarily with people whose demographic characteristics are similar to his or her own. This relatively closed system of interpersonal contacts and communications was assumed to produce mutual reinforcement of 'opinions' and thus to maintain demographically determined voting patterns.

As in the first study, the campaign was again found to have little impact on the election. Most voters were found to be neither interested in, nor informed about, the issues of the campaign. This finding raised doubts about more than the qualities of the voter. It constituted a challenge to the classical theory of democracy, a theory that emphasized the role of intellectual factors. Berelson and his associates (Berelson, 1952; Berelson *et al.*, 1959) pointed out that the textbook model of democracy required that the citizen (1) be interested and participate in political affairs; (2) be capable of and engage in discussion; (3) be well-informed about political affairs, know what the issues are, what alternatives are proposed and the likely consequences of those various alternatives, and what the party stands for; (4) cast his vote on the basis of principle—not fortuitously or frivolously or impulsively or habitually, but with reference to standards not only of his own interest but of the common good as well; and (5) exercise rational judgement in coming to his voting decision.

Berelson *et al.* (1954) concluded that the average American voter fails virtually all the above qualifications of a citizen in a democratic society. According to these authors, 'the ordinary voter, bewildered by the complexity of modern political problems, unable to determine clearly what the consequences are of alternative lines of action, remote from the arena, and incapable of bringing information to bear on principle, votes the way trusted people around him are voting' (p.309).

The Michigan School

In the 1950s a group of scholars working at the University of Michigan's Survey Research Centre examined the voting behaviour research produced by Columbia University's Bureau of Applied Social Research and found it wanting. They argued persuasively that the sociological approach favoured by Lazarsfeld, Berelson, McPhee, and Gaudet at Columbia had produced low-level, time bound generalizations and pointed to a number of cases 'in which earlier sociological propositions, *as formulated*, had become period pieces in the span of a few years' (Campbell, Converse, Miller, and Stokes, 1960). They challenged as inadequate one of the basic conclusions of the Columbia group — that social characteristics determine political preference — by pointing out that 'the distribution of social characteristics in a population varies but slowly over a period of time — yet crucial fluctuations in the national vote occur from election to election' (Campbell *et al.*, 1960, p.17).

As an alternative, they proposed that psychological factors serve as the immediate determinants of voting behaviour. They identified several 'psychological forces' or 'motivating factors' which were assumed to mediate the effects of social characteristics. The first major study by the Michigan group was a nationwide survey of potential voters in the 1952 presidential election (Campbell, Gurin, and Miller, 1954). In this study, voting choice was found to be determined primarily by three partisan motivational orientations:

Party identification — the individual's sense of personal attachment to one party or the other.

Issue partisanship — a person's pro-Democratic or pro-Republican orientation as reflected in his responses to a series of questions about the issues of the campaign.

Candidate partisanship — the difference between the person's attitudes toward the two candidates.

Although they did not compare the relative influence exerted on the vote by each of these three factors, Campbell, Gurin and Miller (1954) suggested that party identification played a major role in the 1948 and 1952 presidential elections. They argued further that 'given a continuation of the present party division, this factor may be expected to contribute a substantial portion of the total motivation in any presidential election in this country. In any particular year, the more variable factors of issues and candidates may have unusual importance . . .' (pp.183–84).

The Michigan school increased their emphasis upon the role of party identification in *The American Voter* (Campbell, Converse, Miller, and Stokes, 1960). In what is generally regarded as the most important single contribution to the study of voting behaviour, Campbell *et al.* reaffirmed their position that voting choice depends in an immediate sense on a system of psychological forces. In contrast to the earlier research, these forces are now conceptualized as a set of six partisan attitudes: (1) toward the Democratic candidate; (2) toward the Republican candidate; (3) toward the parties as managers of government; (4) toward the parties and candidates in relation to foreign issues; (5) toward the parties and candidates in relation to domestic issues; and (6) toward the parties and candidates in relation to reference group interests. Each of these partisan attitudes locates the respondent on a bipolar dimension from pro-Democratic to pro-Republican. Consistent with the position taken by Campbell *et al.*, the six partisan attitudes were found to be highly related to voting choice.

Note that party identification is no longer considered to be one of the forces that serve as an *immediate* determinant of voting behaviour but rather as an antecedent of these forces. Defined as the sense of personal or psychological attachment which the individual feels toward the party of his choice, party identification has been measured by simply recording a respondent's answer to the question: 'Generally speaking, do you usually think of yourself as a Republican, Democrat, Independent, or what?' (Campbell *et al.*, 1960, p.122). If the respondent answers Republican or Democrat he is further asked: 'Would you call yourself a strong Republican (Democrat) or not very strong Republican (Democrat)?' If the answer is Independent, he is asked: 'Do you consider yourself closer to the Republican or Democratic party?' On the basis of these responses, a person is classified into one of seven groups: Strong Republican, weak Republican, Independent leaning toward the Republicans, true Independent, Independent leaning toward the Democrats, weak Democrat, or strong Democrat.[1]

Campbell (1964) has described a person's party identification as 'remarkably constant through the life of the individual'. The Michigan school thus views party identification as a long-term force that influences a person's short-term partisan attitudes.[2] The stability of electoral behaviour is attributed to the long-term influence of party identification and changes in voting patterns from one election to another are explained by short-term variations in the six partisan attitudes. Consistent with this view, Campbell *et al.* (1960) reported that in the 1956 presidential election, party identification was related to the six 'partisan attitudes' and that it could also be used to predict voting behaviour. Moreover, consistent with the assumption that the effect of party identification is mediated by the partisan attitudes, prediction of voting choice from party identification was less accurate ($r = 0.64$) than was prediction on the basis of the six partisan attitudes ($R = 0.71$).

In conclusion, the Michigan school focused attention on the role of *partisanship* in American voting behaviour. The concept of party identification assumes an electorate divided along party lines and an underlying long-term commitment to the ideology and policies of a political party. In the context of a given election, partisanship is reflected in the six short-term attitudes that represent preferences for the candidates or issues of one party as opposed to those of the other.

It may appear at first glance that the findings reported by the Michigan school contradict the Columbia school's conclusions concerning the American voter since attitudes based on domestic and foreign issues were among the psychological forces determining voting choice. Campbell *et al.* (1960), however, did not attribute a great deal of importance to the issues of the campaign. According to these investigators, 'many people know the existence of few if any of the major issues of policy (p.98). 'The widespread lack of familiarity with predominant issues of public policy, along with confusion on party position that remains even among individuals familiar with an issue attests to the frailties of the political translation process' (p.109). Furthermore, they found virtually no evidence for the kind of structured political thinking they felt should characterize a well-informed electorate. In their words, 'Our failure to locate more than a trace of "ideological" thinking . . . emphasizes the general impoverishment of political thought in a large proportion of the electorate' (p.282).

Although the Columbia and Michigan schools differed in the importance they attributed to social versus psychological factors, the Michigan school provided further support for the position that the average American voter fails almost every test of citizenship. The majority of voters were again found to have reached their voting decisions prior to the campaign. As Rossi (1966) pointed out, these findings support the contention that 'electoral campaigns do not accomplish dramatic shifts among the electorate and have as their main function the reactivation of long standing party loyalties' (p.71).

Finally, just as the Columbia group had revised the image of the 'changing' voter, Campbell *et al.* challenged the classic view of the Independent as a voter with high interest in the election but low partisanship. 'Far from being attentive, interested, and informed, independents tend as a group to be somewhat less involved in politics. They have a somewhat poorer knowledge of the issues, their image of the candidate is jointed, their interest in the campaign is less, their concern over the outcome is relatively slight . . .' (p.83).

The American voter was thus pictured as an apathetic, uninformed individual who has developed an attachment to a political party (largely because his family is attached to that party) and tends to vote for the candidate of that party, paying little attention to the issues of the campaign, having no real conception of the differences between the parties, and little or no political ideology. This portrait was created largely from analyses of presidential elections. Presumably the average citizen is even more distant from the textbook ideal when elections of 'lesser importance' (congressional or local) are considered. This view of the American voter was almost unanimously accepted among political scientists and it completely dominated thinking and research about voting behaviour in the 1960s.

Recent Developments

In recent years a few scholars have questioned the widely shared non-intellectual portrait of the American voter. The role of intellectual factors and 'rationality' in the voting process, once dismissed as bases for voting choice, now form the nexus for the current debate in voting behaviour. The influence of policy issues and questions of ideology and rationality have received increasing attention in studies of electoral behaviour. Key (1966) was especially instrumental in reopening the question of how much responsibility could be attributed to the American voter in arriving at his voting decision, but a new generation of scholars interested in the formation of public policy has argued for and tested the importance of issue voting in recent elections (e.g. Boyd, 1972; Page and Brody, 1972; Pomper, 1972; RePass, 1971; Fishbein and Coombs, 1974). There has also been renewed concern with the role of ideology in voting behaviour (Field and Anderson, 1969; Pierce and Rose, 1974) and the notion of a rational voter, inherent in Downs's (1957) theorizing, is attracting increasing attention (Goldberg, 1969; Klecka, 1971; Shapiro, 1969).

Very few investigators, however, have criticized the conclusions reached by the Michigan group or the methodology on which these conclusions were based. The predominant view seems to be not that the Michigan group's portrait of the American voter was incorrect, but that the voter has changed. The political upheavals of the 1960s are usually credited with this change. In their overview of voting behaviour, Mulcahy and Katz (1976) have described this transition as follows:

> Voters can only react to the issues of their times. If no serious problems threaten, why should voters pay attention to issues? If party differences are nonexistent, why bother to be informed? Looking back, the 1950s seem made to inspire political apathy . . . Civil rights, Viet Nam, and the war on poverty changed all this. Issues and ideologies were hotly debated . . . Given a dialogue between competing viewpoints, voters became more interested in policy, and their opinions acquired a new consistency (p.84).

Along the same line, Converse (1974) argued that 'the voter has been rehabilitating himself' (p.660).

Although there can be little doubt that there is an increased awareness of politics, the question remains as to whether the voter was ever as apathetic and uninformed as he was portrayed by the Columbia and Michigan schools. Perspective in such matters might be more easily obtained if research findings could be treated not just as disjointed facts but as elements of a more embracing theory of voting. Despite the tremendous amount of research that has been conducted on the American voter, 'our ability to predict how voters will vote is far more solidly based than our ability to explain why they vote as they do' (Kelly and Mirer, 1974, p.572). While there is evidence that people with similar demographic characteristics tend to vote for the same candidate in a given election, we do not know *why* they vote for that candidate or why they may vote for the opposition candidate in another election. To be sure, Campbell *et al.* (1960) tell us that people vote for a given candidate because of the direction and intensity of their partisan attitudes and they state that these attitudes are influenced by party identification. They do not tell us, however, how voters who identify with the same party can have different attitudes or whether and how their attitudes can be changed.

Even critics of the Michigan school's research have tended to approach empirical questions in an ad hoc manner and have frequently relied upon reanalyses of the Survey Research Centre data. Sullivan's (1966) observation that 'despite the increasing volume of studies relating attitudes to voting behavior, political science lacks a psychology of political attitudes', appears as true today as it was then. Kelley and Mirer (1974) have argued that 'some of the most interesting questions about voting and elections cannot at present be given satisfactory answers. What particular attitudes actually bear on voting, the character and quality of such attitudes and perceptions, the impact of campaigns . . . must wait upon a securely established theory of voting. At present, there is no such theory' (p.572).

Despite the lack of an adequate theory of attitudes, the Michigan school has been remarkably successful in using their measures of partisan attitudes to predict voting behaviour. Such global measures of attitude toward people and institutions are rarely found to be related to specific actions (see Ajzen and Fishbein, 1977). The high relations are even more remarkable in light of the fact that the procedures used to measure the six 'partisan attitudes' are open to question on both theoretical and methodological grounds. For these reasons we will now take a closer look at the partisan attitudes and the way they are measured.

CRITICAL ANALYSIS OF THE SIX PARTISAN ATTITUDES

In the approach developed by the Michigan school, partisan attitudes are measured by analysing the responses to a series of eight open-ended questions, two with respect to each party and two for each candidate (see Campbell *et al.*, 1960). The questions concerning the parties are worded as follows.

1. 'I'd like to ask you what you think are the good and bad points about the two parties. Is there anything in particular that you like about the Democratic party? (What is that?)'
2. 'Is there anything in particular that you don't like about the Democratic party? (What is that?).

The same two questions are also asked about the Republican party.

Later in the questionnaire, respondents are asked,

1. 'Now I'd like to ask you about the good and bad points of the two candidates for president.[3] Is there anything in particular about (name of Democratic candidate) that might make you want to vote for him? (What is that?)'

2. 'Is there anything in particular about (name of Democratic candidate) that might make you want to vote against him? (What is that?)'

The same questions are then asked with respect to the Republican candidate.

Measures of the six partisan attitudes are based on a content analysis of the responses to these open-ended questions. Attitudes toward the Democratic and Republican candidates are obtained by considering only responses to the candidate questions which cite a candidate's experience, abilities, personal attributes, or his relation to his party—but not responses associating the candidate with issues or groups.[4] For example, if a respondent mentioned three personal attributes as reasons for wanting to vote for the Democratic candidate and one personal attribute as a reason for voting against him, his attitude toward that candidate would be scored as + 2.

Rather than developing separate measures of attitude toward each party as a manager of government, a single difference score is derived. This score is based only on responses to the party questions which refer to corruption, to the collective leadership of the parties, and to their capacities to govern. Responses referring to a party's association with issues or groups are again excluded from consideration.[5] To illustrate, suppose that in response to the questions about the parties, a person gave only two answers that referred to the parties as managers of government. Specifically, if he liked the Republican party because 'it has good leaders' and he disliked the Democratic party because 'it is corrupt', his attitude toward the parties as managers of government would be scored as in favour of the Republican party (+ 2). If, on the other hand, he mentioned one reason for liking the Democratic party and one for disliking the Republican party, his score would be –2 (in favour of the Democratic party).

All responses not used to measure the first three attitudes are then classified into three categories: domestic issues, foreign issues, and group references. The responses within each category are used to construct attitude scores in the manner described for the attitude toward the parties as managers of government. These scores thus represent differential attitudes toward two compound stimulus objects—the Democratic party and candidate versus the Republican party and candidate.

Let us examine these measurement procedures in the context of our information-processing theory of attitude formation (see Fishbein, 1963; Fishbein and Ajzen, 1975). There seems to be agreement among investigators that attitudes toward any object are determined by beliefs about that object. A person's belief about an object may be defined as his or her subjective probability that the object has a given attribute. The terms 'object' and 'attribute' are used in the generic sense and they refer to any discriminable aspect of the individual's world. In the context of politics, the object of interest may be a particular candidate, a political party, or an issue. For example, an individual might indicate an 80 percent chance that John Smith (the Republican candidate) is honest. The belief object 'John Smith' is linked to the attribute 'honest' with a subjective probability of 0.80.

Although a person may hold a large number of beliefs about any given object, it appears that he can attend to only a relatively small number of beliefs — perhaps five to nine — at any given moment. According to our theory, these *salient* beliefs are the immediate determinants of the person's attitude. It is of course possible for more than nine beliefs to be salient and to determine a person's attitude; given time and incentive, a person may take a much larger set of beliefs into account. We are here merely suggesting that under most circumstances, a small number of beliefs serve as the determinants of a person's attitude.

The implication of this discussion is that in order to understand why a person holds a certain attitude toward an object it is necessary to assess his salient beliefs about that object. Perhaps the simplest and most direct procedure involves asking the person to describe the attitude object using a free-response format. For example, he could be asked to list 'the characteristics, qualities, and attributes' (Zajonc, 1954) of John Smith. Since salient beliefs are uppermost in the individual's mind, we can assume that the first five to nine beliefs he elicits are his salient beliefs about this candidate.

According to our theory, a person's attitude toward an object is a function of his salient beliefs about that object. Each belief links the object with a valued attribute. The attitude is determined by the person's evaluation of the attributes associated with the object and by the strength of these associations. Specifically, the evaluation of each salient attribute contributes to the attitude in proportion to the person's subjective probability that the object has the attribute in question.[6] By multiplying belief strength and attribute evaluation, and summing the resulting products, we obtain an estimate of attitude toward an object based on the person's salient beliefs about that object. This information-processing theory of attitude is presented symbolically in equation 1, where A stands for attitude, b_i is the belief

$$A = f\left[\sum_{i=1}^{n}\right] b_i e_i \qquad (1)$$

(subjective probability) that the attitude object has attribute i, e_i is the evaluation of attribute i, and the sum is over the n salient beliefs.

Viewing the eight open-ended questions used by the Michigan school from this perspective, it can be seen that they elicit positive and negative attributes of four attitude objects:[7] the Democratic party, the Republican party, the Democratic candidate, and the Republican candidate. Instead of using these beliefs to assess attitudes toward the four targets (the two parties and the two candidates), they classified them into six rather arbitrary categories. Although the categories selected represent traditional areas of concern for political scientists, there is no psychological basis for viewing the beliefs in these categories as indicants of different attitudes, i.e. attitudes toward different 'political elements'.

Examination of the measures used by the Michigan school reveals that the six so-called partisan attitudes can best be described as incomplete measures of attitudes toward partly overlapping targets.

1. An incomplete measure of attitude toward the Republican candidate—incomplete because only some of the salient beliefs about that candidate are used to estimate the attitude.

2. An incomplete measure of attitude toward the Democratic candidate.

3. An incomplete measure reflecting the difference in attitudes toward the Democratic and Republican parties. Again, this measure is incomplete because only some of the beliefs about the parties are used.

4, 5, and 6. Three incomplete measures reflecting the difference in attitudes toward the Democratic party and candidate on the one hand and the Republican party and candidate on the other. Although these measures are based on beliefs arbitrarily classified into three different categories (domestic issues, foreign issues, group references), the beliefs all concern either the parties or the candidates. These three measures thus represent three alternative ways of assessing the same incomplete differential attitude.

Note first that these measures are methodologically unsophisticated since they quantify neither belief *strength* nor *degree* of attribute evaluation. Furthermore, it should be clear that these measures do not constitute six separate dimensions or psychological forces that influence an individual's vote decision. On both theoretical and methodological grounds, responses to the eight questions should have been employed only to measure attitudes toward each party and toward each candidate. Such an approach would not deny the importance of foreign issues, domestic issues, or group references. On the contrary, issues and group references clearly constitute some of the salient attributes associated with the candidates and parties. In this fashion they may influence attitudes toward these objects. For example, a voter's attitude toward a candidate may be influenced by his/her beliefs about the candidate's stands on various domestic and foreign issues. Depending on the voter's own evaluations of these stands (i.e. depending on his/her own position) s/he may develop a favourable or unfavourable attitude toward the candidate. In short, attitudes toward a candidate may be influenced by beliefs about his personal characteristics, beliefs about his associations with various interest groups, or beliefs about his position on various domestic and foreign issues. The important point, however, is that these different types of beliefs are best viewed as contributing to the voter's overall attitude toward a candidate rather than as defining separate partisan preferences.

Our reconceptualization of the measures used by the Michigan school has been based on a consideration of attitude theory and measurement. However elegant theoretically, our analysis has little utility unless we can show that more appropriate measures of attitudes toward parties and candidates based on the Michigan data can predict voting intentions and behaviour as well as or better than can the original six partisan attitudes.

Stokes (1966) also recognized that 'since a presidential campaign confronts the voter with four main objects — the two parties and the two candidates — it is natural to place each respondent along four dimensions of attitude . . .' (p.19). He thus constructed one attitude index for each candidate and one for each party, based on all the responses elicited with respect to the candidate or party in question. Although Stokes did not present the appropriate comparison data, his discussion suggests that he did make these comparisons and found that the four attitudes toward candidates and parties permitted predictions of voting behaviour that were as accurate as those obtained on the basis of original six partisan attitudes.[8]

To enable a more precise comparison, we reanalysed the Michigan data for the 1968 presidential election with respect to the two major candidates, Humphrey and Nixon.[9] In addition to the six *partisan attitudes* used by the Michigan school, we computed attitudes toward each candidate and each party, using all references to that candidate or party (to be called *revised attitude*). Furthermore, since most of the measures used by the Michigan school reflect partisan *differences* in attitudes, we also computed two difference scores on the basis of the revised attitude measures. The first is a 'candidate differential', representing the relative preference for one candidate over the other, and the second a 'party differential' doing the same for attitudes towards the parties. Note that the party differential parallels the Michigan school's measure of attitude toward the parties as managers of government, except that it is based on all references to the parties.

To test the validity of our reanalysis, three multiple correlations were computed in which voting behaviour was regressed on (1) the six partisan attitudes, (2) the four revised attitudes, and (3) the two differential attitudes. These analyses revealed that both the four revised and the two differential attitudes predicted voting behaviour ($R = 0.75$ in each case) as well as did the six partisan attitudes ($R = 0.74$). It thus seems to make little difference whether beliefs about parties and candidates are combined to obtain the six partisan attitudes, the four revised attitudes, or the two differential attitudes. The prediction is equally accurate so long as it is based on *all* of an individual's responses to the eight open-ended questions.

Perhaps of greater theoretical importance, voting behaviour could be predicted almost as accurately from the candidate differential alone ($r = 0.73$). That is, most of the variance in voting behaviour was explained by appropriate measures of attitudes toward the candidates, and little additional information was gained by a consideration of attitudes toward the parties. Finally, in support of our previous arguments concerning the appropriate ways of using the Michigan data to measure attitudes toward candidates and parties, revised attitude measures actually yielded a better prediction of voting behaviour than did their counterparts among the partisan attitudes. Thus, appropriate measures of attitudes toward Nixon and Humphrey (based on all of a respondent's beliefs about these candidates) led to a somewhat more accurate prediction of voting choice ($r = 0.66$ and 0.61, respectively) than did the partisan attitudes toward these candidates as measured by the Michigan scholars ($r = 0.60$ and 0.52). Similarly, when the party differential was measured appropriately, it significantly increased correlations with voting behaviour from 0.46 to 0.62.

In sum, our analysis suggests that at least in the 1968 presidential election, appropriate measures of attitudes toward the candidates permitted a highly accurate prediction of voting behaviour, and considering any of the additional attitude measures did not improve the prediction.

Determinants of Attitudes Toward Political Candidates

Given the strong relation between attitudes toward presidential candidates and voting behaviour, it would be of interest to know the determinants of these attitudes. According to our theory, a person's attitude toward a candidate is a function of his beliefs that the candidate possesses certain attributes and his evaluations of those attributes. The Michigan data suggests that these beliefs deal with the candidate's personal characteristics, his affiliations with a party and other reference groups, and his stands concerning various domestic and foreign issues.

We have attempted to test this theory of attitudes in a number of elections by assessing people's beliefs concerning the candidates' attributes and their evaluations of the attributes. For example, in 1964 a small sample of respondents was asked to list the 'characteristics, qualities, and attributes of Goldwater (Johnson), including his position on various issues'. The most frequently mentioned attributes were identified and used to construct a list of modal salient beliefs. On the basis of these beliefs, a standard questionnaire was constructed and administered to a new sample of 236 respondents[10] (see Fishbein and Coombs, 1974).

Beliefs about Goldwater and Johnson

The set of modal salient beliefs in the 1964 election is shown in Table 1. They include references to personal characteristics (e.g. conservative, physically healthy, consistent in his views), party affiliation, other reference group affiliations (e.g. John Birch Society, Americans for Democratic Action), and

Table 1   Mean beliefs, attribute evaluations, and $b \times e$ products one week prior to 1964 presidential election ($N = 236$)

Salient attribute	Belief strength (b) Goldwater	Belief strength (b) Johnson	Attribute evalua-tions (e)	$b \times e$ products Goldwater	$b \times e$ products Johnson
1. Republican	2.24	-2.72	0.70	1.89	-1.94
2. Democrat	-2.67	2.74	0.37	-0.96	1.02
3. Consistent in his views	-0.50	1.11	2.22	-1.09	2.54
4. Conservative	1.23	-1.19	0.34	0.48	-0.37
5. Moderate	-1.27	0.22	0.65	-0.84	0.57
6. Liberal	-1.86	0.82	0.13	-0.48	0.21
7. Physically healthy	2.47	1.62	2.64	6.63	4.36
8. Mentally healthy	1.75	2.37	2.85	5.16	6.96
9. Political opportunist	0.42	1.07	-0.97	0.57	-0.35
10. Our present foreign policy in Vietnam	-2.38	2.08	-0.81	2.09	-1.50
11. The anti-poverty bill	-2.00	2.69	0.60	-1.40	1.84
12. Reducing the power of the Supreme Court	1.46	-1.68	-0.98	-1.65	1.81
13. Allowing military personnel to make decisions about the use of nuclear weapons	1.05	-1.38	-0.91	-1.22	2.86
14. Medicare	-1.82	2.33	0.29	-0.66	0.86
15. Selecting a well-qualified running mate	-0.40	1.08	2.72	-1.13	3.00
16. Political extremism	0.47	-1.23	-1.83	-0.99	3.09
17. Price supports for farm products	-1.05	1.80	0.21	0.10	0.38
18. Using nuclear weapons in Vietnam	0.66	-2.02	-1.71	-0.78	4.09
19. Swift enforcement of the Civil Rights Act	-1.11	1.72	0.67	-0.48	1.78
20. Increased social security benefits	-0.94	1.87	1.07	-0.81	1.99
21. Reducing the power of the federal government	1.63	-1.88	0.00	0.71	0.01
22. John Birch Society	0.17	-2.31	-1.99	-0.22	4.99
23. The nuclear test ban treaty	-0.77	2.35	1.73	-1.19	4.55
24. Americans for Democratic Action	-1.88	1.31	0.17	-0.13	0.84
			Total	3.62	43.57

stands on various domestic issues (e.g. Medicare, increased social security benefits, swift enforcement of the Civil Rights Act), and foreign issues (e.g. present foreign policy in Vietnam, nuclear test ban treaty).

The standard questionnaire first asked respondents to evaluate each of the characteristics, groups, and issues on a seven-place *good–bad* scale, such as:

Use of nuclear weapons in Vietnam

good $\underline{\quad +3 \quad}$: $\underline{+2}$ $\underline{+1}$: $\underline{\quad 0 \quad}$: $\underline{-1}$: $\underline{-2}$: $\underline{\quad -3 \quad}$ bad
      extremely quite slightly neither nor slightly quite extremely

In addition, the respondents indicated how probable or improbable it was that Lyndon B. Johnson had each of the characteristics and was in favour of each of the policy issues. The following illustration will serve as an example:

Lyndon B. Johnson selected a well-qualified running mate for vice president

probable $\underline{\quad +3 \quad}$: $\underline{+2}$: $\underline{+1}$ $\underline{\quad 0 \quad}$: $\underline{-1}$ $\underline{-2}$: $\underline{\quad -3 \quad}$ improbable[11]
        extremely quite slightly neither slightly quite extremely
                                    nor

This procedure was then repeated with respect to the second candidate, Barry Goldwater.

Following equation 1, these measures were used to compute estimates of attitudes toward each candidate. This is done by multiplying the strength of each belief about a candidate by its corresponding attribute evaluation, and then summing the products across the total set of 24 beliefs. To be able to validate our theory of attitudes, we also obtained more direct measures of attitudes toward Johnson and Goldwater. Respondents were asked to rate each candidate on a set of five evaluative semantic differential-type scales, whose endpoints were *good–bad*, *harmful–beneficial*, *wise–foolish*, *clean–dirty*, and *sick–healthy*. Consistent with our theory, the estimates of attitude based on the 24 beliefs were found to be highly accurate predictors of these more direct attitude measures. The correlation between the relatively direct (semantic differential) and indirect (belief-based) measures of attitude were 0.87 for Goldwater and 0.69 for Johnson.

Having obtained evidence for the validity of the attitude estimates, we can now gain further insight into the determinants of attitudes toward candidates by examining the underlying beliefs. The first two columns in Table 1 show the strength with which our respondents held various beliefs about Goldwater and Johnson. In contrast to the view that American voters are apathetic and uninformed, these data show that, on the average, the American voter distinguished clearly between the two candidates and, more importantly, that their beliefs about the candidates' stands on the various issues were remarkably accurate. For example, respondents accurately believed that Goldwater was in favour of reducing the power of the Supreme Court and of the federal government while Johnson opposed these policies. Similarly, Goldwater was correctly viewed as opposing the anti-poverty bill, Medicare, and swift enforcement of the Civil Rights Act while Johnson was correctly perceived to favour these policies. In fact, rather than being unable to discriminate between the two candidates, the respondents correctly saw them as taking diametrically opposed stands on every major policy issue. The respondents were also very accurate in their belief about each candidate's party affiliation and approval or disapproval of political groups.

The effects of these beliefs on attitudes toward the candidates depend on the evaluations of these associated attributes. These evaluations can be seen in column 3 of Table 1. The fact that many of these evaluations are, on the average, close to the neutral point should not be taken as an indication of the public's lack of concern with these issues. In fact, we shall see below that they often reflect strong disagreements in evaluation between different segments of the population. For example, in 1964 Medicare was a hotly debated issue; its mean value of 0.29 reflects the fact that just as there were many people who had a favourable evaluation of Medicare, there were many who evaluated it unfavourably.

The last two columns in Table 1 show the average effects of each belief on attitudes toward the two candidates. It can be seen that, with only one exception (present foreign policy in Vietnam), Johnson's stands on the issues made positive contributions to the respondents' attitudes toward him. In marked contrast, almost every position taken by Goldwater served, on the average, to lower people's attitudes toward him. Consistent with this pattern, estimates of attitude based on the 24 beliefs in Table 1 resulted, on the average, in more favourable attitudes toward Johnson than toward Goldwater.[12]

These findings suggest that the American voter, far from making uninformed judgements about the candidates solely on the basis of the candidates' personal characteristics, forms his attitudes toward the candidates by considering their stands on various issues. If voters come to like a candidate because he supports an issue they favour and to dislike a candidate because he opposes such an issue, the voters' judgements of the candidates is neither uninformed nor capricious. For example, in Table 1 it can be seen that most voters in 1964 were strongly opposed to the use of nuclear weapons in Vietnam. Columns 1 and 2 show that one of the reasons that Johnson was liked more than Goldwater was that the former was generally viewed as opposed to this policy while the latter was seen as slightly in favour of it.

It might be suggested that these findings which portray a favourable image of the American voter merely reflect the voters' increased interest in issues that is assumed to have taken place since the 1964 presidential election. Data from a 1962 congressional election contradict this assertion.[13] In that election, Springer (the Republican encumbent) was challenged by Wilson (the Democratic candidate) for the congressional seat for the 21st congressional district of Illinois. Again, a set of modal salient beliefs about the two congressional candidates was identified and a standard questionnaire was administered to 263 voting-age residents in Illinois. The questionnaire also included semantic differential measures of attitudes toward the two candidates.

Beliefs about Springer and Wilson

In support of our theory, estimates of attitudes based on beliefs and attribute evaluations were found to predict these more direct semantic differential measures; the correlations were 0.46 and 0.52 ($p < 0.001$) for Wilson and Springer, respectively.[14] We can thus examine these beliefs in an attempt to understand the determinants of attitudes toward the two candidates. Mean beliefs, attribute evaluation, and $b \times e$ products are presented in Table 2. The table shows not only that voters were able to distinguish between candidates prior to 1964 but that, in contrast to most expectations, they could do so in the context of an off-year congressional election. In addition to knowing each candidate's party affiliation, voters correctly believed that Springer had legislative experience and that he was not being supported by a local peace group and that the opposite was true for Wilson. In addition, voters believed that the candidates took different positions on many of the issues and these beliefs were generally quite accurate.[15] For instance, Springer was indeed opposed to ending atmospheric nuclear testing and to Medicare, while Wilson was in favour of these issues. Similarly, the voters correctly believed that both candidates were in favour of blockading Cuba but that only Springer favoured an invasion.[16]

Changes in Beliefs and Evaluations

Accompanying the view of the American voter as ill-informed and unthinking is the notion that campaigns do not matter very much. We have always found it inconceivable that a political campaign which plies voters with a vastly accelerated flow of information and presents a dialogue about the central issues of the day could have no effect on the electorate. If one assesses the effects of a campaign only in terms of changes in voting preferences, this assertion is not without merit. As noted by Lazarsfeld, Berelson, and Gaudet (1944), relatively few voters shift their voting intentions from one candidate to another. Our theory suggests, however, that even though an individual's choice intention or his attitude toward the two candidates may not change during the course of a political campaign, this does not mean that his beliefs

Table 2   Mean beliefs, attribute evaluations and $b \times e$ products one week prior to the 1962 congressional election in Illinois's 21 congressional districts ($N = 263$)

	Belief strength (b) Springer	Wilson	Attribute evaluations (e)	$b \times e$ products Springer	Wilson
1. Republican	2.19	-1.88	0.64	1.67	-1.57
2. Democrat	-1.92	2.08	0.37	-0.26	0.71
3. Veteran	1.46	0.45	1.20	1.94	0.76
4. Having legislative experience	2.06	-0.46	1.56	3.36	-0.48
5. Being suggested by voters for peaceful alternatives	-0.32	0.66	0.35	0.80	0.68
6. Ending atmospheric nuclear testing	-0.47	0.37	0.46	0.50	0.57
7. Eliminating offensive nuclear weapons	-0.81	0.01	-0.84	1.32	0.91
8. Ridding the Americas of Communist-dominated governments	1.77	1.45	1.82	3.53	3.03
9. Blockading Cuba	1.59	1.04	1.90	3.43	2.45
10. Invading Cuba	0.18	-0.52	0.03	0.69	0.54
11. Providing economic—not military—assistance to underdeveloped countries	0.38	0.83	0.79	0.86	1.02
12. Selling agricultural surpluses to Communist and Socialist countries	-0.69	0.02	-0.53	1.12	0.76
13. Meeting between Kennedy and Kruschev	0.87	1.41	1.26	2.17	2.29
14. Government buying and storing of farm surpluses	0.33	1.19	0.01	0.55	0.42
15. Government ownership of communications satellites	-0.22	0.94	0.64	0.63	0.90
16. Medicare	-0.73	1.79	0.60	0.05	1.00
17. Televising political debates	0.25	1.58	1.23	0.92	2.27
			Total	23.28	16.26

about the candidates or his attribute evaluations have also remained stable. A given individual may have the same attitude at two different points in time even when his underlying beliefs have changed considerably.

When attention is paid to beliefs and attribute evaluations that underlie attitudes toward candidates, campaigns are found to have considerable impact on the voter. Consider, for example, the 1964 presidential election in which Johnson opposed Goldwater. Although changes in evluations and beliefs over the last month of the 1964 campaign were not dramatic, we can, with our approach, examine those beliefs which determined the attitudes toward the candidates. We looked first for changes in the way respondents evaluated the personal characteristics of the candidates and the campaign issues. Table 3 shows that there was a significant increase, over the last month of the campaign in the number of respondents who favourably evaluated 'being consistent' and 'reducing the power of the federal government'. The 'anti-poverty bill' and the 'nuclear test ban treaty' were also more favourably evaluated by a larger percentage of our sample, but the changes were small. Indeed, the evaluations of most respondents remained relatively stable over the last month of the campaign.

Table 3   Change over the last month of the 1964 campaign in the percentage of respondents who evaluated issues as good and rated belief statements about the candidates as probable (from Fishbein and Coombs, 1974)

Item	Change in		
	Evaluation of characteristics and issues (%)	Beliefs about Goldwater (%)	Beliefs about Johnson (%)
Consistent in one's views	+9.6[a]	+0.2	+0.1
Liberal	−2.1	−0.3	+7.8[a]
Political opportunist	−2.4	+13.9[a]	+3.3
Anti-poverty bill	+3.3	−4.2[a]	+2.1
Reduce power of Supreme Court	−2.2	+4.5	−8.6[a]
Allow military to make decisions on use of nuclear weapons	+0.5	−5.7	−6.4[a]
Use nuclear weapons in Vietnam	+0.1	+5.6	−5.8[a]
Reduce power of federal government	+7.1[a]	+6.7[a]	−2.9
John Birch Society	−1.1	+8.2[a]	−2.8
Nuclear Test Ban Treaty	+5.1	+0.2	+5.5[a]
Americans for Democratic Action	+3.6	−6.9[a]	+7.5[a]

[a]Percent change statistically significant at less than the 0.05 level.

On 10 of the 24 items (see Table 1) we found a significant increase or decrease in the number of respondents who held a given *belief* about one candidate or the other. With respect to Goldwater, significantly more people perceived him as a 'political opportunist', as 'approving of the John Birch Society', and as being 'in favour' of reducing the power of the federal government' one week prior to the election than had a month earlier. On the other hand, significantly fewer people saw him as 'approving of the Americans for Democratic Action' and as supporting the 'anti-poverty bill'. With respect to Johnson, there were significant increases in the number of people who believed he was a 'liberal', believed he favoured the 'nuclear test ban treaty', and believed he 'approved of the Americans for Democratic Action'. At the same time, significantly fewer people believed he was in favour of 'reducing the power of the Supreme Court', 'allowing military personnel to make decisions about the use of nuclear weapons', and 'using nuclear weapons in Vietnam'.

The findings in Table 3 thus make it clear that even in the last month of a presidential campaign there are occasionally significant net changes in voters' evaluations of issues and that a number of their beliefs about the candidates change. These changes in beliefs are not random but in almost all cases appear to be in the direction of increased accuracy. Disregarding, for the moment, attributes such as 'consistent', 'liberal', and 'political opportunist', and looking at those issues upon which a significant change in beliefs about candidates occurred during the last month of the campaign, the shift toward greater accuracy is apparent. More respondents saw Goldwater as opposing the anti-poverty bill and Johnson as favouring it. More respondents saw Goldwater as favouring the reduction of the Supreme Court's power and Johnson as opposing such a reduction. More saw Goldwater as favouring the use of nuclear weapons in Vietnam and Johnson opposing their use. More saw Goldwater as favouring the reduction of the power of the federal government and Johnson as opposing that reduction. Voters in our sample, we contend, more accurately perceived, at the time of the election than they had one month earlier, the positions of the two candidates on the major issues which distinguished them.[17]

These findings demonstrate that a political campaign can have marked effects on beliefs about the candidates and on attribute evaluations. Examination of our 1962 congressional data again shows that these effects cannot be attributed solely to the voters' increased concern about issues that presumably began in the mid-sixties. For example, as a result of the debate concerning government versus private ownership of communication satellites, 10 percent more voters favoured government ownership just prior to the election than did a month earlier. Even more dramatic, the number of people who favoured selling agricultural surpluses to communist and socialist countries increased by nearly 30 percent in the same period. This change seems to have been due in part to the debate surrounding President Kennedy's decision to sell wheat to the Soviet Union.

Since voters often know much less about the candidates in congressional elections than they know about presidential candidates,[18] a congressional election campaign can also produce very large shifts in beliefs about the personal attributes of the candidates and about their positions on the issues. For example, in our 1962 congressional election study we found that in the course of the last month of the campaign, the number of respondents who believed that Wilson, the Democratic challenger, was not a veteran increased by 18 percent.[19] During the same period, beliefs that Wilson did not have legislative experiences and that Springer was not supported by the local peace group (Voters for Peaceful Alternatives) each increased by 12 percent.

Perhaps even more dramatic was the change in beliefs about Wilson's stands on various issues. For example, while one month prior to the election only 31 percent of our sample believed that the challenger was in favour of selling agricultural surpluses to communist and socialist countries, 53 percent held this belief in the week prior to the election. Substantial shifts also occurred, for example, with respect to beliefs about Wilson's positions on government ownership of communications satellites, Medicare, and providing economic — but not military — assistance to underdeveloped countries. Once again it is important to note that with only one exception all changes in beliefs that took place were in the direction of increased accuracy.[20]

These findings, along with those from the presidential election discussed earlier, clearly demonstrate that the American voter is informed about the issues and is aware of major policy differences between the candidates. Although political scientists have in recent years begun to credit the voter with paying some attention to the issues, the claim that campaigns have little or no effects on the voter is still widely shared. Our results seriously challenge this conclusion by showing that voters are receptive to the information made available to them in a political campaign and use that information to form accurate beliefs about the candidates. We saw that these beliefs about candidates serve as the determinants of attitudes toward those candidates. That is to say, appropriate beliefs and attribute evaluations permit accurate prediction of attitudes toward presidential, senatorial, and congressional candidates.

Determinants of Attitudes Toward Political Parties

Our analysis of the Michigan school's partisan attitudes indicated that in addition to attitudes toward candidates it is possible to obtain estimates of attitudes toward the parties. Given that parties are often considered the most important institutions in the electoral system, it is surprising that over the last two decades political scientists have paid little if any attention to the American voter's attitudes toward the political parties. This may have been due in part to the fact that the Michigan school's conceptualization of party attitude stripped away everything except the differences in the way respondents evaluated the two major parties as managers of government. From our point of view, the formation of attitudes toward political parties is equivalent to the formation of attitudes toward any other object. That is, people's attitudes toward parties are determined by their beliefs that parties are associated with certain attributes and positions on issues and by their evaluations of these attributes and issues.

The 1976 election campaign will serve as an illustration. In addition to indicating their beliefs about Gerald Ford and Jimmy Carter, the presidential candidates, 88 Illinois residents of voting age were also asked to state their beliefs about the Republican and Democratic parties. Table 4 shows the average belief strength, attribute evaluations, and $b \times e$ products obtained by means

Table 4   Mean beliefs, Attribute evaluations, and $b \times e$ products with respect to political parties one month prior to the 1976 presidential election

Salient attribute	Belief strength (b)		Attribute evaluations (e)	$b \times e$ products	
	Republican party	Democratic party		Republican party	Democratic party
National health care system	−0.76	1.48	0.84	0.09	0.10
Constitutional amendment prohibiting abortion	−0.19	−0.99	−1.27	0.41	1.83
Pardon for Vietnam draft evaders	−1.27	0.58	0.01	−0.33	0.39
Being more concerned with inflation than unemployment	0.80	−1.00	−0.13	0.17	−0.02
Guaranteed annual income for the poor and aged	−0.70	1.14	0.57	−0.47	0.94
Constitutional amendment prohibiting busing to desegregate schools	0.25	0.70	0.16	0.16	0.56
Registration of all hand-guns	−0.60	0.82	1.53	−0.33	1.24
Reducing the sale of arms to foreign countries	−0.88	0.34	1.31	−0.94	0.69
Providing moral leadership	0.22	0.33	2.06	1.13	1.17
Keeping a careful watch on Congressional spending	0.67	−0.55	2.20	1.76	−1.07

of a standard questionnaire. The sum of the products for each party served as an estimate of attitude toward that party. More direct measures of attitudes toward the parties were again obtained by means of an evaluative semantic differential. As in the case of attitudes toward candidates, the estimates based on beliefs and attribute evaluations permitted quite accurate predictions of the direct measures of party attitudes. The correlations between estimates and direct measures were 0.63 for the Republican party and 0.51 for the Democratic party.

Since the beliefs measured were found to be related to the attitudes under investigation, we can now turn to a closer examination of these beliefs. Inspection of Table 4 shows that the respondents clearly discriminated between the two parties and that their beliefs tended to reflect reality quite accurately. For example, respondents correctly viewed the Republican party as favouring, and the Democratic party as opposing, a constitutional amendment prohibiting busing. The Democratic party was believed to favour, and the Republican party to oppose, pardons for Vietnam draft evaders, a national health care system, and registration of hand guns.[21]

These findings again contradict the view that the American voter is uninformed and unable to distinguish between the positions of the political parties. Instead, the voters' beliefs about the parties are quite accurate and serve as the basis for their attitudes toward the parties.

Attitudes Toward Candidates and Parties as Predictors of Voting Behaviour

We saw earlier in our reanalysis of the Michigan data that in the 1968 presidential election attitudes toward the candidates were somewhat better predictors of voting choice than were attitudes toward the parties. Our own research — using the measurement procedures described in the previous section — has shown a similar pattern of results in the 1968 as well as in other presidential elections. For example, Fishbein and Coombs (1974) reported that voting choice in the 1964 presidential election correlated 0.74 with attitudes toward Goldwater and 0.72 with attitudes toward Johnson. In the same election study, attitudes toward the Republican and Democratic parties also permitted quite accurate prediction of voting choice (r = 0.63) and 0.57, respectively), but they did not improve the predictions obtained on the basis of attitudes toward the candidates alone.

It might be argued that these results would not hold for elections at state or local levels. Political scientists have usually assumed that people vote more along party lines in local than in national elections. This implies that attitudes toward parties may be more highly related to voting behaviour as one moves from presidential elections to senatorial and congressional levels.

To examine this question, different groups of voting-age residents in Champaign County, Illinois, were interviewed about the 1968 presidential, senatorial, or congressional elections. Using the procedures described previously, we measured the respondents' modal salient beliefs about the Democratic and Republican candidates and parties. In addition, the respondents' attribute evaluations were also assessed. These measures were then used to obtain an estimate of each voter's attitude toward the Democratic party and candidate and toward the Republican party and candidate.[22] Differential candidate and party attitude scores were then computed and used to predict voting behaviour independently and in combination.

Table 5   Prediction of voting choice from attitudes toward candidates and parties in 1968 elections

	Candidate differential	Party differential	Multiple correlation
Presidential election	0.75	0.67	0.75
Senatorial election	0.71	0.65	0.71
Congressional election	0.65	0.62	0.66

Table 5 shows the accuracy of these predictions at each level of the 1968 election. It can be seen that at all three levels of election, differential attitudes toward the candidates predicted voting behaviour with a high degree of accuracy, and that the additional consideration of party attitudes did not improve the prediction.

It thus appears that in the context of partisan elections in the United States, attitudes toward candidates are superior to attitudes toward parties as predictors of voting behaviour. In other electoral systems (such as those of Germany, Israel, and Great Britain) that pose a choice among parties rather than among candidates, or where the formation of a government is based on the number of seats won by a party, a different pattern of results may be obtained. In fact, a study conducted during the 1974 general parliamentary election in Great Britain (Fishbein, Thomas, and Jaccard, 1976) found that attitudes toward the political parties yielded a better prediction of voting choice than did attitudes toward either the candidates in the voter's constituency or the party leaders. Consideration of the latter two attitudes in addition to attitudes toward the parties did not improve prediction of voting behaviour.

TOWARD A GENERAL THEORY OF VOTING BEHAVIOUR

The theory and methods introduced by the Michigan school have had a major impact on studies of American voting behaviour. Party identification and the six partisan attitudes continue to play a central role in most analyses of the voting process. It is important to realize that the concepts and methods introduced by the Michigan school were developed in the context of partisan elections within the American electoral system. There can be little doubt that in this context the Michigan approach has enabled an accurate prediction of voting choice. According to this approach, an individual's voting decision is determined in an immediate sense by his partisan attitudes. These political preferences are viewed as relatively short-term forces based on separate considerations of the candidates' personal characteristics, the parties' abilities to manage the government, and the candidates' and parties' positions with respect to various issues and interest groups. Whereas partisan attitudes are assumed to reflect the events and circumstances of a given election, party identification is viewed as a more stable long-term partisan force that underlies the voter's political preferences.

In our analysis we have tried to show that the idea of partisanship which underlies the Michigan approach is really unnecessary for the prediction of voting behaviour. We have seen that in the context of partisan elections in the United States appropriate measures of attitudes toward the two candidates predict voting choice at least as well as does the total set of six partisan attitudes. The reason that the Michigan approach has been successful is that embedded within their measures of the six partisan attitudes are several indices that in part reflect the voter's attitudes toward the candidates.

As we interpret it, the Michigan school has focused on three basic concepts: party identification, attitudes toward the parties, and attitudes toward the candidates. Despite the widespread acceptance of the Michigan approach, we would argue that this set of concepts cannot provide the basis for a general theory of voting behaviour. It should be obvious that an emphasis on partisanship and assessment of related concepts can be of only limited utility in the context of non-partisan elections. For example, the candidates in primary elections are all members of the same party and there are many other non-partisan contests, such as elections to the school board and to various municipal and county offices. In such elections, measures of party attitudes and party identification will not provide much insight into the voting process, although attitudes toward the candidates might still be appropriate. Even attitudes toward candidates, however, become irrelevant in the context of a referendum and since most referenda are explicitly non-partisan, party identification and party attitudes are also unlikely to provide an accurate prediction of voting choice. By the same token, the emphasis on partisanship may be less useful in the electoral systems of other nations. For example, one may question the meaningfulness of the concept of party identification in a one-party system or in a multi-party system where the composition and political alignments of parties are in constant flux. Even in the United States, the concept of party identification may be losing its utility since an increasing number of voters classify themselves as Independents.

Perhaps more important, we will try to show that party identification and attitudes toward such objects as candidates, parties, issues, and interest groups do not serve as immediate determinants of voting behaviour. Like demographic characteristics, variables of this kind can influence voting choice only indirectly. We will return to this point below. First, however, let us consider an alternative approach to predicting and understanding voting behaviour.

A Theory of Reasoned Action

Our analysis of the voting process is based on a general theory of human behaviour, the theory of reasoned action (see Fishbein, 1967, 1980; Fishbein and Ajzen, 1975; Ajzen and Fishbein, 1980).

The ultimate goal of the theory is to predict and understand an individual's behaviour. We make the assumption that most behaviours of social relevance are under volitional control and, consistent with this assumption, the theory views a person's intention to perform (or not to perform) a behaviour as the immediate determinant of that action. Thus, barring unforeseen events, a person's intention should permit a highly accurate prediction of his behaviour. It should be obvious, however, that intentions can change over time; the longer the time interval, the greater the likelihood that events will occur which will produce changes in intentions. It follows that accuracy of prediction will usually increase as the time interval between measurement of intention and behavioural observation decreases.

Since our goal is to *understand* human behaviour, not merely to predict it, the second step in our analysis requires that we identify the determinants of intentions. According to the theory, a person's intention is a function of two basic determinants, one personal in nature and the other reflecting social influence. The personal factor is the individual's positive or negative evaluation of performing the behaviour; this factor is termed *attitude toward the behaviour*. Note that the theory of reasoned action is concerned with attitudes toward behaviours and not with the more traditional attitudes toward objects, people, or institutions. The second determinant of intention is the person's perception of the social pressures put on him to perform or not perform the behaviour in question. Since it deals with perceived prescriptions, this factor is termed *subjective norm*. Generally speaking, people will intend to perform a behaviour when they evaluate it positively and when they believe that important others think they should perform it.

Our theory assumes that the relative importance of these factors depends in part on the intention under investigation. For some intentions, attitudinal considerations may be more important than normative considerations while for other intentions normative considerations may predominate. Frequently, both factors are important determinants of the intention. In addition, the relative weights of the attitudinal and normative factors may vary from one person to another. The discussion of our theory up to this point can be summarized symbolically as follows:

$$B \sim I = f[w_1 A_B + w_2 SN] \qquad (2)$$

In equation 2, B is the behaviour of interest, I is the person's intention to perform behaviour B, A_B is the person's attitude toward performing behaviour B, SN is the person's subjective norm concerning performance of behaviour B, and w_1 and w_2 are empirically determined weighting parameters that reflect the relative importance of A_B and SN.

For many practical purposes, this level of explanation may be sufficient. However, for a more complete understanding of intentions it is necessary to explain why people hold certain attitudes and subjective norms.

We saw earlier that any attitude is a function of beliefs (see equation 1). When dealing with attitude toward a behaviour, most salient beliefs link the behaviour to positively or negatively valued outcomes. Generally speaking, a person who believes that performing a given behaviour will lead to mostly positive outcomes will hold a favourable attitude toward performing the behaviour while a person who believes that performing the behaviour will lead to mostly negative outcomes will hold an unfavourable attitude. The beliefs that underlie a person's attitude toward the behaviour are termed *behavioural beliefs*.

Subjective norms are also assumed to be a function of beliefs, but beliefs of a different kind, namely the person's beliefs that specific individuals or groups think he should or should not perform the behaviour. These beliefs underlying the subjective norm are termed *normative beliefs*. Generally speaking, a person who believes that most referents with whom he is motivated to comply think he should perform the behaviour will perceive social pressure to do so. Conversely, a person who believes that most referents with whom he is motivated to comply think he should not perform the behaviour will have a subjective norm that puts pressure on him to avoid performing the behaviour. The relation between normative beliefs and subjective norm is expressed symbolically in equation 3. Here again, SN is

$$SN = f\left[\sum_{j=1}^{n} b_j m_j \right] \qquad (3)$$

the subjective norm, b_j is the normative belief concerning referent j, m_j is the person's motivation to comply with referent j, and n is the number of salient normative beliefs.

Our discussion of the theory of reasoned action shows how behaviour can be explained in terms of a limited number of concepts. Through a series of intervening constructs it traces the causes of behaviour back to the person's beliefs. Each successive step in this sequence from behaviour to beliefs provides a more comprehensive account of the factors underlying the behaviour. That is to say, each step represents a different level of explanation for a person's behaviour. At the most global level, behaviour is assumed to be determined by intention. At the next level, these intentions are themselves explained in terms of attitudes toward the behaviour and subjective norms. The third level explains these attitudes and subjective norms in terms of beliefs about the consequences of performing the behaviour and about the normative expectations of relevant referents. In the final analysis, then, a person's behaviour is explained by reference to his or her beliefs. Since people's beliefs represent the information (be it correct or incorrect) they have about their worlds, it follows that their behaviour is ultimately determined by this information.

APPLICATION OF THE THEORY OF REASONED ACTION TO VOTING IN PARTISAN ELECTIONS

In the remainder of this chapter we will try to show how this theory can be applied to the study of voting behaviour. According to our theory, a voter's choice can be predicted from his or her voting intention. That is, respondents can be asked for whom they intend to cast their votes (choice intention) or to indicate separately their intentions to vote for each of the candidates (voting intentions). In the latter case, we would expect the voting choice to correspond to the strongest voting intention.

The intention to vote for a given candidate is, according to our theory, determined by the person's attitude toward voting for that candidate and by his/her subjective norm, i.e. his/her belief that most important others think s/he should or should not vote for the candidate in question. Attitudes toward voting for a given candidate are in turn determined by beliefs that voting for the candidate will lead to certain consequences and the evaluations of these consequences. Similarly, beliefs that specific referents think one should or should not vote for the candidate in question and motivations to comply with the specific referents are viewed as determining the subjective norms.

Prediction of Voting Behaviour from Intentions

As a first step toward an understanding of voting behaviour we have to examine the extent to which a person's choice between candidates can be predicted from his intentions to vote for each of the candidates. In a number of congressional, senatorial, and presidential elections in the United States we have assessed intentions to vote for each major candidate and have used these measures to predict actual voting behaviour. Approximately one week prior to the election, and in some cases also one month prior to the election, different samples of respondents of voting age residing in Champaign County, Illinois, indicated their intentions to vote for each of the candidates. These intentions were assessed on seven-point scales, such as the following:

I will vote for Jimmy Carter

likely __+3__ : __+2__ : __+1__ : __0__ : __-1__ : __-2__ : __-3__ unlikely

In the week following the election the respondents were contacted again and were asked to reveal for whom they had voted. For example, in the 1976 presidential election about 43 percent of the respondents in our sample reported they had voted for Ford, another 43 percent for Carter, and about 14 percent either did not vote or refused to reveal their choice. These voting decisions were found to correspond closely to voting intentions measured one week prior to the election. Ford voters had significantly stronger intentions to vote for Ford ($M = 2.29$) than for Carter ($M = -2.18$), and the opposite was true for respondents who had voted for Carter ($M = 1.87$ and -1.92 for intentions to vote for Carter and Ford, respectively).

To obtain measures of the strength of the association between voting intentions and actual voting choice in different elections, we computed the difference between each voter's intentions to vote for the two major candidates and used this differential intention score to predict his self-report of voting choice. In every election, intentions to vote for the two candidates predicted actual vote with a high degree of accuracy. For example, in 1968 different samples of respondents were interviewed in an attempt to predict voting choice not only in the presidential race but also in a senatorial and a congressional election. Voting in the presidential race correlated 0.81 with the differences in intentions to vote for Humphrey and Nixon. In the senatorial race, the correlation between differential intention and behaviour was 0.83, and in the congressional election it was 0.75. Similarly, in the 1976 presidential election the difference between intentions to vote for Carter and Ford correlated 0.76 with actual voting choice.

The findings also support the argument that intentions can change over time and that a measure of intention taken just prior to the election will yield the most accurate prediction. For example, over the four-week period preceding the 1976 presidential election, our respondents' intentions were found to change in the direction of their subsequent voting choices. One week prior to the election, Ford voters had a stronger intentions to vote for Ford ($M = 2.29$) than they had four weeks prior to the election ($M = 1.79$); similarly, their intentions to vote for Carter decreased from -1.39 to -1.92 during this period. Comparable results were obtained for Carter voters. As might be expected, intentions were somewhat better predictors of voting behaviour when measured one week prior to the election ($r = 0.76$) than when they were obtained one month prior to the election ($r = 0.71$).

Prediction of Voting Intentions

The next step in our attempt to understand voting behaviour is to examine the determinants of a person's intention to vote for a given candidate, namely his attitude toward voting for the candidate and his subjective norm concerning this behaviour.

We have argued that the relative importance of attitudinal and normative considerations as determinants of intentions will depend upon the behaviour in question and may vary as a function of the population under investigation. Our earlier discussion of the Columbia and Michigan schools suggests two points of view with respect to the relative importance of the attitudinal and normative components. The Columbia school's conclusion that people vote the way trusted others vote seems to imply that normative considerations will be predominant. In contrast, the Michigan school de-emphasized the role of interpersonal influence while stressing the importance of 'partisan attitudes'. Despite the difference between these attitudes and attitudes toward voting for a given candidate, the Michigan approach can be viewed as implying that the attitudinal component is a more important determinant of voting intentions than is the normative component.

Table 6 Prediction of voting intention from attitude toward the behaviour and subjective norm.

| | Correlation coefficients | | Relative weights[a] | | |
	Attitude	Subjective norm	Attitude	Subjective norm	Multiple correlation
1966 senatorial election ($N = 81$)					
Douglas	0.69	0.70	0.38	0.43	0.75
Percy	0.76	0.86	0.28	0.65	0.88
1976 presidential election ($N = 88$)					
Carter	0.72	0.65	0.51	0.32	0.76
Ford	0.77	0.65	0.60	0.24	0.79

[a]Standardized regression coefficients.
Note: All cell entries are significant ($p < 0.01$).

Columns 1 and 2 in Table 6 show that there is some merit in both positions; in each election both components were highly related to intentions. It can be seen in columns 3 and 4, however, that although both components did carry significant weights in the prediction of intentions, their relative importance varied from one election to the other. While normative considerations were more important than attitudinal considerations in the senatorial election, the reverse pattern emerged in the presidential election. Interestingly, this pattern of results is consistent with the general notion that interpersonal influence may become more important as one moves from national to local elections. Note, however, that no firm conclusion can be reached on the basis of a single comparison. In fact, the observed difference could just as well reflect changes in the American electorate over time (from 1966 to 1976) as differences in electoral levels. Nevertheless, these findings illustrate the importance of distinguishing between attitudinal and normative considerations and they show how various assumptions or hypotheses concerning the relative importance of these components can be tested.

We have seen that a person's intention to vote for a given candidate is determined by his/her attitude toward voting for that candidate and by his/her subjective norm concerning this action. Since voting intentions were found to predict accurately the person's actual voting choice, consideration of the attitudinal and normative determinants of that intention provide a new level of explanation for the behaviour under investigation.

Table 7   Mean attitudes and subjective norms with respect to voting for Ford and Carter in the 1976 presidential election

| | Attitudes[a] toward voting for | | Subjective norms[b] concerning voting for | |
	Ford	Carter	Ford	Carter
Total sample ($N = 88$)	1.13	0.05	0.07	−0.28
Ford voters ($N = 38$)	4.76	−3.50	1.08	−1.50
Carter voters ($N = 38$)	−2.29	3.60	−0.89	0.84

[a]Attitude scores can range from −9.0 to +9.0.
[b]Subjective norms can range from −3.0 to + 3.0.

Table 7 shows the mean attitudes and subjective norms for the total sample as well as the Ford and Carter voters one week prior to the 1976 presidential election. Consistent with the fairly equal distribution of Ford and Carter voters in our sample, there were only small and non-significant overall differences in attitudes and subjective norms concerning voting for the two candidates. However, marked differences between the candidates emerged when Ford and Carter voters were considered separately. It can be seen that respondents who ultimately voted for Ford had significantly more positive attitudes and subjective norms with respect to voting for Ford than with respect to voting for Carter. The reverse pattern found for Carter voters. At this level of explanation, then, we can say that people intend to, and actually do, vote for a given candidate if they hold favourable attitudes toward voting for the candidate and if they believe important others think they should do so.

Prediction of Attitudes toward Voting for a Candidate

We have suggested that a person's attitude toward any concept—be it a person, an institution, or a behaviour—is determined by his salient beliefs associating the concept with various attributes or outcomes and by his evaluations of these attributes or outcomes. Consistent with this argument, we saw earlier in this chapter that voters' attitudes toward political parties and candidates can be predicted from their beliefs and attribute evaluations with respect to a given party or candidate.

By the same token, a person's attitude toward voting for a given candidate should be a function of his/her beliefs about the consequences of this behaviour and his/her evaluation of the consequences. In order to test this hypothesis, we elicited a set of modal salient beliefs that associated various outcomes with the act of voting for Carter or Ford in the 1976 presidential election. (Table 9 below shows the ten outcomes elicited most frequently.) One month prior to the election, and again one week prior to the election, belief strength and outcome evaluations were assessed.

To illustrate, consider the outcome 'a five to seven billion dollar cut in the defence budget'. Evaluation of this outcome was measured as follows:

A five to seven billion dollar cut in the defence budget

good _____ : ___ : ____ : ____ : ____ : ___ : _____ bad
   extremely quite slightly neither slightly quite extremely

Responses to this scale were scored from +3 (good) to −3 (bad). Measures of belief strength were obtained by linking each outcome to the act of voting for the two candidates:

1. Casting my vote for Jimmy Carter will lead to a five to seven billion dollar cut in the defense budget

likely _____ : ___ : ____ : ____ : ____ : ___ : _____ unlikely
   extremely quite slightly neither slightly quite extremely

2. Casting my vote for Gerald Ford will lead to a five to seven billion dollar cut in the defense budget

likely _____ : ___ : ____ : ____ : ____ : ___ : _____ unlikely
   extremely quite slightly neither slightly quite extremely

As in the case of attribute evaluations, responses to these scales were also scored from +3 (likely) to −3 (unlikely).

With respect to each candidate, products were computed by multiplying belief strength and corresponding attribute evaluations. The ten products for each candidate were then summed as an estimate of a voter's attitudes toward 'casting my vote for' the candidate in question. Thus, for each respondent we obtained four estimates of attitude: his attitudes toward casting his vote for Ford and for Carter at two points in time—one month and one week prior to the election.

The correlations between these estimates and the more direct measures of attitude described earlier are shown in Table 8. It can be seen that beliefs and attribute evaluations permitted highly accurate predictions of attitudes toward voting for Ford and Carter at both points in time.

Table 8   Correlations between estimates and direct measures of attitude toward voting for a candidate in the 1976 presidential election ($N = 88$)

Candidate	One month prior to the election	One week prior to the election
Ford	0.75	0.74
Carter	0.75	0.69

Note: All correlations are significant ($p < 0.01$).

Having established the validity of the indirect attitude measures, we can take a closer look at beliefs and attribute evaluations to increase our understanding of the factors that determine a person's voting behaviour. Table 9 summarizes the relevant findings. The first two columns show the average belief strength associated with voting for each candidate, followed by the average evaluations of the consequences of this behaviour and the average contribution of each belief to the overall attitude (i.e. the average products of belief strength and attribute evaluation).

Clearly, with respect to each of the outcomes considered, voting for Carter was viewed as more likely to lead to the outcome than was voting for Ford.[24] Examination of these behavioural beliefs shows that beliefs about the consequences of voting for the two candidates were not arbitrary or frivolous but based, at least in part, on available information about the candidates and parties. For example, one of Carter's campaign promises had been to cut the defence budget by five to seven billion dollars whereas Ford had come out against this policy. It thus stood to reason that voting for Carter would be more likely to result in this outcome than would voting for Ford. Similarly, one item in the Democratic party's platform called for the institution of a national health care system whereas the Republican party was known to oppose this policy. It was thus reasonable for voters to infer that voting for Carter would be more likely to result in the institution of a national health care system than would be voting for Ford.

Table 9   Mean beliefs, outcome evaluations, and cross products one week prior to the 1976 presidential election ($N = 88$)

Outcome	Belief strength (b)		Outcome evaluations (e)	$b \times e$ products	
	Voting for Ford	Voting for Carter		Voting for Ford	Voting for Carter
$5–7 billion cut in defence budget	−1.64	0.65	0.28	−0.08	0.01
National health care system	−1.11	1.16	0.75	−0.26	1.06
Reduction in unemployment	−0.15	0.54	2.34	−0.44	1.39
Amnesty for Vietnam deserters	−1.27	0.79	0.20	−0.59	0.56
Major reform in the tax system	−0.53	0.74	1.98	−0.89	1.57
Increased price supports for farm products	−0.09	0.67	0.00	0.30	−0.33
Increased presidential control of foreign policy	−0.15	0.30	0.26	0.17	0.50
Good working relationship between the President and Congress	−0.51	0.82	2.18	−1.11	1.90
Increased federal spending for welfare programmes	−1.24	1.47	−0.90	0.76	−1.11
Reduction in U.S. troops stationed abroad	−0.93	0.59	0.39	−0.20	0.13

Since most outcomes were evaluated positively by our sample, the behavioural beliefs tended to make negative contributions to attitudes toward voting for Ford and positive contributions to attitudes toward voting for Carter (see columns 4 and 5).

We can further enhance our understanding of voting decisions in the 1976 presidential election by comparing the beliefs and outcome evaluations of Ford and Carter voters. Table 10 shows that respondents who eventually voted for Ford or Carter differed considerably in their behavioural beliefs concerning both candidates. Consider first beliefs about voting for Carter. With respect to five of the ten outcomes, Carter voters were significantly more certain than were Ford voters that casting their votes for Carter would lead to the outcomes in question. For example, Carter voters believed it more likely that voting for Carter would lead to a national health care system and to a major reform in the tax system than did Ford voters. With respect to beliefs about voting for Ford, four significant differences were observed. In each case the Carter voters believed that voting for Ford was more unlikely to produce the outcome than

Table 10   Mean beliefs and outcome evaluations for Ford and Carter voters one week
prior to the 1976 presidential election

Outcome	Voting for Ford		Voting for Carter		Outcome evaluations	
	Ford voters	Carter voters	Ford voters	Carter voters	Ford voters	Carter voters
$5–7 billion cut in defence budget	−1.42	−1.87	0.11	1.11[b]	−0.24	1.03[b]
National health care system	−0.42	−1.68[b]	0.84	1.50[a]	0.24	1.24[a]
Reduction in unemployment	0.76	−1.11[b]	−0.26	1.18[b]	2.26	2.37
Amnesty for Vietnam deserters	−0.92	−1.71	0.37	1.26	−0.53	1.26[b]
Major reform in the tax system	0.58	−1.58[b]	0.11	1.24[b]	2.00	2.03
Increased price supports for farm products	0.24	−0.42	0.71	0.55	0.05	−0.11
Increased presidential control of foreign policy	0.26	−0.42	−0.05	0.50	0.26	0.03
Good working relationship between the President and Congress	0.24	−1.13[b]	0.18	1.39[b]	2.39	1.95
Increased federal spending for welfare programmes	−0.89	−1.63	1.61	1.39	−1.61	−0.21[b]
Reduction in U.S. troops stationed abroad	−0.74	−1.21	0.53	0.68	0.13	0.86[a]

[a]Difference between Ford and Carter voters significant at $p < 0.05$.
[b]Difference beteween Ford and Carter voters significant at $p < 0.01$.

did Ford voters. Thus, although both Ford and Carter voters believed that
voting for Ford was unlikely to lead to a national health care system or
amnesty for Vietnam deserters, Carter voters held these beliefs more strongly
than did Ford voters.

Note that the behavioural beliefs considered here may be based in part on
beliefs about candidates or parties. For example, the belief that voting for a
candidate will lead to the adoption of a certain policy can be viewed as an
inference based largely on (a) the belief that the candidate is in favour of or
opposed to the policy in question, and (b) the belief that he is capable of
implementing it. A well-informed electorate should be able to agree on a
candidate's expressed position with respect to a given policy, but voters may
well disagree about the likelihood that he will be able to implement it.

Consistent with this argument, we noted earlier that voters do accurately perceive a candidate's position on the issues. The present results show that there are, however, considerable differences in beliefs concerning the consequences of voting for a candidate. Even though a voter may believe that a candidate favours a given policy, he need not believe that voting for the candidate will lead to the implementation of that policy since he may doubt the candidate's ability to get Congress to approve the policy in question.

To illustrate, it was found that Carter was viewed as being in favour of a national health care system by both Ford voters ($M = 1.73$) and Carter voters ($M = 1.79$). However, as can be seen in Table 10, Carter voters were more confident that voting for Carter would lead to a national health care system ($M = 1.50$) than were Ford voters ($M = 0.84$). This difference presumably reflects stronger beliefs among Carter than Ford voters that Carter could implement the policy in question.

Despite the differences between Ford and Carter voters, their behavioural beliefs are found to be responsive to reality. For example, we noted above that in the course of the campaign Carter had expressed his support for a national health care system while Ford had opposed it. As might therefore be expected, all voters believed that casting their votes for Carter was more likely to lead to a national health care system than was casting their votes for Ford. Similarly, although Carter had expressed his opposition to amnesty for Vietnam deserters, his support of a pardon for draft evaders seemed to have led voters to believe that amnesty was more likely if they voted for Carter than if they voted for Ford.

With respect to four outcomes, voters were not in agreement that voting for one candidate would be more likely to produce the outcomes than would voting for the other. As might be expected, Ford voters believed that a reduction in unemployment, a major reform in the tax system, increased presidential control of foreign policy, and a good working relationship between the Presidential and Congress were more likely to occur if they voted for Ford than if they voted for Carter. The reverse was true for Carter voters who believed that these outcomes were more likely if they voted for Carter than if they voted for Ford. Note, however, that these differences in no way contradict the notion of a well-informed electorate since there was in fact no objective way of knowing whether voting for Ford or Carter was more likely to lead to these outcomes.

Differences in beliefs that voting for one candidate is more likely to produce certain outcomes than voting for the other can help explain the observed differences in attitudes toward voting for the two candidates. But even if Ford and Carter voters held similar beliefs concerning the consequences of voting for the two candidates, their attitudes toward voting for the candidates could differ if they evaluated these consequences differently. The last two columns in Table 10 show that Ford and Carter voters did indeed differ significantly in the way they evaluated many of the issues in the campaign. For example, respondents who eventually voted for Carter were in favour of a five to seven billion dollar cut in the defence budget and amnesty for Vietnam deserters, while respondents who ultimately voted for Ford were opposed to these policies. Although all voters tended to favour a national health care system and a reduction in U.S. troops stationed abroad, Carter voters had significantly more favourable evaluations of these outcomes than had Ford voters. Finally, Ford voters were more opposed to increased federal spending for welfare programmes than were Carter voters, even though the latter also had a somewhat negative evaluation of this policy.

By considering both beliefs and evaluations we can now provide a more complete explanation as to why some respondents voted for Carter and others for Ford.[25] Generally speaking, a person voted for Carter if s/he believed that the outcomes s/he valued favourably were more likely to occur as a result of this choice than as a result of voting for Ford. Similarly, a person voted for Ford, rather than Carter, if s/he believed that doing so would be more likely to result in the outcomes s/he valued favourably.

Consider, for example, a reduction in unemployment. As can be seen in Table 10, all voters had very favourable evaluations of this outcome. Respondents who believed that voting for Carter was more likely to achieve this outcome tended to vote for Carter, while the respondents who believed that a vote for Ford was more likely to achieve this outcome tended to vote for Ford. A somewhat more interesting case is the question of amnesty for Vietnam deserters. We saw above that all respondents viewed this outcome as more likely to occur if they voted for Carter than if they voted for Ford. Table 10 shows that people who favoured amnesty tended to vote for Carter while those who opposed amnesty tended to vote for Ford.

It must be realized that the voting decision is based on the total set of beliefs and not one or two isolated instances. The attitude toward voting for a given candidate is determined by the sum over all salient beliefs concerning the consequences of this behaviour and need not be related to any given belief. Consider, for example, increased federal spending for welfare programmes. Although Carter voters had a negative evaluation of this policy, they nevertheless believed that voting for Carter would be more likely to bring about this outcome than would voting for Ford. In the same fashion, although Ford voters had, on the average, a positive evaluation of a national health care system, they believed nevertheless that a vote for Ford was unlikely to produce this outcome.[26]

These findings demonstrate that voters are aware of both the advantages and disadvantages of voting for a given candidate and that their voting decisions take these considerations into account. This is an eminently rational strategy for making a voting choice. It is neither frivolous nor arbitrary to attempt to maximize the likelihood of achieving valued outcomes.

Prediction of Subjective Norms with Respect to Voting for a Candidate

We have seen above that subjective norms also served as significant determinants of voting intentions in the 1976 presidential election. According to our theory, people's subjective norms are a function of their normative beliefs, i.e. their beliefs that specific referents think they should vote for a given candidate, and their motivations to comply with those referents.

To investigate the relation between specific normative beliefs and the overall subjective norm, we assessed beliefs concerning four salient referents: spouse (or present date), parents, three closest friends, and co-workers. As an illustration, consider the referent 'my three closest friends'. Motivation to comply with this referent was measured as follows:

When it comes to politics, I usually want to do what my three closest friends think I should do

likely _____ : _____ : _____ : _____ : _____ : _____ : _____ unlikely

Responses to this scale were scored from 1 (unlikely) to 7 (likely).

Measures of belief strength were obtained by linking each referent to the act of voting for the two candidates:

1. My three closest friends think I should vote for Jimmy Carter

likely _____ : _____ : _____ : _____ : _____ : _____ : _____ unlikely

2. My three closest friends think I should vote for Gerald Ford

likely _____ : _____ : _____ : _____ : _____ : _____ : _____ unlikely

Responses to these scales were scored from $+3$ (likely) to -3 (unlikely).

With respect to each candidate, products were computed by multiplying belief strength and corresponding motivations to comply. The four products for each candidate were then summed as an estimate of the voter's subjective norm with respect to voting for the candidate in question (see equation 3). For each respondent, we obtained four estimates of subjective norm: subjective norm with respect to voting for Ford and for Carter one month and one week prior to the election.

The correlations between these estimates and the direct measures of subjective norms described earlier are shown in Table 11. It can be seen that normative beliefs and motivations to comply permitted accurate predictions of subjective norms with respect to voting for Ford and Carter at both points in time.

Table 11   Correlations between estimates and direct measures of subjective norm with respect to voting for a candidate in the 1976 presidential election ($N = 88$)

	One month prior to the election	One week prior to the election
Ford	0.63	0.69
Carter	0.60	0.73

Note: All correlations are significant ($p < 0.01$).

Having established the validity of the indirect measure of subjective norm, we can now turn to an examination of the specific normative beliefs and motivations to comply to increase our understanding of the normative factors that determine voting behaviour. Table 12 summarizes the relevant findings

Table 12   Mean normative beliefs, motivation to comply, and cross products one week prior to the 1976 presidential election ($N = 88$)

Referent	Belief strength		Motivation to	Cross products	
	Voting for Ford	Voting for Carter	to comply	Voting for Ford	Voting for Carter
Spouse (date)	0.10	−0.53	2.76	0.28	−1.07
Parents	0.03	−0.45	2.65	0.18	−0.63
Three closest friends	−0.11	−0.49	2.64	−0.20	−1.01
Co-workers	−0.01	−0.56	2.47	−0.22	−0.86

for the total sample one week prior to the election. Although on average the respondents believed that their referents were less likely to think they should vote for Carter than for Ford, these differences were relatively small and not significant. Interestingly, when it comes to politics people have relatively low motivations to comply with their relevant referents. Moreover, they seem to be no more motivated to comply with their spouses and parents than with their close friends and co-workers.

The differences in normative beliefs were reflected in the products such that each referent made a more negative contribution to subjective norms with respect to voting for Carter than with respect to voting for Ford. Again, however, the differences were relatively small.

In an attempt to further our understanding of voting decisions in the 1976 presidential election, we can compare the normative beliefs and motivations to comply of Ford and Carter voters. Table 13 shows that the differences in subjective norms reported earlier were due almost entirely to differences in normative beliefs rather than motivations to comply. Ford voters believed that

Table 13 Mean normative beliefs and motivations to comply for Ford and Carter voters one week prior to the 1976 presidential election

Referent	Voting for Ford		Voting for Carter		Motivation to comply	
	Ford voters	Carter voters	Ford voters	Carter voters	Ford voters	Carter voters
Spouse (date)	1.32	−1.11[a]	−1.89	0.87[a]	2.82	2.89
Parents	0.89	−0.71[a]	−1.47	0.45[a]	2.74	2.74
Three closest friends	0.79	−0.87[a]	−1.63	0.55[a]	2.53	2.82
Co-workers	0.66	−0.68[a]	−1.50	0.39[a]	2.34	2.72

[a]Difference between Ford and Carter voters is significant ($p < 0.01$).

each referent thought they should vote for Ford and not for Carter while the opposite was true for Carter voters. In other words, an individual tended to vote for a given candidate if he believed that his relevant referents thought he should vote for that candidate.

Changes Over Time

By examining changes in beliefs over time, we can assess the impact of the election campaign on the factors that ultimately determine the voter's choice. Although a campaign may not produce large shifts in voting intentions and actual voting decisions, or even in general measures of attitudes and subjective norms with respect to voting for the candidates, it may nevertheless have considerable impact on beliefs about voting for a candidate, outcome evaluations, or normative beliefs. As we pointed out earlier, attitudes and subjective norms are determined by sets of beliefs, and changes in some of these beliefs may be offset by changes in others.

Our data concerning the 1976 presidential election support these arguments. Although intentions, attitudes, and subjective norms did not change greatly in the course of the four-week period prior to the election, the changes that did take place were in the direction of subsequent voting choices. For example, the attitudes of Ford voters toward voting for Ford tended to become more favourable and their attitudes toward voting for Carter tended to become more unfavourable, while the opposite was true for people who in the election voted for Carter. Exactly the same trends were evident in the subjective norms and intentions of Ford and Carter voters.

Our data also revealed some changes in the beliefs underlying attitudes toward voting for the two candidates and subjective norms. For example, during the last month of the campaign all voters became more certain that 'casting my vote for Jimmy Carter will lead to a five to seven billion dollar cut in the defence budget'. This change in belief, however, did not have the same effect on all respondents' attitudes toward voting for Carter, since some people were in favour of a cut in the defence budget while others were opposed. Recall that respondents who eventually voted for Ford had, on the average, a negative evaluation of this policy while respondents who eventually voted for Carter evaluated it favourably. It follows that the change in this belief can account in part for the changes in attitudes toward voting for Carter.

Changes also were found with respect to normative beliefs, but only in the case of voting for Carter. The respondents' beliefs that various referents thought they should vote for Ford remained relatively stable over time. In contrast, all respondents came to view as more unlikely that their spouses (or dates) thought they should vote for Carter. While this change contributed negatively to all respondents' subjective norms with respect to voting for Carter, changes in other normative beliefs made differential contributions to the subjective norms of respondents who eventually voted for Ford and Carter. Specifically, in the course of the campaign people who ultimately voted for Carter increased the strength of their beliefs that their three closest friends and their co-workers thought they should vote for Carter; Ford voters, on the other hand, came to believe more strongly that these two referents thought they should not vote for Carter. These findings are consistent with the changes in subjective norms of voting for Carter.

To summarize briefly, we have seen that people form beliefs about the likely consequences of voting for one candidate or another in a political contest, as well as normative beliefs concerning the prescriptions of relevant referents. Generally speaking, these beliefs tend to be quite reasonable in light of the information available to the voters and they tend to change in accordance with new information to which the voters are exposed. Beliefs that voting for a candidate will lead to certain outcomes, and the evaluations of those outcomes, were shown to serve as the determinants of attitudes toward voting for that candidate. Consistent with common sense, the more a person believed that casting his/her vote for a given candidate will lead to outcomes s/he desired, the more favourable was his/her attitude toward voting for that candidate. Similarly, normative beliefs and motivations to comply were found to determine subjective norms. In further support of the theory of reasoned action the attitudinal and normative components predicted voting intentions with a high degree of accuracy, and these intentions were found to determine actual voting behaviour.

Effects of External Variables

Note that in applying our theory to voting behaviour we have not found it necessary to consider such traditional variables as attitudes toward the parties or candidates, party identification, interest or involvement in the election campaign, liberalism–conservatism, or any of the numerous demographic characteristics (religious affiliation, income, socio-economic status, education, etc.) that have been assumed to influence voting behaviour. From our point of view these variables external to our model can influence voting only indirectly by influencing one or more of the underlying determinants of this behaviour. An external variable may be related to voting in one election, but it may be found to be unrelated to voting in another election. For example, one of the candidates in a given election may be viewed as an intellectual and highly educated people might have more favourable attitudes toward voting for that candidate than people with less education. In another election, the candidates may be perceived as intellectual equals and there might be no relation between the voters' educational level and attitudes toward voting for either candidate. In the former election, level of education is more likely to be related to voting choice than in the latter.

In the study of the 1976 presidential election described earlier a wide variety of external variables were assessed. Within our sample of respondents the majority of these variables were unrelated to voting choice. For example, religiosity, income, socio-economic status, age, interest and involvement in the election, and marital status seemed to have little effect on people's voting choices.

Several other variables, however, were found to correlate significantly with voting behaviour, as can be seen in the first column of Table 14. The correlations presented in this table are based only on the 76 respondents who reported

Table 14 Relations of external variables to voting choice and the determinants of voting choice one week prior to the 1976 presidential election ($N = 76$)

External variables[a]	Voting choice	Differential[b] voting intention	Multiple correlation[c] with behaviour	Differential[b] voting attitude	Differential[b] subjective norm
Candidate differential	0.66	0.58	0.84	0.68	0.64
Party differential	0.60	0.56	0.82	0.74	0.65
Party identification	0.69	0.62	0.84	0.65	0.65
Prior voting history	0.50	0.40	0.82	0.28	0.31
Liberalism–conservatism	0.62	0.55	0.83	0.55	0.52
Educational level	0.26	0.32	0.80	0.17[d]	0.27

[a]Descriptions of the external variables are provided in the text.
[b]Differences with respect to Ford and Carter.
[c]Prediction of behaviour from intention and external variable; effect of the external variable is indicated by the increment above 0.80, the intention–behaviour correlation.
[d]Not significant; all other correlations are significant ($p < 0.05$).

their voting choices. As in other studies of American elections, attitudes toward candidates and parties were found to be strongly related to voting choice. Consistent with the findings reported earlier in this chapter, the differential attitude toward the two candidates was a somewhat better predictor of voting behaviour ($r = 0.66$) than was the party differential ($r = 0.60$); considering the party differential in addition to the candidate differential did not improve prediction appreciably ($R = 0.66$). Interestingly, and consistent with our theory, differential attitudes toward *voting* for the two candidates provided a significantly better prediction of voting behaviour ($r = 0.74$) than either or both the candidate and party differentials. This finding supports our argument that the attitude toward an action is more highly related to that action than is the attitude toward the target at which the action is directed.

Also consistent with findings in other American elections, voting choice was found to be highly related to party identification and history of voting for the Republican or Democratic candidates in past elections. In addition, the voters' self-reports of their liberalism–conservatism and of their educational levels were found to correlate significantly with voting behaviour; liberals and the more educated voters were more likely to cast their votes for Carter than were conservatives and voters of lower educational achievement.

From our point of view, the immediate and most important determinants of voting choice are the person's intentions to vote for each of the candidates. For the present sample of respondents (excluding the 12 respondents who either did not vote or refused to reveal their choices), the differences between intentions to vote for Ford and Carter correlated 0.80 with actual behaviours. Our theory implies that when external variables are found to influence voting behaviour, this influence is due to their effects on voting intentions. In column 2 of Table 14 it can be seen that each of the external variables that was found to correlate with voting choice was also highly related to the choice intention. In fact, considering these external variables in addition to intentions did little to improve the prediction of behaviour. This is evidenced by the fact that the multiple correlations (column 3) were the same or only slightly higher than the correlations based on the intentions alone. For example, consideration of party identification in addition to voting intentions raised the correlation with behaviour from 0.80 to 0.84.

Our theory further implies that since intentions are determined by attitudes and subjective norms, the effects of external variables on intentions must be due to their effects on one or both of these components. The correlations in the last two columns in Table 14 supports this argument. Except for educational level which correlated significantly only with the subjective norm, all external variables correlated significantly with both components. As expected, consideration of the external variables in addition to the two components did little to improve the prediction of intentions.[27] In the case of party identification, this external variable was highly related to both the differential attitudes toward voting for the two candidates and the differential subjective norms. For example, people who identified with the Republican party held more favourable attitudes toward voting for Ford than for Carter and believed that their most important others thought they should vote for Ford rather than for Carter. Once these differential attitudes and subjective norms were known, however, little improvement in prediction of voting intentions and behaviour could be gained by also considering party identification since its influence was already reflected in the two components. Despite its high correlation with intentions, the added consideration of party identification was found to produce only a minimal increment in the predictability of intentions (from 0.72 to 0.74).

As a final step, our approach allows us to explain why the external variables influenced the attitudinal and normative components. Generally speaking, such influence must be due to the effects of the external variables on the determinants of these components, i.e. on beliefs about voting for the candidates, outcome evaluations, normative beliefs, and motivations to comply. It seems reasonable to assume that people who hold different attitudes toward the candidates or parties will also hold different beliefs about the consequences of voting for the candidates. Similar hypotheses can be formulated about the likely effects of other external variables on the determinants of the attitudinal and normative components. One of the important implications of our approach is that unless the investigator can link the external variable of interest to one or more of these determinants, there is little justification for predicting that the external variable will have an effect on voting behaviour.

Consider, for example, the question of the voter's interest in the election campaign. There seems to be no reason to assume that interested and disinterested voters will differ systematically in their outcome evaluations or in their beliefs that voting for one candidate will lead to more positive outcomes than will voting for the other candidate. Furthermore, interested and disinterested voters are unlikely to differ in their perceptions that relevant referents think they should vote for one candidate rather than the other, or in their motivations to comply with the referents. Consequently, there is no basis for assuming that interest in the campaign will be related to voting choice and, consistent with this argument, voters' interest in the 1976 presidential campaign had only a low and non-significant correlation ($r = 0.11$) with voting behaviour.

In contrast, let us again consider the effects of party identification in the 1976 presidential election. It is easy to see that a person's identification with one party or the other may influence some of the determinants of attitudes toward voting for the candidates or of the subjective norms with respect to this behaviour. First, and foremost, it is very likely that Democrats and Republicans will differ in their evaluations of certain policies. Since implementation of these policies constitutes the possible outcomes of voting for a given candidate, Democrats and Republicans are likely to hold different attitudes toward voting for the candidate. Moreover, they are likely to differ in their

Table 15 Mean behavioural beliefs and outcome evaluations for Republicans, Independents, and Democrats one week prior to the 1976 presidential election (N = 76)

Outcome	Voting for Ford			Voting for Carter			Outcome evaluations		
	Repub-licans	Indepen-dents	Demo-crats	Repub-licans	Indepen-dents	Demo-crats	Repub-licans	Indepen-dents	Demo-crats
$5–7 billion cut in defence budget	-1.29	-2.08	-1.88	0.17	0.92	1.11	-0.22	0.08	0.94[a]
National health care system	-0.71	-1.00	-1.63[a]	0.82	1.42	1.46[b]	0.07	1.17	1.40[b]
Reduction in unemployment	0.68	-0.58	-0.97[a]	-0.02	1.17	1.00[a]	2.22	2.42	2.46
Amnesty for Vietnam deserters	-0.71	-1.83	-1.74	0.68	0.25	1.11	-0.44	0.00	1.03[a]
Major reform in the tax system	0.27	-0.42	-1.51[a]	0.24	0.83	1.29[a]	2.00	2.17	1.86
Increased price supports for farm products	0.15	0.42	-0.54	0.54	1.17	0.66	-0.17	1.00	-0.14
Increased presidential control of foreign policy	0.15	-0.58	-0.34[b]	0.05	0.50	0.51	0.46	0.25	0.03[b]
Good working relationship between the President and Congress	-0.02	-0.67	-1.03[a]	0.41	1.17	1.17[a]	2.17	2.75	2.00
Increased federal spending for welfare programmes	-0.85	-1.00	-1.77[b]	1.63	1.00	1.43	-1.46	-0.58	-0.34[a]
Reduction in U.S. troops stationed abroad	-0.63	-1.33	-1.14[b]	0.39	0.67	0.80	-0.02	0.58	-0.80[b]

[a]Difference between Republicans, Independents, and Democrats is significant at $p < 0.01$.
[b]Difference between Republicans, Independents, and Democrats is significant at $p < 0.05$.

beliefs that a given candidate will be able to implement these policies. For example, in comparison to Democrats, Republicans may be more likely to believe that voting for Ford will lead to a policy he supports while the reverse may be true with respect to the Democratic candidate. All of these possible effects could explain the obtained relation between party identification and attitudes toward voting for the candidates.

Table 15 shows the effects of party identification on behavioural beliefs and on outcome evaluations. Party identification was measured by means of the procedure described earlier in this chapter. The seven response categories were collapsed into three: Democratic identifiers and leaners ($N = 35$), Independents with no leanings toward either party ($N = 12$), and Republican identifiers and leaners ($N = 41$).

In the last three columns of Table 15 we can see that Democrats, Republicans, and Independents differed greatly in their evaluations of certain policies. As might be expected, in comparison to Republicans, Democrats had more favourable evaluations of a cut in the defence budget, a national health care system, amnesty for Vietnam deserters, and a reduction in U.S. troops stationed abroad. In each case, evaluations of Independents fell between those of the Democrats and Republicans.

At the same time, it is also important to note that party identification did not significantly affect evaluations of all issues. Irrespective of party identification, respondents had, on the average, strong positive evaluations of a reduction in unemployment, major reforms in the tax system, and a good working relationship between the President and Congress.

Turning to the beliefs about the consequences of voting for the two candidates, it can be seen that irrespective of party identification, there was general agreement that voting for Carter was more likely to lead to each of the ten outcomes than was voting for Ford. For example, respondents generally believed that voting for Carter was more likely to result in a national health care system, increased federal spending for welfare programmes, and a reduction in U.S. troops stationed abroad. This agreement seems to reflect relatively accurate perceptions of the candidates' positions on the issues.

Party identification did, however, influence some of the voters' behavioural beliefs. Considering first beliefs about voting for Ford, Table 15 shows that Democrats believed it unlikely that voting for Ford would result in any of the ten outcomes, while Republicans believed that voting for Ford was likely to produce at least some of these outcomes. For example, Republicans believed that voting for Ford would lead to a reduction in unemployment, whereas Democrats thought this was rather unlikely. Most differences, however, simply reflect the fact that, although all voters agreed that voting for Ford was unlikely to result in the various outcomes, Democrats held those beliefs with greater strength. With respect to voting for Carter, all respondents believed that this behaviour had some likelihood of producing the various outcomes, although again Democrats held many of these beliefs more strongly than did Republicans. For example, Democrats and Independents believed it was quite likely that voting for Carter would lead to a national health care system (M = 1.46 and 1.42, respectively), while Republicans thought that this outcome was much less likely (M = 0.82). In sum, although party identification may influence beliefs about voting for a candidate, its potential impact is limited by the fact that these beliefs are responsive to reality.

By looking at the differences in beliefs and attribute evaluations, we can understand why Democrats, Republicans, and Independents held different attitudes toward voting for the two candidates. To illustrate, consider the outcome 'a reduction in U.S. troops stationed abroad'. While Republicans were relatively neutral with respect to this policy, Democrats evaluated it favourably. Since both Democrats and Republicans believed that a vote for Carter was more likely to lead to this outcome than was a vote for Ford, these beliefs had relatively little effect on Republicans' attitudes toward voting for the two candidates,' but they made a positive contribution to Democrats' attitudes toward voting for Carter and a negative contribution to their attitudes toward voting for Ford.

The same approach can be used to explain the effects of party identification on subjective norms. Democrats, Republicans, and Independents are unlikely to differ greatly in their motivations to comply with such referents as their spouses, parents, or their three best friends. Consistent with this argument, party identification was found to be unrelated to respondents' motivations to comply with any of the four referents considered in our study of the 1976 presidential election.[28]

In contrast, we can expect that the families and friends of Democrats will have different political philosophies than the families and friends of Republicans or Independents. As a result, it is reasonable to assume that Democrats will believe their referents think they should vote for the Democratic candidate while Republicans will tend to believe that their referents think they should vote for the Republican candidate.

Table 16 provides strong support for these expectations with respect to all four referents. It is interesting to note that in our sample of respondents, Independents reported more normative pressure to vote for Ford than for Carter. These differences in normative beliefs among Democrats, Independents, and Republicans explain the finding that the subjective norms of Republicans favoured voting for Ford while those of Democrats favoured voting for Carter.

The above discussion illustrates how we can explain the effects of an external variable such as party identification on voting choice. Similar analyses could be performed in an attempt to explain the effects of other external variables, such as demographic characteristics (e.g. socio-economic status, sex, age, education), personality factors (e.g. liberalism–conservatism,

Table 16   Mean normative beliefs for Republicans, Democrats, and Independents one week prior to the 1976 presidential election ($N = 76$)

Referents	Voting for Ford			Voting for Carter		
	Republicans	Independents	Democrats	Republicans	Independents	Democrats
Spouse (date)	1.10	0.33	−1.14	−1.44	−0.83	0.63
Parents	0.68	−0.33	−0.60	−1.22	−0.25	0.37
Three closest friends	0.59	0.25	−1.06	−1.20	−1.00	0.51
Co-workers	0.73	0.00	−0.89	−1.24	−0.67	0.29

Note: The differences between Republicans, Independents, and Democrats are significant ($p < 0.01$) with repsect to each referent.

authoritarianism), or traditional attitudes toward candidates, parties, issues, or interest groups. In each case we would expect that the effect of the external variable on voting choice is mediated by the determinants of this behaviour as specified in the theory of reasoned action. A detailed analysis will reveal which of these determinants (intentions, attitudes, subjective norms, behavioural beliefs, normative beliefs, outcome evaluations, and motivations to comply) are influenced by the external variable under consideration. That is to say, our approach allows an investigator to identify the loci of an external variable's effects on voting behaviour.

Voting in American Partisan Elections: Some Conclusions

In this chapter we have tried to show how our approach can be used to understand voting decisions in American elections.[29] This analysis has led to the following view of the processes underlying the decision to vote for a given candidate. As a result of their interactions with others and their exposure to the mass media and other sources of information, people acquire various beliefs about our political institutions, prominent political figures, and numerous issues and policies. At any point in time, therefore, people associate various attributes with the political parties and public figures; they hold beliefs as to the positions of the political parties and public figures with respect to some of the issues of the day; and they assume that the implementation of certain policies would lead to desirable or undesirable outcomes. On the basis of these beliefs, they form attitudes toward the public figures, the parties, and the policies.

Whenever a new political figure attracts our attention, we tend to form beliefs about him even if we have only very limited information. For example, on the basis of his party affiliation or geographic origin we may infer that he favours certain policies and opposes others, or that he is liberal or conservative.

Often, these inferences, although based on very little information, turn out to be quite accurate.

When the time for an election draws near, there is a rapid increase in the amount of information concerning the political parties, the potential candidates, and the issues of the day. This information reinforces some beliefs and contradicts others, thus producing changes in existing beliefs, or it may provide the basis for the formation of new beliefs.

We have tried to show that voters take account of the information available to them. By the time of the election, most voters hold quite accurate beliefs about the political candidates and parties. Perhaps more important, the campaign induces people to consider the likely consequences of *voting* for the different candidates. Such behavioural beliefs are based in part on the information the person has about the candidate and the party to which the candidate belongs. For example, the belief that voting for a candidate will lead to the implementation of a certain policy depends partly on the belief that the candidate in question favours that policy.

On the basis of these beliefs, the voter forms an attitude toward the act of voting for each candidate. The process whereby these attitudes are formed is eminently reasonable. A person who believes that voting for a candidate will lead to mainly positive outcomes will form a favourable attitude toward voting for that candidate; a person who believes that voting for the candidate will lead to mostly negative outcomes will form a negative attitude. When confronted with different candidates, a person will feel most positive toward voting for the candidate whom s/he believes can do the most for him/her. In support of this position, we have shown that people's attitudes toward voting for a candidate can be predicted with considerable accuracy from a knowledge of their beliefs that voting for the candidate will lead to certain outcomes and their evaluations of these outcomes.

In the course of interacting with other people, we often discuss not only the political candidates, parties, and issues but also the likely consequences of voting for a given candidate. As a result of these discussions we may infer that our friends, families, co-workers, or other referents think we should vote for one candidate rather than another. In conjunction with the individual's motivations to comply with each referent, these normative beliefs determine his/her subjective norm, i.e. his/her belief that most important others think s/he should vote for one candidate or the other. Even though a person may believe that a specific referent thinks s/he should vote for a certain candidate, this belief will influence his/her subjective norm only to the extent that s/he is motivated to comply with the referent. We presented data showing a strong relation between normative beliefs and motivations to comply on the one hand and subjective norms on the other.

We also showed that attitudes and subjective norms with respect to voting for a given candidate provide the basis for intentions to vote for that candidate.

From our point of view, the attitudinal and normative components serve as the only determinants of voting intentions. We realize, of course, that people hold attitudes toward the parties, candidates, and issues in a campaign and that these attitudes as well as such other external variables such as party identification, liberalism–conservatism, or any of a number of demographic variables may influence the beliefs on which the two determinants of intentions are based. However, all of these effects are incorporated within, and are taken into account by, the measures of the attitudinal and normative components. Although consideration of external variables may help explain the origin of certain beliefs, we saw that the two components of our theory are sufficient to predict voting intentions.

In arriving at his voting intention, a person may place more weight on his attitude toward voting for the candidates or on his subjective norm. We have at present little information about the factors that determine these relative weights. Generally speaking, they are likely to be influenced by individual differences and by the particular election under consideration. In fact, we saw that within our samples of respondents, the normative component was given more weight in a 1966 senatorial race while the attitudinal component was more important in the 1976 presidential election. It is not clear, however, whether this shift in weights was due to the level of the election, to changes in the electorate over time, or to some other uncontrolled factor.

Finally, we demonstrated that a person's choice among the candidates is determined by his intentions to vote for them. The best prediction is afforded when the intentions are measured immediately prior to the election. The reason for this finding is that intentions often change over time. It must be stressed, however, that these changes in intentions are not arbitrary, but rather they follow systematically from changes in beliefs brought about by exposure to new information. If the new information produces changes in one or more beliefs about the consequences of voting for a candidate, these changes may affect attitudes toward voting for the candidate and, hence, voting intentions. Similarly, new information may influence beliefs about the normative prescription of a relevant referent; this change in normative belief may affect the subjective norm and ultimately the voting intention.

Note that even relatively large changes in a person's intentions to vote for each candidate may not be sufficient to shift his choice intention from one candidate to another. Imagine a person who initially thought it quite likely that he would vote for Carter and quite unlikely that he would vote for Ford. This person could lower his intention to vote for Carter and raise his intention to vote for Ford, but the difference in intentions could still favour Carter. Moreover, as we saw in our discussion of the 1976 election, changes in intention may often serve to increase, rather than decrease, the initial difference. The absence of reversals in choice intentions cannot therefore be taken as evidence that intentions did not change or that the campaign had no effects on the voters. Indeed, it is our contention that political campaigns have large and significant effects on the beliefs of the electorate.

Contrast this view of voting behaviour with the view held by most social scientists. The traditional approach has been to explain voting behaviour in terms of such demographic variables as social class, religion, income, age, and education; attitudes toward parties, candidates, and issues; and party identification and political ideology (e.g. liberalism–conservatism). Although the prediction of voting choice from variables of this kind has usually been quite successful, this approach has led to a view of American voting behaviour which appears to us incompatible with the bulk of available evidence. First, in light of the data discussed in this chapter, we find it hard to accept the portrait of the American voter as an apathetic uninformed individual who pays little attention to the issues of the campaign, who has no real conception of the differences between the parties or candidates, and who tends to vote for a candidate merely because the candidate represents the party with which the voter identifies or because he blindly follows the dictates of trusted others. Secondly, as indicated above, we also reject the argument that political campaigns have little or no effect on the voter.

In short, although quite successful in predicting voting behaviour, the traditional approach has failed to provide an acceptable description or explanation of the process whereby people arrive at their voting decisions. In part, this is due to the fact that the traditional approach has focused on what we have called external variables, i.e. variables which from our point of view can have only an indirect effect on voting behaviour. To be sure, if you assess a large enough number of demographic variables, other individual difference variables such as party identification, previous voting record, personality traits, or political ideology, and attitudes toward candidates, issues, parties, or other institutions, you will find that many of these variables are in fact related to voting decisions in a given election. Unfortunately, the relations obtained in one election often do not hold in other elections and it is thus impossible to arrive at a clear and systematic understanding of the factors that determine voting decisions.

Even the six 'partisan attitudes' and party identification which, according to the Michigan school, represent the basic determinants of voting choice cannot provide an adequate explanation of the process whereby voters reach their decisions. First, like other external variables, the relative importance of these 'attitudes' varies considerably from election to election, although it is often possible to provide interesting and quite reasonable post-hoc explanations for these shifts.

Moreover, as we noted earlier, there is no way these variables could account for the voting process in other types of elections or electoral systems. Clearly, partisan attitudes and party identification are irrelevant in non-partisan elections such as within-party primaries, some municipal elections, and referenda on various issues. Similarly, partisan attitudes and party identification are largely irrelevant in a one-party electoral system.

In marked contrast, our approach can be applied to the prediction and understanding of voting behaviour in any kind of election. To illustrate the generality of the theory of reasoned action, we will briefly describe its application in the context of political referendum.

Application of the Theory of Reasoned Action to Voting in a Referendum

In recent years the general public has taken an increasingly active role in the political decision-making process. No longer content to leave decisions that impact on their lives solely in the hands of their elected representatives, individuals and interest groups have turned to the use of referenda as a means of expressing their concerns. From our point of view, the decision to vote *yes* or *no* on a given proposition is reached on the basis of the same process that leads to the decision to vote for or against a given candidate. As a result of exposure to the mass media, campaign literature, and discussions with various people, the voter forms beliefs that voting for (or against) the proposition would lead to certain outcomes and that certain individuals or groups think he should vote for (or against) the proposition. By considering the relative advantages and disadvantages of voting for the proposition, he forms an attitude toward this behaviour. Similarly, his normative beliefs and motivations to comply lead to the formation of a generalized belief that most important others think he should or should not vote for the proposition (i.e. the subjective norm). The person's intention to vote for (or against) the proposition is based on these attitudinal and normative considerations and ultimately determines his actual vote.

As a result of the 1973 oil embargo, questions concerning energy production and conservation have become the focus of considerable attention. The public has become quite vocal in expressing its concerns about the impact of energy decisions upon the price of energy, the safety and environmental consequences of the power production methods proposed, and the requirements for a change in lifestyle. Nuclear energy in particular has aroused a great deal of public concern. This concern has increased to the point where it threatens to restrict or halt the expansion of the nuclear industry. For example, among the various voting decisions that confronted Oregon voters in the election of 1976 was Ballot Measure No. 9—The Oregon Nuclear Safeguards Initiative. This measure was designed to place restrictions on the construction of nuclear power plants.

Prior to the election, interviews were conducted by telephone with 89 potential voters in order to elicit salient outcomes and referents associated with voting for or against the proposition. Since at the time of the interview public opinions on the issue were just beginning to crystallize, it was decided to supplement the obtained outcomes and referents with information from newspaper items and the campaign literature. A content analysis of all the materials yielded lists of 20 salient consequences and 7 referents that were used to construct a standard questionnaire.

Just prior to the election, 89 respondents completed and returned a questionnaire they had received through the mail.[30] The respondent's voting intention was assessed by means of the following scale:

I intend to vote *yes* on the Oregon Nuclear Safeguards Initiative — Ballot Measure No. 9.

likely_____:_____:_____:_____:_____:_____:_____unlikely

In addition, using procedures similar to those described for presidential elections, the questionnaire also assessed the following variables: attitudes and subjective norms with respect to voting *yes* on the proposition, beliefs that voting *yes* would lead to each of the 20 outcomes and that each of the 7 referents thought the respondent should vote *yes*, as well as evaluations of each outcome and motivations to comply with each referent.[31]

In the week following the election, follow-up telephone calls were made to all respondents in order to ascertain their actual voting behaviour. Of the 89 respondents, 39 voted *yes* (in favour of placing restrictions on nuclear power plant construction), 38 voted *no*, 4 did not vote in the referendum, 4 refused to reveal their votes, and 4 could not be contacted.

The results of the study provided strong support for our theory. Consistent with findings in other voting situations, a person's intention to vote *yes* on the nuclear safeguards proposition accurately predicted actual voting behaviour ($r = 0.89$). In turn, voting intentions were strongly related to attitudes ($r = 0.91$) and subjective norms with respect to voting *yes* on the proposition ($r = 0.72$). Although both components made significant contributions to the prediction of intentions, the attitude toward the act of voting *yes* was more important ($w_1 = 0.80$) than was the subjective norm ($w_2 = 0.17$); their multiple correlation with intentions was 0.92. Finally, both the attitude and the subjective norm were accurately predicted from considerations of their underlying cognitive structures. The correlation between the direct (semantic differential) and indirect (belief-based) measures of attitude toward voting *yes* was 0.74, and the corresponding correlation for the subjective norm was 0.79.

These findings demonstrate that the salient beliefs considered in this study ultimately determined how a person voted on the Oregon nuclear safeguards initiative. To gain insight into the considerations that led people to vote *yes* or *no* on the proposition, we divided the respondents into those who intended to and actually did vote *yes* and those who intended to and actually did cast a *no* vote. Looking first at the behavioural beliefs, it was found that the voters in our sample were very well informed about the issues involved in the referendum. They realized, among other things, that adoption of the proposition (i.e. a *yes* vote) would mean a change in Oregon's present system for regulating nuclear power and would require new tests of nuclear safety systems and a decision on a permanent nuclear waste disposal method. Furthermore, they also knew that passage of the proposition would give regulatory control of nuclear power to state legislators, would make nuclear power plant operators financially responsible for nuclear accidents, and would essentially give full compensation to victims of such accidents. Finally, although not directly part of the referendum proposal, media coverage and general public debate had made it clear to most voters that passage of the proposition would not ensure low-cost electricity and would probably lead to a court battle over the constitutionality of the proposition.

These findings again demonstrate that a concerned public is much better informed than it has usually been given credit for, and that irrespective of their eventual voting decisions, respondents recognized some of the advantages and disadvantages of the proposed measure.

The major factors that distinguished between *yes* and *no* voters were differences in beliefs concerning three basic issues: the state's economy, the energy crisis, and the safety of nuclear power plants. Some people believed that adoption of the proposed measure (a *yes* vote) would hurt economic development in Oregon and increase unemployment, while others were uncertain about its effects on economic development and believed it would *not* increase unemployment. The first group of respondents was likely to vote *no* while the second was likely to vote *yes*. There was also considerable disagreement about the effects of the proposition on the energy crisis in general. There were some who believed that passage of the proposal (a *yes* vote) would reduce funds for the development of alternative energy sources, would eliminate a needed energy source, and would ultimately lead to a future energy shortage. Others felt these outcomes were unlikely. Those in the former group were more likely to vote *no* on the proposition than those in the latter group. The final area of disagreement concerned the likelihood that passage of the proposition (a *yes* vote) would make new nuclear power plants safer than present ones, would set up realistic standards for nuclear waste management, would decrease danger from radioactive materials and waste, and would reduce the threat of nuclear sabotage. In general, if a person believed that voting *yes* would lead to the outcomes listed, he or she was very likely to cast a *yes* vote. On the other hand, people who felt that risk reductions were unlikely outcomes of voting *yes* typically cast their votes against the proposition.

In sum, respondents who believed that a *yes* vote would reduce nuclear hazard and increase safety *without* harming the economy or increasing the probability of an energy crisis supported the proposed measure (i.e. voted *yes*). In contrast, respondents who believed that a *yes* vote would harm the economy and increase the likelihood of a future energy shortage without reducing nuclear risk or increasing safety voted against the proposition.

Normative beliefs underlying subjective norms concerning a yes *vote.* Although of less importance, normative considerations were also found to contribute significantly to the voting decision. Although voters did not differ in their motivations to comply with their personal referents (family, friends, co-workers), there were significant differences in normative beliefs, and these differences were reflected in the voting decisions. Individuals were likely to vote *yes* if they believed that their personal referents thought they should vote *yes* and to vote *no* if they believed that these referents thought they should vote *no*.

General agreement was found with respect to the normative prescriptions of four public referents. Voters believed that the power companies, most government officials, and most nuclear experts thought they should vote *no* and believed that the environmentalists thought they should vote *yes*. Voters differed, however, in their motivations to comply with these referents. Predictably, those who were more motivated to comply with the power company, the government, and most nuclear experts (all of whom opposed the proposition) and were less motivated to comply with the environmentalists were more likely to cast a *no* vote.

To summarize briefly, when confronted with the decision to support or oppose the Oregon Nuclear Safeguards Referendum, voters considered the likely consequences of voting *yes* and, to a lesser extent, the normative prescriptions of important referents. Attitudes and subjective norms based on these beliefs led to accurate predictions of intentions, and these intentions were, in turn, highly related to actual voting behaviour. By examining the beliefs of supporters and opponents of the initiative, we were able to account for their differential voting behaviour. Although voters were in general agreement about the legislative and legal implications of the proposition, they disagreed markedly in their beliefs concerning the effects of a *yes* vote on the economy, on the energy shortage, and on nuclear safety.

SUMMARY AND CONCLUSION

Following a brief overview of the two major approaches to research on American voting behaviour, we identified some of their major shortcomings. In particular, we questioned the way in which attitudes have been conceptualized and measured, and we tried to show that the traditional approaches could not provide the basis for a general theory of voting behaviour. As an alternative, we proposed that a general theory of human behaviour—the theory of reasoned action—could usefully be applied to the prediction and understanding of behaviour in the political domain. We presented data from two studies which provided support for the theory with respect to a presidential election and a political referendum. These studies illustrate the way in which the same fundamental set of variables can be used to analyse voting behaviour in very different contexts. To be sure, comparing different types of elections uncovers some very important substantive differences. In an American presidential election, voting behaviour is strongly influenced by beliefs that voting for a given candidate will lead to the implementation of certain policies. Different considerations are involved in the case of voting in a referendum. Here the voter appears primarily concerned with the consequences of implementing the proposed policy. Even within a given type of voting situation, the content of the particular beliefs that are salient will vary from election to election. These beliefs will reflect the concerns of the public at the time of the election and the issues that are raised in the course of the campaign.

According to the theory of reasoned action, voting choice can ultimately be explained only by examining the content of the beliefs that are salient in a given election. Although these beliefs differ from election to election, they all represent beliefs about the act of casting a vote, be it a vote for a given candidate or a vote for or against a proposition. These beliefs provide the basis for the voter's attitude toward the vote and, in conjunction with the subjective norm, this attitude leads to the formation of a voting intention and eventually determines the voting choice. Although the explanation of voting behaviour differs substantively from one election to another, the basic psychological processes underlying the vote are identical.

Application of the theory of reasoned action results in a portrait of the voter that is very different from that often found in the literature. The data presented in this chapter provide evidence for a rather complimentary view of the American voter as a person who is informed about the candidates or issues involved in the election and who used this information to arrive at a voting decision in a reasonable manner.

ACKNOWLEDGEMENTS

Portions of this chapter are based in part on the following publications: Fishbein and Coombs (1974), Ajzen and Fishbein (1980, chs. 13 and 14), and Bowman and Fishbein (1978).

NOTES

1. Often a five-category scale is obtained by combining Independents who lean toward a given party with weak identifiers of that party.

2. It is unclear whether identification as an Independent is to be considered a long-term force or whether voters without a clear party identification are assumed to base their voting choices solely on the short-term effects of partisan attitudes.

3. In 1968 these questions were also asked about the third major candidate (George Wallace).

4. These latter responses are used to measure some of the remaining attitudes.

5. These responses are also used to construct the remaining attitude measures.

6. Theories of a similar nature have been proposed by Edwards (1954), Rosenberg (1956), and others (see Feather, 1959; Fishbein and Ajzen, 1975).

7. Note, however, that we would phrase our belief elicitation questions differently in order to avoid restricting the range of responses to *particular* things people like about parties or to particular things about a candidate that 'would make you want to *vote* for (against) him'.

8. Specifically, Stokes (1966, p.28) stated that 'the multiple correlation of the several predictors with partisan choice has varied in the range of 0.72 to 0.75 over the four presidential elections studied'.

9. Wallace voters were excluded from our analysis.

10. Like the Columbia school we concentrated our efforts on a single county. This analysis is based on a representative sample of voting-age residents in Champaign County, Illinois. Although Champaign-Urbana is a college community, our samples were drawn to represent different levels of various demographic characteristics (e.g. socio-economic status and education).

11. The numbers on the two scales indicate how responses were scored; they did not appear in the questionnaire. Note that, like evaluation, our measure of subjective probability is scaled from -3 to $+3$ and not from 0 to 1. This scoring system is essential for an expectancy-value model since it permits a disbelief that an object has a negative attribute to contribute positively to the overall attitude i.e. $(-2) \times (-2) = +4$.

12. The $b \times e$ products in columns 4 and 5 are not obtained by multiplying average belief strength and average attribute evaluation. Instead, these products are computed separately for each respondent and the numbers in columns 4 and 5 represent the average of these individual products. Thus, even where the candidates are, on the average, perceived to take different positions on an issue, the positions taken may, across respondents, have the same effects on the attitudes toward each candidate. For example, although Goldwater and Johnson were viewed as taking opposite stands on price supports for farm products, the average effect of these stands was to produce a slight increment in attitudes toward both candidates.

13. See note 10.

14. Note that the degree of accuracy was somewhat lower than in the 1964 presidential campaign. Evidence from other elections suggests that the lower correlations do not reflect differences in the level of the election. Instead, they may be due in part to the fact that six-place scales without a neutral point were used to measure beliefs and attitudes in the 1962 election.

15. For a complete discussion of accuracy on this election, See Colldeweih (1968).

16. The candidates' stands on the issues were ascertained by means of interviews with Wilson and with Springer's campaign manager.

17. It should also be noted that by considering only the percentage of respondents who changed their evaluation from one side of an issue to another, or who changed their beliefs about whether a candidate was positively or negatively associated with the issue, large changes in beliefs and evaluations may go undetected. For example, while the proportion of voters who believed Goldwater was in favour of 'our present foreign policy in Vietnam' remained relatively constant [5.8% at time 1 (t_1) and 3% at time 2 (t_2)], people were significantly more certain of his opposition at t_2 (mean belief at $t_1 = -2.09$; mean belief at $t_2 = -2.33$). This change in average belief strength is statistically significant. While shifts of this latter type are not as dramatic as changes from one side to the other, they are assigned equal importance in terms of their ultimate influence upon attitude according to the theory we have suggested. In a closely contested election, people may hold similar attitudes toward the two candidates, and changes in the

strength (but not the direction) of beliefs may ultimately decide the election.

18. One possible exception to this generalization occurs if one of the congressional candidates is a long-standing incumbent or a person who has attracted national recognition.

19. This change reflects the fact that, during the course of the campaign, it became known that Wilson had been a conscientious objector. Because we foresaw the possibility that this information could be made public we included the belief about being a veteran in the questionnaire.

20. For a more detailed discussion of the effects of the 1962 congressional election campaign in Champaign County, Illinois, see Colldeweih (1968).

21. In fact, the respondents' beliefs about the two parties differed significantly with respect to nine of the ten issues.

22. As in the reanalysis of the Michigan data reported above, Wallace voters were excluded from the analysis of the presidential election. Details of the attitude measurement procedure will be given below.

23. Actually, the concept of an overall subjective norm was not developed until 1975. In the 1966 election, separate normative beliefs with respect to four reference groups (friends, family, co-workers, and respondent's political party) were obtained, weighted by motivation to comply, and the sum of the products was used as an estimate of subjective norm.

24. The finding that the likelihood was always higher for Carter than for Ford is a function of the way in which the items were phrased. For example if 'increased federal spending for welfare programmes' had been reversed to read 'reduced federal spending for welfare programmes' voting for Carter would probably have been viewed as less likely to lead to this outcome than voting for Ford.

25. We can do this only because we have shown earlier that the total set of beliefs and outcome evaluations did in fact determine attitudes toward voting for the two candidates, that these attitudes were significant determinants of voting intentions, and that intentions were accurate predictors of voting choice.

26. These findings are clearly inconsistent with the argument that people bring their beliefs into line with their attitudes or intended behaviours.

27. In the present sample of respondents, differential attitudes toward voting for the candidates and differential subjective norms had a multiple correlation of 0.72 with differential intentions. Considering any one of the external variables in addition to attitudes and subjective norms raised the correlation to no more than 0.74.

28. Had the set of salient referents included the Democrats or Republican parties, we probably would have found that Democrats and Republicans differ in their motivations to comply with each party.

29. The utility of the theory of reasoned action was also demonstrated in a study of the 1974 general parliamentary election in Great Britain (see Fishbein, Thomas, and Jaccard, 1976). One interesting finding of that study was that the British voters' behavioural beliefs are in part concerned with the strategic implications of a vote for the formation of the government. In most other respects, the following description of the American voter is equally applicable to the electorate of Great Britain.

30. Questionnaires were mailed to 500 addressees randomly selected from the 1976 telephone directory for Portland, Oregon. Of the 500 questionnaires, 47 were returned by the post office as undeliverable, 12 were returned unanswered, and 92 were returned answered, but three of these had been completed after the respondent had voted in the election. Viewed within the context of comparable mail surveys with no special incentive for responding, this response rate of 18 percent is not atypical, although it is slightly lower than average (see, for example, Kanuk and Berenson, 1975).

31. In keeping with a conventional approach, a limited number of demographic

characteristics and more traditional attitudes were also assessed. Readers interested in the effects of those variables on voting decisions are directed to Bowman and Fishbein (1978).

REFERENCES

Ajzen, I. and Fishbein, M. (1977) 'Attitude-behavior relations: A theoretical analysis and review of empirical research', *Psychological Bulletin*, **84**, 888-918.
Ajzen, I. and Fishbein, M. (1980) *Understanding Attitudes and Predicting Social Behavior*, Prentice-Hall, Englewood Cliffs, N.J.
Berelson, B. (1952) 'Democratic theory and public opinion', *Public Opinion Quarterly*, **16**, 313-30.
Berelson, B., Lazarsfeld, P. F., and McPhee, W. N. (1954) *Voting: A Study of Opinion Formation in a Presidential Campaign*, University of Chicago Press, Chicago.
Bowman, C. H. and Fishbein, M. (1978) 'Understanding public reactions to energy proposals: An application of the Fishbein model', *Journal of Applied Social Psychology*, **8**, 319-40.
Boyd, R. W. (1972) 'Popular control of public policy: A normal vote analysis of the 1968 election', *American Political Science Review*, **66**, 429-49.
Campbell, A. (1964) 'Voters and elections: Past and present', *Journal of Politics*, **26**, 745-57.
Campbell, A., Converse, P. E., Miller, W. E., and Stokes, D. E. (1960) *The American Voter*, Wiley, New York.
Campbell, A., Gurin, G., and Miller, W. E. (1954) *The Voter Decides*, Row, Peterson, Evanston, Ill.
Colldeweih, J. H. (1968) 'The effects of mass madia consumption on accuracy of beliefs about the candidates in a local congressional election', Unpublished doctoral dissertation, University of Illinois.
Converse, P. E. (1974) 'Comment: The status of nonattitudes', *American Political Science Review*, **68**, 650-60.
Downs, A. (1957) *An Economic Theory of Democracy*, Harper & Row, New York.
Edwards, W. (1954) 'The theory of decision making', *Psychological Bulletin*, **51**, 380-417.
Feather, N. T. (1959) 'Subjective probability and decision under uncertainty', *Psychological Review*, **66**, 150-54.
Field, J. O. and Anderson, R. E. (1969) 'Ideology in the public's conceptualization of the 1964 election', *Public Opinion Quarterly*, **33**, 380-398.
Fishbein, M. (1963) 'An investigation of the relationships between beliefs about an object and the attitude toward that object', *Human Relations*, **16**, 233-40.
Fishbein, M. (1967) 'Attitude and the prediction of behavior', in *Readings in Attitude Theory and Measurement* (Ed. M. Fishbein), Wiley, new York, 477-492.
Fishbein, M. (1980) 'A theory of reasoned action: Some applications and implications', in *Nebraska Symposium on Motivation, 1978* (Eds. H. Howe and M. Page), University of Nebraska Press, Lincoln.
Fishbein, M. and Ajzen, I. (1975) *Belief, Attitude, Intention, and Behavior: An Introduction to Theory and Research*, Addison-Wesley, Reading, Mass.
Fishbein, M. and Coombs, F. S. (1974) 'Basis for decision: An attitudinal analysis of voting behavior', *Journal of Applied Social Psychology*, **4**, 95-124.
Fishbein, M., Thomas, K., and Jaccard, J. J. (1976) 'Voting behavior in Britain: An attitudinal analysis', *Occasional Papers in Survey Research*, **7**, SSRC Survey Unit, London, England.

Goldberg, A. S. (1969) 'Social determinism and rationality as bases of party identification', *American Political Science Review*, **63**, 5–25.

Kanuk, L. and Berenson, C. (1975) 'Mail surveys and response rates: A literature review', *Journal of Marketing Research*, **12**, 440–53.

Kelley, S., Jr and Mirer, T. W. (1974) 'The simple act of voting', *American Political Science Review*, **68**, 572–91.

Key, V. O., Jr (1966) *The Response Electorate*, Harvard University Press, Cambridge Mass.

Klecka, W. R. (1971) 'A comparative analysis of rational voting behavior: U.S., Canada, and Britain', Paper presented at the Annual Meeting of the North East Political Science Association, Saratoga Springs.

Lazarsfeld, P. F., Berelson, B., and Gaudet, H. (1944) *The People's Choice: How the Voter Makes Up His Mind in a Presidential Campaign*, Columbia University Press, New York.

Mulcahy, K. V. and Katz, R. S. (1976) *America Votes*, Prentice-Hall, Englewood Cliffs, N.J.

Page, B. I. and Brody, R. A. (1972) 'Policy voting and the electoral process: The Vietnam war issue', *American Political Science Review*, **66**, 979–1005.

Pierce, J. C. and Rose, D. D. (1974) 'Nonattitudes and American public opinion: The examination of a thesis', *American Political Science Review*, **68**, 626–49.

Pomper, G. M. (1972) 'From confusion to clarity: Issues and American voters, 1956–1968', *American Political Science Review*, **68**, 415–28.

RePass, D. E. (1971) 'Issue salience and party choice', *American Political Science Review*, **65**, 389–400.

Rosenberg, M. J. (1956) 'Cognitive structure and attitudinal affect', *Journal of Abnormal and Social Psychology*, **53**, 367–72.

Rossi, P. H. (1966) 'Trends in voting behavior research', in *Political Opinion and Electoral Behavior* (Eds. E. C. Dreyer and W. A. Rosenbaum), Wadsworth, California, 67–78.

Shapiro, M. J. (1969) 'Rational political man: A synthesis of economic and social psychological perspectives', *American Political Science Review*, **63**, 1106–19.

Stokes, D. E. (1966) 'Some dynamic elements of contests for the presidency', *American Political Science Review*, **60**, 19–28.

Sullivan, D. G. (1966) 'Psychological balance and reactions to the presidential nominations in 1960', in *The Electoral Process* (Eds. M. K. Jennings and L. H. Ziegler), Prentice-Hall, Englewood Cliffs, N.J.

Zajonc, R. B. (1954) 'Structure of the cognitive field', unpublished doctoral dissertation, University of Michigan.

Progress in Applied Social Psychology, Volume 1
Edited by G. M. Stephenson and J. M. Davis
© 1981 John Wiley & Sons, Ltd.

9

*Interpersonal Coordinations and Sociological Differences in the Construction of the Intellect**

GABRIEL MUGNY†, ANNE-NELLY PERRET-CLERMONT,
and WILLEM DOISE

Translated from the French by Alma Dorndorf, University of Bristol, and
Diane Mackie, University of Auckland.

INTRODUCTION

Psychosociological experimentation seeks to elucidate the many links which
exist between different levels of analysis of the same phenomenon: links which
connect functions at the individual level; functions which develop at the level
of interpersonal relations; implications of different category memberships and
the intergroup relations in which they are manifest; and the influence of the
most widely held values in a society (or ideology) (Doise, 1976; Doise, 1978).
In this chapter we shall try to distinguish the links which exist between several
of these levels in the sphere of the development of cognitive processes which is
usually studied at the intra-individual level (if only on account of the
individualistic nature of the tests). We will deal first of all with the interpersonal bases of the development of cognitive mechanisms in the child,
illustrating experimentally the chain of circular (or spiral) causality which

---

*Most of the research referred to in this chapter was carried out as part of a programme sponsored
by the Fonds National Suisse de la Recherche Scientifique, no. 1.343.0.76.
†Authors' address: Faculté de Psychologie et des Sciences de l'Education, Université de Genève,
1211 Genève 4, and Faculté des Lettres, Université de Neuchâtel, Switzerland.

connects individual cognitive functions with the interpersonal interactions in which the child participates. Secondly, we will examine this first connection as it relates to differences between social categories via a demonstration that although inter-individual elaboration of cognitive functions is manifest at different times in children from different social categories, the developmental pattern governing them is the same for all social categories.

TRENDS IN THE EXPERIMENTAL STUDY OF THE LINKS BETWEEN SOCIAL INTERACTION AND COGNITIVE DEVELOPMENT

There is no lack of theoretical and experimental work concentrating on the problem of the acquisition of intellectual notions, and essentially of operational notions such as conservation (for a review of this work, see especially Brainerd and Allen, 1971; Strauss, 1972; Brainerd, 1973; Inhelder, Sinclair, and Bovet, 1974). The notion of conflict (in its more general sense) is of importance here, although this concept has been operationalized in widely divergent ways. Thus, a first type of conflict emerges between hypotheses and observations of findings which may disconfirm them creating intellectual dissatisfaction (Lefebvre and Pinard, 1972; Inhelder, Sinclair, and Bovet, 1974). A second type of conflict, studied in depth by the Piagetian school (Inhelder, Sinclair, and Bovet, 1974), arises when different schemata are simultaneously brought into play but are contradictory. To these two very general types of conflicts can be added a third type which is of specific interest to us, i.e. 'socio-cognitive' conflict, where a change in the individual's strategy of responses has its explicit source in a conflict between his initial response and the response strategy of one or several others.

The paradigm commonly used in research into the role of social interaction in cognitive development consists of confronting the subjects, after having evaluated their cognitive levels in a pre-test, with other possible responses to a problem during an interaction phase, in order finally to evaluate any subsequent progress during one or more post-tests. The interaction situations can be categorized according to several criteria: according to the nature of the social situation (e.g. observation of a model or reciprocal interaction between subjects); according to the nature of the partner allocated to the child (e.g. peer or adult); and according to the cognitive level of the responses presented to the child. It can be noted at this point (Mugny, Lévy, and Doise, 1978) that although the interactions between children are studied more frequently than situations where one child merely observes another, the converse is true when one partner is an adult: although adults participate frequently in these experimental paradigms as models to be observed by the child, they do not interact with the child (in the sense of reciprocal exchanges). It is indeed interesting to note that until recently real interactions with the child have been ignored as far as the adult partner is concerned even when the latter plays an important part in the child's history. However, one can easily guess than an omission of this kind arises in reality from a very narrow conception of the pedagogic relationship as the social transmission of a cultural heritage, abstracted from all contexts of elaboration, exchange, and cooperation between child and adult.

A similar perspective can be perceived in the too-frequent usage of certain models of response, and in the no less systematic omission of other types of models. In effect, four types of cognitive models can be distinguished, which can be presented to the child in one form or another. Thus, we will use the term *progressive* model to indicate a model of response which is developmentally superior to that used by the child in the pre-test; a progressive model can be *correct* or *incorrect (intermediate)* when we are dealing with a method of resolving the problem which mediates between the subject's solution and the correct solution. A model is said to be *similar* when it is based on the same scheme as the child's responses; it may or may not be contradictory to that of the child. For example, two subjects may both incorrectly judge one stick to be 'longer' than another stick in a conservation of length test, but may either agree or differ as to which stick is 'longer'. Finally, we speak of a *regressive* model to indicate that the alternative model is at a cognitively inferior level in relation to the level of which the child is actually capable. Let us then examine the previous research concerning these various types of models (the work carried out by the present authors will not figure at this point of the analysis, since it will be discussed later).

(a) A condition utilizing a *progressive correct model* is integral to virtually all of the experimental designs used, and is in fact very often an essential condition of any demonstration. Moreover, in the majority of cases the effects of such a model appear to be positive. Indeed, children benefit from observation of a correct response model by a peer (J. P. Murray, 1974; Botvin and F. B. Murray, 1975; Cook and F. B. Murray, 1975), or by an adult (Beilin, 1965; Waghorn and Sullivan, 1970; Rosenthal and Zimmerman, 1972; Zimmerman and Lanaro, 1974) as much as they do from observation of a correct response by a peer with whom they interact reciprocally (F. B. Murray, 1972; Silverman and Stone, 1972; Silverman and Geiringer, 1973; Botvin and Murray, 1975; Miller and Brownell, 1975).

(b) Few experiments have studied the impact of a *progressive incorrect* (or *intermediate) model*, and, furthermore, their results have in general been inconsistent: J. P. Murray (1974) found that such a model has no beneficial effect, whereas Kuhn (1972), who predicted that children would benefit from such a model, found that they did progress in terms of cognitive development. There appears to exist in fact an optimal 'cognitive distance' between the cognitive level of the model and that of the child, outside of which the child will not progress.

(c) No progress is expected, nor has been found, in the experiments which examine a *similar model* (Kuhn, 1972; J. P. Murray, 1974). Let us note with regard to this point that the models used were in no way conflictual (as is *a priori* the case for the three other types of models) since those used proposed identical responses to those of the subject.

(d) The *regressive model* does not seem to have been studied to any great extent. It can certainly be implicitly assumed that the subject who serves in an experiment as partner to a child at an inferior cognitive level is able to observe reciprocally a regressive model in the latter. However, no progress has been reported by the researchers for the superior child in such cases (although there are indications that such progress may have occurred in F. B. Murray, 1972, and Kuhn, 1972), but the data presented do not allow for conclusions to be drawn. One could also cite the work on the 'tutoring effect' (Allen, 1976) in which, however, the progress is attributed to the *individual* cognitive activity and not to the interaction which is merely the pretext for its appearance. The case of Rosenthal and Zimmerman (1972) is a very special one: they appeal to the notion of the vicarious acquisition of learning in their study of cognitive development from a behavioural perspective, and from this perspective are able to predict a regression of level of performance for the conserving subjects who observed a non-conserving model. The confirmation of this hypothesis is based, however, on an operationalization which continues to present problems (Silverman and Geiringer, 1973; Mugny, Doise, and Perret-Clermont, 1975–76; Perret-Clermont, 1980), particularly the difficulty of differentiating merely compliant responses from some underlying change in cognition.

Taking into consideration all the points discussed and especially when we consider the predominance of correct models in the conditions designed to elicit progress, it seems justifiable for us to conclude that even when social interaction has been introduced as an agent of progress, it has been introduced as an integral part of an approach which postulates, at least implicitly, a process of imitation as a necessary condition for progress to occur.

It was partially in reaction, on the one hand, to a certain domination of individualistic concepts of development and, on the other hand, to a reduction of social interaction to imitation processes, that a new psychosociological perspective of cognitive development was developed. Such an approach was prompted by reflections initiated by the crisis in social psychology; as emphasized by Moscovici (1972, p.141), the task of a new social psychology is partly to develop from 'a bipolar psychology (ego-object) to a tripolar psychology (ego-other-object), a necessary change because it conforms more to reality'.

A PSYCHOSOCIOLOGICAL APPROACH
TO COGNITIVE DEVELOPMENT

The central idea of our approach is that cognitive development does not result simply from the interaction of the child with his surroundings in his non-social environment, but that this interaction is always mediated by, and therefore derives its meaning from, his social interactions with his peers and with the adults of his acquaintance. In this sense we are dealing with a socio-interactive approach, which is also a constructivist perspective, since we maintain (with Piaget) that cognition is not a copying process, a passive appropriation, but that it is indeed a construction by the active subject (or, to emphasize the psychosociological perspective, *inter*active subject), which therefore takes place during social interaction.

This perspective, which will now be developed further, is based on an important collection of experiments which for the most part involve a pre-test, test, and post-test procedure. Several experiments employ the same situation, which of course varies according to what we wish to demonstrate, but which is nevertheless based on the same paradigm. The principles of these paradigms are summarized in the Appendix. Four paradigms are presented: *Paradigm I*, spatial transformations experiments: *Paradigm II*, conservation of length experiments; *Paradigm III*, conservation of liquids experiments; and *Paradigm IV*, the 'cooperative game'. The reader is therefore invited to refer to the Appendix to obtain the information which is required for complete understanding of the experiments, but which is too cumbersome to repeat each time one of these paradigms is referred to.

Our basic hypothesis, namely that intra-individual cognitive structuring develops from inter-individual cognitive coordination, led us to develop those ideas both theoretically and experimentally in five directions.

1. The inter-individual elaboration of cognitive strategies initially precedes their intra-individual elaboration. It is evident when considered from a developmental perspective that individual cognitive levels evidenced in the post-test constitute the principal dependent variable; social interaction itself can in effect be considered as of only secondary importance as a dependent variable, even though it is precisely at the level of the inter-individual interaction that the independent variables are most frequently manipulated. However, several experiments have been directly concerned with the evaluation of collective performances. To the extent that the general hypothesis specifies that the inter-individual interactions are beneficial to cognitive development, it is legitimate to suppose that inter-individual coordinations would consequently be superior to intra-individual coordinations in one way or another. This is indicated by several experiments, employing the paradigm of spatial transformations (Doise, Mugny, and Perret-Clermont, 1975; Mugny and Doise, 1978), the paradigm of the conservation of length (Mugny, Giroud, and Doise, 1979), and the paradigm of the cooperative game (Doise and Mugny, 1975; Mugny and Doise, 1979).

The results achieved in an interaction situation cannot be equated with the performance of the better of the partners. This is an important point, and is one that was already being debated in the 1950s when the findings of authors such as Shaw (1932) or Taylor and Faust (1952) were contrasted with the findings of Macquart (1955) or Faust (1959). It is in fact from the first model of Lorge and Solomon (1955) that we have borrowed the formula enabling us to compare the collective performance with the performance of fictitious or nominal groups, randomly composed according to the probability that one of the partners could discover the correct solution by himself. Indeed, the collective performances exceed this possibility (Doise, Mugny, and Perret-Clermont, 1975).

Another method of demonstrating the cognitive originality of the collective solutions is offered in an experiment using the same paradigm of spatial transformations (Mugny and Doise, 1978). After the subjects had participated in a pre-test, they were divided into those subjects responding correctly or incorrectly; then two groups of two of these latter were formed. One of them was 'inferior' at this task and the other one was 'intermediate', but gave no correct responses whatsoever. Observation of the behaviour during the interaction shows that in the majority of cases these pairs were capable of completing at least one item correctly. It should be remembered that no subject was capable of making these coordinations by himself.

A series of experiments using the paradigm of the cooperative game (Doise and Mugny, 1975) elucidates further the conditions under which the performance of the group is superior to that of the individual. First, it appears that the group is superior essentially in the initial stages of the elaboration of a notion. On this task the group performance is superior to the individual performance when the subjects are about 7 to 8 years old, but is no longer superior when they are about 10 years old (this result is corroborated by some new research on this paradigm; Mugny and Doise, 1979). This indicates that cognitive progress is based on an initial interdependence of actions which decreases to the extent that the individual internalizes his interactively established coordinations.

In a similar way, communication has an essential part to play in the elaboration of a notion. When subjects in a group are prevented from communicating verbally, the collective performances are distinctly inferior to those evidenced in a free communication condition. Once again, this difference is no longer apparent with older subjects. Finally, a similar result is observed for the groups where a hierarchical structure is imposed: the performances of these groups are inferior to those of groups which have been able to interact more spontaneously.

2. Participation in a social interaction can produce individual progress in the partners in the post-tests. Our experimental paradigms, based for the most part on three observation sessions (pre-test, experimental situation, post-test), enable us to elucidate the problem of distinguishing between the quality of the collective performances from the consequent acquisition or learning during

social interaction. Since we maintained, in the work previously mentioned, that the collective performances can be superior to those previously achieved in the pre-test by the same subjects working alone, or by other individuals working alone in a 'control' situation, the comparative study of the individual performances in the pre-test and the post-test should enable us to evaluate the nature of the learning thus produced.

It should be made clear right away that the correlation between any progress evidenced in the post-tests and the progress (compared with performances in the pre-tests) demonstrated during social interaction cannot always be ascertained. In effect, the level attained during the collective activity does not enable us to directly predict the level which will be attained by those same individuals when they next work alone. The psychosociological characteristics of the collective situation and of the interactions which it produces can in fact prevent the child from developing cognitive coordinations at the same level as those on which the collective achievement is based. One can imagine social situations which are too constrained for progress to be even temporarily manifest (Lévy, Doise, and Mugny, in press), or in which such progress is not apparent even when the correct solution has been elaborated during the collective situation. This was the case in one of our experiments (Mugny and Doise, 1978) where the subjects with the correct response imposed it without discussion on the subjects with the incorrect response.

What is the nature of the learning observed when the comparison between the initial abilities of the subjects in the pre-test and the abilities they displayed in the post-test reveals that the individuals concerned have progressed? Are we dealing here with the mere imitation of a pattern of behaviour cumulatively added to the already established behavioural repertoire of the subject? Or can these new abilities be termed 'operations' in the sense that they result from a more general cognitive restructuring of which the individual has now become capable? Three of our experiments were particularly concerned with finding an answer to this question (Doise, Mugny, and Perret-Clermont, 1975; Perret-Clermont, 1980). These experiments relied on the notions of the conservation of liquids and the conservation of number. The analysis of behaviour in the post-tests enabled us to elaborate, in several ways, our theory that the progress achieved as a result of interaction does not result from the simple imitation of a behaviour pattern, but from a much more extensive restructuring of cognitions.

The results of post-tests which included tests of operations other than the one being examined in the experiment show that the subjects' progress tends to become generalized to other, related notions: progress in the elaboration of the notion of the conservation of liquids tends to be accompanied by the acquisition of the notion of the conservation of number, by similar progress in the test for the conservation of matter, and by eventual progress in the sphere of the conservation of length (Perret-Clermont, 1980).

Furthermore, a comparison between the behaviour of the subjects during the post-tests and the behaviour of their partners during the interaction emphasizes that any progress evidenced by the former cannot be solely ascribed to imitation. Thus, in an experiment examining the notion of the conservation of liquids, we recorded all the arguments that the conserving children (i.e. those who had mastered the notion in question) gave to their less advanced partners (non-conservers). We were able to observe that during the post-test, these former non-conservers did not limit themselves to repeating the arguments they had heard (all of which they do not always repeat), but that in half the cases they offered novel arguments which they had not been capable of offering in the pre-test. In the same way, it is not possible to explain, by reference to processes of imitation, the progress demonstrated by the subjects who had interacted with their less advanced companions but who did not at that time display the behaviour of which they were finally capable in the post-test. This is particularly the case for the children at the 'intermediate' level who interacted with the non-conserving or 'inferior' subjects in the conservation of number experiment (Perret-Clermont, 1980) and in a spatial transformation task (Mugny and Doise, 1978).

It would therefore seem that these different analyses combine to demonstrate that the learning acquired in social interaction arises from fundamental cognitive restructuring, and goes beyond imitative adoption of situation-specific and 'superficial' behaviour patterns.

Using a series of operational tests and a detailed analysis of the behaviour of non-conserving subjects during the pre-test has, on the other hand, enabled us to show that for each notion examined it is only at a particular stage in the development of this notion (or of the cognitive operations related to it) that the individual is likely to benefit from the social interactions taking place. Thus, we observed that only those children already capable of numerical conservation succeeded in progressing to the conservation of quantities, after having participated in a period of social interaction. In the same way, only those children who were capable of recognizing the equivalence of two series of elements by putting them in one-to-one correspondence and who knew how to 'count' (in the sense of declining the sequence of numbers) were likely to progress subsequent to the social interaction in the experimental stage. This means that in order for the predicted cognitive acquisition to take place, the child should already possess certain 'pre-requisites' which render him capable in some way of playing a significant part in an active confrontation and discussion with his partner. These results support a social constructivist interpretation of development; if the cognitive elaboration of a notion actually occurs in successive stages, each conditional upon the other, these stages would not, however, arise from the simple display of innate, individual potentialities, but from the elaboration of these abilities in previous social interactions. The appropriate model of development should therefore emerge as a cycle of reciprocal causality extending from the collective to the individual and vice versa.

3. In order to produce progress, social interaction should be conflictual. This was the post-hoc hypothesis put forward after an initial experiment on the effects of groups (Doise, Mugny, and Perret-Clermont, 1975, experiment 1). A clinical analysis of the interactions in this experiment seemed to show that the collective performances increased in superiority as a function of the amount of conflict between the partners' responses. It is towards a confirmation of this hypothesis that several new experiments have been directed, introducing situations and variables likely to manipulate directly the existence (or indeed the intensity) of a socio-cognitive conflict of this kind. One piece of research within the spatial transformation paradigm (Mugny and Doise, 1978) utilized an experimental design enabling both the opposition of subjects at different cognitive levels and the juxtaposition of subjects at the same level. The subjects were categorized during a pre-test into three cognitive levels; we shall call them inferior, intermediate, and superior or correct (see Appendix). During a collective interaction phase, two children worked side by side (and thus saw the problem from the same point of view) and had to reach agreement concerning a copy of the village they had to reproduce. In three experimental conditions an inferior subject worked either with a partner at the same inferior level or with a partner at an intermediate level, or with a partner giving the correct response. A final condition opposed two children at the same intermediate level. The results indicated that during the interaction the collective performances were all the better if one of the partners was at a higher level than the other. However, as we have already seen, even pairs in which a subject at an inferior level is opposed to one at an intermediate level succeed for the most part in solving at least one item correctly. None of the members was able to do this individually. Moreover, this experimental condition shows that the progress is produced as much by the inferior subjects as by the intermediate subjects, emphasizing the active constructivist nature of this cognitive elaboration. However, when the inferior subject is in partnership with a 'correct' subject, he does not progress, despite the conflict. It is clear therefore that although conflict is necessary for the production of progress, it is an insufficient condition. In this specific case the absence of progress seems to be attributable to the nature of the conflict: the superior subject, to whom the solution seemed obvious, actively imposed it on the inferior subject, whereas in the condition with the inferior and the intermediate subjects the latter, unsure of the solution, explained the dimensions which they found problematic in more detail to their partner. The inferior subjects were therefore given an opportunity to be active in the situation and to participate in the elaboration of the collective solution. Finally, when two subjects at the same inferior level worked together, no cognitive conflict was apparent and thus, as predicted, no resulting progress was found. It should be noted that the

condition with two intermediate subjects was more conflictual than was predicted, given that the two participants were at the same level. However, in this case the fluctuation characteristic of the behaviour of intermediate subjects is such that there is some probability of conflict occurring. Other observations (Perret-Clermont, 1980) confirm these different results in other respects.

Progress therefore only appears as a function of inter-individual conflict, where the partners' respective solutions are opposed. We have demonstrated the way in which differences between cognitive levels of partners sharing the same point of view allow a conflict of this nature to be introduced. We further showed (Doise and Mugny, 1979) how a similar conflict can be introduced between subjects at the same cognitive level simply by opposing their viewpoints in the same task of spatial transformations. After the pre-test only the inferior and intermediate subjects were retained for the experimental stage. As was the case in the preceding experiment, two subjects at the same cognitive level were asked to work together, but this time they were not placed in the same position (i.e. did not work side by side) but in positions opposite each other across the table on which the experimental equipment was arranged (so that the level of difficulty of the task was the same for both partners, cf. Figure 1, Item 2). This meant that if the two subjects both wished to use the same incorrect response strategy, a conflict of responses would result. A control condition allowed children to complete the same experimental items alone by successively changing their points of view, thus enabling us to see whether a subject working from successively opposed points of view also experiences conflict. The results show that this is not the case, since different responses may arise from the different points of view, without the child being aware of a contradiction. By contrast, as predicted, significant progress was observed in the collective condition. Thus, the hypothesis of the importance of socio-cognitive conflict in cognitive development is illustrated, in a new way, by a situation which moreover has the advantage of eliminating the modelling effect as an explanation. The two subjects were at the same cognitive level, and were confronted with each other's similar incorrect responses. As was shown in the preceding experiment, it is not necessarily the case that a correct model is also a beneficial model and, furthermore, progress can be achieved without a correct model being presented.

The same effect was observed again using the paradigm of the conservation of length (Mugny, Doise, and Perret-Clermont, 1975–76). In this paradigm a non-conserving child who states that one of the two sticks had grown longer after it had been displaced is told by the adult experimenter that one of the sticks is indeed longer than the other, but that it is in fact the other one, the one not chosen by the child. The child is therefore confronted once again with a model of response involving a similar strategy (the evaluation of length as a function of a topological strategy of over-estimation), but one leading to contradictory responses. As before, progress was once again produced without the presentation of a correct, or even a progressive, model. And, in effect, socio-cognitive conflict is the only explanation that can be proposed to account for these results.

Two other experiments made use of the same paradigm (Mugny, Giroud, and Doise, 1979). The first demonstrated that the occurrence of progress is linked to intensity of the conflict: the conflict was operationalized in this case by the experimenter's persistence in questioning the child, by means of the similar but contradictory incorrect response. Subjects who consistently opposed the contradictions of the experimenter progressed, until they reached the conservation stage. However, for some subjects a different social dynamic emerged, as it were, to 'counteract' the positive effect on the conflict. These subjects evidenced compliance by systematically accepting the contradictory responses of the adult and did not progress.

The second experiment demonstrates that conflicts also appear spontaneously between children placed on different sides of the table on which the sticks are lying (this ensures a probability for the occurrence of opposed centrations). Moreover, progress was observed in the groups where this conflict appeared but did not appear when the interaction was non-conflictual.

It may be noted that the effectiveness of a socio-cognitive conflict is dependent upon certain social norms, such as assigning larger objects to an adult, and smaller objects to a child. Thus, in an experiment also involving the notion of the conservation of length (in this case, unequal length, Doise, Dionnet, and Mugny, 1978) the experimenter systematically questioned the child's incorrect responses. In one condition the child had to assign one of two bracelets to the experimenter and the other one to himself, the instructions specifying that the bracelets had to fit their respective wrists. In a control condition the assignment was to one of the two cylinders, one small and the other large. One of the contradictions pointed out by the experimenter was between the judgement of length (incorrect for the non-conservers when the configurations were modified, cf. Appendix) and its, often correct, assignment. The results showed that most progress was produced when the socio-cognitive conflict has some direct general relevance, i.e. when the bracelets are attributed to the experimenter and to oneself, rather than to cylinders.

The results of all the experiments described here clarify the conditions under which an interpersonal interaction will produce cognitive progress. Essentially, the occurrence of a conflict of a social nature is necessary. A socio-cognitive conflict is created when the responses to the same situation differ among the members of a group. This conflict can appear between members at the same cognitive level, provided that the responses are given from different points of view or when the centrations issuing from the same reasoning are contradictory. The resolution of this conflict can lead to cognitive progress, notably as a function of the intensity and the social significance of this conflict, and providing that it is not resolved by prima facie social influence processes, such as compliance (Kelman, 1958) or even obedience. Socio-cognitive conflict therefore leads to collective and/or individual cognitive restructuring when these cognitive coordinations are directly involved in the establishment, maintenance, or reconstruction of an inter-individual relationship, which itself fits into a larger system of relationships and of social norms.

An inter-individual conflict of this kind involves processes at different levels. Thus, the subject is emotionally activated when he is involved in interpersonal conflict, because of the contradictory responses which are made salient to him. He becomes aware of the existence of different centrations, and must come to view his own centration relativistically. We have specified conditions which lead a group member to combine different centrations and to produce new coordinations. This occurs only if the subject is actively involved in the situation. The subject finds himself confronted with cognitive models which, although they do not offer him the correct response, suggest to him some relevant dimensions for a progressive elaboration of a cognitive mechanism new to him.

4. In our experiments we created social situations in which neither the collective nor the individual results could be explained in terms of the processes of imitation. Let us assume, at this point, that the processes involved in a socio-cognitive conflict could indeed be explained within a socio-constructivist perspective. How, then, can we interpret the results obtained with different types of models? First of all, it can be stated that even in the cases where the progress resulting from the imitation of a correct or intermediate model has been accounted for by the cognitive nature of the models on the one hand, and by the intervention of the imitation process on the other, it remains no less true that a conflict of a socio-cognitive nature was implicitly present, or at least could have been so. In our view, it is this inter-individual conflict which is the essential cause of these so-called modelling effects. Thus, we can state, for example, that it is not necessary for a correct model to be presented for progress to occur; this fact seems to have been largely proved. A system of similar but opposed responses can lead the subject to a new cognitive elaboration. Equally, one could assume therefore that even a regressive model would result in socio-cognitive conflict, which in turn would give rise to progress. One of our experiments illustrates just these ideas (Mugny, Lévy, and Doise, 1978).

In the spatial transformation task subjects at the inferior cognitive level were again questioned by the experimenter, who also constructed a copy of the village after the child had completed his. Three different conditions were used. The experimenter's solution was either correct, progressive but incorrect (intermediate), or regressive. Subjects confronted with either the correct or intermediate solution progressed. However, the regressive solution also produced as much progress as the intermediate model (and, it can be emphasized, not significantly less than a correct model!). There is no doubt that it is therefore the nature of the socio-cognitive conflict induced by the presentation of a model which determines whether progress will occur and not the mere presentation of something that can be copied.

Moreover, this last result has also been found in several other experiments. We have shown, for example (Carugati, Mugny *et al.*, 1978), that a socio-cognitive conflict can cause progress even in subjects for whom the task presents no difficulty at all. In an experiment using the spatial transformation task, the orientations of the base of the village to be copied and of those of the base on which it is to be reconstructed were arranged in such a way that the task is made easy for a child in position X (Figure 1, Item 1), but is made complex for the subjects in the other position (Y). Only one subject was in the easy position, while, according to the experimental conditions, either one or two children were placed in the complex position. As expected, the subjects in the position posing a cognitive problem progressed (it is significant that they were able to observe the correct placing of one or more houses at one point or another by the subject in the easy position); but the most striking result is that the subject in the easy position could also progress, despite the fact that for him the solution seemed obvious. In this case, also, only conflictual interaction can account for such progress, all the more so as this progress appeared especially when the subject in the easy position was opposed to two subjects in the difficult position—which increased the probability of conflict (see also Carugati, De Paolis, and Mugny, 1979).

5. As we have already observed, the respective status of the partners plays an important part in the resolution of socio-cognitive conflicts. One of the important variables at this level appears to be status differences between adults and children. Thus, current research (Lévy, Doise, and Mugny, in press) tries to show how different methods of questioning influence cognitive development in different ways, according to whether the source of conflict is a peer or an adult (Lévy, in preparation). Other data examining the concept of 'foreigner' (Jacq, in preparation) showed that subjects understood the reciprocal nature of this notion when Swiss children were confronted with a foreigner, but not when they had to work with a compatriot. Furthermore, foreign children tend to progress more in such a situation, probably because the very fact that they are outsiders renders them more sensitive to the 'injustice' or the 'inferiority' which arises from a failure to recognize the reciprocal nature of the notion. Finally, we may ask whether or not socio-economic or socio-cultural category membership is also likely to be a factor in the process of the elaboration of the cognitive abilities which we have examined in our experiments.

SOCIOLOGICAL AND PSYCHOSOCIOLOGICAL FACTORS

Although we had hypothesized even from our initial experiments that a relationship existed between the category membership of subjects and the intellectual abilities they developed, this aspect of the work had not been our main focus of attention. However, the compelling nature of some of our findings finally led us to analyse more systematically the effect of social category membership. A comparison of pre-test data obtained from two different schools showed that despite similarity in age and number of years at school, there were more non-conservers among children attending an inner-city school than among the children attending a school in the suburbs. This difference seemed to correlate with a difference in the social background of pupils attending these schools.

This led us to re-analyse the data from two previous experiments carried out in suburban schools (Perret-Clermont, 1980), in relation to the subjects' sociological background, as defined by the socio-professional category to which their parents belonged. This analysis of the two experiments (which deal with the conservation of liquid and of number) was therefore conducted *a posteriori*. Although it is unlikely that this analysis was directly influenced by our expectations (no hypothesis having been formulated as to the nature of this variable's influence and the social background of the subjects being at that time unknown to the experimenters), its validity is however limited. This is mainly due to the fact that since no analysis in terms of category membership had been envisaged, the number of subjects in the different social categories was not always large enough to ensure the validity of significant results. We felt justified, however, in accepting the results of the analysis as illustrative of possible effects and used them in the elaboration of hypotheses which were later largely confirmed experimentally.

As had generally been the case in other studies (particularly Coll Salvador, Coll Ventura, and Miras Mestres, 1974), pre-test results from these two experiments revealed differences in the percentage of children from different social backgrounds who attained the various cognitive levels — in a population of working-class children 40–50 percent were non-conservers, while in a population of similarly aged children whose parents were engaged in middle and higher management only 25 percent were non-conservers. What was of specific interest to us, however, was that the amount of progress evidenced by subjects subsequent to social interaction was such that in the post-test, the percentage of 'low' category children mastering more advanced strategies was similar to the percentage of the 'high' category subjects using them in the pre-test. This recovery seems all the more remarkable when one considers that the 'compensatory' intervention represented by the social interaction lasted no more than 15 minutes. Before investigating further the nature of these differences in the cognitive performances of subjects from different social backgrounds, it was necessary to see if these results could be replicated. In other research involving the conservation of liquid, care was taken to select comparable numbers of children from two dissimilar social backgrounds, one of which was termed a high category, where the parents were managers, directors, or have specialized technical skills, while the other was called a low category, where the parents were working class. All the subjects were the same age and had just started school (Perret-Clermont and Schubauer-Leoni, 1981).

All the children were given the same tests in the pre-test, which included a certain number of items from the classic test for conservation of liquid. This enabled us to divide them into two groups: the non-conservers (who had not mastered this notion of conservation at all), and the intermediate and conserving subjects who have either partly or fully elaborated the cognitive operations relevant to the invariance of quantity during successive decantings. Table 1 shows the number of subjects from the two social categories whose pre-test performance manifested the two operational levels just described. The difference in the levels achieved during the pre-test was highly significant, with the 'high' group being more advanced than the 'low' status group.

Table 1   Number of non-conserving (NC) and intermediate (I) or conserving subjects (C) in the pre-test, according to social category

Social category	Cognitive level	
	NC	I + C
Low	78	30
High	20	31

After this pre-test, all the available non-conserving subjects (70 percent of the original sample) took part in social interaction (either with a peer at the same or at a different level, or with an adult who acted as a model), so that any difference in the effect of these collective conditions could be seen. Finally, each subject was again individually post-tested two weeks later, allowing us to note in particular any subsequent change in the operational level demonstrated in the test for the conservation of liquid (see Table 2).

Table 2   Percentages of non-conserving (NC) and intermediate (I) or conserving subjects (C) in the pre-test, high social category, and in the post-test, low social category, all conditions and collective condition NC × C

Social category	Cognitive level	
	NC (%)	I + C (%)
Low, post-test (all conditions, $N = 58$)	53	47
Low, post-test (NC × C condition, $N = 12$)	33	67
High, pre-test ($N = 51$)	39	61

Once again the results confirmed our hypothesis that the post-test performance level of subjects from a 'low' social category would approach the level attained in the pre-test by 'high' category subjects, despite different experimental conditions, whereas the difference in pre-test performance of subjects in the two social categories had been highly significant, the difference between the performance of the 'low' category subjects in the post-test and that of the high category subjects in the pre-test was now only slight.

It should be remembered that these data relate to all 'low' category subjects, not all of whom participated in the collective interaction condition with a conserving peer—the condition more likely to effect progress. When only those subjects from the low category who participated in this condition were considered, it was clear that the percentage of them attaining the various levels at the post-test phase was similar to those attained by the children from the high category in the pre-test. A spatial-transformation experiment involving a similarly adequate number of subjects allowed us to confirm these results: it was clear that the cognitive levels attained in the post-test by children in the low category were equivalent to the levels of the children evidenced in the pre-test by the high category (Mugny and Doise, 1978).

Table 3   Number of subjects attaining inferior (NC), intermediate (PC), and superior (TC) cognitive levels in the pre-test, according to social category

Social category	Cognitive level		
	NC	PC	TC
Low	26	17	20
High	14	19	37

Table 3 shows the number of children in the two social categories evidencing the three possible cognitive levels (see Appendix) in the pre-test. The overall results revealed a distinct superiority in the performance of 'high' social category subjects. However, it should be noted that this difference varied as a function of age. Although for younger children (average age, 5 years and 9 months) no difference in performance was apparent, a marked difference emerged in older children (average age 7 years 9 months), at that very age at which the type of notion under examination is usually acquired.

After this pre-test, the NC and PC subjects participated in one of two experimental conditions. In the first, each individual child constructed a copy of a model village from one point of view and then had to decide whether his reconstruction (which he could change if he thought it necessary) was satisfactory after seeing both it and the model from a different point of view. A situation involving intra-individual conflict was thus possible. In the second condition, two children of the same cognitive level were placed in positions opposite each other to complete the same task (positions X and Y, see Figure 1, Item 2), so that a situation involving inter-individual conflict was possible. Table 4 shows the progress achieved by subjects of the two sociological categories in the two conditions. An inferior subject was deemed to have progressed if he used at least one intermediate or correct strategy, while an intermediate subject was deemed to have progressed if he used at least one correct strategy.

Table 4   Number of subjects progressing (+) or not (o) according to the experimental condition and the social category

Social category	Conflict:			
	Intra-individual		Inter-individual	
	o	+	o	+
Low	13	9	6	13
High	8	9	4	10

The results confirmed our psychosociological hypothesis that inter-individual conflict would induce more progress than a situation producing intra-individual conflict. However, when the data from the two sociological categories were considered separately, it was clear that the difference between the two experimental conditions was significant for only the low social category. In fact, an intra-individual conflict situation did not produce significantly less progress than an inter-individual conflict situation for the high category subjects. The results of these experiments seem to indicate that subjects from 'inferior' sociological environments benefit more from social interactions than from individual activity, whereas those from a 'superior' social environment benefit almost as much from the one as from the other. Although its distribution varied in relation to experimental condition, the similar proportion of progress evidenced by members of the two social categories led us to predict that the difference established in the pre-tests, although reduced, would remain (see Table 5).

Table 5   Number of subjects attaining inferior (NC), intermediate (PC), and superior (TC) cognitive levels in the post-test, according to social category

Social category	Cognitive level		
	NC	PC	TC
Low	14	13	36
High	9	9	52

Although the difference between the sociological categories was significant (Kendall's S test, $z = 1.955$ $p < 0.03$), it had considerably diminished in comparison with the pre-test where the value of z was 2.758 ($p < 0.003$). Firm conclusions were not possible however since this result could easily have been due to a 'ceiling effect'—while there was room for improvement in the performance of 43 of the 63 'low' category subjects, this was the case for only 33 of the 70 'high' category subjects.

We therefore compared the post-test performance of the children in the low sociological category with the pre-test performance of the children in the high category. Table 6 shows the percentage of members of the social categories attaining each cognitive level in the pre-test and in the post-test. The raw data are shown in Tables 3 and 5.

Table 6   Percentages of subjects attaining inferior (NC), intermediate (PC), and superior (TC) cognitive levels, according to social category

Social category	Cognitive level		
	NC (%)	PC (%)	TC (%)
Low, pre-test	41	27	32
High, pre-test	20	27	53
Low, post-test	22	21	57
High, post-test	13	13	74

The data fully confirmed the prediction, inferred from the previous experiments, that such a simple exercise (participation in an experimental activity) would result in the children from an 'inferior' social group responding at the same cognitive level in a post-test as had children from a 'superior' social group in a pre-test. Even if we limit ourselves for the moment to a consideration of one specific notion, as has been the case in our experiments, it is obvious that the notion of a social 'deficit' in cognition is no longer straightforward.

Several questions remain unanswered, however. As already noted, our results were necessarily inconclusive because of the large number in the 'high' category who could not 'improve' their already correct performances. Moreover, the proportion of subjects participating in the inter-individual experimental condition, which produced the most progress, was very small. However, it is essentially a matter of ascertaining first whether members of an 'inferior' social group do in fact benefit more from a situation involving inter-individual activity than they do from individual activity, and secondly, whether members of a 'superior' social group do in fact benefit as much from individual as from inter-individual activity. If this proves to be the case, the validity, or at least the generality, of our psychosociological interpretation of cognitive development must be questioned, since it would seem to be applicable only to disadvantaged socio-economic categories where social interactions function to compensate for a 'deficit' (the inability of these children to develop their cognitive mechanisms autonomously). Such arguments (previously discussed by Perret-Clermont, 1980) are invalidated by the results of a final experiment to be presented in detail here, which attempted to deal with the remaining contentious issues (Mugny and Doise, 1979).

The experiment was within the cooperative game paradigm but involved one modification not detailed in the Appendix. All measurements were obtained from the game with the three pulleys but, in contrast to an earlier series of experiments (Doise and Mugny, 1975), the pulleys were set up during the individual pre- and post-tests so that they jammed automatically whenever they were not being directly manipulated. This meant that a subject could not move the marker towards him simply by pulling on one pulley: this could only be done if he first 'let out' either one or both other pulleys and then pulled on his (otherwise of course the pulleys jammed, as often occurred if a subject did not coordinate his actions). This automatic jamming did not occur during the experimental phases.

While the pre- and post-test involved subjects manipulating the equipment individually, it was the collective experimental conditions which were of obvious importance, given our previous results. This phase comprised an individual as well as two collective conditions, the results of which were combined as they produced the same effects.

In the first collective condition, two subjects had to work together to move the marker along the circuit. One of the children worked using one pulley, while the other child (who had been instructed not to 'let out' any of his pulleys) manipulated the other two pulleys. In the second collective condition, three subjects had to work together. In these conditions the subjects working together were class-mates of the same age and sex. The experimental phase took place one week after the pre-test, and one week before the post-test.

The children tested came from two very dissimilar social environments within the one southern European country. Ninety-five came from a working-class, immigrant urban school (who are termed the 'low' category) and 95 others were pupils at a private school and came from well-to-do families. The extension of the subject population to include another age group allowed more detailed analysis than had been previously possible.

In the experimental phase, 23 children from each social group were assigned to the individual condition (8 from each age group, except 7–8 years, where there were 7 subjects), and 72 children to the collective condition (for each age group, 6 groups of two and 4 groups of three children). In contrast to the previous experiments, therefore, a large number of subjects were in the collective condition.

Table 7 shows the median scores for the subjects in the pre-test. It is clear that the performances improved as a function of age. However, the rate of this improvement is not the same for the two social groups. Although the performances

Table 7   Median performance scores according to age and social category in the pre-test

Age	Social category	
	Low	High
5–6 years	–22.5	–18.5
6–7 years	–8.5	+7.0
7–8 years	+9.0	+14.0

were at the same level in the 5–6 year age range, they improved more rapidly in the high social category who achieved a level of performance at 6–7 years of age which subjects from the 'low' social group did not achieve until 7–8 years of age. This confirmed that a considerable number of differences between social groups exist during the initial stages of the elaboration of cognitive notions. It must be emphasized that such differences only became significant at that developmental period when the notions or coordinations under examination are usually being spontaneously elaborated, which in this case is at 6–7 years of age.

The results of the post-tests, as shown in Table 8, allowed us to see whether the interactions in which 72 of the 95 children in each group had participated had led to any significant modification in this situation.

Table 8   Median performance scores according to age and social category in the post-test

Age	Social category	
	Low	High
5–6 years	–33.0	0.0
6–7 years	+23.0	+17.0
7–8 years	+23.0	+28.0

As can be seen, important improvements in performance have occurred within both social groups and in fact the overall difference between the two social groups is no longer significant. (According to the Mann–Whitney U test, the value of z is 1.229 in the post-test ($p < 0.12$), whereas in the pre-test it was 1.934 ($p < 0.03$).) However, a comparison of the individual age groups reveals a significant difference at the 5–6 year old level (where the 'high' category subjects progress while the 'low' category subjects do not) which starts to disappear from the 6–7 year old level on. This shows therefore that not only are differences in performance as a function of social group membership only significant in the initial stage of the elaboration of a notion, but that such differences also actually become less clearly defined during the course of development. No potential intellectual differences could therefore be said to exist between the members of social categories. If such differences do appear, they may merely be the result of differences between social groups in the amount of and/or the significance accorded to social interactions between children, or between children and adults, with regard to a given notion.

Even though our work is limited in that it deals with only a single notion, rather than several at once, it obviously calls into question the nature of social category differences so frequently observed and alluded to. We will return to this point in the final discussion.

We must look first, however, at the differential effect of the individual and collective conditions at the different age levels in the two social groups. Table 9 shows the average progress made in each condition. It appears that the inter-individual activity condition is not automatically effective but that its effectiveness is essentially a function of the stage of development of the notion being examined.

Table 9   Median progress between the pre-test and the post-test according to age, social category, and experimental condition

Social category		Condition	
		Individual	Collective
Low	5–6 years	−8.5	−2.3
	6–7 years	−2.0	+ 35.3
	7–8 years	+ 24.0	+ 19.8
High	5–6 years	−2.5	+ 10.1
	6–7 years	+ 8.5	+ 14.6
	7–8 years	+ 24.0	+ 8.6

At an initial pre-elaboration stage in the development of a notion neither individual nor inter-individual activity enables the child to progress, which seems to confirm our belief that there are necessary cognitive prerequisites for progress to occur subsequent to interaction, as discussed above. Thus, neither condition benefited children of 5–6 years of age in the 'low' category (and one can conjecture that results would be similar for children of 4–5 years in the 'high' social group). At a second stage, which apparently corresponds to the phase at which the cognitive mechanisms necessary for successful completion of this task are first being elaborated, social interaction alone induces progress, whereas individual activity is not capable of doing so. This is apparent in the results of 6–7-year-old children in the 'low' social group and in children of 5–6 years of age in the 'high' social group. Finally, at a third stage, both the individual and the collective activity conditions enable the child to progress, as can be seen in the results of the 7–8-year-old children in the 'low' social group and of the children from 6–7 years of age in the 'high' social group.

The experiment thus confirmed the hypotheses developed from our socio-psychological perspective: social interaction appears to be an essential condition of progress at the initial stage of the elaboration of a notion and, furthermore, it is from this social interdependence that autonomy in development is progressively acquired. Finally, it follows from the data that this progressive acquisition of autonomy, which for both groups is grounded in initial interdependence, develops with a time-lag (of about one year in this case) between the high social group and the low social group. Even though these differences may be obliterated to some extent when the potentialities of the groups are developed, it still remains the case that the social class membership influences the rate of cognitive acquisition; while the experiment enables us to 'de-mystify' the nature of certain social differences, it does not however eliminate the effects of discrimination which occur in other spheres of social organization. Despite this 'de-mystification', we are still unable to account for these differences, and further research on this problem is necessary.

We can now try to draw some conclusions about the interaction between individual cognitive levels, inter-individual processes, and social category membership.

CONCLUSION

As stated in the Introduction, several levels of analysis of the same 'phenomenon' are possible. The research just described suggests that the study of cognitive functions (which at first glance appear to be intra-individual phenomena) cannot be examined independently of analysis at other levels. If this is true, even the notion of the cognizing individual ('le sujet épistémique' in Piagetian terms) becomes an abstraction — an abstraction both from the inter-individual relations which underly the formation of cognitive mechanisms, and from the more general social conditions prevailing in the society in which both individual development and inter-individual relations evolve.

We have in fact demonstrated experimentally that cognitive functions are initially elaborated in inter-individual relationships before being 'internalized' by each individual. The individual, as an autonomous, cognizing subject, does therefore not exist, a priori, before any development has taken place. Paradoxically, he is the product of a social interdependence which creates and ensures his subsequent autonomy. Since explanations at the intra-individual level of analysis do not embrace inter-individual social relations, any conception of cognition as a purely intra-individual phenomena is based on an abstraction.

Just such an abstraction is typical in work on cognitive development and provides the underpinning for traditional methodology, on which much of the research which reports the superiority of children from certain social categories and the inferiority of children from other relies. It is not a matter here of becoming embroiled in the debate concerning the causality of, or the relative contribution of heredity and environment to such differences; our paradigms do not provide, and make no claim to provide, any answer to this question. We proceeded from the simple truth that when the results of only the individual pre-testing are considered, there is ample evidence for a correlation between performance and social category memberships, with members of 'high' social groups performing better than members of 'low' social categories. The originality of our paradigms lay, however, in the introduction of a phase which allowed us to reintegrate the individual with the social context of his development. To achieve this, children from the various social categories were put in a socio-psychological context of development involving social and, more specifically, inter-individual interaction. We were able to demonstrate experimentally the existence of those very processes that our theoretical model suggested would operate in the child. This proper reintegration of the child with the context inducing development, led to a general reduction in, or even the almost complete disappearance of, the cognitive differences between children from different social categories. The potentialities of both groups would thus seem to be comparable, even if their rate of development, particularly at the initial stages of a notion's elaboration, can differ. It follows from these observations that the majority of the research dealing with intellectual differences between social groups and, in particular, that grounded in traditional test methodology, is based on an abstraction which distorts the object being studied. In effect, these tests scientifically create and justify social discrimination; in that it uncovers such inadequacies by demonstrating the interaction between various levels of analysis, social psychological research remains an invaluable tool.

APPENDIX: SOME EXPERIMENTAL PARADIGMS

Paradigm I: The Spatial Transformation Task

In every phase of these experiments, 5–8-year-old subjects construct a copy of a model village comprising three or four houses on a base. Every base has the same clearly visible mark as a point of reference for the orientation of the base, presented in the form of a lake, a mountain, or a pool (see Figure 1). The subjects are placed in certain positions from which they may not move, and thus see their own base and the experimenter's village from only one perspective. The items are either simple (Item 1 in Figure 1 is a simple item for a subject in position X, requiring only a simple rotation of 90 degrees for successful reproduction of the village), or complex (the same configuration is a complex item for a subject in position Y, since, in addition to the visual rotation of 90 degrees, a reversal of the left/right relationship and the front/back relationship is required for the village to be correctly reproduced). Item 2 in

Plan of the experimental situation

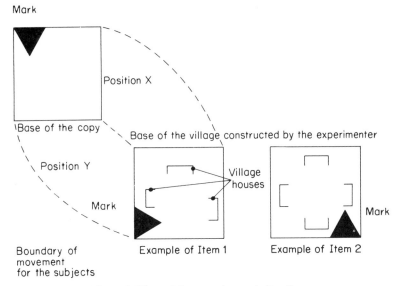

Figure 1. Plan of the experimental situation

Figure 1 confronts subjects in positions X and Y with the same degree of difficulty. The subject's cognitive levels are ascertained from his pre-test performance on two complex items (Item 1, position Y, for example). In general, only those children whose pre-test performances on both items evidence the same cognitive level are retained as experimental subjects.

Three levels are distinguished: subjects categorized as 'inferior' (NC or non-compensating) simply rotate the configuration of houses through 90 degrees, thus making no compensation for the different orientations of the two bases; intermediate subjects (PC or partially-compensating) successfully reverse either the left/right or the near/far dimension but cannot compensate for both; and subjects categorized as 'superior' (TC or totally-compensating) reverse both dimensions and produce a correct model of the village. During the experimental phase and depending on the experimental condition, subjects work either individually or in groups of two or three, and are placed either side by side (i.e. both in position Y) or opposite one another (e.g. one in X, one in Y). Evaluation of individual test performance is based on the better of two items, and progress is deemed to occur when a more advanced strategy (on the NC–PC–TC scale) is used.

Paradigm II: The Conservation of Length

The two different types of experiment reported here both comprised individual pre- and post-testing, with an intervening experimental phase. In the individual tests subjects are tested on the notions of both equality and inequality of length.

(a) *The conservation of equal lengths.* Two sticks of equal length are placed parallel to each other (⸺⸺⸺): children of 5–8 years of age confirm the equality of the lengths of the two sticks. When one of the two sticks is displaced so that the sticks are no longer co-terminous, the responses differ (⸺⸺⸺) : non-conservers judge one of the sticks to be longer than the other, focusing on one of the displaced end-points; intermediate subjects either agree that the sticks are equally long but cannot say why, or are undecided; conservers judge the two sticks to be equally long independently of their spatial configuration, and can produce arguments to support their judgement.

In the collective situations, a child and an experimenter (or two children) sit at different sides of the table on which the sticks are placed. When the subject claims that one displaced stick is longer, the experimenter points to the other end of the other ruler and says 'I think this one is longer, you see, it goes further there'. (This response is of course also incorrect but is symmetrically opposed to the subject's.) If the subject complies, the experimenter reminds him of his previous response.

(b) *The conservation of unequal lengths.* The procedure and the category evaluation methods are similar to those for the conservation of equal lengths. Two bracelets of unequal length are placed parallel to each other (⸺⸺⸺): all the children confirm the inequality of the lengths. Then, the longer bracelet is folded so the two bracelets are co-terminous (⌒): non-conservers then judge both bracelets to be equal while intermediate subjects frequently go on judging them to be unequal (but give the incorrect response to the next item). Finally, the longer bracelet is folded again so that its extremities are contained by those of the shortest bracelet (〰). Both non-conservers and intermediate subjects now judge the longer bracelet to be the one which is actually the shorter as they consider only the relative positions of the ends of the bracelets. The conservers conserve the inequality of the lengths correctly, independently of the configurations they perceive, and can argue to support their judgement.

Subjects participated in an experimental stage between the pre-test and the post-test(s) in which they had to judge unequal lengths. In general the collective experimental condition opposed the subject and an adult collaborator who, after the child had given his answer, responded to each question according to a pre-established programme of responses intended for the most part to contradict the child's responses.

Paradigm III: The Conservation of Liquids

This paradigm is adapted from the test used by Piaget and Szeminska (1941) for the acquisition of the notion of the conservation of quantities of liquids. The experiment has three phases, in the first of which children (6–7 years old) are individually pre-tested. Each subject has to pour an equal amount of juice into two different shaped glasses so that both he and the experimenter have the same amount to drink. The child's operational level for the elaboration of the notion of the conservation of the liquid, as deduced from his performance, is evaluated according to the criteria defining three specific levels: non-conservers (NC) do not comprehend the notion of conservation and assert that the initial quantity of liquid increases or decreases according to the size of the glass into which it is poured; conservers (C) comprehend this notion and are therefore able to justify the invariance of the quantity judged; and intermediate subjects (I) who oscillate between both these cognitive levels. The level of the subjects in acquiring other operational notions (e.g. matter, number) is evaluated in the same way.

About one week later, in the collective experimental conditions, the children are organized in groups of two or three to share the juice out among themselves using different shaped glasses. The composition of the groups of two or three children at the same or differing cognitive levels differs according to experimental conditions. The instructions given to the subjects specify that they can only drink the contents of their different shaped glasses when they reach agreement that the distribution of the juice is 'equitable' and when they agree that everyone has the same amount to drink. When the partners are at different cognitive levels this produces a certain amount of conflict between the children as the non-conservers justify the amounts they have distributed by reference to the equal 'heights' of the juice in the glasses while the conservers claim that their distributions are fair because they have taken the unequal shapes of containers into account.

About ten days after this, each subject is again individually post-tested to see if any improvement in the level of cognitive development of notions of conservation has taken place. (A second post-test may take place some time later.)

Paradigm IV: The Cooperative Game

The principle of the cooperative game is very simple: a moving part holding a pencil is attached to three pulleys by means of which one or several subjects can move this part along a given path (see Figure 2) with the pencil making the precise course it follows.

Plan of the co-operative game

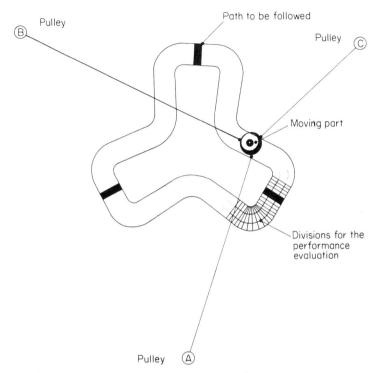

Figure 2. Plan of the cooperative game

This game can be played alone (the subject having to walk around the game in order to manipulate the pulleys), or by two or three children. Individual tests, like collective performances, are evaluated in the following manner. The path to be followed is divided breadth-wise into three equal thirds, and length-wise into units, the circuit being divided into 44, 60, or 180 units, as the case may be. When the pencil mark is wholly within the middle third, this unit is considered to be a successful coordination (score +1); when the mark encroaches on or is in either of the outside thirds the unit is considered as causing average difficulty in coordination (score 0); when the pencil mark is outside the path altogether, the unit is considered as presenting a serious difficulty (score –1). Progress is evaluated in terms of a comparison of pre- and post-test scores.

REFERENCES

Allen, V. L. (1976) *Children as Teachers*, Academic Press, New York.

Beilin, M. (1965) 'Learning and operational convergence in logical thought development', *Journal of Experimental Child Psychology*, **2**, 317-39.

Botvin, G. J. and Murray, F. B. (1975) 'The efficacy of peer modelling and social conflict in the acquisition of conservation', *Child Development*, **46**, 3, 796-99.

Brainerd, C. J. (1973) 'Neo-piagetian training experiments revisited: Is there any support for the cognitive-developmental stage hypothesis?', *Cognition*, **2**, 3, 349-70.

Brainerd, C. J. and Allen, T. W. (1971) 'Experimental inductions of the conservation of "first-order" quantitative invariants', *Psychological Bulletin*, **75**, 2, 128-44.

Carugati, F., De Paolis, P., and Mugny, G. (1979) 'A Paradigm for the study of social interactions in cognitive development', *Italian Journal of Psychology*, **7**, 147-55.

Carugati, F., Mugny, G. *et al.* (1978) 'Psicologia sociale dello sviluppo cognitivo: imitazione di modelli o conflitto socio-cognitivo?', *Giornale Italiano di Psicologia*, **5**, 2, 323-52.

Coll Salvadore, C., Coll Ventura, C., and Miras Mestres, M. (1974) 'Genesis de la clasificacion y medio socioeconomico; Genesis de la seriacion medios socio-economicos', *Anuario de Psicologia*, **10**, 53-99.

Cook, H. and Murray, F. B. (1975] 'The acquisition of conservation through the observation of conserving models', roneo.

Doise, W. (1976) *L'articulation psycho-sociologique et les Relations Entre Groups*, De Boeck, Bruxelles.

Doise, W. (1978) 'Images, représentations idéologiques et expérimentation psychosociologique', *Information sur les Sciences Sociales*, **17**, 41-69.

Doise, W., Dionnet, S., and Mugny, G. (1978) 'Conflit socio-cognitif, marquage social et developpement cognitif', *Cahiers de Psychologie*, **21**, 4.

Doise, W. and Mugny, G. (1975) 'Recherches socio-génétiques sur la coordination d'actions interdépendantes', *Revue Suisse de Psychologie*, **34**, 160-74.

Doise, W. and Mugny, G. (1979) 'Individual and collective conflicts of centrations in cognitive development', *European Journal of Social Psychology*, **9**, 105-8.

Doise, W., Mugny, G., and Perret-Clermont, A. N. (1975) 'Social interaction and the development of cognitive operations', *European Journal of Social Psychology*, **5**, 3, 367-83.

Faust, W. L. (1959) 'Group versus individual problem solving', *Journal of Abnormal and Social Psychology*, **59**, 68-72.

Inhelder, B., Sinclair, H., and Bovet, M. (1974) *Apprentissage et Structure de la Connaissance*, P.U.F., Paris.

Jacq, V. (1980) Développement cognitif et élaboration d'une représentation sociale dans différentes situations d'interaction. Doctoral dissertation (in preparation).

Kelman, H. C. (1958) 'Compliance identification and internalization, three processes of attitude change', *Journal of Conflict Resolution*, **2**, 51-60.

Kuhn, D. (1972) 'Mechanisms of change in the development of cognitive structures', *Child Development*, **43**, 833-44.

Lefebvre, M. and Pinard, D. (1972) 'Apprentissage de la conservation des quantités par une méthode de conflit cognitif', *Revue Canadienne des Sciences du Comportement*, **4**, 1-12.

Lévy, M. (1980) 'Necessité du dépassement du conflit socio-cognitif et développement cognitif', Doctoral dissertation (in preparation).

Lévy, M., Doise, W., and Mugny, G. (1980) 'Remise en question, modèle régressif et progrès cognitif' (to be published).

Lorge, I. and Solomon, H. (1955) 'Two models of group behaviour in the solution of Eureka-type problems', *Psychometrika*, **20**, 139-48.

Macquart, D. (1955) 'Group problem solving', *Journal of Social Psychology*, **41**, 103-13.

Miller, S. A. and Brownell, C. A. (1975) 'Peers, persuasion and Piaget: Dyadic interaction between conservers and non conservers', *Child Development*, **46**, 992-97.

Moscovici, S. (1972) *Introduction à la Psychologie Sociale*, vol. 1, Larousse, Paris.

Mugny, G. and Doise, W. (1978) 'Socio-cognitive conflict and structuration of individual and collective performances', *European Journal of Social Psychology*, **8**, 2, 181-92.

Mugny, G. and Doise, W. (1978) 'Factores sociologicos y psicosociologicos en el desarollo cognitivo', *Anuario de Psicologia Social*, **18**, 1, 21-40.

Mugny, G. and Doise, W. (1979) 'Factores sociológicos y psicosociológicos en el desarollo cognitivo: una nueva ilustración experimental', *Anuario de Psicologia*, **21**, 5-25.

Mugny, G., Doise, W., and Perret-Clermont, A. N. (1975-76) 'Conflit de centrations et progrès cognitif', *Bulletin de Psychologie*, **29**, 321, 199-204.

Mugny, G., Giroud, J. C., and Doise, W. (1973) 'Conflit de centrations et progrès cognitif, II: nouvelles illustrations expérimentales': *Bulletin de Psychologie*, **32**, 978-85.

Mugny, G., Lévy, M., and Doise, W. (1978) 'Conflit socio-cognitif et développement cognitif: L'effet de la présentation par un adulte de modèles "progressifs" et de modèles "régressifs" dans une épreuve de représentation spatiale', *Revue Suisse de Psychologie*, **37**, 1, 22-43.

Murray, F. B. (1972) 'Acquisition of conservation through social interaction', *Developmental Psychology*, **6**, 1-6.

Murray, J. P. (1974) 'Social learning and cognitive development: Modelling effects on children's understanding of conservation', *British Journal of Psychology*, **65**, 1, 151-60.

Perret-Clermont, A. N. (1980) *Social Interaction and Cognitive Development in Children*, Academic Press.

Perret-Clermont, A-N. and Schubauer-Leoni, M-L. (1981) 'Conflict and cooperation as opportunities for learning', In: P. Robinson (ed.), *Communication in development*, Academic Press, London.

Piaget, J., Inhelder, B., and Szeminska, A. (1948) *La Géometrie Spontanée chez l'Enfant*, P.U.F., Paris.

Piaget, J. and Szeminska, A. (1941) *La Genèse du Nombre*, Delachaux et Niestlé, Neuchatel, Paris.

Rosenthal, T. L. and Zimmerman, B. J. (1972) 'Modelling by exemplification and instruction in training conservation', *Developmental Psychology*, **6**, 392-401.

Shaw, M. E. (1932) 'A comparison of individuals and small groups in the rational solution of complex problems', *American Journal of Psychology*, **44**, 491-504.

Silverman, I. W. and Geiringer, E. (1973) 'Dyadic interaction and conservation induction: A test of Piaget's equilibration model', *Child Development*, **44**, 815-20.

Silverman, I. W. and Stone, J. (1972) 'Modifying cognitive functioning through participation in a problem-solving group', *Journal of Educational Psychology*, **63**, 603-8.

Strauss, S. (1972) 'Inducing cognitive development and learning: A review of short-term training experiments I. The organismic developmental approach', *Cognition*, **1**, 4, 329-57.

Strauss, S. (1974) 'A reply to Brainerd', *Cognition*, **3**, 2, 155-85.

Taylor, D. W. and Faust, W. L. (1952) 'Twenty questions: Efficiency in problem solving as a function of size of group', *Journal of Experimental Psychology*, **44**, 360-68.

Waghorn, L. and Sullivan, E. (1970) 'The exploration of transition rules in conservation of quantity (substance) using film mediated modelling', *Acta Psychologica*, **32**, 75-80.

Zimmerman, B. J. and Lanaro, P. (1974) 'Acquiring and retaining conservation of length through modelling and reversibility cues', *Merill-Palmer Quarterly of Behavior and Development*, **20**, 3, 145-61.

Progress in Applied Social Psychology, Volume 1
Edited by G. M. Stephenson and J. H. Davis
© 1981 John Wiley & Sons, Ltd.

10

An Experimental Analysis of Teaching by Telephone: Theoretical and Practical Implications for Social Psychology

D. R. RUTTER

Social Psychology Research Unit, University of Kent, Canterbury, England

and

B. ROBINSON

Faculty of Educational Studies,
The Open University, Walton Hall, Milton Keynes, England

INTRODUCTION

Applied social psychology has two main aims. The first, which perhaps most closely identifies it among social scientists, is practical: it tries to help solve and prevent a range of problems in everyday life. The second is theoretical. Traditionally, experimental social psychologists worked in the laboratory, where they set up theories, derived hypotheses, and tested them by means of carefully controlled experiments. Research was often conducted in a 'vacuum' (Tajfel, 1972), and the results were seldom re-examined in everyday settings. What is more, the very questions which experimenters chose to examine increasingly stemmed from the laboratory, so that a cycle was set up—from theory to experiment to theory—at no stage impinged upon by issues or observations from the everyday world. The theoretical purpose of applied social psychology is to test and extend existing theories by taking them outside the laboratory and, at the same time, to use everyday problems as its source of new issues and theory.

What follows in this chapter is a progress report of our experimental work on teaching by telephone. Throughout the research our aims have been both theoretical and practical, and our purpose will be to draw out both sets of implications for social psychology. For some years the first author has been working on theoretical and empirical questions in non-verbal communication, particularly the role which visual communication plays in social interaction. Most of the research has been conducted in the laboratory and, while a body of reliable findings has emerged, there remains the question whether they will extend beyond the laboratory into everyday life.

This stage in the research coincided with the British Open University's decision to make a large investment in teaching by telephone. A small number of telephone teaching projects had been underway since 1973 but, in 1976, the Open University decided to fund telephone teaching throughout Britain. This both offered an everyday setting in which previous laboratory findings could be tested, and raised questions about the feasibility of teaching effectively by telephone.

At the same time, the second author joined the Open University as a Staff Tutor. She was researching into learning and teaching in tutorials, as well as developing materials for briefing and training part-time staff. The advent of telephone tutorials raised many practical questions about the nature of teaching by telephone which previous research had not answered. Given our related interests, it was clear that we should combine our resources, and this chapter presents the first results of our collaboration. First, we shall outline previous research on the role of visual communication in social interaction; then we shall discuss the development of telephone teaching in the Open University; and finally we shall present our own experimental research on telephone tutoring in the Open University and discuss some of the ways in which we hope the work will develop.

THE ROLE OF VISUAL COMMUNICATION IN SOCIAL INTERACTION

For many years, non-verbal cues communicated by the visual channel have been thought to play an important part in social interaction (Harper *et al.*, 1978). Initially, in the early 1960s, experimental interest centred on gaze. In most types of encounter we look at one another in the region of the eyes from time to time, and sometimes our eyes meet to form eye-contact. The early evidence suggested that we use looking and eye-contact for a number of functions: to express our interpersonal attitudes and emotions, to gain information about how the other person is responding to what we say, and to help synchronize switches from speaker to speaker (Argyle and Cook, 1976). More recent research, however, has led to a re-evaluation of much of the early evidence, partly as a result of greater methodological sophistication (Stephenson and Rutter, 1970; Rutter, Morley, and Graham, 1972; Stephenson, Rutter, and Dore, 1973), and it is now doubted whether gaze plays quite so important a role (Rutter *et al.*, 1977, 1978; Rutter and Stephenson, 1979b; Pennington and Rutter, in press). Increasingly, attention has turned to a second line of research. Visual contact between people allows more to occur than just looking and eye-contact: it makes possible the communication of a host of cues from the face, head, hands, and so on, all of which may serve important social functions; indeed, precisely those functions once attributed to gaze. If these cues *are* important, then removing the opportunity for visual communication, on which they rely, should have marked consequences. If, that is to say, we were to compare face-to-face encounters with encounters in which the speakers could not see one another, as for example over the telephone, we ought to find measurable behavioural differences.

The purpose of this section of the chapter is to report our laboratory findings on visual communication, a programme of research in which the principal investigators have been Derek Rutter, Geoffrey Stephenson, and Ian Morley. Initially, we shall concentrate on three separate sets of findings: the *outcome* of conversations; their *content*; and the speech *style* the participants use. However, by the end of the section we hope to have demonstrated two things: (a) that the three sets of findings ought not to be regarded separately since they are closely bound together and can all be considered within one theoretical framework; and (b) that the findings lead us to a new theoretical interpretation which relies on more than visual communication alone.

Outcome

The first stsudies of outcome were conducted by Morley and Stephenson (1969, 1970). They were interested in negotiation, and the setting they chose to explore was a simulated plant-level negotiation between a union representative and a management representative. The subjects were students, and the union and management roles were assigned at random. Each read a detailed description of the dispute (which was based on a genuine case) and, unknown to the subjects, the descriptions were so worded that one side was given what was objectively the stronger case, in half the pairs the union side, in half the management side. The pair was then given 30 minutes to try to reach a settlement. Half the pairs negotiated face-to-face and half communicated over an audio link, in which each member of the pair sat in a separate room and spoke to his partner over a microphone–headphone intercom which precluded visual communication.

The findings were very clear: the side with objectively the stronger case was found to have an advantage in the audio condition. That is, there were more settlements in favour of the side with the stronger case in the audio condition than the face-to-face condition, and there was a marked tendency for face-to-face negotiations to end in compromise. Morley and Stephenson have themselves replicated the finding (Morley and Stephenson, 1977), and similar results were also reported by Short (1974).

The interpretation which Morley and Stephenson offered was as follows.

The audio condition, they argued, was characterized by a lack of social cues, among them cues transmitted visually, and this lack of cues they termed 'formality'. Negotiations include both interparty and interpersonal dimensions (Douglas, 1957), and the effect of formality is to enable negotiators to disregard interpersonal considerations to a great extent and concentrate on the interparty issues. That is to say, formality enables one to behave impersonally and keep to the task of negotiating and pursuing victory. As one concentrates on the issues, the relative merits of the case come to the fore and are evaluated objectively, with the result that the stronger case prevails. Face-to-face, when visual communication is free to occur and the setting is less 'formal', interpersonal considerations are less easy to ignore, the objective merits of the case are less prominent, and compromise is the common outcome.

Content

The next stage in the argument was developed by Stephenson, Ayling, and Rutter (1976). If, they reasoned, Morley and Stephenson were correct, and the audio condition differed from face-to-face in encouraging participants to behave impersonally and keep to the task, it ought to be possible to detect corresponding differences in what people said. That is, in comparison with the content of face-to-face discussions, audio discussions should be *depersonalized* and more *task-oriented*. Accordingly, Stephenson, Ayling, and Rutter set up a series of two-person student debates, half of them conducted face-to-face, half over the audio link. The debates were about union–management relationships, but this time were not aimed at reaching an outcome. Students first completed a questionnaire which tapped union–management attitudes, and pairs were then formed with one pro-union subject and one pro-management subject. Their task was to spend 15 minutes discussing one or two prescribed items from the questionnaire on which their answers had differed.

The content of the discussions was scored by means of Conference Process Analysis, which was devised by Morley and Stephenson and described in full in Morley and Stephenson (1977). The system is rooted in exchange theory (Homans, 1961), and was intended for use particularly with industrial types of meeting and negotiation. First, full verbatim transcripts of the discussions were made, and prepared in typescript. The transcripts were then divided into 'acts', each act conveying one point, and every act was coded on three dimensions: Mode; Resource; and Referent. The mode dimension indicates whether or not participants are *offering*, *accepting*, *rejecting*, or *seeking* a resource. The Resource dimension allocates to each act one of five categories: *outcome* (or settlement point), *procedure* (way of conducting the interaction), *praise*, *blame*, or *information*. The Referent dimension indicates whether or not any person or party directly involved in the negotiation is described in the act: *self*, *opponent*, *own party*, *opponent's party*, *both persons*, or *both parties.* Individual categories from any one dimension, as well as interactions among them, may be examined.

The results of the content analysis were very much as the outcome data from Morley and Stephenson (1969, 1970) had led us to expect, i.e. audio discussions were depersonalized in comparison with face-to-face discussions and more task-oriented. Depersonalization was reflected in significantly less praise for the opponent in the audio condition than face-to-face and significantly more references to party, and also by trends toward greater blame for opponent, fewer self references, and more disagreement (measured by the Reject mode). Task orientation was reflected in significantly more frequent offers of information in the audio condition than face-to-face, especially union offers of information about the opponent's party.

Style

So far, then, the findings indicated that, when visual communication was precluded, both the outcome of discussions and their content were affected. Might there also be effects on speech style? Kendon (1967) argued that one function of visual communication or more strictly gaze was to synchronize transitions from speaker to speaker. When the speaker had finished what he wanted to say, he would send a non-verbal signal to this effect, and the partner would return a signal accepting or rejecting the offer. Remove visual communication and speech style ought to be disrupted. Either there should be more interruption or silence as the participants disentangle themselves, or it may be that subjects compensate for the lack of visual communication in the structure of their speech perhaps by adding redundancy or ending their utterances with a question so that the partner is under pressure to take over. Preliminary evidence had already been published by Argyle, Lalljee, and Cook (1968) and Cook and Lalljee (1972) and the alternative hypotheses were now tested by Rutter and Stephenson (1977).

The material which Rutter and Stephenson analysed was the conversations collected by Stephenson, Ayling, and Rutter (1976), and a large number of stylistic measures were taken. These included the frequency and duration of simultaneous speech (which is usually the result of interruption); the duration of silence between utterances; the number and length of utterances; the ratio of nouns to verbs (the more nouns proportionately, the closer to written text the material and so the more redundant); the proportion of floor changes (switches from speaker to speaker) which immediately followed a question; the frequency of acknowledgement signals ('Mmhmm', 'Yes', 'I see', and so on); the filled pause ratio (an index of 'ers' and 'ums' generally regarded as a measure of linguistic planning and preparation, Maclay and Osgood, 1959); and the speech disturbance ratio (introduced by Mahl, 1956, as an index of stutters, false starts, slips of the tongue, and so on, generally regarded as a measure of situational anxiety, Cook, 1969).

The findings were quite different from what Kendon had led us to expect. Certainly there *were* stylistic differences between the face-to-face and audio discussions, but they indicated neither disruption nor compensation. First, there was *less* interruption in the audio condition than face-to-face, with significantly fewer occurrences of simultaneous speech and less time spent in simultaneous speech in total. There was no difference between conditions in the duration of silence, and the only other significant effects were that the word-length of utterances was greater in the audio condition and speech disturbance was more marked.

Although neither hypothesis was supported, there seemed to us at the time to be a clear interpretation. Face-to-face, interruption can occur freely because visual communication allows the transmission of non-verbal signals which maintain the interaction and prevent the breakdown which interruption might otherwise threaten. In the absence of visual communication, the non-verbal signals cannot be received, and speech assumes greater significance in regulating the flow of conversation. Since interruptions might prove disruptive, they are made less frequently. Utterances are longer in the audio condition simply because they are less often broken by interruption, and speech disturbance is greater because subjects are more anxious than face-to-face, perhaps because of the novel setting or even because the absence of visual communication requires greater concentration on speech, and this causes errors. The role of visual communication, in other words, seemed to us to be to enable subjects to speak *spontaneously* and interrupt freely without threatening the continuity of the encounter.

Physical Presence: Rutter, Stephenson & Dewey (1981)

Taking our three sets of findings together, we now had evidence that, when the opportunity for visual communication was removed, *outcomes* changed, *content* became more impersonal and task-oriented, and *style* became less spontaneous. Much of the work has subsequently been replicated, and reviews are to be found in Argyle and Cook (1976) Short, Williams, and Christie (1976), and Williams (1977). At the empirical level, it is clear what sorts of prediction we ought to make about differences between face-to-face and telephone tutorials. But, at the theoretical level, there arises a major problem for interpreting differences between face-to-face and audio conditions, and that is that visual communication is confounded with a second variable, namely physical presence. Face-to-face, subjects are visually together *and* physically together; in the audio or telephone condition, they are visually separate *and* physically separate. Being physically in the same room as the other person gives one a number of cues, quite apart from those transmitted visually, which may well influence discussion but which are absent or at least distorted in the audio condition—auditory cues from the voice, drawing breath, shuffling, and so on. Cues of this sort may affect discussion directly, or they may have an indirect influence by affecting the participants' cognitive set or feeling that the partner is 'there'; but, in either case, visual communication and physical presence had to be disentangled if any differences we subsequently found between face-to-face and telephone tutorials were to be interpreted.

The first approach we adopted was to study pairs of blind people. If the critical variable in our work was indeed physical presence and not visual communication, blind pairs face-to-face should show the same pattern of differences from blind pairs in the audio condition as we had found for sighted pairs since physical presence is varied while visual communication is absent in both conditions. Pairs of students from a College of Further Education for the Blind, some of them congenitally blind and others adventitiously blind, completed a Braille version of a short socio-political questionnaire and were then asked to spend 15 minutes debating one or two of the issues which divided them. Half the pairs met face-to-face, half over an audio link, and the discussions were tape-recorded and their content and style analysed as in Stephenson, Ayling, and Rutter (1976) and Rutter and Stephenson (1977). There were no differences between conditions in the content of the discussions, and this argued against the physical presence hypothesis. However, four differences in style were revealed: greater duration of simultaneous speech face-to-face than in the audio condition and more speech disturbance, but fewer changes of speaker and a slower speech rate.

This was a very odd pattern of findings and, while any difference between conditions is consistent with the physical presence hypothesis, in fact there is an alternative, more plausible, explanation in this particular case. Because of our interest in non-verbal communication, we had decided to video-record some of the conversations, but we chose to record only face-to-face encounters, with the result that cameras were present in all the face-to-face conversations but were absent from the audio sessions. Speech disturbance was very high face-to-face, and this suggests that the cameras made the face-to-face subjects anxious, perhaps a sign of apprehension at the possibility of being evaluated. The other three stylistic findings now fall into place. The face-to-face subjects spoke slowly to ensure that their arguments were clear (quite literally minding their p's and q's in front of the cameras); this in turn meant fewer changes of speaker, and the greater duration of simultaneous speech resulted from the slower speech rate and the consequent delay in yielding to interruption.

While the results ultimately offered no support for the physical presence hypothesis in either content or style, the presence of cameras in the face-to-face condition of course means that the experiment was not entirely satisfactory and that the results cannot be clearly interpreted. Moreover, it might be objected that to try to generalize from blind people to sighted people is hazardous since there is more to being blind than just being unable to engage in visual communication. What we needed was to return to sighted people and find a way of disentangling physical presence from visual communication in the laboratory, and this we did in an experiment which proved to mark a turning-point in the interpretation of all our previous findings. The experiment made use of four conditions: face-to-face; video, in which subjects sat in separate rooms, each with a television monitor displaying a head-and-shoulders image of the partner conveyed by a camera in the other room; curtain, in which subjects sat in the same room, a curtain pulled between them part-way across the room; and audio. The four conditions formed a 2 × 2 design (Figure 1).

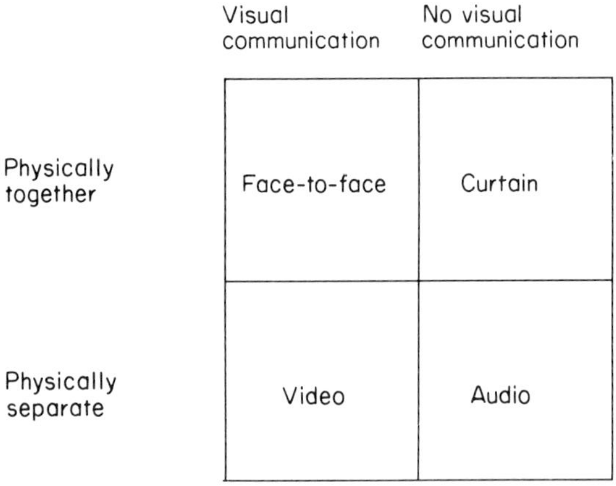

	Visual communication	No visual communication
Physically together	Face-to-face	Curtain
Physically separate	Video	Audio

Figure 1. Experimental design

The procedure was very similar to that in the previous experiment, on blind people. Subjects first completed an expanded version of the same questionnaire, including items on politics, social issues, religion, and so on, and then pairs discussed one or two items on which their individual opinions were divided. The discussions lasted 20 minutes, and pairs were randomly allocated to one of the four conditions. Measures of both content and style were taken, using the same indices as before. If physical presence were the critical variable in our previous work, conversations in which subjects sat in separate rooms (video and audio) should differ from those where they sat together (face-to-face and curtain). If visual communication were critical, the difference should be between face-to-face and video on the one hand and curtain and audio on the other. Whichever is the case, or even if neither holds, we should at least replicate our findings that audio conversations are depersonalized in comparison with face-to-face conversations and more task-oriented, and also less spontaneous in style.

In the event, there was no support for the physical presence hypothesis, and no support either for the visual communication hypothesis. Of the sixty main effects examined by analysis of variance, three were significant at the 5 percent level, exactly what was to be expected by chance. However, in contrast to these two hypotheses, there was good support for the third, that our original differences between face-to-face and audio would be replicated. Planned comparisons (Winer, 1970) revealed both that content in the audio condition was depersonalized in comparison with face-to-face and more task-oriented, and that style was less spontaneous. Depersonalization was reflected principally in a lack of acknowledgement signals, and task-orientation was reflected in greater discussion of procedures and more frequent references to those present, presumably about what procedures to follow. Spontaneity of style was reflected in a variety of measures. As in Rutter and Stephenson (1977), the time spent in simultaneous speech was significantly less in the audio condition than face-to-face, and speech disturbance was greater. In addition, the proportion of utterances which ended in a question and the proportion of floor changes which were preceded by a question were greater in the audio condition, both of them findings which had tended in the same direction in Rutter and Stephenson (1977) but had not reached significance.

In summary, while face-to-face and audio again differed in the ways we had predicted, the differences could be attributed to neither visual communication *nor* physical presence. What then was the critical variable? The answer comes from the other two conditions, video and curtain. Whenever there was a significant difference between face-to-face and audio, whether in depersonalization, task-orientation, or style, video and curtain lay somewhere *between* face-to-face and audio (with just one exception in the seven significant results). Moreover, Kemp (1977), in an experiment which replicated the procedures of Stephenson, Ayling, and Rutter (1976) and Rutter and Stephenson (1977) and followed up his own pilot work, found exactly the same for a condition in which a wooden screen was placed on the table between the two participants: in every case where there was a significant difference between face-to-face and audio, the wooden screen condition lay somewhere between them.

Combining the experiments, what emerges is a consistent rank-ordering of conditions from face-to-face to video, curtain, and wooden screen, to audio. What can we say about this rank-ordering? It is this. Face-to-face, cues are available from both visual communication *and* physical presence; in video, curtain, and wooden screen, one set each is available, visual cues in the video condition, and cues from physical presence in the curtain and wooden screen conditions; and, in the audio condition, neither set of cues is available. In other words, as we move from face-to-face to video, curtain and wooden screen, to audio, the conditions become increasingly 'cueless' — and it is this, 'cuelessness', we believe, which explains all our previous results from content and style. The smaller the aggregate number of available social cues from whatever source—visual communication, physical presence, or, indeed, any other—the more depersonalized and task-oriented the content, and the less spontaneous the style (Rutter and Stephenson, 1979a).

While 'cuelessness' is a new term, there already exist in the literature two related concepts. The first, 'social presence', was introduced by Short, Williams, and Christie (1976). Social presence is a perceived characteristic of media, and is defined as the extent to which a medium is perceived to allow psychologically close, interpersonal communication. Subjects take part in encounters over one medium or another, and are then asked to complete a 'social presence' questionnaire. Face-to-face is found to have considerable social presence, video rather less, and audio very little—the same rank-order as cuelessness.

Unfortunately, while the concept has its attractions, there are two major difficulties. The first is that, since ratings of social presence are made *after* the encounter, they are very likely to be influenced by whatever effect the medium may have had on the encounter. Any attempt subsequently to use the concept to account for findings for content, style, and outcome, or, indeed, any other aspect of the encounter, will therefore be circular. The second, and related, difficulty for the concept is that Short, Williams, and Christie are unable to say how the subject arrives at his subjective impression of the magnitude of a medium's social presence. Our own suggestion is that he derives his impression from the objective number of cues the medium makes available, so that social presence is underpinned by cuelessness. The more cueless a medium, the less its social presence.

The second concept related to cuelessness is 'formality', which Morley and Stephenson (1969, 1970) introduced to account for their outcome findings. Formality was defined 'in terms of the numbers of social cues available' (Morley and Stephenson, 1969, p.543) and is therefore exactly equivalent to our concept of cuelessness. What this means, of course, is that cuelessness can now be used to interpret all three sets of measures we have considered—not just content and style, but also outcome. How cuelessness has its effects we do not yet know, but the likely answer, we believe, is that, from the start of the encounter, the available social cues aggregate to produce an impression of psychological proximity or distance—the feeling that someone is 'there' or not —and it is this which determines the effects on content, style, and outcome.

Cuelessness and Content, Style, and Outcome

At the start of this section of the chapter we said that we hoped to demonstrate two things. One was that content, style, and outcome could be interpreted within one theoretical framework: that framework has been offered. The role of visual communication, we now believe, has traditionally been overstated — by ourselves in the 1976 and 1977 papers as much as by any other writers — and a more satisfactory framework is provided by cuelessness.

Our second aim was to show that content, style, and outcome ought not to be regarded as separate but are closely bound together. Earlier in this section we suggested that audio outcomes differ from face-to-face outcomes because what the participants *say* is different in the two conditions. That is, cuelessness leads subjects to be impersonal and task-oriented in the content of what they say, and it is content which in turn produces the different outcomes. Might it be that style also is the product of content, so that when we are being impersonal and task-oriented we use a deliberate, unspontaneous style?

To test this possibility, we re-examined the data from the experiment outlined above, in which face-to-face, video, curtain, and audio were incorporated and, for each pair of subjects, we correlated the score for every C.P.A. category with every stylistic index. The pattern of correlations revealed good support for the prediction. Throughout our research we have always taken interruption, measured by the frequency and duration of occurrences of simultaneous speech, as the principal index of spontaneity. The critical question was therefore how well interruption correlated with measures of depersonalization and task-orientation. In conversations which are inter-personal rather than depersonalized, speakers frequently praise one another and are inclined to accept one another's contributions. The more the *accept* category was used, the longer were the interruptions; and the more *praise*, the longer and more frequent they were. Task-orientation, we have argued, is revealed by a concern with outcomes, procedure, and relevant information, as well as avoidance of irrelevant information, and here too the prediction was supported. The more subjects discussed *outcomes*, the shorter their interruptions; and the greater their concern with *procedure*, the somewhat less frequent and shorter they were. There were no correlations with *information*, but there was a tendency for the introduction of *irrelevant information* to be associated with long interruptions.

Correlation does not, of course, necessarily mean cause–effect. To establish a causal relationship we will have to manipulate content experimentally and demon-strate corresponding effects on style — but it is at least plausible to argue that content determines style. What we have, then, is the suggestion that the relation-ship between cuelessness and *both* style and outcome is mediated by content (Figure 2). Cuelessness produces a certain content which, in turn, produces a particular style and particular outcomes. This suggestion, we believe, is some-thing quite new, and a very interesting issue which will be well worth pursuing.

Figure 2. Cuelessness

Current Developments

The research outlined in this section has led us to a number of theoretical and empirical conclusions and, as we made clear at the start of the chapter, much of our attention has now turned to extending and evaluating them in everyday life and exploiting some of their practical implications — hence our work with the Open University. At the same time, there remain a number of issues which we are continuing to explore in the laboratory.

In one experiment we are looking at a further measure of outcome, namely opinion change, and testing whether this, like the outcomes of negotiations, is influenced by cuelessness. The same experiment is comparing pairs of subjects with four-person groups, so that we shall be able to test the extent to which group size may relate to cuelessness. Content and style, as well as outcome, are being measured, thus allowing us for the first time to examine all three at once. Another question we are exploring is whether impression-formation is influenced by cuelessness. As with opinion change, a number of writers have already examined impression-formation in relation to visual communication (Argyle and Cook, 1976; Short, Williams, and Christie, 1976), but there has been no systematic attempt to relate it to cuelessness more broadly. Finally, following up our earlier interest, Nigel Kemp has recently completed an extensive study of social interaction in blind people. There has been almost no experimental research in this area, yet there are very important questions to ask. How do blind people open and maintain conversations given the limited number of social cues they are able to receive? How accurately and confidently do they form impressions of strangers? Are there detectable differences from sighted people in their competence and performance at non-verbal signalling? Does their behaviour with other blind people differ from their behaviour with sighted people? Each of these studies is still in progress and runs parallel with our applied research. The results will be reported in due course.

THE DEVELOPMENT OF TELEPHONE TEACHING IN THE OPEN UNIVERSITY

The theoretical questions and findings discussed above have considerable practical implications for the use of telecommunications in teaching. The Open University is a distance learning system in which students and staff do not come together on a campus. Instead, a central core of academics and administrators at the University's headquarters produce distance teaching materials which are sent directly to students' homes throughout the country. Open University students are working adults who live at home and study in their spare time. The University is, at the time of writing, in its ninth teaching year and has over 70,000 students. It offers 117 undergraduate and 51 associate student (non-degree) courses.

The teaching approach is a multi-media one, using correspondence materials, radio and television broadcasts, audio cassettes and, more recently, interactive computer learning programmes. Open University students also have access to tutorial and counselling support at Study Centres, of which there are about 260 throughout Britain. However, the use students can make of these services is very much affected by the distances they live from their tutor or counsellor or Study Centre, or by personal circumstances such as being housebound, ill or disabled, or on shift-work. Isolation from contact with other students or a tutor can play a significant part in a student's decision to withdraw from a course.

The Open University has, for administrative purposes, thirteen regions, varying in geographical size and student population: for example, the Open University in Scotland constitutes one 'region', the London conurbation another. The number of 'remote' students in any one region varies. In Scotland, there are more than 600 students who are unable to meet regularly with their part-time tutors; more than 300 of these cannot reach a Study Centre without an overnight stay. Similarly, in Wales, the geographical isolation of students makes the provision of face-to-face tutorials uneconomic in many cases. Geographical scatter and personal circumstances are not the only reasons for a student finding himself at some distance from a tutor or other students. With the provision of an increasing number of courses, sometimes specialist ones, the student population for a course within a region may be comparatively small; thus, a tutor will not be available at the student's nearest Study Centre, and indeed there may be only one or two tutors for a course for a whole region. For students and tutor to meet in these circumstances would involve considerable time, travel, and expense.

Difficulties such as these have led the Open University to experiment with telephone teaching, using the public Post Office telecommunications system as a means of solving problems of distance and isolation. The Open University venture is neither the first nor the only one of its kind: distance learning systems in America, Canada, and Europe have used the telephone for teaching in varying ways. However, the use has been rather different from that within the Open University. For example, Wisconsin University—Extension uses a dedicated telephone network as its main means of teaching a course with little or no correspondence course material; in Sweden, the University of Lund uses one-to-one telephone calls together with correspondence material, as well as using the telephone as a means for students at home to listen to a class tutorial (Flinck, 1978). In the Open University, correspondence and broadcast materials form the main means of teaching, and are designed to enable a student to complete a course successfully by studying them alone, together with writing essays or assignments. Within this framework, tutorials are intended to be of a 'remedial' nature, an opportunity for students to raise problems they have encountered in the course material or with assignments, and to discuss them with their tutor and fellow students. Attendance at tutorials is not compulsory for students. 'Telephone teaching' in an Open University context is therefore 'telephone tutoring' relating to correspondence and broadcast materials.

There are a number of ways in which a tutor can hold a telephone tutorial. The most frequent is the one-to-one call, where a student consults his tutor about a particular problem with course material or an assignment. To encourage the development of this form of contact, students in Scotland who could not attend face-to-face tutorials were each allocated vouchers for about two hours' telephone time with their tutors. This form of contact has also been found to be particularly valuable on project courses, or courses where a student negotiates with his tutor the kind of assignment he does. As well as individual contact, a group tutorial can be held by means of a conference call (sometimes called a 'teleconference'). This involves several participants (usually a tutor and up to about seven students) each on an individual line, usually a domestic telephone line. The lines are linked together by a 'conference bridge' into a common network. The bridging is done by a Post Office operator at the exchange, but recently the Open University has begun to install bridging equipment at some of its regional offices so that conference calls can be activated directly from there. With the conference call arrangement, everyone can hear, and speak to, everyone else on the network. A third kind of telephone tutorial can be conducted using a loudspeaking telephone. This usually involves two locations: at one, the tutor uses an ordinary telephone hand-set; at the other, a group of students at a Study Centre sit around a telephone fitted with an amplifier and microphones (an LST 4 set) so that all students can hear and speak to the tutor. This kind of tutorial has been used frequently in Wales, where the concentration of tutors tends to be in the south of the region, while students are scattered throughout. In Scotland, long distances have been overcome, for example linking a group of students at Stornoway, in the Outer Hebrides, with a tutor at St Andrews (Robinson and Carr, 1978).

Since the first series of telephone tutorials in 1973, tutoring by telephone has been set up in all thirteen regions. Regional Reports (1977) indicates a widespread growth of its use on a variety of courses, from music to technology. In some regions, and for some courses, telephone tuition is built in at the start of the academic year as part of the tutorial programme, substituting for face-to-face tutorials. In some cases, students opt in to a telephone tutorial group in preference to a face-to-face group. In others, telephone tuition is offered as a supplement to face-to-face tuition where the particular circumstances of a course, or group of students, warrant it.

Although the use of telecommunications appears to offer considerable potential as a tutoring resource, it raises a number of questions. Is telephone tutoring as effective a learning–teaching medium as face-to-face? How does the use of a different medium affect the nature of the tutorial process and outcomes? How is the telephone tutorial perceived by tutors and students in comparison with the face-to-face tutorial? Does the medium require the tutor to change his role and structure the meeting in a special way? What special skills, if any, does he need to develop? Are there subject differences which affect the use of telephone tutorials: for example, can Mathematics or Science be effectively tutored by telephone?

Research into teleconferencing is comparatively new (a little over a decade old), and research into teleconferencing for educational purposes is even newer. Only recently have researchers begun to examine systematically the possible effects of media on psychological processes. Much of the research into new telecommunications systems or media has been done by their designers, and has been set up to demonstrate the feasibility of a particular system. But, as Williams and Chapanis (1977) point out, this kind of evaluation fails to answer three important questions: how effectively can people use a medium; how does the system compare with its alternatives from the users' point of view; will people choose to use the medium, given a choice?

Laboratory studies have suggested that tasks which figure frequently in educational settings (information exchange, questioning, and certain kinds of problem solving) are as effectively managed by telephone as face-to-face. Field studies, measuring differences in the effectiveness of face-to-face and telephone 'instruction' have again generally found that the telephone is as effective and, sometimes, more effective in terms of learning outcomes. However, many of the studies are no more than descriptive, and the uses of the telephone which they describe are often not comparable. Studies of users' attitudes to teleconferencing (sometimes of groups which have no alternatives open to them) have generally been restricted to broad surveys with little detailed investigation. Moreover, much of the research comes from North America, where the educational context is very different from that of the Open University and where the focus has been on the 'tele-lecture' rather than the tutorial. What this means is that we still know very little about the content, style, and outcome of telephone tutorials. To try to answer some of the questions posed earlier in this section we therefore set up a project of our own, and it is to this that we now turn.

AN EXPERIMENTAL ANALYSIS OF TEACHING BY TELEPHONE

The aims of the project were threefold: to test whether our theoretical and empirical conclusions from the laboratory would be verified; to exploit the new setting as a source of further hypotheses; and to try to help tutors and students with the practical problems of teaching and learning by telephone. We shall first discuss the two studies we have completed, and then, in the concluding section of the chapter, outline some proposals for further research.

First Experiment: Telephone Tutoring in the Open University

The first experiment took place in the East Midlands Region of the Open University, and five tutorial groups were studied, all from Course E201, 'Personality and Learning'. The experiment began at the start of the academic year, when students had already been allocated to tutors, three to six a group. Tutorials in the East Midlands are usually held face-to-face, and a random selection of six groups were asked if they would agree to hold two of their meetings by telephone conference call instead. One group was subsequently excluded because of the poor technical quality of the tape-recordings. The first tutorial was held face-to-face, and the following four meetings were the sessions which made up the experiment. For three groups, two face-to-face tutorials were followed by two telephone tutorials and, for the other two groups, the order was reversed (Figure 3), giving a cross-over design to help control for participants' familiarity with one another and with the tutorial material. From the four meetings for each group, one face-to-face tutorial and one telephone tutorial were selected for analysis, and, so far as recording quality would allow, the first tutorial of each type was chosen.

	Face-to-face tutorials	Telephone tutorials
Groups		
1	2,3	4,5
2	2,3	4,5
3	2,3	4,5
4	4,5	2,3
5	4,5	2,3

Figure 3. Open University experiment: design

The tutorials lasted, on average, just over one hour, and for each, a full tape-recording was made and a typewritten verbatim transcript was prepared. Three analyses were carried out: of *content*, of *style*, and of *outcome* in the form of participants' perceptions of the tutorials. For the content analysis, a 20-minute segment of each meeting was analysed beginning 20 minutes into the tutorial, while, for the stylistic analysis, the full transcript was scored. The perceptual measures were based on diary reports. Students and tutors were asked to keep a tape-recorded diary of their reactions to each tutorial by making a recording immediately after the session. A checklist of questions was provided and, in addition, participants were asked to note anything else which they felt they wanted to report.

Content was measured by a modified form of C.P.A. which was designed

Mode	0	unclassifiable
	1	offer
	2	accept
	3	reject
	4	seek

Resource	0	unclassifiable
	1	procedure
	2	procedure for topic (academic)
	3	procedure for course (OU)
	4	evaluation (academic)
	5	evaluation of course (OU)
	6	information (academic)
	7	information about course (OU)
	8	information (relevant)
	9	information (irrelevant)
	10	praise
	11	blame

Referent	0	unclassifiable/no referent
	1	self
	2	student (or students as individuals)
	3	students as a group
	4	tutor
	5	tutor + student (or students as individuals)
	6	tutor + students (as a group)
	7	third party (academic)

Figure 4. Open University experiment: Conference Process Analysis (C.P.A.) categories

especially for this experiment (Figure 4). The Mode categories were unchanged, and the Referent categories were specially tailored to the tutorial setting. The principal changes were to the Resource dimension, and the intention was to allow discussion of the academic substance of the tutorial to be distinguished from discussion of Open University matters. The result was an expanded set of Resource categories, and examples of each have been selected from the transcripts and reproduced in Figure 5. Style was analysed in the usual way: measures were taken of the number of interruptions, the number of words spoken, the number of utterances and their mean word-length, the number of questions and acknowledgement signals, the filled pause ratio and, for students, the proportion of utterances which immediately followed a question

0. *Unclassified*

And, er ———————
So ————————
Which must be for ———

1. *Procedure*

Let's have a think about Block 4 first
What would you like to concentrate on first?
Can I just make one point?
Can I just try and sum up so far about what we've said
    about Block 4?

2. *Procedure for topic* (academic)

Now, I think it would be a good idea, obviously, that when
    you're coming to revise Piaget, if you can have in your
    mind certainly an idea of how Piaget describes the
    evolution of one particular concept
I mean I wouldn't try and remember all the details of all
    the experiments that Piaget goes on about
I think the main point to grasp is that Bryant and others
    have found some weaknesses in the way Piaget gathers
    his data
That's probably quite useful when you're thinking about
    the formal operational stage of Piaget

3. *Procedure for course* (OU)

I'd want really to try and look in a bit more detail at Block
    5, although obviously people will want to perhaps tidy
    up things in Block 4

4. *Evaluation* (academic)

I find his work quite interesting really
But I think Bryant was very difficult to understand
Were you surprised at that way of looking at children?
It's very interesting, but he felt it was quite remote from a
    remedial classroom in a local school
It's very useful for remedials

5. *Evaluation of course* (OU)

The radio broadcast Piaget announced seems to give
    Bryant's point of view pretty well
Do you think that covers most of what he wanted to say?
From what you've said already it seems your reaction to

Block 4 has been, you've felt a little overwhelmed by the actual amount of detail you need to assimilate

I think there's an awful lot of clouding as well in some of the backup information that goes with this course, particularly in the personality and learning book

6. *Information* (academic)

Bryant and Bower, Bryant particularly, have made a number of criticisms of Piaget

He fairly recently has published a book in which he went into great detail across a whole range of Piaget's experiments

Could you explain conservative focusing strategy as opposed to scanning strategy?

And then when you're in the start of 3rd stage you're talking about the child having a memory almost, a sort of primitive plan so he can look for objects that he loses

7. *Information about course* (OU)

How much do we have to remember each detailed test?

I hope you'll find there'll be quite a few connections in the substsance of Block 5 with the Piaget work

They go into some detail about Bryant's work

This is Block 5, isn't it?

I don't think you've had Block 5 for very long anyway

8. *Information* (relevant)

Is Piaget completely fresh to everyone? Or have you come across this work before?

I teach remedial children

Very small babies can't hold anything can they?

9. *Information* (irrelevant)

What's your first name?

I've just got back after a long absence

10. *Praise*

The possibility's remote, very obviously as far as you're concerned, of lack of success

11. *Blame*

I think I phrased it very badly, actually, come to think

Figure 5. Open University experiment: examples of C.P.A. resource categories

by the tutor. The perceptual data were based on the checklist questions and participants' spontaneous comments.

The first prediction was that *content* would be depersonalized in the telephone condition in comparison with face-to-face, and more task-oriented. Depersonalization has two principal meanings. The first is 'impersonal', and tutorials which are depersonalized in this sense should be characterized by remarks which make no personal references or perhaps refer only to third parties. The second meaning is 'antagonistic', and depersonalization in this sense should be evident in the speaker's rejection of his partner's contributions and unwillingness to accept what he says, and in criticism and lack of praise. Task-orientation, it was expected, would appear as a large amount of evaluation, information, and discussion of procedures, the latter particularly about the academic substance of the tutorial and, perhaps, the Open University.

Table 1　Open University experiment. Content analysis: Mean proportion (%) acts allocated to each resource

	Face-to-face		Telephone		df	t
	Mean	S.D.	Mean	S.D.		
Tutor						
0. Unclassifiable	17.6	3.0	14.8	3.7	4	1.4
1. Procedure	1.9	1.1	2.0	1.5	4	0.2
2. Procedure (academic)	0.0	0.0	0.0	0.0	4	0.0
3. Procedure (OU)	0.0	0.0	0.0	0.0	4	0.0
4. Evaluation (academic)	16.9	3.6	23.5	8.5	4	1.9
5. Evaluation (OU)	0.4	0.4	1.6	2.7	4	1.0
6. Information (academic)	38.6	15.5	24.4	11.3	4	2.4
7. Information (OU)	3.4	2.6	7.4	9.2	4	1.3
8. Information (relevant)	20.9	15.9	22.0	12.0	4	0.2
9. Information (irrelevant)	0.0	0.0	0.0	0.0	4	0.0
10. Praise	0.0	0.0	0.0	0.0	4	0.0
11. Blame	0.0	0.0	0.0	0.0	4	0.0
Students						
0. Unclassifiable	11.5	5.9	14.0	3.0	4	0.9
1. Procedure	0.2	0.4	0.3	0.3	4	0.6
2. Procedure (academic)	0.0	0.0	0.0	0.0	4	0.0
3. Procedure (OU)	0.0	0.0	0.0	0.0	4	0.0
4. Evaluation (academic)	18.4	8.3	21.9	9.9	4	1.9
5. Evaluation (OU)	6.9	14.8	4.1	7.1	4	0.7
6. Information (academic)	34.3	18.4	26.0	13.2	4	1.1
7. Information (OU)	3.1	6.0	6.3	8.4	4	1.9
8. Information (relevant)	32.2	24.7	26.4	15.2	4	0.5
9. Information (irrelevant)	0.0	0.0	0.0	0.0	4	0.0
10. Praise	0.0	0.0	0.0	0.0	4	0.0
11. Blame	0.0	0.0	0.0	0.0	4	0.0

The findings for each resource category, for tutors and students separately, are presented in Table 1. The tutor values are the mean of the five tutors condition by condition; for the students, the total score for each group was calculated, and the mean was then taken across the five groups. The conditions were compared by t-tests, and no significant effects were revealed either for tutors or for students: that is, there was no evidence that telephone tutorials were either depersonalized or more task-oriented. Task orientation was very high in both settings, and there was little interpersonal discussion: resources 4–8 (the academic substance of the tutorials) combined with resource zero (unclassifiable or incomplete) accounted for around 95 percent of acts in both conditions. However, the way in which so high a degree of task-orientation was achieved differed markedly between conditions. In the telephone meetings, tutors sought contributions from students more than face-to-face ($t = 6.6$; df 4; $p < 0.01$), and students responded with more offers ($t = 4.4$; df 4; $P < 0.05$). Tutors were also more likely to call on particular students ($t = 5.8$; df 4; $p < 0.01$), and students made more self references ($t = 3.6$; df 4; $p < 0.05$) as they offered their contributions. Face-to-face, students sought resources from the tutor more than in the telephone condition ($t = 2.9$; df 4; $p < 0.05$), especially academic information, and tutors correspondingly made more offers ($t = 4.3$; df 4; $p < 0.05$), especially offers of academic and other relevant information. In other words, the main difference between conditions was in the way the task was approached. Tutors made more effort to elicit contributions in the telephone condition, and students responded by offering more.

The second prediction was that *style* would be less spontaneous in the telephone condition than face-to-face, with less interruption and, as Kemp (1977) had reported, a greater degree of filled pausing as participants planned what to say. The results are presented in table 2, and offer good support for the prediction. Students interrupted almost twice as frequently face-to-face as in the telephone condition, and tutors and students alike used filled pauses more frequently over the telephone. In addition, students used fewer acknowledgement signals over the telephone than face-to-face, perhaps a measure of reduced spontaneity or even depersonalization. Finally, there were some very interesting findings concerning questions and the amount which participants said. Students asked significantly fewer questions in the telephone condition than face-to-face, while proportionately more of their utterances were replies to questions by the tutor; and tutors said significantly less in the telephone condition than face-to-face (measured by the number of words spoken) while students tended in the opposite direction. What this suggests is a concern on the part of tutors to impose structure on the telephone tutorials, as was evident in the content analysis. Over the telephone it is easy for reticent students not to contribute, and tutors seemed to anticipate this and ask direct questions to draw them out. Indeed, some tutors kept a check-list of contributions

Table 2   Open University experiment. Stylistic analysis: Mean values

	Face-to-face		Telephone		df	t
	Mean	S.D.	Mean	S.D.		
Tutor						
No. utterances	157.2	33.4	148.0	30.5	4	0.7
No. words	748.0	1071.5	4942.2	755.5	4	5.4[a]
Word length of utterances	50.0	18.4	33.5	8.0	4	2.0
No. interruptions	17.8	11.1	12.0	7.1	4	1.2
No. questions	48.6	12.4	69.0	19.8	4	2.0
No. acknowledgement signals	86.6	46.1	100.6	52.3	4	0.5
Filled pause ratio (% words)	2.5	1.4	4.9	2.8	4	3.3[b]
Students						
No. utterances	186.4	47.4	173.4	38.9	4	0.5
No. words	3990.0	678.0	4706.0	857.0	4	2.7
Word length of utterances	23.1	9.9	28.5	9.1	4	1.7
No. interruptions	33.4	20.0	17.6	10.2	4	2.9[b]
No. questions	36.4	12.4	20.0	8.0	4	5.0[a]
% utterances which =						
response to tutor question	23.2	4.9	36.4	10.0	4	2.8[b]
No. acknowledgement signals	68.0	29.5	41.0	17.3	4	3.2[b]
Filled pause ratio (% words)	1.9	0.6	3.4	0.6	4	14.0[a]

[a]$p < 0.01$ (two-tailed).
[b]$p < 0.05$ (two-tailed).

and tried to ensure that every student was encouraged. While this certainly seems to have produced a large number of responses, the associated reduction in questions by students may not be something which tutors would wish.

One final aspect of the stylistic results also deserves comment. Stephenson, Ayling, and Rutter (1976) reported that one consequence of removing social cues was to diminish role effects. Behavioural differences between 'union' and 'management' were less marked in the audio condition than face-to-face. A similar pattern was revealed here. For both the length of utterances and the number of words spoken, the difference between tutors and students was smaller in the telephone condition than face-to-face (t = 4.4; df 4; $p < 0.05$ and t = 7.5; df 4; $p < 0.01$, respectively). Lacking cues to personal identity, participants treated the meetings relatively impersonally, and role differences were less salient for them.

The third prediction was that the two conditions would differ in *outcome*, as measured by the participants' perceptions of the tutorials. Telephone tutorials were seen as the more 'business-like', 'structured', and 'formal', and most students thought that the material was covered 'more efficiently'. Both students and tutors reported spending longer on preparation, the students because they felt more exposed to tutors' questions — perhaps reflecting their greater frequency in the telephone condition. Tutors were generally seen by both tutors and students as more 'chairman-like' in the telephone condition, and necessarily so. Almost all participants reported greater anxiety in telephone tutorials — consistent with findings for speech disturbance. Overall, as Hammond *et al.* (1978) have recently reported, face-to-face tutorials were generally 'preferred', even if they were regarded as academically less effective.

In summary, content, style, and outcome all differentiated between face-to-face and telephone. While the tutorials were highly task-oriented and relatively impersonal in both conditions, there were marked differences in the way the task was approached, tutors seeking contributions and students responding to them more in the telephone tutorials than face-to-face. Stylistically, telephone tutorials were the less spontaneous, and tutors imposed a greater degree of structure. Outcome, measured by participants' perceptions, corresponded closely to the findings for both content and style.

Second Experiment: A Laboratory Analogue

The second experiment was designed and conducted by Janet Taylor. The first study had made use of the Open University tutorial setting, from which, it might be argued, it is difficult to generalize, given the special nature of the Open University. Furthermore, it was not possible to say whether the telephone findings were attributable to cuelessness generally or to the absence of visual communication in particular. The second experiment was therefore designed as a laboratory analogue which would draw on a conventional university and also allow a direct test of the visual communication hypothesis. Content, but not outcome, was again examined, and the experiment was also designed to make possible a more detailed analysis of style and structuring.

Six tutorial groups in the Department of Psychology at the University of Nottingham agreed to take part in the experiment. Four consisted of three students (though one student was absent from one of the tutorials) and the tutor, and two consisted of four students and the tutor. The experiment took place part-way through the year, and the students and tutors knew one another reasonably well. Each group was asked to hold two of its regular, time-tabled meetings in the Social Psychology Laboratory, one face-to-face, the other from behind screens. The participants sat in the same positions for the two sessions but, in the screen condition, cloth screens approximately 2 metres by 1 metre were placed between the chairs so that visual communication was precluded but physical presence was retained. As was also the case in the Open University experiment, the discussion topic could not be held constant across the tutorials, but the meetings were all part of the same introductory course. Three groups held their screen tutorial first, two their face-to-face tutorial. Each session lasted about 45 minutes, and tape-recordings and verbatim transcripts were made. Opening and closing remarks which did not contribute to the

Table 3   Laboratory analogue. Content analysis: Mean proportion (%) acts allocated to each resource

	Face-to-face		Screen		df	t
	Mean	S.D.	Mean	S.D.		
Tutor						
0. Unclassifiable	11.8	3.5	10.3	4.0	5	1.0
1. Procedure	1.6	1.6	5.9	3.3	5	2.9[a]
2. Procedure (academic)	0.2	0.4	1.4	1.6	5	2.1
3. Procedure (university)	2.9	3.9	2.9	7.1	5	0.0
4. Evaluation (academic)	11.6	8.3	13.4	9.2	5	1.3
5. Evaluation (university)	1.4	3.0	0.3	0.8	5	0.9
6. Information (academic)	23.8	12.0	30.1	17.3	5	0.8
7. Information (university)	7.7	9.8	3.1	6.8	5	1.2
8. Information (relevant)	36.7	19.0	29.3	21.0	5	0.9
9. Information (irrelevant)	0.6	1.0	2.5	2.4	5	2.2
10. Praise	1.5	3.3	0.2	0.3	5	1.0
11. Blame	0.1	0.2	0.6	1.0	5	1.1
Students						
0. Unclassifiable	11.8	3.2	9.9	3.6	5	1.0
1. Procedure	0.7	0.6	4.6	2.4	5	4.0[a]
2. Procedure (academic)	0.0	0.0	1.2	1.9	5	1.6
3. Procedure (university)	1.2	2.2	1.6	4.0	5	0.3
4. Evaluation (academic)	10.1	5.9	11.4	5.2	5	0.6
5. Evaluation (university)	2.5	5.7	0.3	1.0	5	0.9
6. Information (academic)	29.5	12.0	29.9	12.5	5	0.1
7. Information (university)	4.6	4.9	1.3	3.3	5	1.8
8. Information (relevant)	37.7	14.2	34.2	13.6	5	0.6
9. Information (irrelevant)	0.6	0.8	3.2	2.9	5	2.1
10. Praise	1.3	2.9	0.9	2.3	5	0.3
11. Blame	0.0	0.0	1.3	2.6	5	1.2

[a] $p < 0.05$ (two-tailed).

discussion were excluded. Both the content analysis and the stylistic analysis were based on the first, middle, and final 5-minute periods. The same measures were taken as in the Open University experiment and, in addition, pausing between utterances was measured by means of an electronic timer-counter operated by push-buttons (Rutter, Morley, and Graham, 1972).

The results for each resource category of *content* are given in Table 3. For tutors and students alike there was more exchange of procedures in the screen condition than face-to-face, indicating greater task-orientation. Tutors offered procedures more ($t = 2.7$; df 5; $p < 0.05$) as they attempted to structure the meetings, and students correspondingly accepted them more than face-to-face ($t = 2.8$; df 5; $p < 0.05$). Task-orientation was again high in both conditions, and there was no evidence of depersonalization in the screen condition.

Categories 4–8 and zero in combination again accounted for around 95 percent of acts face-to-face, but the figure of 87 percent for the screen condition was unexpectedly significantly lower ($t = 2.6$; df 5; $p < 0.05$ for tutors, and $t = 6.9$; df 5; $p < 0.001$ for students). There was no evidence this time that the task was approached differently in the two conditions.

Table 4   Laboratory analogue. Stylistic analysis: Mean values

	Face-to-face		Screen		df	t
	Mean	S.D.	Mean	S.D.		
Tutor						
No. utterances	33.5	10.6	27.8	8.1	5	1.5
No. words	1662.5	504.1	1646.3	253.4	5	0.1
Word length of utterances	56.5	33.6	65.9	29.9	5	0.6
No. questions	9.5	5.5	10.8	3.2	5	0.5
Filled pause ratio (% words)	2.1	1.2	2.5	1.6	5	1.3
Students						
No. utterances	40.8	9.2	35.2	12.5	5	0.9
No. words	775.5	269.7	684.8	371.5	5	0.6
Word length of utterances	19.1	6.4	18.5	4.6	5	0.2
No. questions	3.3	1.6	3.3	2.3	5	0.0
Filled pause ratio (% words)	1.7	1.0	2.4	1.6	5	1.6
% utterances = response to tutor question	29.0	—	42.5	—	5	3.4[a]
Tutor + students						
No. occurrences simultaneous speech	19.8	8.3	10.8	5.2	5	2.3
Length pauses (sec. mean)	3.8	—	2.6	—	5	2.7[a]
No. acknowledgement signals	9.5	4.4	6.8	4.9	5	1.3

[a] $p < 0.05$ (two-tailed).

The results for *style* are given in Table 4. The face-to-face tutorials were somewhat more spontaneous, with a greater readiness to allow silences to develop, and a tendency towards more frequent interruption. They were also less structured than the screen sessions, consistent with the content findings. Fewer of the students' contributions were direct answers to the tutor's questions, and students were more likely to talk to one another than in the screen condition, where tutor–student–tutor was the norm.

In summary, the findings of the laboratory and Open University studies are similar in several respects, indicating that the Open University results are not confined to that particular setting and group of people, but are more readily attributed to the medium of communication. For example, the tutorials were highly task-oriented throughout, and there was no evidence of depersonalization in either the telephone or screen conditions. Furthermore, style was generally more spontaneous face-to-face, and tutors were less inclined to impose their own structure. However, not all the Open University findings were borne out, and the effects were often smaller. Because of differences in procedure and analysis, interpretation is, of course, difficult. Nevertheless, the differences in findings between the experiments are consistent with our model of cuelessness. If visual communication had been the critical variable in the Open University experiment, the differences between the face-to-face and screen conditions in the present experiment should have been just as marked. They were not. The screen condition makes cues available from physical presence but not visual communication. If the cuelessness model is correct, the difference between screen and face-to-face (where cues from both physical presence and visual communication are available) should be less than the difference between face-to-face and telephone (where neither set of cues is available)—and that is precisely what we found.

CONCLUSIONS

The first object of our experimental work with the Open University was to test the validity and generality of our laboratory conclusions. It was predicted that content, style, and outcome would all distinguish between face-to-face and telephone tutorials, and this proved to be the case. The laboratory analogue study went on to indicate that the findings could more readily be attributed to cuelessness than to visual communication alone, offering good support for our previous conclusions.

As we hoped, moving from the laboratory to an everyday setting has led us to several interesting new lines of enquiry. With the support of a recent grant from the Social Science Research Council of Great Britain, we plan to explore three main questions in particular, and the first concerns teaching strategy. Both the Open University experiment and the analogue experiment showed that tutors were concerned to impose their own structure on telephone and screen tutorials in a way which did not happen face-to-face, suggesting that they try to tailor their teaching strategies to the particular setting. Relatively little attention has been paid to telephone teaching strategy, and we hope to examine it in some detail using an approach developed from Wood and Middleton (1975).

Wood and Middleton were concerned with the strategies mothers use in helping their young children to solve certain types of perceptual and intellectual problem. For example, they were interested in how frequently the mothers intervened, what form the intervention took, and how sensitive they were to feedback from their children. The system has subsequently been extended for analysing adult tuition, and it is this revised version which we shall use. Learning and teaching in tutorials are taken to be based, ideally, on a process of disputation or dialogue between participants. The tutor's role is taken to be primarily one of guiding the dialogue in such a way as to assist in bringing about informed changes in the structure of the students' knowledge. Since the tutor's choice of strategies is likely to be determined in part by feedback from the students, differences between telephone and face-to-face tutorials are to be expected given the inequality of available information. In particular, the system will enable us to examine differences in the type of student activity upon which the tutor bases his choice of when and how to intervene, the nature of his interventions, and their consequences.

A second question concerns the outcome of tutorials. So far, we have examined only the participants' perceptions of the meetings, and it is important that other measures are developed so that the effectiveness of telephone teaching can be assessed. In particular, we plan to examine how well students recall and understand what they hear in tutorials. The existing evidence from other settings suggests that the telephone may sometimes be superior (Argyle and Cook, 1976), perhaps because distractions from social cues are fewer. Questionnaires will be posted to students, and they will be asked to complete them immediately after each tutorial. First, they will be asked what they saw as the objectives of the tutorial, and to list the main points discussed. The reports will be assessed against transcripts of the sessions. Secondly, they will be asked to answer a number of specific questions about material covered in the tutorial, probably by forced-choice. Comparisons between face-to-face and telephone tutorials and across time will be made.

Time brings us to one final theoretical question we hope to explore. Previous work, including our own, has looked only at the effects of short-term manipulations. One result of this emphasis is that we know very little about the ways in which people may adapt over time to the absence of visual and other cues. It may be, for example, that visual cues are important initially, but that other cues assume a greater role as time goes on, and people can manage without visual feedback as they grow familiar with one another. As yet, we simply do not know. We therefore plan to conduct a small longitudinal study in which a number of telephone tutorial groups will be examined at regular intervals and changes will be monitored. Content, style, and outcome will all be measured.

At the very start of the chapter we made it clear that our aims were both theoretical and practical, and we should like to conclude with some practical implications. The most common anxiety expressed about telephone teaching is not to do with psychology but instead concerns the primitive quality of the technology: public telephone lines frequently and unpredictably distort speech so badly that it is incomprehensible or even inaudible; and they provide no means of presenting graphic material. To try to overcome these problems, the Open University is currently exploring two possibilities. One is a proposal to establish a dedicated teleconferencing network (Sparkes, 1978) for the whole of Britain, modelled on that used in Wisconsin, where an educational telephone network connects about 200 centres in a State approximately the size of England. Such a system provides much better sound quality than is possible with the Post Office system; and the equipment is simple to use (loudspeaker and microphone speaker-sets rather than hand-held telephones) and could be based at local study centres. The teleconferencing network would also enable greater numbers of students to be linked up to a tutor, either regionally or nationally. Such a teleconferencing network system offers great potential for use in the field of Continuing Education, enabling collaborative ventures between educational providers, and allowing a course to be taught from any location to any number of locations throughout the country.

The second possibility is the use of CYCLOPS, a device which has been developed at the Open University (Liddell and Pinches, 1978). This is an audio-visual system based on a domestic television set and standard cassette recorder. Both audio and visual material can be stored on an *audio* cassette and played back through the television. Besides providing a sophisticated local calculator with visual display and telephone access to a larger computer, CYCLOPS can also be used as a remote blackboard, providing two-way audio-visual communication through a light-pen or keyboard. This allows a student in one place (perhaps at home) to receive graphic material drawn on a television screen in another place by the tutor, and in turn to send visual information back to the tutor, by drawing on his own screen. This device would enable considerable development in telephone teaching in those subjects (for example, Science) which appear to have greater need for a visual channel of communication.

All of these interesting developments in communications technology depend ultimately for their value on the use people make of them. It is a case not only of what the hardware can do, but also how effectively the user can handle it, and how the user and the technology interact. This then leads us to the practical question of how best to help the user adapt to the medium. Experience with telephone teaching within the Open University has shown the need for soundly based briefing and training materials and activities for tutors, many of whom find their adaptation to telephone tutoring a stressful experience; this is particularly so during the first tutorials, when the main anxiety is about how to regulate a group discussion with unseen participants. The kinds of experiences tutors have in adapting both their communication skills and teaching strategies affect their attitudes to the continued use of the medium. We now have a reasonable theoretical understanding of the process of telephone teaching, and our goal is to continue to apply that knowledge through training (Robinson, 1979; Robinson *et al.* 1979).

ACKNOWLEDGEMENTS

The theoretical and laboratory research reported at the start of the chapter was supported by grants from the Social Science Research Council, and the work on tutorial teaching was supported by a grant from the Open University and by a Programme grant to Geoffrey Stephenson from the Social Science Research Council. We are grateful to George Delafield for helping to set up the Open University study, and to Avrille Blecher, Michael Dewey, Ken Giles, Ann Harding, and Ann Morisy for helping to record and analyse the tutorials.

REFERENCES

Argyle, M. and Cook, M. (1976) *Gaze and Mutual Gaze*, C.U.P., London.

Argyle, M., Lalljee, M., and Cook, M. (1968) 'The effects of visibility on interaction in a dyad', *Human Relations*, **21**, 3-17.

Cook, M. (1969) 'Anxiety, speech disturbances and speech rate', *British Journal of Social and Clinical Psychology*, **8**, 13-21.

Cook, M. and Lalljee, M. (1972) 'Verbal substitutes for visual signals in interaction', *Semiotica*, **3**, 212-21.

Douglas, A. (1957) 'The peaceful settlement of industrial and inter-group disputes', *Journal of Conflict Resolution*, **1**, 69-81.

Flinck, R. (1978) 'Correspondence education combined with systematic telephone tutoring, unpublished Ph.D. thesis, University of Lund, Sweden.

Hammond, S., Young, I., and Cook, A. (1978) *Teaching by Telephone*, Final report to Social Science Research Council.

Harper, R. G., Wiens, A. N., and Matarazzo, J. D. (1978) *Nonverbal Communication*, Wiley, London.

Homans, G. C. (1961) *Social Behaviour: Its Elementary Forms*, R.K.P., London.

Kemp, N. J. (1977) 'Visual communication and the synchronisation of conversation', Paper to the Annual London Conference of the British Psychological Society, December, 1977.

Kendon, A. (1967) 'Some functions of gaze direction in social interaction', *Acta Psychologica*, **26**, 1-47.

Liddell, D. C. and Pinches, C. A. (1978) 'The electronic blackboard—a remote teaching aid', Paper to the I.E.R.R. Conference on Microprocessors in Automation and Communication, University of Kent, Canterbury.

Maclay, H. and Osgood, C. E. (1959) 'Hesitation phenomena in spontaneous English speech', *Word*, **15**, 19-44.

Mahl, G. F. (1956) 'Disturbances and silences in the patient's speech in psychotherapy', *Journal of Abnormal and Social Psychology*, **53**, 1-15.

Morley, I. E. and Stephenson, G. M. (1969) 'Interpersonal and interparty exchange: A laboratory simulation of an industrial negotiation at the plant level', *British Journal of Psychology*, **60**, 543-45.

Morley, I. E. and Stephenson, G. M. (1970) 'Formality in experimental negotiations: A validation study', *British Journal of Psychology*, **61**, 383–84.

Morley, I. E. and Stephenson, G. M. (1977) *The Social Psychology of Bargaining*, George Allen & Unwin, London.

Open University (1977) *Regional Reports on Telephone Tuition Schemes*.

Pennington, D. C. and Rutter, D. R. (in press) 'Information or affiliation? Effects of intimacy on visual interaction', *Semiotica*.

Robinson, B. (1979) 'Briefing and training for telephone teaching: some guidelines', Mimeo, Open University.

Robinson, B. and Carr, R. J. (1978) 'Reaching the remote student: Tutoring by telephone', in *Problems of Education in Remote and Sparsely populated Areas*, Scottish Educational Research Association Monograph.

Robinson, B., Harrison, I., Richards, H. R., and Brown, D. (1979) *Tutoring by Telephone: A Handbook*, Open University.

Rutter, D. R., Morley, I. E., and Graham, J. C. (1972) 'Visual interaction in a group of introverts and extroverts', *European Journal of Social Psychology*, **2**, 371–84.

Rutter, D. R. and Stephenson, G. M. (1977) 'The role of visual communication in synchronising conversation', *European Journal of Social Psychology*, **7**, 29–37.

Rutter, D. R. and Stephenson, G. M. (1979a) 'The role of visual communication in social interaction', *Current Anthropology*, **20**, 124–25.

Rutter, D. R. and Stephenson, G. M. (1979b) 'The functions of Looking: effects of friendship on gaze', *British Journal of Social and Clinical Psychology*, **18**, 203–5.

Rutter, D. R., Stephenson, G. M., Ayling, K., and White, P. A. (1978) 'The timing of Looks in dyadic conversation', *British Journal of Social and Clinical Psychology*, **17**, 17–21.

Rutter, D. R., Stephenson, G. M., and Dewey, M. E. (1981) 'Visual communication and the content and style of conversation', *British Journal of Social Psychology*, **20**, 41–52.

Rutter, D. R., Stephenson, G. M., Lazzerini, A. J., Ayling, K., and White, P. A. (1977) 'Eye-contact: A chance product of individual looking?', *British Journal of Social and Clinical Psychology*, **16**, 191–92.

Short, J. A. (1974) 'Effects of medium of communication on experimental negotiation', *Human Relations*, **27**, 225–34.

Short, J. A., Williams, E., and Christie, B. (1976) *The Social Psychology of Tele-communications*, Wiley, London.

Sparkes, J. J. (1978) 'The U.K. Telenet: A proposed telephone conference network for educational and other purposes', Paper to the Committee for Communications Technology, the Open University.

Stephenson, G. M., Ayling, K., and Rutter, D. R. (1976) 'The role of visual communication in social exchange', *British Journal of Social and Clinical Psychology*, **15**, 113–20.

Stephenson, G. M. and Rutter, D. R. (1970) 'Eye-contact, distance and affiliation: A re-evaluation', *British Journal of Psychology*, **61**, 385–93.

Stephenson, G. M., Rutter, D. R., and Dore, S. R. (1973) 'Visual interaction and distance', *British Journal of Psychology*, **64**, 251–57.

Tajfel, H. (1972) 'Experiments in a vacuum', in *The Context of Social Psychology* (Eds. J. Israel and H. Tajfel), Academic Press, London.

Williams, E. (1977) 'Experimental comparisons of face-to-face and mediated communication: A review', *Psychological Bulletin*, **84**, 963–76.

Williams, E. and Chapanis, A. (1977) 'A review of psychological research comparing communications media', in *The Status of the Telephone in Education*, Second Annual International Communications Conference, University of Wisconsin — Extension.

Winer, B. J. (1970) *Statistical Principles in Experimental Design*, McGraw-Hill, London.

Wood, D. J. and Middleton, D. (1975) 'A study of assisted problem-solving', *British Journal of Psychology*, **66**, 181–91.

Author Index

375

Subject Index

accidents (traffic), 192, 194–202, 209, 212
adreno-corticotrophic hormone (ACTH), 161
age, 72–3, 82, 124, 195–7, 204, 208, 214, 223–51, 295, 300, 304, 328, 330, 333–5
aggression, 87, 89, 98, 100–1, 159, 174, 198, 207–11, 215, 218–19
alcoholism, 73–4, 200, 214, 218
altruism, 41–3, 63, 65, 159, 205
 kin-altruism, 43
Americans For Democratic Action, 266–7, 272–3
applied social psychology, 5–7, 31–2, 345
assumed similarity between opposites (ASo), 109, 111–12, 124, 142
attitudes, 9, 191, 197–200
 change, 6
 political, 253–4, 258, 260–78, 283–6, 296–7, 301, 304, 308–10, 312
 toward behaviour, 279–89, 293–7, 300–9
attribution theory, 70, 81–2, 101, 149, 199, 206–8, 210
 dispositional attributions, 82–3, 102
 environmental attributions, 83
avoidance learning, 87

behaviourism, 87–9, 195, 318
behaviour modification, 6
Belgian Navy, 108, 120
beliefs, 226, 244
 behavioural, 280–1, 287–9, 293–4, 297–301, 305–6, 311
 in determining attitudes, 262–4, 266, 268–80, 285–93, 300–11
 normative, 280–1, 291–4, 297, 300–2, 305, 308

candidate partisanship, 257
Carter, Jimmy, 275, 282–301, 303, 311

catholic, 255
ceiling effect, 332
celerity, 90–1, 94
centration, 325, 326
chrystallizers, 255
clinical psychology, 67
civil rights, 260, 267, 269
cognitive distance, 317
collective failure, 40–1
collective goods, 39, 45, 53
Columbia group, the (views on voting), 254–60, 283
commons dilemma, 38–9, 46, 51, 53–4, 63–4
communication effects (in games), 57–8
Conference Process Analysis (CPA), 348, 355, 360
conscience, 50, 61
conservation, 316–8, 328, 342–3
 of length, 319, 321, 324–5, 339–40
 of liquids, 319, 321–2, 328–9, 340
 of numbers, 321–2, 328
cooperative game, 319–20, 333, 340–1
Coronary Heart Disease (CHD), 163, 167, 170, 181
corticosteroids, 161–2
crime clearance rates, 86
criminal history, 80–3
crisis in psychology, 3, 318
crowding (effects on stress), 159, 162, 184
cuelessness, 354–6, 367, 370
CYCLOPS, 372

dangerousness, 82–3, 93, 101
Darwinism, 43, 63
deception study, 14
demand characteristics, 9, 14
Democratic Party, 257–8, 261–4, 267–77, 296–301, 311
depersonalization, 348–9, 353–5, 364, 368–9

387